CW00539921

THE IISS
ARMED CONFLICT SURVEY

2018

published by

 Routledge
Taylor & Francis Group

for

The International Institute for Strategic Studies

The International Institute for Strategic Studies
Arundel House | 6 Temple Place | London | WC2R 2PG | UK

THE IISS ARMED CONFLICT SURVEY 2018

First published July 2018 by **Routledge**
4 Park Square, Milton Park, Abingdon, Oxon, OX14 4RN

for **The International Institute for Strategic Studies**
Arundel House, 6 Temple Place, London, WC2R 2PG, UK

Simultaneously published in the USA and Canada by **Routledge**
711 Third Avenue, New York, NY 10017

Routledge is an imprint of Taylor & Francis, an Informa business

© 2018 The International Institute for Strategic Studies

DIRECTOR-GENERAL AND CHIEF EXECUTIVE Dr John Chipman
EDITOR Dr Anastasia Voronkova
DIRECTOR OF EDITORIAL Dr Nicholas Redman
ASSOCIATE EDITOR Alex Goodwin
EDITORIAL Sara Hussain, Jack May, Nicholas Payne, Kathryn Shaw, Sam Stocker,
Jessica Watson, Carolyn West
DESIGN AND PRODUCTION John Buck, Kelly Verity
RESEARCH ASSOCIATE Nicholas Crawford
CONFLICT AND MAP RESEARCH Chris Bignell, Ally Chandler, Alexandra Dzero, Michael
Hart, Adam Higazi, Andrew Kelly, Alyse Kennedy, Janosch Kullenberg, Zara Jarvinen,
Tareq Megerisi, Akali Omeni, Alexandra Phelan, Eric Reeves, Paula Roque, Christopher
Shay, Jeremy Schetz, Søren Sørensen, Dr Hebatalla Taha, Mohd Tahir, Jens Wardenaer,
Caitlin Vito, Zoha Waseem, Alex Waterman
COVER IMAGES Getty

British Library Cataloguing in Publication Data
A catalogue record for this book is available from the British Library

Library of Congress Cataloguing in Publication Data

ISBN 978-1-85743-956-4
ISSN 2374-0973

Contents

Editor's Introduction

The major armed conflicts in the Middle East and Afghanistan continued to rage in 2017. The strengthening of government forces in Syria and Iraq fostered hope that the conflicts were moving towards a conclusion, although fatalities in both remained high. The conflict in Yemen became appreciably more fierce and there was no sign of Afghanistan's conflict becoming less bloody or closer to an end. Many of the world's other conflicts, likewise, showed little sign of coming to an end.

In Syria, President Bashar al-Assad's regime recovered territory throughout the year, setting its sights on heavily populated, rebel-held enclaves across the country and decimating the rebellion through brutal warfare (including chemical weapons and forced displacement), Russian firepower and foreign personnel. The regime also put greater effort into the campaign against the Islamic State, also known as ISIS or ISIL, in service of its race for territory in eastern Syria against the United States-supported and Kurdish-dominated Syrian Democratic Forces, which seized major cities and oilfields. Regional powers Turkey, Iran and Israel increased their operations and ground presence in an effort to shape the battlefield. The risk of direct confrontation between them increased.

The government of Iraq, with broad international support, drew closer to its objective of defeating ISIS. The liberation of Mosul after months of gruelling urban fighting was a major setback for the jihadi organisation, which adopted insurgent tactics to prolong its survival. Despite the retreat of ISIS, other sources of conflict in the region resurfaced: Kurdish ambitions for independence were met with regional disapproval and were ended swiftly by a government operation that recovered

Kirkuk and other oil-rich areas. The question of what would happen to the alliance between the mostly Shia (and often Iran-backed) militias and the government once their common enemy was defeated also gained prominence.

Yemen's conflict grew bloodier and more fragmented. Lines of battle remained mostly static, including in the city of Taizz. Saudi Arabia carried out airstrikes and implemented a naval blockade, both of which had dramatic consequences on the country's food and water supply and health facilities, raising the numbers of indirect casualties. By late 2017, the break between the forces of Ali Abdullah Saleh and the Houthis was made irreversible when the latter killed the erstwhile state president, auguring a new phase in the conflict. In total, the conflicts in Syria, Iraq and Yemen registered an estimated 72,000 fatalities, more than half of which were recorded in Syria alone.

In Afghanistan, there were an estimated 15,000 fatalities as the government, with the support of the US and other powers, largely held the Taliban in check. By the end of 2017, the Taliban remained in control of 14 districts and were openly present in 263 others, thus threatening at least 70% of the country. The conflict in Myanmar's Rakhine State registered the most dramatic escalation of all major conflicts in 2017. Attacks by the Arakan Rohingya Salvation Army on 25 August led to a massive military response, resulting in a political and humanitarian disaster that displaced hundreds of thousands of Rohingya Muslims, with 12,000 estimated fatalities.

Increasingly, political stalemates became entrenched. In Myanmar, for example, the prospects for peace between the government and the ethnic armed organisations in Shan and Kachin states grew dimmer. The former continued to reject the legitimacy of the latter and refused to engage in any dialogue. Developments in 2017 made more persistent the question as to whether the conflict parties desired to see the peace process, first launched in 2013, to a breakthrough.

Fragmentation, consolidation and adaptation of armed groups

The proliferation and fragmentation of armed groups was a feature of many conflicts, both as a result of internal division within the groups and state intervention. The Congo Research Group mapped more than 120 armed groups operating in the Democratic Republic of the Congo as of October 2017, representing an almost

50% increase since October 2015. In Latin America, the Mexican armed forces have succeeded in fracturing most of the large cartels that had challenged the state, but the subsequent increase in the number of smaller criminal gangs has driven new waves of fighting between the state and organised crime, and among criminal groupings.

Yet in a few conflicts, under-pressure militant groups came together. In March, four of the largest and most influential non-state armed actors in Mali – Ansar Dine, the Macina Liberation Front, al-Mourabitoun and al-Qaeda in the Islamic Maghreb – merged into a single entity, Jamaat Nusrat al-Islam wal Muslimeen. By pooling their resources, the groups were able to project influence over a wider territory.

In the Philippines, Isnilon Hapilon, then leader of the Abu Sayyaf Group (ASG), decided to join forces with the ISIS-aligned Maute group and take over large parts of the city of Marawi in Lanao del Sur province. The security forces underestimated the strength of the combined forces, leading to a five-month siege and the declaration of martial law as the government attempted to retake the city. However, this alignment was likely to be a temporary phenomenon. With the ASG lacking a leader after Hapilon's death, the group was likely to fragment.

Armed groups also showed flexibility in their organisational and operational parameters. In the absence of a leader, the Sudan People's Liberation Movement–In Opposition (SPLM–IO) in South Sudan adopted a decentralised structure in which units of command acted autonomously while remaining under the banner of the SPLM–IO. This reorganisation could impact mediation efforts, as the new structure may allow the SPLM–IO to keep fighting for a long time. While al-Shabaab made no territorial gains in Somalia in 2017, the group exploited the lack of government and military authority outside Mogadishu to assert its influence in key areas in the country. Despite continuing pressure from the Nigerian Army, Boko Haram remained a threat in the Lake Chad Basin by shifting its tactics, including the increasing use of women and children as suicide bombers. ISIS sought to diversify its theatre of activity in the wake of losing most of its territory in the Middle East, and remained a potent threat in Southeast Asia. Despite losing militants in Marawi, the group continues to make attempts to recruit new fighters, and is likely to be able to launch attacks across the region as long as local grievances and unresolved conflicts remain.

Rising incidence of external intervention

While state-on-state conflict remains a rarity in the twenty-first century, it is notable that the number of internal conflicts in which external powers are involved has risen in this decade. In 1997, there were 11 such conflicts active in the world, and six of those were in sub-Saharan Africa. In 2017, by contrast, the number of these internationalised conflicts had risen to 17. There were four in the Middle East and North Africa, six in sub-Saharan Africa, four in the Americas, two in Eurasia and one in South Asia.

Almost all of the external powers involved in the 11 conflicts in 1997 were proximate or neighbouring states – for instance, Pakistan in Afghanistan, Turkey in Iraq's Kurdish regions, Iran in Lebanon, Russia in Abkhazia, and Uganda and Ethiopia in Sudan's secessionist civil war. The US was the only non-regional power active in a conflict (against the Lord's Resistance Army) and the Economic Community of West African States the only regional organisation (in Sierra Leone).

By contrast, in 2017 almost half of the 17 conflicts – namely those in Afghanistan, Central African Republic, Iraq, Libya, Mali, Somalia, Syria and Yemen – involved extra-regional powers. Leading Western states (in particular the US and France) are prominent in this development, yet the tally of such conflicts in 2017 shows that non-Western states have also become more active in this field. Russia has intervened in Afghanistan, Libya and Syria, as well as in neighbouring Ukraine. Saudi Arabia and the UAE have become principal combatants in Yemen, while also exerting influence in Libya and Syria. Egypt and Turkey also have demonstrated an appetite for external intervention in recent years.

It is not accurate to describe all of these interventions as proxy conflicts, in which external powers equip or otherwise aid one side in an internal conflict to further their own objectives. Proxy conflicts were a feature of the Cold War and declined in tandem with US–Soviet competition. In some of the contemporary cases, external powers are deploying their own military resources on the battlefield and very occasionally clash with other external powers. There is almost certainly a connection between the increase in external involvement in domestic conflicts, and rising competition between major powers globally.

There is a more positive aspect to the comparison between 1997 and 2017. In 1997, there were six conflicts in sub-Saharan Africa that featured significant external-state intervention. In five of those cases, the intervention was undertaken to support rebels against the state government. This was the case in Central Africa, the Democratic Republic of the Congo, Senegal, Sierra Leone and Sudan. The sole exception was Uganda's intervention on the side of the government in the closing stages of Angola's civil war. The picture in 2017 was very different. While there were six active conflicts that featured significant external involvement, in all cases – Central African Republic, the Democratic Republic of the Congo, Lake Chad (Boko Haram), Mali, Somalia and South Sudan – the intervention was undertaken in support of the government. United Nations and African Union forces were prominent, alongside regional coalitions. Thus sub-Saharan Africa appeared to have moved away from a regional norm of state interventions directed at weakening neighbouring governments in their internal conflicts.

The picture is different in the Middle East and North Africa. Iraq's conflict was the only one in which all external parties worked to support the government. In Libya, Syria and Yemen there was considerable support for opposition forces by regional and extra-regional powers, although in most cases this was offset by support from other powers for the state combatant.

Stabilisation and reconstruction

In the Chart of Armed Conflict 2018, we address the issue of international assistance and multilateral missions to conflict zones. In recent years, the European Union has deployed numerous missions overseas to train and build the capacity of security forces, as well as naval task forces to address piracy off Somalia and illegal human smuggling from Libya across the Mediterranean. It is now a significant player in the stabilisation response to conflicts. In the north of Africa, regional forces are also playing an important role, including the G5 Sahel Force, the Multinational Joint Task Force (against Boko Haram) and the France-led *Operation Barkhane*.

The Chart shows marked variations in the breakdown of international assistance to conflict-affected countries. International assistance to Syria (which excludes the military support provided to the Syrian government by Russia and Iran, and excludes counter-terrorism operations by the US and its allies) is primarily focused on humanitarian relief, reflecting the catastrophic human impact of the conflict. By contrast, Yemen received markedly lower international assistance per capita in

2016 (including far lower humanitarian-aid spending per capita) despite the rapid spread of disease and famine. Although the number of direct casualties of violence is lower, the conflict had a serious impact on Yemen's wider population. The high level of aid (at a per capita rate) provided to the Palestinian Territories reflects the dependence of the country, and the Gaza Strip in particular, on international aid, which consists primarily of humanitarian assistance and social-infrastructure and services spending.

The level of conflict-related assistance provided to Lebanon is, perhaps, surprisingly high. There are three UN missions deployed in the country – the UN Interim Force in Lebanon (UNIFIL), the Office of the United Nations Special Coordinator for Lebanon (UNSCOL) and the Office of the Special Envoy of the Secretary-General for the Implementation of Security Council Resolution 1559. Only a small proportion of the aid is attributable to efforts made by international partners to insulate the country from the conflict raging in neighbouring Syria.

In sub-Saharan Africa, international aid spending is inversely proportional to income levels in each country, such that the poorest receive the highest levels of per capita assistance. Thus Central African Republic, Somalia and South Sudan receive the highest levels of per capita international assistance. It is notable that multilateral peace and stabilisation missions represent a higher proportion of international assistance spend in sub-Saharan African than in other regions. In Latin American states, by contrast, the main route for conflict-related assistance is the provision of support on security-sector management and reform. The Chart of Armed Conflict 2018 also highlights that, around the world, there is a markedly low level of assistance dedicated to demobilising child soldiers and reintegrating them into society.

Conflicts in this year's *Armed Conflict Survey*

The 2018 edition includes some conflict situations that were not included in the 2017 edition and removes others based on a consistent application of our definition of armed conflict, detailed in our essay on the essence of armed conflict.

The violence in Brazil's Rio de Janeiro meets our criteria for an armed conflict. In Rio, groups in control of the city's *favelas* compete violently for territory, influence and trade (especially, but not only, the trade in drugs), and engage in armed clashes with one another and with the state to this end. The clashes are intense in their frequency and they have been sustained over a considerable period. The limited geographic scope of the fighting is no limit to its qualification as an armed conflict. It is of sufficient scale, intensity and duration to classify as an armed conflict, and indeed affects far more people than many other ongoing armed conflicts.

Armed conflict between communities of pastoralists and farmers was one of the main national-security issues in Nigeria in 2017. Armed clashes occurred in almost every zone of the federation although their scale and intensity varied among the 36 states. Overall, the conflict is of sufficient duration and armed confrontations expanded in number and severity through 2017. As well as resulting in heavy loss of life, this conflict had a negative impact on agricultural and livestock production in the country.

In previous editions of *The Armed Conflict Survey*, the conflict between the Burmese state and ethnic armed groups in Kachin, Rakhine and Shan states was analysed collectively. However, in 2017 the conflict in Rakhine developed into a markedly different conflict from that in Kachin and Shan states, and so the two conflicts are distinguished in this year's edition. Likewise, last year's *Armed Conflict Survey* covered the violence between the Colombian state and the BACRIM (organised criminal groups) in the wider context of the conflict in the country involving FARC and the National Liberation Army (ELN); however, the conflict between the state and the BACRIM has developed and meets our criteria for inclusion separately. *The Armed Conflict Survey* previously recognised the armed violence between MS-13, Barrio 18 and the states of El Salvador, Honduras and Guatemala as a single, cross-border conflict spanning the so-called Northern Triangle. *The Armed Conflict Survey 2018*, recognising important distinctions between these three countries, considers them on a national basis. The situations in El Salvador and Honduras meet *The Armed Conflict Survey* criteria for classification as an armed conflict.

We judged that non-state groups in Ethiopia were not organised sufficiently to mount sustained armed resistance against government repression. In Niger Delta too, there were not enough instances of combat to justify inclusion. In China (Xinjiang), violent incidents continued to decline in frequency and sophistication. The conflict in Russia's North Caucasus also declined in intensity over time and no longer meets our 'frequency of fighting' criterion.

In the case of India's northeastern insurgencies in Assam and Nagaland, a long and drawn-out peace process between the government and the pro-talks factions of the militant groups has led to a gradual diminution of the intensity of the fighting. We have included these conflicts in the publication, pending the conclusion of the negotiations. In Darfur, the major non-state armed groups appeared to be progressively losing cohesiveness, which affected their ability to carry out armed resistance against the Sudanese Armed Forces or the Rapid Support Forces. We continue to monitor the conflict to see whether the armed groups will be able to reconstitute their military cohesion and capability. Meanwhile, the region continued to experience clashes between ethnic militias.

Thematic essays

The Armed Conflict Survey 2018 contains essays that are relevant to armed conflicts across the globe. Dismantling terrorist financial networks and improving counter-terrorist financing measures have been key priorities for the international community. Colin Clarke discusses the challenges facing this endeavour, including the difficulty of passing legislation that criminalises terrorist financing, capacity and resources. He highlights the willingness of terrorist organisations to use new technologies, creating multiple opportunities to raise funds in innovative ways. Drawing on a wide range of empirical contexts, Clarke examines how opportunistic and innovative funding models underpin the continuing ability of non-state armed actors to plan and execute attacks.

Not only does technology change terrorist financing, it is also blurring the boundary between the physical and narrative dimensions of contemporary conflict. David Patrikarakos examines the ways in which social media allows ordinary citizens to influence conflict narratives. The role of social media, he argues, makes modern conflicts more fluid and chaotic, not least because the physical battlefield is arguably no longer the decisive arena in which conflicts are fought. The shift from conflicts that are settled on the battlefield towards more open-ended conflicts waged by non-military methods could mean that peace is increasingly difficult to achieve.

The making of peace is the theme of Stefan Wolff's contribution. Wolff compares peace processes in Colombia, South Sudan and Ukraine, evaluating their successes and limitations. He discusses whether and when the benefits of the status quo outweigh the costs of concessions during bargaining. He highlights the dangers of unrealistic expectations that cannot be fulfilled, thus making implementing peace unviable. This partly explains why a number of peace processes terminate with the resumption of the war they were meant to end.

Mia Bloom's essay focuses on one category of participants in armed conflicts – child soldiers. Child soldiers are increasingly recruited into armed groups worldwide and used in many roles, including as fighters and suicide bombers. She notes the multiplicity of recruitment avenues (both coercive and voluntary), as well as indoctrination mechanisms, including specially tailored education programmes and instilling a sense of pride in belonging to the group. A particularly pressing challenge for policymakers is to maintain and improve deradicalisation and reintegration programmes for children. In this endeavour, Bloom argues, the role of education in unlearning ideas adopted during indoctrination into armed groups is particularly important.

Chapter One: **Thematic Essays**

The Essence of Armed Conflict

Armed conflict profoundly affects the security of states and people. For a state, the deployment of military force in the pursuit or defence of its objectives is a grave decision with potentially ruinous consequences. Armed conflicts result in the loss of life, the displacement of civilian populations and the destruction of national infrastructure. Domestically, they exert a material effect by disrupting the political order or posing an existential challenge to the state. Internationally, they can have a profound impact on international relations and the formulation and conduct of defence and security policy.

We define armed conflict to be a sustained contest between two or more organised adversaries, making purposive use of armed force. Crucially, it involves combat, rather than the one-sided application of lethal force.

The qualities that make a conflict sustained are duration and intensity. Ordinarily, we recognise an armed conflict after it has run for at least three months and that features combat on a weekly or fortnightly basis. In the case of military conflicts between state actors which feature substantial levels of military mobilisation, simultaneous armed clashes and significant fatalities, the duration threshold may be relaxed.

To be included in our definition, armed conflicts must be fought between two or more adversaries, which may be states or non-state actors. The antagonists must demonstrate a level of organisation sufficient to be able to plan and execute attacks. Whether at the strategic or tactical level, these attacks are directed to achieve a purpose that is opposed by the other party or parties to the conflict.

From this definition, we apply three tests to determine whether an armed conflict exists: duration of at least three months; incidents of armed combat on a weekly or fortnightly basis; and that the parties demonstrate the ability to plan and execute military operations. In the case of state actors, the organisational test demands the deployment of armed forces rather than the police.

Our definition of armed conflict, and our purpose, differs from that enshrined in the Geneva Conventions and the Rome Statute. We approach armed conflict as a politico-military phenomenon, rather than a legal one. We do not seek to determine the cases of violence in which international humanitarian law should apply.

Classical conceptions of armed conflict

Traditionally, armed conflict is regarded as the use of armed force by one party against another, with the objective of imposing its will on the target; this is the short definition of war put forward by Carl von Clausewitz. Most students of armed conflict acknowledge certain core elements to the phenomenon of war, at the heart of which is the idea that armed conflict is an attack on the fundamental authority of a state.[1] In this model, the use of armed violence by a non-state grouping or foreign state presents a challenge to the host state's monopoly on the use of force and political power; in the case of a non-state grouping, this challenge often highlights 'the failure of the state to fulfil its side of the social contract'.[2] The state recognises the threat and concentrates on obtaining, maintaining, developing and mobilising resources to resist it.

Often the challenge to state authority involves the control of territory, which is traditionally viewed as the basis of power and authority.[3] The adversary of the host state usually harbours political objectives intended to effect a fundamental change to existing power arrangements, either to the functions (and therefore legitimacy) of the state or the geographical borders of the state (or sometimes both).[4] Economic or social objectives are also possible motivations, but conflict parties are customarily understood to be primarily motivated by political objectives.

A challenge to the authority of the state, control of territory and political intention are key aspects in the classical conception of conflict. However, over time the understanding of these aspects – and others – has changed. There is, for example, debate over whether a party to an armed conflict should have the ability to control territory, or merely to contest control of territory. The presence of effective, sustained territorial governance and provision of public goods such as basic social welfare by rebels is not an essential element of conflict, particularly at the early stages; rather, it some-times emerges in the course of a conflict.[5]

The role of political intention is also less straightforward than some assume. Armed conflicts morph over time and ideological commitments erode. Some actors enter a conflict for reasons of politics or ideology, but are obliged to adopt com-mercial imperatives in order to support the struggle, and later come to be driven by predation and greed. The conflict between the Colombian state and FARC is instruc-tive: FARC resorted to crime in order to generate the funds to continue its armed struggle. Furthermore, the absence of political goals on the part of a non-state actor does not necessarily imply that a conflict cannot have profound political effects. In several parts of the world, most notably Latin America, groups have emerged that employ violence strategically to gain economic control over territory and dominate local communities for predation, especially – but not exclusively – in large urban centres. Their activities have long-term and sustained political effects as they weaken the state, challenge its authority and compete with it for the loyalty of the population.

Our understanding of the duration, intensity, organisation and level of fatalities in an armed conflict has also evolved. Some definitions of duration, for example, hold that the fighting in an armed conflict runs uninterrupted for a considerable period of time. In practice, conflicts rarely demonstrate an unvarying intensity of fighting over an extended period. Episodes of low-level activity or even dormancy (for example, in the depth of winter) are observable in some cases. In Afghanistan, for instance, there is generally less fighting between December and March because of the climate. Throughout history, moreover, there have been conflicts where fight-ing has subsided when the time came to collect the harvest. It is generally accepted that contemporary armed conflicts have become longer, with fluctuating levels of violence over the course of months or even years.[6]

Our understanding of organisation on the part of conflict actors has also pro-gressed. Not all non-state groups engaged in armed conflicts have a distinct and effective chain of command; many are highly decentralised, with an amorphous structure, a transnational network and a global outreach. Sometimes they carry out activities in the name of a markedly transnational agenda. The existence of a hier-archical military structure on both sides is therefore not an essential condition of armed conflict, although access to weapons and other military equipment is clearly required. Nevertheless, in an armed conflict, non-state groups (even decentralised ones) have to be able to devise strategy, carry out operations, effectively coordinate activities and establish a degree of communication between members, frequently by relying on and expanding existing social networks drawn from local and/or national circles. They also have to recruit and train members.

Fatalities are another controversial measure: in classical definitions, an armed conflict must register at least 1,000 battlefield deaths, or 1,000 battlefield deaths per year. However, this measure – with its arbitrary threshold – was developed at a time when conflicts were largely fought on battlefields and were often relatively short, decisive affairs contested between states. Since the end of the Cold War, many of the world's chronic armed conflicts have not met this annual fatality threshold. Examples include Kashmir, the Philippines' fight against the New People's Army and the conflict in Palestine. Moreover, in the age of rapid transmission of information, even a relatively low number of fatalities can have strategic effect, as was the case in 2004 when four US contractors were murdered in Fallujah. Images of the victims circulated in the global media, sparking a public outcry in the US which resulted in a military operation to recapture the city.

Categorising armed conflict

The four 1949 Geneva Conventions and their Additional Protocols identify two types of armed conflict: an international armed conflict (IAC) between states, and a non-international armed conflict (NIAC). An IAC is any declared war or undeclared armed conflict between states that are party to the Geneva Conventions. An NIAC is less well defined, partly because of the difficulty in forging consensus among the states that drafted the conventions; it is described as an armed conflict 'not of an international character'. While an NIAC is understood to involve at most one state party (the state on whose territory the conflict is fought), Article 1 of Additional Protocol II states that 'internal disturbances and tensions, such as riots, isolated and sporadic acts of violence and other acts of a similar nature' do not qualify as an NIAC. That negative definition is echoed in the 1998 Rome Statute, the founding document of the International Criminal Court.

Over time, the understanding of an NIAC has changed. It has come to be accepted, for instance, that an NIAC can be fought between non-state actors. This was endorsed by the signatories to the Rome Statute. Among the many tests put forward over time to determine whether an internal conflict qualifies as an NIAC, two now stand out: intensity and organisation. The first applies where hostilities are of a collective character or where a government relies on its military to fight insurgents. The second applies where the non-state party or parties have a command structure and the capacity to sustain military operations (the state is assumed to meet this criterion; it is not expected that the non-state actor will have an analogous level of organisation). Some scholars argue that the non-state party must control territory.

There is no central authority that determines which incidents of violence count as an IAC or an NIAC. In every case, states and bodies such as the International Committee of the Red Cross (ICRC) make their own determinations, although the ICRC rarely if ever declares an NIAC over the objections of a state. The declaration of an IAC or NIAC is, however, a significant act, because any such declaration has legal implications. The purpose of the Geneva Conventions and their Additional Protocols, and also the Rome Statute, is to determine instances where International Humanitarian Law (IHL) should apply. IHL is more extensive in the case of an IAC than an NIAC, and the threshold for application of IHL is much lower in an IAC than in an NIAC. As noted above, any resort to armed force between states is sufficient to qualify as an IAC and thus make IHL applicable. It would apply even in the case of a brief, uncontested and non-lethal incursion by one state's armed forces onto the territory of another state, without the consent of the host state.

In contrast to the Geneva Conventions, which recognise two types of armed conflict with different qualifying thresholds, we recognise three types of armed conflict and apply a common threshold for inclusion, centred on duration, intensity and organisation. Our categories are based on the types of actor involved and the interactions between them:

- An international or inter-state conflict is waged between one state (or group of states) and another state (or group of states). It can take place on the territory of one or several states, or the global commons.
- An internal conflict is waged principally on the territory of a single state, either pitting the government (and possibly allied militias) against one or more non-state actors; or between several non-state actors.

- An internationalised conflict has the features of an internal conflict, but is one in which an external state is or becomes involved militarily. Such involvement might include training, equipping or providing military intelligence to a conflict party – or even participating in the conflict directly. In some instances, an internationalised conflict can feature the involvement of external powers on both sides of the conflict. External powers may clash directly, or through local proxies or sponsored actors. However, an internationalised conflict differs from an international or inter-state conflict because the kernel of the conflict is an internal dispute.

Armed violence beyond armed conflict

Our definition of armed conflict excludes a large number of cases involving lethal armed force. The repression of a population by its government, with the application of lethal force, is not covered by this definition unless the population displays a capacity for armed, organised resistance. The Khmer Rouge regime in Cambodia killed more than one million of its own people between 1975 and 1979, but we do not regard this as an armed conflict because the regime did not encounter armed, organised resistance prior to the Vietnamese invasion. The same applies to the one-sided killing of civilians in East Timor by pro-Indonesia militias in the late 1990s, which prompted the dispatch of a United Nations peacekeeping force to protect civilians. Armed stand-offs between state or non-state actors, including the militarisation of the border between the Koreas and intermittent military incidents between the two states, do not meet the definition because there is no combat. Furthermore, many instances of criminal violence and associated high homicide rates do not meet our criteria concerning organisation. We exclude terrorist attacks of the kind seen in recent years in West European states, because although they have led to the domestic deployment of the armed forces in Belgium and France, there are not enough armed clashes in any given year to meet the criteria of duration and intensity. Terrorist attacks are a feature of some conflicts that we do recognise, but without sustained combat there is no armed conflict under our definition.

On the other hand, our definition includes cases of internal conflict where organised criminals, rather than revolutionaries or separatists, fight each other and the state. In Brazil, Colombia, El Salvador, Honduras and Mexico, there are organised groups using armed violence in a purposive manner against one another and against the state. In all cases, the state has responded by deploying its military forces against armed groups that have demonstrable logistical and operational capacity.

Some conflicts over time lose the qualities of intensity, duration or organisation that merit inclusion in *The Armed Conflict Survey*. In such cases we remove the conflict from the publication after a period of two years.

The search for a single definition of armed conflict is both limiting and enlightening. Limiting, in that there are instances of serious violence which, due to decisions over thresholds and classification, are not considered instances of armed conflict. However, the search for a definition is also enlightening because it forces us to engage more closely with the phenomenon. The outward form of conflict has changed considerably over time, from the set-piece battles of the nineteenth century and the total wars of the mid-twentieth century. The development of society and technology has wrought considerable change. Yet the nature of conflict remains a clash of wills through the medium of combat.

Notes

[1] Stathis Kalyvas, *The Logic of Violence in Civil War* (Cambridge: Cambridge University Press, 2006); Charles Tilly, *The Politics of Collective Violence* (Cambridge: Cambridge University Press, 2003); Matthew Levitt, 'Hamas from Cradle to Grave', *Middle East Quarterly*, vol. 11, Winter 2004, pp. 1–12, https://www.meforum.org/articles/2004/hamas-from-cradle-to-grave.

[2] Alexus G. Grynkewich, 'Welfare as Warfare: How Violent Non-State Groups Use Social Services to Attack the State', *Studies in Conflict and Terrorism*, vol. 31, no. 4, 2008, p. 353.

[3] Robert David Sack, *Human Territoriality: Its Theory and History* (Cambridge: Cambridge University Press, 1986).

[4] Nicholas Sambanis, 'What Is Civil War? Conceptual and Empirical Complexities of an Operational Definition', *Journal of Conflict Resolution*, vol. 48, no. 6, December 2004, pp. 814–58.

[5] Zachariah Cherian Mampilly, *Rebel Rulers: Insurgent Governance and Civilian Life During War* (Ithaca, NY: Cornell University Press, 2011); Anna Arjona, *Rebelocracy: Social Order in the Colombian Civil War* (Cambridge: Cambridge University Press, 2016).

[6] Paul Collier, *Breaking the Conflict Trap: Civil War and Development Policy* (Washington DC: World Bank and Oxford University Press, 2003); Paul Collier, Anke Hoeffler and Mans Soderbom, 'On the Duration of Civil War', *Journal of Peace Research*, vol. 41, no. 3, May 2004, pp. 253–73; James Fearon, 'Why Do Some Civil Wars Last So Much Longer Than Others?', *Journal of Peace Research*, vol. 41, no. 3, May 2004, p. 276.

The Financing of Armed Groups in Conflict

Colin P. Clarke

At its peak, the Islamic State, also known as ISIS or ISIL, controlled more than 100,000 square kilometres of territory containing more than 11 million people.[1] The United States, and the West in general, were caught completely by surprise by the rapid development of this new jihadist group, which attracted legions of recruits – including 40,000 foreign fighters from more than 120 countries worldwide – as it transformed into a formidable fighting force. Its social-media presence was ubiquitous and its propaganda compelling, both in its extremely high production values and also in the way in which it offered a bold vision of a new state founded on extremist ideals.[2] But above all else, perhaps the most surprising statistic about ISIS was that in 2015, the group's gross domestic product (GDP) was estimated at over US$6 billion. That figure put the Islamic State's GDP on a par with actual nation-states, including Lichtenstein, in terms of the size of its economy.[3] Through taxation and rent extraction, this violent non-state armed group amassed a huge war chest.

Although ISIS is perhaps an exceptional case, the issue of the financing of armed groups in conflict is one that draws together a plethora of motives and methods. This essay will explore the central role financing plays in the character and concerns of armed groups across the world. After a brief introduction to the subject of terrorist financing, this essay will focus on case studies in the Middle East, sub-Saharan Africa, South Asia, Asia-Pacific and Latin America to explore the variability in how terrorists, insurgents and other armed groups finance their operations and sustain their organisations. Finally, the essay will conclude with an analysis of how the international community, as well as individual nation-states and regional bodies, have approached the issue of terrorist financing, and what challenges lie ahead.

Terrorist financing defined and explained

Terrorist financing – defined here as the process of raising, storing and moving funds obtained through legal or illegal means for the purpose of terrorist acts or sustaining the logistical structure of a terrorist organisation – is an ongoing game of 'cat and mouse'.[4] Just as terrorists and insurgents are continually creating new financing networks to evade law enforcement, security officials tasked with countering the financing of irregular warfare must continually adapt their range of countermeasures in order to disrupt these networks. The challenges faced by security officials involved in countering terrorist financing are exacerbated by globalisation, the proliferation of failed states, the ubiquity of porous borders and the shifting of ungoverned and alternatively governed spaces.[5] Although groups engaged in terrorist financing exist largely outside of the licit economy, in many cases their illicit activities are connected in a variety of ways to more formal aspects of the global economy. For example, armed groups take advantage of globalisation by commingling their money with the voluminous amounts of capital transfers that total trillions of dollars daily.[6] By combining their resources and profits with legitimate funds, armed groups make it difficult to detect where criminal funds end and where legitimately earned funds begin.[7]

Terrorist financing is used to augment the ability of armed groups to execute attacks successfully, while some of the money is allocated towards organisational components aimed to increase group cohesion. In order to survive, armed groups must generate significant levels of income in order to sustain their operational capabilities and fund their organisations. In general, terrorists, insurgents, warlords, criminals and militias do not possess the ability to tax citizens legally, although again the case of ISIS between 2014 and 2017 proved an exception, with the group generating nearly 80% of its vast fortune by mimicking the functions of an actual nation-state, collecting taxes and tariffs from the citizens living in the territory it controlled. It also extorted individual citizens, specific ethnic groups, private corporations, local businesses and the Iraqi government.[8]

The case of ISIS could turn out to be an historical anomaly or, more likely, a model for armed groups to emulate in the future. But before looking at how armed groups might finance their organisations in the future, it is critical to evaluate how they have done so in the past and how this phenomenon has evolved over time.

Armed groups and income generation

The superpower proxy conflict between the US and the Soviet Union came to a close with the collapse of the Soviet Union in 1991, leading then US president George H.W. Bush to declare a 'new world order'. With such ambitious declarations dominating the headlines, one lesser noticed by-product of the end of the Cold War was the termination of sponsorship for a number of armed groups throughout the world, from Africa to Latin America. The end of the Cold War also resulted in a proliferation of cheap weapons flooding the global arms market, making it easier for non-state actors to address their funding deficits through armed criminal acts ranging from extortion to robbery.[9] Insurgents and criminals began cooperating more frequently out of necessity.[10] What were once top-down, hierarchical and parochial organisations deliberately sought to flatten their organisational structures in an attempt to become more networked, decentralised and transnational in both scope and scale.[11] To compensate for the withdrawal of external state sponsorship and patronage, those terrorist and insurgent groups which were determined to keep fighting sought to undertake most of their financing operations themselves, in part to mitigate vulnerabilities, but more importantly, to achieve a certain level of self-sufficiency.[12] The transnational-crime scholar Phil Williams was among the first to recognise the trend, and presciently labelled it 'do-it-yourself (DIY) organised crime'.[13]

Scholars have attempted to categorise armed groups by differentiating between criminal and political violence; in essence, by seeking to determine whether the motive of the group is chiefly profit (as is the case with criminals), or more ideologically based (as it is with insurgents and some terrorist groups). This is often simplified into the greed versus grievance debate. However, reducing the causes of war to an either/or scenario imposes analytical limitations by creating a dichotomy on what are instead extremely complex systems of social interaction.[14]

In contrast, Tamara Makarenko's 'crime–terror nexus' suggests that the relationship between armed rebellion and organised crime is flexible and exists on a sliding scale wherein groups can move back and forth between the extremes of crime and ideological insurgency, occupying any number of intermediate stages along the way.[15] Furthermore, the transition from a focus on politics to profits can change both the group's financial condition as well as its motivational structure.[16] Wars serve complex functions for armed groups, and in many cases belligerents craft strategies to prolong the conflict as a means of continuing to reap its economic benefits.[17] Accordingly, this can impact the evolution of the conflict, the development of the group itself and the prospects of various measures of conflict resolution. It is therefore impossible to separate the commercial interests and political aspirations of armed groups, since both are necessary for the group's existence and dictate the group's behaviour.

The allocation of finances and resources

Daniel Byman observes that insurgent groups are less likely to continue fighting if they believe they have little chance of success on the battlefield.[18] As success on the battlefield derives from a group's operational and organisational capabilities, it is therefore critical that armed groups maintain the funds that underpin these capabilities.[19] The operational capacity of an insurgent organisation is comprised of the activities that allow the insurgents to sustain a series of successful attacks, and include many of the things towards which insurgents dedicate financing, such as weapons, training, sanctuary, logistics and intelligence.[20] The organisational capacity of an insurgent group is comprised of those activities that sustain the group's existence as a cohesive entity and foster decision-making. Organisational capabilities include leadership, group structure, the dissemination of propaganda and the ability to recruit new members.

How an insurgent group finances itself has a major impact on the motivation of its members, overall group morale, political legitimacy and the trajectory of the conflict.[21] To illustrate how various armed groups raise funds and then deploy their resources, the next section of this essay analyses several armed groups from various regions of the world: ISIS, al-Shabaab, the Afghan Taliban, the Abu Sayyaf Group (ASG) and FARC.

Middle East: ISIS

As mentioned above, ISIS is unique in recent history as being one of the few insurgent groups to earn most of its revenue based on the territory it held, which was in turn connected to taxation and extortion, oil, looting, confiscation of property and cash, and fines levied against the population for perceived offences. (There are also some indications that ISIS has been involved with trafficking drugs.)[22] However, there is scant evidence that foreign donations were a significant funding source during the group's peak, while the sale of antiquities and kidnap for ransom (KFR) were also 'unlikely to have been major sources of income'.[23]

Although recent developments suggest that the period of extensive territorial control is now over, it also appears clear that ISIS is determined to fight to the death.[24] This stance may have broader implications than the fate of the group's fighters on the battlefield, with the group seeking to move pre-existing funds and diversify its income sources. Some figures estimate that ISIS successfully managed to smuggle as much as US$400m out of Iraq and Syria over the course of 2017, while also investing in legitimate businesses throughout the region, including hotels, hospitals, farms and car dealerships. ISIS militants have also made large purchases of gold in Turkey.

As the organisation continues to evolve, the group's sources of revenue could very well expand, with the group working to secure external funding from sympathetic donors throughout the Arab and Islamic world, or nation-states in the Middle East that view ISIS as a useful proxy in the region's ongoing internecine conflict.[25]

Sub-Saharan Africa: al-Shabaab

Al-Shabaab ('The Youth') is a radical faction that split off from the Islamic Courts Union (ICU) in Somalia, which itself was an outgrowth of al-Ittihad al-Islamiya (AIAI).[26] Al-Shabaab was formally created when a network of Afghan war veterans of Somali origin, ex-AIAI militants and al-Qaeda remnants throughout the Horn of Africa coalesced around 2005.[27] The group has waged an on–off insurgency throughout Somalia for more than a decade, relying on a range of ambush-style attacks, improvised explosive devices, assassinations and bombings (the group introduced suicide bombing to Somalia).[28]

Even by the standards of notoriously adaptive armed groups, al-Shabaab's funding model is innovative and opportunistic. The group makes money from the smuggling of sugar through Somalia into Kenya, a trade worth approximately US$200m–US$400m per year, although not all of this goes to al-Shabaab (other actors, including the Kenyan military, are also allegedly involved).[29] Al-Shabaab militants tax the transit of sugar as it passes through Somalia on its way to be repackaged and sold in wholesale markets in Nairobi.[30] The group also earns money from the illegal ivory trade, as well as significant sums of money – perhaps as much as US$25m a year – from the charcoal-smuggling business.[31] When armed groups have sizeable war chests, it allows them to maintain a high operational tempo of attacks, which in turn signals to group members that the organisation has a robust capacity. In turn, this attracts more recruits and can serve as a self-fulfilling prophecy, emboldening existing members and allowing terrorists and insurgents to be more audacious in planning spectacular attacks.

South Asia: the Afghan Taliban

The United Nations Office on Drugs and Crime (UNODC) estimates the Taliban's annual income at around US$400m, approximately half of which is earned through the illicit narcotics economy in Afghanistan.[32] Donations from wealthy sheikhs and hardline Islamist philanthropists have also helped sustain the Taliban, although exact figures on how much the Taliban has received from external financing are unclear.[33] Afghan émigrés and members of the diaspora who are sympathetic to the Taliban's cause have also helped finance the insurgency.[34]

Part of the Taliban's war chest is also derived from a multibillion-dollar trade in goods, including minerals and precious metals, smuggled from Dubai to Pakistan.[35] Complicating the situation in Afghanistan is the emergence of the Islamic State in Khorasan Province (ISIS–KP), which has received an influx of fighters and funding from the core ISIS movement and will inevitably seek to establish its own provincial revenue streams in the country, likely through extortion, smuggling and KFR operations, similar to the Afghan Taliban, thus bringing this new group into direct competition with the Taliban.[36]

Asia-Pacific: Abu Sayyaf Group

In Southeast Asia, KFR operations by the ASG and the Moro Islamic Liberation Front (MILF) provide further evidence of the blurred lines between criminality and terrorism.[37] The ASG is thought to have earned an estimated US$35m from KFR operations between 1992 and 2008. In the Philippines, the average ransom settlement for a foreigner is listed as US$250,000–US$3m (and up to US$5m), while the average ransom demand for a local is between US$2,000 and US$50,000.[38] The ASG has also been known to finance its activities through arms smuggling and drug trafficking, enabled by the geography throughout Southeast Asia where archipelagos and islands make maritime security a serious challenge.[39] Armed groups in the Asia-Pacific region have also relied on charities and investments through front companies, while regularly utilising bulk cash transfers and informal value transfer systems, such as hawalas, to transfer funds throughout their networks.[40]

In 2017, elements of the ASG joined forces with the ISIS-affiliated Maute group, composed of former MILF fighters, to seize Marawi, the largest city in Mindanao's autonomous region with a population of 200,000 people. The militants held Marawi for roughly five months despite intense assaults from the Philippines' security forces (which was even more impressive considering the counter-insurgent force included elite US-trained special-operations forces). The effectiveness of the insurgents was apparently bolstered by material support from ISIS – the core ISIS organisation in Iraq and Syria reportedly sent nearly US$2m to help finance the battle for the city, a particularly worrisome trend given ISIS's remaining war chest, thought to be in the hundreds of millions of US dollars, and apparent ability to maintain command-and-control nodes in franchise groups in disparate locations.[41] An infusion of funding in a post-Marawi environment could provide militants in the Philippines with the confidence to launch a new wave of attacks and challenge government security forces in areas where they are already weak or underrepresented, especially in areas where the population is sympathetic to the Islamic State's clarion call.

Latin America: FARC

FARC is a guerrilla movement that has been active in Colombia since the mid-1960s, motivated by Marxist-Leninist ideology and funded through rents from a range of sources, including smuggling and trafficking narcotics, extortion of both local government and other narco-traffickers, as well as investments in front companies and money laundering.[42] While some armed groups in Colombia, such as the National Liberation Army (ELN), have targeted multinational oil companies with intimidation and extortion, FARC set its sights on gold and other mining companies.[43]

Colombia has experienced a fragile peace since the signing of a landmark agreement between FARC and the Colombian government in November 2016, although the peace process suffered a major setback in March 2018 when Rodrigo Londoño (aka Timochenko) of the Common Alternative Revolutionary Force (the political party which succeeded FARC following the group's disarmament) exited the electoral race due to health concerns and was never replaced.[44] Many fear that if the peace process continues to stall, the country will descend once again into violence and chaos. Most of the armed groups in Colombia could quickly ramp up their operations, buoyed in large part by easy access to financing through participation in the illicit narcotics economy and widespread availability of extortion schemes and rackets targeting lucrative industries such as energy and mineral extraction.

Countering the financing of armed groups

In his essay entitled 'Don't Follow the Money: The Problem with the War on Terrorist Financing', Peter Neumann argues that, with respect to the global campaign to combat terrorist financing, 'there is no evidence that it has ever thwarted a terrorist campaign'.[45] However, it could be argued that even if a counter-insurgent force is unable to identify a measurable return from targeting the finances of armed groups, the alternative – completely eschewing this line of effort – seems even worse. In other words, it is always worth trying to prevent the funding of armed groups, even if empirical evidence of its efficacy proves elusive in many cases, not least because countering the funding of armed groups has ramifications beyond the finances themselves. As Brian Gordon and J. Edward Conway recognise, in the case of Afghanistan, the Taliban's taxation of the poppy harvest is not merely an issue of either counter-narcotics or counter-insurgency, but rather 'a threat finance and counterinsurgency issue – it both funds the Taliban and establishes the Taliban as the legitimate source of governance for the people'.[46]

Significant steps have been taken to counter the funding of armed groups. Following the al-Qaeda attacks of 11 September 2001, the Bush administration signed Executive Order 13224, an order which the then-president stated was specifically designed to 'starve the terrorists of funding' by blocking property and prohibiting transactions with persons who commit, threaten to commit or support terrorism.[47] For good measure, the United Nations Security Council unanimously adopted Resolution 1373, which called on all UN member states to criminalise the use or collection of funds intended, or known to be intended, for terrorism, in addition to freezing funds and assets; prohibiting aid or provision to terrorists; refraining from providing any support; and denying safe haven to those who finance, plan, support or commit terrorist acts.[48] Moreover, the USA PATRIOT Act, also signed in 2001, expanded the ability of law-enforcement officials and the intelligence community to access and share financial information regarding terrorist investigations.[49]

Yet even with enhanced tools, countering the financing of armed groups will remain an area with serious challenges, as the fight against ISIS demonstrates. Since early 2016, coalition forces have conducted targeted, intelligence-driven strikes on ISIS's oil operations and its bulk-cash stores in Iraq and Syria; to keep crippling the group's main sources of wealth, these operations will need to continue well into the foreseeable future. As ISIS continues to lose territory, it might attempt to compensate for losses in certain revenue streams by increasing revenue generation in other areas. Every potential facet of ISIS revenue should be considered for targeting or sanctioning, with the most difficult areas to counter – taxation and extortion of the local population – a longer-term objective that is closely tied to post-conflict reconstruction and the training of an effective security force in areas where rebels are still active. In Iraq, it will be crucial for coalition forces to move beyond advising, assisting, training and equipping Iraqi military efforts and instead dedicate more resources to training law-enforcement entities. In Syria, the situation is far more difficult, since President Bashar al-Assad remains in power and there is no semblance of state-security services capable of policing large swathes of eastern Syria.

Although the international community has made significant progress in countering the financing of terrorism, many challenges still lie ahead. In some cases, the challenges are more fundamental and include getting countries to pass legislation criminalising the financing of terrorism in the first place. These challenges are compounded by issues of capacity, as many developing countries, even if they are able to pass legislation, struggle with implementation, often relying on nascent and underfunded judicial infrastructures to investigate and prosecute individuals and groups conducting these activities.

As the case of ISIS highlighted, very little can be done to prevent a group from self-financing its activities when it is able to control large swathes of territory. While the international community has become much better at isolating armed groups from the international financial system, short of military intervention, there are few avenues that can be reliably counted upon to disrupt groups that raise and spend money locally. Furthermore, many armed groups are technologically savvy, and continue to explore new and innovative ways to raise and transfer funds, including through the use of virtual currencies and the exploitation of social media. Finally, there is the challenge of maintaining the momentum and capitalising upon the successes of the past two decades. As China, Iran, North Korea and Russia rise to the top of the global security agenda, armed groups and violent non-state actors will have more freedom of movement to exploit power vacuums in weak states and ungoverned spaces.

Colin P. Clarke is a political scientist at the RAND Corporation, a lecturer at Carnegie Mellon University's Institute for Politics & Strategy, an associate fellow at the International Centre for Counter-Terrorism (The Hague) and a non-resident Senior Fellow in the Program on National Security at the Foreign Policy Research Institute (FPRI). Twitter: @ColinPClarke.

Notes

[1] Seth G. Jones et al., *Rolling Back the Islamic State* (Santa Monica, CA: RAND Corporation, 2017), https://www.rand.org/pubs/research_reports/RR1912.html.

[2] Colin Clarke and Charlie Winter, 'The Islamic State May Be Failing, But Its Strategic Communications Legacy Is Here to Stay', *War on the Rocks*, 17 August 2017, https://warontherocks.com/2017/08/the-islamic-state-may-be-failing-but-its-strategic-communications-legacy-is-here-to-stay/.

[3] 'Islamic State Has Been Stashing Millions of Dollars in Iraq and Abroad', *The Economist*, 22 February 2018, https://www.economist.com/news/middle-east-and-africa/21737302-their-so-called-caliphate-crumbles-jihadists-are-saving-up-fight.

[4] Kevin D. Stringer, 'Tackling Threat Finance: A Labor for Hercules or Sisyphus', *Parameters,* vol. 41, no. 1, Spring 2011, pp. 101–19, http://ssi.armywarcollege.edu/pubs/Parameters/articles/2011spring/Stringer.pdf.

[5] Mark Duffield, 'Post Modern Conflict: Warlords, Post-Adjustment States, and Private Protection', *Civil Wars*, vol. 1, no. 1, Spring 1998, p. 68, http://site.uit.no/warandpeacedynamics/files/2013/03/Postmodern-Conflict.pdf; Phil Williams, *From the New Middle Ages to a New Dark Age: The Decline of the State and US Strategy* (Carlisle, PA: USAWC Strategic Studies Institute, 2008), p. 11, https://ssi.armywarcollege.edu/pubs/display.cfm?pubID=867.

[6] Sidney Weintraub, 'Disrupting the Financing of Terrorism', *Washington Quarterly*, vol. 25, no. 1, Winter 2002, pp. 53–60, https://www.tandfonline.com/doi/pdf/10.1162/016366002753358311.

[7] Louise I. Shelley and John T. Picarelli, 'Methods Not Motives: Implications of the Convergence of International Organized

Crime and Terrorism', *Police Practice and Research*, vol. 3, no. 4, 2002, p. 308.

8 Renad Mansour and Hisham al-Hashimi, 'ISIS Inc.', *Foreign Policy* blog, 16 January 2018, http://foreignpolicy.com/2018/01/16/isis-inc-islamic-state-iraq-syria/.

9 Stathis N. Kalyvas and Laia Balcells, 'International System and Technologies of Rebellion: How the End of the Cold War Shaped Internal Conflict', *American Political Science Review*, vol. 104, no. 3, 2010, pp. 415–29, https://pdfs.semanticscholar.org/ab6f/6a40ee839944089ae13471e7c3decd8f86a2.pdf.

10 Steve Hutchinson and Pat O'Malley, 'A Crime–Terror Nexus? Thinking on Some of the Links Between Terrorism and Criminality', *Studies in Conflict & Terrorism*, vol. 30, no. 12, 2007, pp. 1095–107.

11 Chris Dishman, 'The Leaderless Nexus: When Crime and Terror Converge', *Studies in Conflict & Terrorism,* vol. 28, no. 3, 2005, pp. 237–52, https://www.tandfonline.com/doi/pdf/10.1080/10576100701670870?needAccess=true.

12 Chris Dishman, 'Terrorism, Crime and Transformation', *Studies in Conflict & Terrorism,* vol. 24, no. 1, 2001, pp. 43–58, https://www.tandfonline.com/doi/abs/10.1080/10576100118878?journalCode=uter20.

13 Phil Williams, 'Terrorist Financing and Organized Crime: Nexus, Appropriation or Transformation?', in Thomas Biersteker and Susan Eckert (eds), *Countering the Financing of Terrorism* (London: Routledge, 2008), pp. 126–49.

14 Karen Ballentine and Heiko Nitzschke, 'Beyond Greed and Grievance: Policy Lessons from Studies in the Political Economy of Armed Conflict', International Peace Academy Policy Report, October 2003, p. 2, https://reliefweb.int/sites/reliefweb.int/files/resources/6765C3D3477FE91C8525742400689BD7-IPA_ArmedCoflict_Oct03.pdf.

15 Tamara Makarenko, 'The Crime–Terror Continuum: Tracing the Interplay between Transnational Organized Crime and Terrorism', *Global Crime*, vol. 6, no. 1, 2004, pp. 129–45, https://www.iracm.com/wp-content/uploads/2013/01/makarenko-global-crime-5399.pdf.

16 Svante Cornell, 'Narcotics and Armed Conflict: Interaction and Implications', *Studies in Conflict & Terrorism*, vol. 30, no. 3, 2007, p. 208, https://www.tandfonline.com/doi/abs/10.1080/10576100601148449.

17 David Keen, *Useful Enemies: When Waging Wars Is More Important than Winning Them* (New Haven, CT: Yale University Press, 2012).

18 Daniel Byman, 'Talking with Insurgents: A Guide for the Perplexed', *Washington Quarterly*, vol. 32, no. 2, 2009, p. 126, https://www.tandfonline.com/doi/pdf/10.1080/01636600902775565.

19 Colin P. Clarke, *Terrorism, Inc.: The Financing of Terrorism, Insurgency and Irregular Warfare* (Santa Barbara, CA: ABC–CLIO, 2015).

20 Kim Cragin et al., *The Dynamic Terrorist Threat: An Assessment of Group Motivations and Capabilities in a Changing World* (Santa Monica, CA: RAND Corporation, 2004), p. 25.

21 See the considerable body of literature devoted to the effect of resources on conflict: Paul Collier and Anke Hoeffler, 'Greed and Grievance in Civil War', *Oxford Economic Papers*, vol. 56, 2004, pp. 563–95, https://

www.econ.nyu.edu/user/debraj/Courses/ Readings/CollierHoeffler.pdf;   Richard Snyder, 'Does Lootable Wealth Breed Disorder? A Political Economy of Extraction Framework', *Comparative Political Studies*, vol. 39, no. 8, October 2006, pp. 943–68; Michael L. Ross, 'How Do Natural Resources Influence Civil War? Evidence from Thirteen Cases', *International Organization*, vol. 58, no. 1, Winter 2004, pp. 35–67, http://www.uky. edu/~clthyn2/PS439G/readings/ross_2004. pdf; Michael L. Ross, 'What Do We Know About Natural Resources and Civil War?', *Journal of Peace Research*, vol. 41, no. 3, 2004, pp. 337–56.

22 Colin P. Clarke, 'Drugs & Thugs: Funding Terrorism Through Narcotics Trafficking', *Journal of Strategic Security*, vol. 9, no. 3, Fall 2016,   http://scholarcommons.usf.edu/cgi/ viewcontent.cgi?article=1536&context=jss.

23 Stefan Heißner et al., 'Caliphate in Decline: An Estimate of Islamic State's Financial Fortunes', International Centre for the Study of Radicalisation and Political Violence (ICSR),   2017,   http://icsr.info/wp-content/ uploads/2017/02/ICSR-Report-Caliphate-in-Decline-An-Estimate-of-Islamic-States-Financial-Fortunes.pdf.

24 Phil Williams and Colin P. Clarke, 'Iraqi and Syrian Networks', in Kim Thachuk and Rollie Lal (eds), *Terrorist Criminal Enterprises* (Santa Barbara, CA: ABC–CLIO, forthcoming 2018).

25 Colin P. Clarke et al., *Financial Futures of the Islamic State of Iraq and the Levant* (Santa Monica, CA: RAND Corporation, 2017), https://www.rand.org/content/dam/rand/ pubs/conf_proceedings/CF300/CF361/ RAND_CF361.pdf.

26 Daveed Gartenstein-Ross, 'The Strategic Challenge of Somalia's Al-Shabaab', *Middle East Quarterly*, vol. 16, no. 4, Fall 2009, pp. 25–36. For a more robust discussion of AIAI, see Kenneth J. Menkhaus, 'Somalia and Somaliland: Terrorism, Political Islam, and State Collapse', in Robert I. Rotberg (ed.), *Battling Terrorism in the Horn of Africa* (Cambridge: World Peace Foundation, 2005), pp. 35–6.

27 Stig Jarle Hansen, *Al-Shabaab in Somalia: The History of a Militant Islamist Group, 2005–2012* (New York: Oxford University Press, 2013), pp. 28–32.

28 Ken Menkhaus, 'Non-State Actors and the Role of Violence in Stateless Somalia', in Klejda Mulaj (ed.), *Violent Non-State Actors in World Politics* (New York: Columbia University Press, 2010), p. 373.

29 Tom Keatinge, 'Sugar Not Ivory Is the Real "White Gold" of Al-Shabaab', *Royal United Services Institute Commentary*, 27 November 2015,   https://rusi.org/commentary/sugar-not-ivory-real-%E2%80%98white-gold%E2%80%99-al-shabaab.

30 Tom Keatinge, 'Gimme Some Sugar', *Foreign Affairs* blog, 3 December 2015, https://www. foreignaffairs.com/articles/2015-12-03/ gimme-some-sugar.

31 'A Charred Harvest: Charcoal and Terrorism in Somalia', *The Economist*, 11 October 2014,   https://www.economist.com/news/ middle-east-and-africa/21623793-unlikely-link-between-gulf-lounges-and-somalias-jihadists-charred-harvest.

32 United Nations Office on Drugs and Crime, *World Drug Report 2017*, see Executive Summary, p. 23, http://www.unodc.org/ wdr2017/.

33 Carlotta Gall, 'Saudis Bankroll Taliban, Even as King Officially Supports Afghan Government', *New York Times,* 6 December 2016, https://www.nytimes.com/2016/12/06/world/asia/saudi-arabia-afghanistan.html.

34 Council on Foreign Relations, 'The Taliban: A CFR InfoGuide Presentation', 17 August 2017, see 'Profiteers and Ideologues' section, https://www.cfr.org/interactives/taliban?cid=marketing_use-taliban_infoguide-012115#!/taliban?cid=marketing_use-taliban_infoguide-012115.

35 Barnett R. Rubin, 'The Political Economy of War and Peace in Afghanistan', *World Development,* vol. 28, no. 10, 2000, pp. 1,789–803, https://pdfs.semanticscholar.org/c36f/7be485354bca2bc1991280c4cb5204a3914f.pdf.

36 Bennett Seftel, '"Persistent, Expanding and Worrisome": ISIS Rebounds in Afghanistan', *Cipher Brief* blog, 5 January 2018, https://www.thecipherbrief.com/persistent-expanding-worrisome-isis-rebounds-afghanistan; see also Amanda Erickson, 'How the Islamic State Got a Foothold in Afghanistan', *Washington Post,* 21 March 2018, https://www.washingtonpost.com/news/worldviews/wp/2018/03/21/how-the-islamic-state-got-a-foothold-in-afghanistan/?utm_term=.043e2337a6ae.

37 Thomas M. Sanderson, 'Transnational Terror and Organized Crime: Blurring the Lines', *SAIS Review,* vol. 24, no. 1, Winter–Spring 2004, p. 52.

38 McKenzie O'Brien, 'Fluctuations Between Crime and Terror: The Case of Abu Sayyaf's Kidnapping Activities', *Terrorism & Political Violence,* vol. 24, no. 2, 2012, p. 321, https://www.tandfonline.com/doi/pdf/10.1080/09546553.2011.648679?needAccess=true.

39 Wade A. Germann et al., 'Terrorist Financing in the Philippines', in Michael Freeman (ed.), *Financing Terrorism: Case Studies* (London: Ashgate, 2012), p. 149.

40 Aurel Croissant and Daniel Barlow, 'Terrorist Financing and Government Responses in Southeast Asia', in Harold A. Trinkunas and Jeanne K. Giraldo (eds), *Terrorism Financing and State Responses: A Comparative Perspective* (Palo Alto, CA: Stanford University Press, 2008).

41 Patrick B. Johnston and Colin P. Clarke, 'Is the Philippines the Next Caliphate?', *Foreign Policy* blog, 27 November 2017, http://foreignpolicy.com/2017/11/27/is-the-philippines-the-next-caliphate/.

42 Nazih Richani, 'Fragmentation of Sovereignty and Violent Non-State Actors in Colombia', in Klejda Mulaj (ed.), *Violent Non-State Actors in World Politics* (New York: Columbia University Press, 2010), p. 37; see also Jennifer Holmes et al., 'A Subnational Study of Insurgency: FARC Violence in the 1990s', *Studies in Conflict and Terrorism,* vol. 30, no. 3, 2007, pp. 249–65, https://www.tandfonline.com/doi/pdf/10.1080/10576100601148456?needAccess=true.

43 Francisco Gutiérrez Sanin, 'Criminal Rebels? A Discussion of War and Criminality from the Colombian Experience', London School of Economics Working Paper no. 27, April 2003, p. 9, https://assets.publishing.service.gov.uk/media/57a08cfd40f0b652dd0016bc/WP27FG.pdf.

44 Nicholas Casey, 'Colombia Rebel Ends Presidential Campaign, in Blow to Peace Process', *New York Times,* 8 March 2018, https://www.nytimes.com/2018/03/08/world/americas/colombia-election-timochenko-farc.html.

45 Peter Neumann, 'Don't Follow the Money', *Foreign Affairs,* vol. 96, no. 4, July/August 2017, https://www.foreignaffairs.com/articles/2017-06-13/dont-follow-money.

46 Brian A. Gordon and J. Edward Conway, 'Cost Accounting: Auditing the Taliban in Helmand Province, Afghanistan', in David M. Blum and J. Edward Conway (eds), Counterterrorism and Threat Finance Analysis During Wartime (Lanham, MD: Lexington Books, 2015), p. 82.

47 Aimen Dean et al., 'Draining the Ocean to Catch One Type of Fish: Evaluating the Effectiveness of the Global Counter-Terrorism Financing Regime', *Perspectives on Terrorism*, vol. 7, no. 4, 2013, http://www.terrorismanalysts.com/pt/index.php/pot/article/view/282/570.

48 Jonathan M. Winer and Trifin J. Roule, 'Fighting Terrorist Finance', *Survival*, vol. 44, no. 3, 2002, p. 91.

49 Jeffery M. Johnson and Carl Jensen, 'The Financing of Terrorism', *Journal of the Institute of Justice & International Studies*, no. 10, 2010, p. 111.

Child Soldiers in Armed Conflict

Mia Bloom

This essay defines a child soldier as anyone under 18 years of age who is part of any regular or irregular armed force.[1] This definition includes youth who are forcibly recruited, as well as those who join voluntarily. (The idea of voluntary enrolment, however, must be understood in the specific context of armed conflict, as discussed below.) All child participants, regardless of function (for example, cooks, porters, messengers, 'bush wives' or other support roles), are included in the definition. Customary international humanitarian law clearly forbids the utilisation of child soldiers, stating that 'children must not be recruited into armed forces or armed groups' and that 'children must not be allowed to take part in hostilities' in either international armed conflicts or civil wars.[2]

Despite the legal prohibition, the use of child soldiers in armed conflict has risen over the past 20 years. The phenomenon of child soldiers in Africa has been well documented and the exploitation of children by such armed groups as the Liberation Tigers of Tamil Eelam (LTTE) has garnered international condemnation. The Islamic State, also known as ISIS or ISIL, is perhaps the most notorious of the armed groups, having trained hundreds if not thousands of children for military engagement since the group came to global prominence in 2014.[3] The group has also featured child soldiers extensively in its propaganda. A video from January 2015 showed 12-year-old Ryan Essid from Toulouse executing two Russian prisoners accused of being spies for Russia's Federal Security Service.[4] A follow-up video featured a 13-year-old boy shooting Muhammad Mossalam, an Arab Israeli from Jerusalem, several times, including once in the head.[5] On 4 July 2015, 25 boys shot

25 Syrian-regime soldiers before a packed crowd at the ancient Roman theatre in Palmyra.[6]

The current prevalence of children in armed conflict is also accompanied by a trend for armed groups to use younger children, a fact reflected in the continuing decline in the overall median age of suicide bombers.[7] As well as adolescents, groups now often use 12-year-olds (and sometimes children as young as seven) as suicide bombers. By exploiting children, armed groups gain comparative advantages, notably the element of surprise and increased media attention for the shock value of breaching previous societal and psychological barriers.

The recruitment of child soldiers remains a major issue, with the internet offering a way for armed groups to reach young people not located in the vicinity of the conflict. Efforts at grooming the next generation have been uncovered in diaspora communities in the United States and the United Kingdom. Perhaps the most well-known case was the disappearance of Burhan Hassan and six of his Somali-American friends from Minneapolis between 2007 and 2009 to join al-Shabaab, the militant Islamist group based in Somalia.[8] In August 2013, young al-Shabaab members from Minnesota were featured in a recruitment video using the tagline '*This* is the *real* Disneyland'.[9] However, the recruitment drives of armed groups are still most tangible at ground level. Schools dedicated to churning out 'martyrs' have been established in Iraq, Pakistan, Syria and Sudan; football teams, streets, parks and summer camps in Palestine are named after terrorists.[10] Some groups kidnap children, while others lure them with incentives.

This essay will explore the issue of child soldiers in armed conflict by examining the various methods of recruitment, indoctrination and initiation used by armed groups, as well as the different roles undertaken by girls and boys. The essay will conclude with an assessment of the challenges facing the disarmament, demobilisation and reintegration (DDR) of child soldiers. As will be seen, the diverse range of experiences of child soldiers means that it is difficult if not impossible to ascertain a set of assumptions about the experience of child soldiers, posing difficult questions for those trying to address the phenomenon at the policy level.

Recruitment

The role of family is a key factor accounting for variation in child-recruitment practices, although this differs from conflict to conflict. As a general rule, parents or caregivers in sub-Saharan Africa are not willing participants in the recruitment process, with children often being abducted or forcibly separated from their guardians. By contrast, the children in ISIS-controlled schools tend to be those whose families volunteered them or who have been found in orphanages.[11] Mohammed, a young ISIS member, said that he was recruited by his uncle: 'he took me to Sharia classes and then he told me: "Son, now you have to go to the training camp."'[12] Some ISIS parents appear not only to be willing to permit their children's participation but to encourage it openly. *Muhajiroun* ('emigrant', i.e., people who have travelled to Iraq and Syria to join the caliphate) parents have taken to Western social media to post images of their children posing with mutilated corpses and severed heads[13] and encourage their children to become martyrs in video propaganda. In this regard, ISIS recruitment parallels that of the Moro Islamic Liberation Front (MILF) in the Philippines, which encourages children to engage in militant activities along with their family.

In other cases, parents might sell their children to militias voluntarily or because they are coerced. In 2009, Baitullah Mehsud, then leader of the Tehrik-e-Taliban Pakistan (TTP), was reported to be buying children aged between seven and 16 to serve as suicide bombers against US, Pakistani and Afghan targets. Pakistani officials confirmed that children were being sold for prices between US$7,000 and US$14,000 in a nation where the per capita income is US$2,600 per year.[14] Child trafficking also occurs in the Philippines. In a January 2018 report in the *Manila Times*, Drei Toledo and Mimi Fabe interviewed a Filipina mother who was given 150,000 pesos (US$3,000) in exchange for her 11-year-old son to join an ISIS-backed group in Marawi.[15] In the Swat Valley region of Pakistan, however, Taliban commanders often did not give parents an option. Given widespread poverty, the TTP would demand financial payments equivalent to two years' salary from the local civilian population in return for protection. If families could not pay this extortionate amount, the group demanded a child for the movement instead.[16]

Despite these variables, Scott Gates and Simon Reich have identified common themes across a variety of cases that relate to the vulnerability of children to recruitment in their edited volume *Child Soldiers in the Age of Fractured States*. In chapter one, Barry Ames explains that 'children become especially vulnerable with the breakdown of the traditional extended family'; that 'schooling can mitigate the risk of child soldiering';[17] and that 'children are more likely to become child soldiers if one or both parents are dead'.[18]

Some child soldiers may be said to join armed groups voluntarily, although it is important to note the argument of Lisa Alfredson, who states that 'voluntary' participation may be only an illusion in situations where political or economic forces leave children with no other option.[19] Children may perceive joining violent organisations as a safer option compared to being preyed upon.[20] In Afghanistan, the need for food and shelter are strong motivations for children to enlist, as reported by Hujjatullah Zia in 2014: 'Taliban insurgents are bribing starving children to plant roadside bombs, act as decoys and to be suicide bombers against Afghan and foreign forces in the country. They recruit the young boys from the ranks of homeless and orphaned children.'[21]

Youth who joined the LTTE cited multiple motivations, including feelings of discrimination or inequality. Often the inadequate provision of state benefits – especially education – instilled a sense of outrage. One interviewee explained:

> Youngsters [of] school age know … as Tamils they are discriminated [against]. Even if you study you are going to be under suppression. Tamils need a higher cut off point than the Sinhalese, to get to the University. So we see that we have no future.[22]

Myriam Denov stresses that girls join armed groups to satisfy basic needs (such as food) or to exact revenge for lost loved ones. The desire for protection may inspire girls to join militant groups such as FARC in Colombia in order to escape domestic abuse at home as well as develop skills.[23] In Sierra Leone, girls joined the Civil Defence Forces as fighters along with their boyfriends or husbands, while in societies that oppress women girls may join for real or perceived empowerment. This author observed one such example in northeastern Sri Lanka, where the LTTE made it explicit that the regime would sexually abuse women at checkpoints and thus joining the terrorist group was the best prophylactic.

ISIS notably recruits children using non-coercive means by gradually exposing them to the group's ideology, worldview and apocalyptic vision. The organisation convenes public events aimed at raising awareness of the group, attracting children by offering them toys, candy or ice cream just for showing up. [24] Local children help out at these events by waving the ISIS flag or distributing leaflets to passers-by. This 'soft' approach by ISIS illustrates the extent of its propaganda campaign, which blurs the distinction between recruitment and indoctrination.

Education and indoctrination

The different methods of indoctrination employed by armed groups often point towards the different role child soldiers are expected to play in the broader context of the conflict. This is most evident in a group's approach to education, particularly in the case of ISIS.

As a result of the civil war breaking out in 2011, the Syrian state descended into chaos and in 2014 ISIS assumed de facto authority over schools in the areas under its control. Although a significant portion of Syrian teachers remained in their positions, they were forced to teach an ISIS-controlled curriculum to gender-segregated pupils, a curriculum which included weapons training and intense ideological conditioning. According to the head of the Syrian Observatory for Human Rights, Rami Abdulrahman, '[ISIS] uses children because it is easy to brainwash them. They can build these children into what they want, they stop them from going to school and send them to ISIS schools instead.'[25] As well as indoctrinating children, these schools also provided recruiters with access and opportunity to scout for talent. Children with an aptitude for communication were deployed as recruiters themselves, adopting public-speaking roles to conscript others. Child recruiters not only goad adults but also more children into the fold with the promise of status, purpose and admiration from adults and the public alike.

ISIS intends to engender a sense of pride, prestige and competition among the students to achieve status as a 'cub'. Students earn cub status in one of the dedicated training camps where they learn the skills needed to become a militant.[26] Since its rise, ISIS has used footage of child soldiers being trained as part of its propaganda. Between May and July 2015, the group released three videos featuring children aged between ten and 15 years old. In the videos, children are trained as snipers and taught how to ambush moving targets: one video depicted young boys in a live-fire exercise inside an ISIS 'kill house' (an indoor firing range). A video from February 2015 featured 80 children – some as young as five – wearing camouflage, standing in formation and engaging in military exercises.[27] They were also taught how to behead people and use AK-47s.

ISIS has pioneered a unique form of resilience by combining intense physical and military training with deep levels of ideological and psychological indoctrination. The group has designed a systematic process that produces competent militants who embrace every aspect of its teachings, not just mindless drones. This is because ISIS's priority is ensuring the continuity and longevity of the group: the ISIS cubs represent the group's best chance for survival. In October 2017, as ISIS began to lose vast stretches of its territory in Syria and Iraq, their propaganda centred on expansion into Southeast Asia. Recruiters posted the following message in ISIS chat rooms:

> Remember: 'Marawi is just the beginning!' as of those who survives Walahi we will train those new cubs and soldiers migrated from different countries for the knowledge we gain inside for more than 4 month of intense fighting against your crusader forces. Walahi the next seige [sic] you will never see it coming bi'idnillah.[28]

Educational programmes organised in ISIS-controlled schools stand in contrast to the experiences of child soldiers in Liberia and Uganda, who were often perceived as mere cannon fodder – efforts to educate them were irrelevant. In general, African militias in Sierra Leone and the Democratic Republic of the Congo often regard children as low-skilled members of the group, valuable only because of their youth and availability. These militias are not interested in creating an ideological legacy – they simply require bodies to fight. In contrast, the LTTE combined military with ideological training; the group trained children with wooden rifles to prepare them for using a real gun. Children first served as messengers and spies, before becoming combatants by the age of ten (once they were strong enough to shoot a real gun). The LTTE, however, also stressed ideological conformity and education.

In the same way that each group approaches the ideological indoctrination of their recruits in a different way – including sometimes not at all – so too do different groups use different initiation procedures to turn a child recruit into a child soldier.

Initiation

Historically, terrorist groups have formalised the inclusion of children by creating youth wings or dedicated brigades, with the intention of providing ideological preparation to ensure consistent and unified political views. (Examples come from Hamas, Ogra Sinn Féin and Hizbullah.) In most of the groups, children are not 'activated' for front-line activities until after they turn 16. In fact, some of the left-wing European groups (such as the Italian left-wing group the Red Brigades) refused to engage youth altogether. By contrast, ISIS targets very young children and engages them on the front-lines as young as six.

Once organised into the structure of an armed group, children must then be initiated and prepared for the realities of conflict. Perpetrating acts of extreme violence, including forcing children to kill their own parents or perform acts of brutality against family members, can be a crucial mechanism in the initiation process. Dara Cohen writes that an act of violence by a group, such as gang rape, helps cohere the recruits, fosters kinship, builds bonds and creates a macabre 'band of brothers', especially in situations where recruitment was coerced.[29] Forcing children to kill members of their own family can cause a psychological break and result in them attaching to a new entity. Militias accordingly socialise the children to form close ties to the group, replacing family with members of the militia to create a new 'family'. This intimate form of violence also cuts the child off from a possible exit from the militia, leaving them nowhere to go. Child soldiers in African conflicts were often moved from their traditional villages or forced to kill family members in order to destroy their option of fleeing home.[30]

ISIS exposes children to corporal punishment of prisoners or those accused of being apostates (i.e., other Muslims who do not subscribe to the doctrine of ISIS) – the routine spectacle of such events forces children to internalise the violence. Although some children may get physically ill from attending the beheadings,[31] the vast majority become immune to violence, representing what the psychologist Albert Bandura described as 'moral disengagement and the process of desensitization'.[32] In propaganda, children are carefully posed and coached by those filming on how to behave and what to say. In some cases, the children are praised for wielding a weapon or holding up a decapitated head.

Corporal punishment also forms a part of the training for ISIS child recruits. Accounts of former ISIS recruits paint a bleak picture of life in the camps. Children were pushed to their mental and physical limits during the training sessions, beaten to 'toughen them up' and forced to sleep on flea-infested mattresses. Yet despite the hardships, or maybe as a result of them, the experiences fostered an intense sense of camaraderie among the cohort. In northern Uganda, however, McKay and Mazurana report that the severity of the training process often leads to the death of the children:

> All children and youth, except those females with very small children or who are pregnant, begin early every morning with forced singing and dancing at a frenzied pace. After hours of singing and dancing, at noon in the heat of the day the children are then forced to run in wide circles or up and down hills until the middle of the afternoon. Any boy or girl who drops from exhaustion, is left to die … the training continues from one to three months. The majority of abductees die before or during this initial training period.[33]

A significant difference in the mechanisms of initiation between armed groups relates to the role of narcotics and alcohol. Myriam Denov and Richard Maclure describe how African militias use drugs and alcohol in the early stages of initiation to sow confusion and fear, and to prepare children for violent attacks.[34] Drug use was prevalent in the Revolutionary United Front (RUF) in Sierra Leone, where some children reported being injected with cocaine, hallucinatory drugs, alcohol or gunpowder as a means of gearing them up for fighting.[35] According to UNICEF's Tanya Zayed, one of the first lessons for new recruits was how to roll a joint, smoke drugs and how to rape a woman.[36] By contrast, there are virtually no reports of ISIS children using illegal substances. Many terrorist groups eschew drug use because it diminishes the capacity of operatives to carry out basic instructions, whereas African militias often used drugs to dull, reward, calm or ramp up child soldiers.

Gender and role differentiation

Different groups structure the training of children in different ways according to the child's gender and intended role. Denov and Maclure's life history of RUF child soldiers in Sierra Leone outlines the process of role development and compares the experiences of a male and female RUF fighter.[37] Isata was abducted at the age of nine and immediately gang raped and sexually abused until she became the 'wife' of a commander. Although the effects of being raped were harmful for boys and girls, it had especially negative effects on boys: post-traumatic stress disorder (PTSD), social dysfunction and suicidal tendencies were present among male rape survivors, but not female survivors. This differential effect may be attributable to shame and internalising of negative emotions.[38] Isata's initial role was domestic and included cooking, cleaning and portage. After a year, she received weapons training and became a combatant, which she found to be empowering. She eventually took part in killings and mutilations, and used drugs and alcohol along with the rest of the group. She exited the group after being abandoned by the commander who impregnated her, and she was rescued by UN troops.[39]

Girls have often played a significant role in armed conflict, constituting as much as 30% of child soldiers globally. McKay and Mazurana document that in northern Uganda, 72% of the girls received military training immediately upon arrival to a base. However, as Isata's case demonstrates, the roles for girls in armed groups tend to be multifaceted, involving 'domestic work, sexual slavery, and combat activities. Importantly, in all of the contexts, girls' roles were multiple and fluid most often carrying out a variety of roles and tasks simultaneously.'[40] Domestic work was critical to the successful functioning of the groups and would not have been considered a lesser task.

Although al-Qaeda in Iraq (AQI) inspired ISIS's ideology,[41] there is one key difference between the groups, namely that ISIS excludes girls from its recruitment of child soldiers. This exclusion makes it unique compared to other groups that have employed children on the front-lines, such as the Irish Republican Army (IRA), the LTTE, the North Caucasus group Imarat Kavkaz (IK) and the Palestinian groups the al-Aqsa Martyrs' Brigade (AMB) and the Popular Front for the Liberation of Palestine (PFLP). ISIS enforces gender hyper-segregation of boys from girls and men from women, and refuses to engage women in combat. It is worth noting that Salafi jihadist ideology is not the key reason accounting for the difference of whether or not to engage female combatants, as AQI and other jihadi groups, including Boko Haram, have all used women (and girls) to deadly effect.[42] It appears that ISIS values women more as commodities than as front-line activists. In contrast to this, in 2014,

UNICEF reported that Boko Haram used women and girls to carry out three-quarters of the attacks in Nigeria.[43]

It is useful to compare ISIS with Boko Haram. Despite Boko Haram's pledge of allegiance (*bay'ah*) in March 2015, the two organisations remain worlds apart in terms of strategy. Recent research has illustrated that the vast majority of suicide attacks against civilians in Nigeria have been perpetrated by females. Jason Warner and Hilary Matfess have reported that in the period between April 2011 and June 2017, Boko Haram deployed 434 bombers in 238 attacks, of which at least 56% were women (243) and at least 81 were children or teenagers.[44] Boko Haram has used girls as young as seven to carry out attacks. One girl blew herself up along with a baby strapped to her back.

Demobilisation and deradicalisation

Child soldiers in Africa are recruited not for the future but for the present. Many, if not most, children are killed in battle and few survive to progress through the ranks to become leaders. By contrast, ISIS takes a longer strategic view of their child recruits. This difference in approach has significant implications for those actors attempting to rehabilitate former child soldiers: what may have worked for several DDR programmes in Africa – transformative roles for children aided by family, community, educational and religious authorities – may not work as seamlessly in Syria, as these institutions have been co-opted, controlled and distorted by ISIS.

If the international community is to have any hope of reintegrating those children who survive and leave ISIS, one thing is certain: it will require a level of coordination and creativity not seen in any DDR programme to date. Demobilisation will require a multi-pronged approach that addresses the psychological trauma suffered by the children from watching executions, in addition to the effects of having participated in acts of violence. The *Telegraph* interviewed former 'cubs of the Caliphate' who are now orphans or wounded; some of them are depressed or suffer from PTSD.[45]

Given that indoctrination in many cases started at a very young age, the children will need to unlearn the distortions of the Islamic faith and re-learn basic life skills along with participating in vocational training. (Gates and Reich have noted that 'former child soldiers as a general rule suffered from a lack of education and vocational skills'.)[46] This is a long-term process, longer than the three-month rehabilitation standard that already exists. These children will likely have problems with socialisation, lack empathy and suffer from attachment problems, and normalisation will be all the more challenging.

Two cornerstones of successful DDR programmes of the past – the Catholic Church and reunifying child soldiers with their extended families – are not good options for children who have been soldiers under ISIS. For one, the children's knowledge and experience of religion has been profoundly distorted (as was the case among Pakistani children abducted by the Taliban), meaning that there would need to be a significant re-education in the Islamic faith. More problematic is the role that parents and families played in providing the terrorist organisation with access to children. One cannot guard against recidivism if the children are returned to the families that exposed them to the violence in the first place. The experiences of children at Sabaoon in Pakistan are instructive. While the programme has been extraordinarily successful, the one case where the child returned to the militants was one in which a brother had recruited his younger sibling. When the child returned from the deradicalisation programme, his brother once again pulled him into the group. In cases where families have been the source of radicalisation, an extreme solution – separating children from their families – might have to be entertained, making DDR all the more challenging.

However, while the endeavour of reintegrating children who have been soldiers into society will certainly be complicated, we have no choice but to begin planning for it. The increasing prevalence of armed groups using children as combatants, the challenges deriving from the varying practices of child soldiering and the psychological effects suffered by children who participate in armed conflict all indicate that DDR is an urgent issue for both the present and the future.

Mia Bloom is Professor of Communication and Middle East Studies at Georgia State University and the author of *Small Arms: Children and Terrorism*, forthcoming from Cornell University Press. Twitter: @miambloom.

Notes

1 The Fourth Geneva Convention and Additional Protocol I hold that children affected by armed conflict are entitled to special respect and protection; the latter instrument also states that children must 'not take a direct part in hostilities' and that 'conscripting or enlisting children' into armed forces or groups constitutes a war crime in any armed conflict. (The International Criminal Court's Rome Statute says roughly the same thing.) https://www.icrc.org/customary-ihl/eng/docs/v1_rul_rule135.

2 Jean-Marie Henckaerts and Louise Doswald-Beck (eds), *Customary International Humanitarian Law* (Cambridge: International Committee of the Red Cross (ICRC) and Cambridge University Press, 2005), rules 136 and 156; Rome Statute of the International Criminal Court, adopted 17 July 1998, UN. Doc.A/CONF.183/9 (1998), entered into force 1 July 2002, arts. 8(2)(b)(xxvi) and 8(2)(e)(vii), http://legal.un.org/icc/statute/99_corr/cstatute.htm; see also https://ihl-databases.icrc.org/customary-ihl/eng/docs/home.

3 'ISIL Terrorists recruit children for war in Syria', Alalam News, 25 December 2013, http://en.alalam.ir/news/1548067.

4 https://www.youtube.com/watch?v=aljxSxvqC6I; see also 'Latest ISIS executioners linked to 2012 France attack', CBS News, 11 March 2015, https://www.cbsnews.com/news/isis-teen-militant-execution-video-toulouse-mohammed-merah-jewish-school/.

5 Elise Labott, 'New ISIS video claims to show child killing Palestinian captive', CNN, 11 March 2015, http://www.cnn.com/2015/03/10/middleeast/isis-video-israeli-killed/.

6 'Isis video shows killing of Syrian troops at Palmyra amphitheatre', *Guardian*, 4 July 2015, https://www.theguardian.com/world/2015/jul/04/isis-video-killing-palmyra-amphitheatre.

7 Einav Yogev and Yoram Schweitzer, 'Suicide Attacks in 2015', Institute for National Security Studies Insight no. 789, 26 January 2016, http://www.inss.org.il/publication/suicide-attacks-in-2015/; for average age, see https://ctc.usma.edu/depictions-of-children-and-youth-in-the-islamic-states-martyrdom-propaganda-2015-2016/.

8 Dina Temple-Raston, 'Missing Somali Teens May Be Terrorist Recruits', NPR, 28 January 2009, https://www.npr.org/templates/story/story.php?storyId=99919934.

9 'Al Shabaab's American Pipeline for Terrorism', ABC, http://abcnews.go.com/WNT/video/al-shabaabs-american-pipeline-terrorism-20351030.

10 Souad Mekhennet and Joby Warwick, 'For the "children of ISIS", target practice starts at age 6. By their teens, they're ready to be suicide bombers,' *Washington Post*, 7 October 2016, https://www.washingtonpost.com/world/national-security/for-the-children-of-isis-target-practice-starts-at-age-6-by-their-teens-theyre-ready-to-be-suicide-bombers/2016/10/06/3b59f0fc-8664-11e6-92c2-14b64f3d453f_story.html?utm_term=.7934edf4b661; see also http://www.palwatch.org/main.aspx?fi=362.

11 John G. Horgan, Max Taylor, Mia Bloom and Charlie Winter, 'From Cubs to Lions:

A Six Stage Model of Child Socialization into the Islamic State', *Studies in Conflict and Terrorism*, vol. 40, no. 7, 2017, pp. 645–64.

12 Wilson Fache, 'Cigarettes, music and shaking women's hands: how to rehabilitate Isil's child soldiers', *Telegraph*, 30 December 2017, http://www.telegraph. co.uk/news/2017/12/30/cigarettes-music-shaking-womens-hands-rehabilitate-isils-child/.

13 Heather Saul, 'Khaled Sharrouf: Mother of boy pictured holding severed head "wants to return to Australia" – but PM warns family will face full force of law', *Independent*, 28 May 2015, http://www.independent.co.uk/news/world/australasia/khaled-sharrouf-mother-of-boy-pictured-holding-severed-head-wants-to-return-to-australia--but-pm-warns-family-will-face-full-force-of-law-10281994.html.

14 'Taliban buying children for suicide bombers', *Washington Times*, 2 July 2009, https://www.washingtontimes.com/news/2009/jul/02/taliban-buying-children-to-serve-as-suicide-bomber/.

15 Drei Toledo and Mimi Fabe, 'Terrorists Recruiting Child Warriors from Sabah and Marawi', *Manila Times*, 5 January 2018, http://www.manilatimes.net/terrorists-recruiting-child-warriors-sabah-marawi/372351/.

16 John Horgan, 'Child Suicide Bombers Find Safe Haven', CNN, 27 March 2013, http://www.cnn.com/2013/03/27/world/asia/pakistan-anti-taliban/index.html.

17 Scott Gates and Simon Reich (eds), *Child Soldiers in the Age of Fractured States* (Pittsburgh, PA: University of Pittsburgh Press, 2010), pp. 8, 10 and 15.

18 Barry Ames, 'Methodological Problems in the Study of Child Soldiers', in Gates and Reich (eds), *Child Soldiers in the Age of Fractured States*, p. 16.

19 Lisa Alfredson, 'Child soldiers, displacement and human security', *Children and Security*, 3, 2002, pp. 17–27.

20 David M. Rosen, *Armies of the Young: Child Soldiers in War and Terrorism* (New Brunswick, NJ: Rutgers University Press, 2005).

21 Hujjatullah Zia, 'The Psychological Effects of War on Children', *Daily Outlook*, 17 March 2014, http://outlookafghanistan.net/topics.php?post_id=9665#ixzz4zxCvkDfS.

22 P. Kanagaratnam, M. Raundalen and A. Asbjørnsen, 'Ideological commitment and posttraumatic stress in former Tamil child soldiers', *Scandinavian Journal of Psychology*, vol. 46, no. 6, 2005, p. 515.

23 J. Rice, 'Girls at War: Historical Perspectives and Representations', in Helga Embacher et al. (eds), *Children and War: Past and Present* (West Midlands, England: Helion & Company Limited, 2013).

24 John Horgan and Mia Bloom, 'This Is How the Islamic State Manufactures Child Militants', *Vice*, 8 July 2015, https://news.vice.com/article/this-is-how-the-islamic-state-manufactures-child-militants.

25 'Islamic State recruits 400 children since Jan – Syria monitor', Reuters, 24 March 2015, http://in.reuters.com/article/2015/03/24/mideast-crisis-syria-children-idINKBN0MK0U620150324.

26 'Inside ISIS Training Camps for Terror's Next Generation', Fox News, 20 July 2015, http://www.foxnews.com/world/2015/07/20/beat-us-everywhere-inside-isis-training-camps-for-terror-next-generation/.

27 Richard Engel, 'Child Soldiers, or "Cubs," Shown in Latest ISIS Video', NBC News, 22

February 2015, http://www.nbcnews.com/storyline/isis-terror/child-soldiers-or-cubs-shown-latest-isis-video-n310646.

28 Alnasseri, 'Sons of the Khilafah', Telegram, posted 17 October 2017.

29 Dara K. Cohen, *Sexual Violence During War* (Ithaca, NY: Cornell University Press, forthcoming).

30 Christopher Blattman and Jeannie Annan, 'The consequences of child soldiering', *Review of Economics and Statistics*, vol. 92, no. 4, November 2010, pp. 882–98.

31 Arwa Damon, 'Child fighter tormented by ISIS', CNN, 13 November 2014, http://www.cnn.com/2014/11/12/world/meast/syria-isis-child-fighter/.

32 Albert Bandura, 'Moral disengagement in the perpetration of inhumanities', *Personality and Social Psychology Review*, vol. 3, 1999, pp. 193–4.

33 Susan McKay and Dyan Mazurana, *Where are the Girls? Girls In Fighting Forces In Northern Uganda, Sierra Leone and Mozambique: Their Lives During and After War*, technical report, Rights & Democracy (International Centre for Human Rights and Democratic Development), 2004, Montreal, p. 74, https://www1.essex.ac.uk/armedcon/story_id/000478.pdf.

34 Myriam Denov and Richard Maclure, 'Turnings and Epiphanies: Militarization, life histories, and the making and unmaking of two child soldiers in Sierra Leone,' *Journal of Youth Studies*, vol. 10, no. 2, 2007, pp. 243–61.

35 T. Betancourt, S. Simmons, I. Borisova, S. Brewer, U. Iweala and M.D.L. Soudière, 'High hopes, grim reality: Reintegration and the education of former child soldiers in

Sierra Leone', *Comparative Education Review*, vol. 52, no. 4, November 2008, pp. 565–87; Richard Maclure and Myriam Denov, '"I didn't want to die so I joined them": Structuration and the process of becoming boy soldiers in Sierra Leone', *Terrorism and Political Violence*, vol. 18, no. 1, 2006, pp. 119–35, https://www.tandfonline.com/doi/full/10.1080/09546550500384801?scroll=top&needAccess=true.

36 Interview with the author, New York City, May 2015.

37 Myriam Denov and Richard Maclure, *Child Soldiers in Sierra Leone: Experiences, Implications and Strategies for Community Reintegration*, 2005, technical report for the Canadian International Development Agency, http://www.operationspaix.net/DATA/DOCUMENT/5552~v~Child_Soldiers_in_Sierra_Leone__Experiences_Implications_and_Strategies_for_Rehabilitation_and_Community_Reintegration.pdf.

38 Theresa S. Betancourt, Ivelina I. Borisova, Marie de la Soudière and John Williamson, 'Sierra Leone's Child Soldiers: War Exposures and Mental Health Problems by Gender', *Journal of Adolescent Health*, vol. 49, no. 1, 2011, pp. 21–8.

39 Maclure and Denov, '"I Didn't Want to Die So I Joined Them"'.

40 Roles girls perform include 'cooking, washing dishes, fetching water and firewood, laundering, and taking care of younger children . . . and pillaging villages for food and other goods. Most girls were required to carry heavy loads of small arms, ammunition, food, young children, and looted goods over extremely long distances': Myriam Denov, 'Girl Soldiers

and Human Rights: Lessons from Angola, Mozambique, Sierra Leone and Northern Uganda', *International Journal of Human Rights*, vol. 12, no. 5, 2008, pp. 813–36, 819.

41 Michael Weiss and Hassan Hassan, *ISIS: Inside the Army of Terror* (New York: Regan Arts, 2015).

42 Mia Bloom and Hilary Matfess, 'Women as Symbols and Swords in Boko Haram's Terror', *Prism: A Journal of the Center for Complex Operations*, vol. 6, no. 1, March 2016, p. 104.

43 UNICEF, 'Northeast Nigeria: Alarming spike in suicide attacks involving women and girls', 26 May 2015, http://www.unicef.org/media/media_82047.html.

44 Jason Warner and Hilary Matfess, 'Exploding Stereotypes: The Unexpected Operational and Demographic Characteristics of Boko Haram's Suicide Bombers', Combatting Terrorism Center, 9 August 2017, p. iv, https://ctc.usma.edu/posts/report-exploding-stereotypes-the-unexpected-operational-and-demographic-characteristics-of-boko-harams-suicide-bombers.

45 Anugrah Kumar, 'Cubs of the Caliphate: Rehabilitating ISIS' Child Soldiers', *Christian Post*, 31 December 2017, https://www.christianpost.com/news/cubs-of-the-caliphate-rehabilitating-isis-child-soldiers-211985/; see also Fache, 'Cigarettes, music and shaking women's hands: how to rehabilitate Isil's child soldiers'.

46 Gates and Reich, *Child Soldiers in the Age of Fractured States*, p. 6.

Web 2.0: The New Battleground

David Patrikarakos

It is now clear to scholars, policymakers and practitioners alike that the digital revolution has greatly influenced conflict in the twenty-first century, and that social media stands at the centre of this revolution. For the purposes of this essay I use Andreas Kaplan and Michael Haelein's definition of social media as 'a group of Internet-based applications that build on the ideological and technological foundations of Web 2.0, and that allow the creation and exchange of user-generated content'.[1]

Social media has changed war irretrievably; platforms like Facebook, Twitter and YouTube have become the latest battlegrounds in conflict. Whether you are a president, a soldier or a terrorist, the power of social media can no longer be ignored. You may still win the odd battle if you don't understand how to effectively deploy social media, but you will lose a twenty-first-century war, or at least a major part of it.

This essay will primarily examine the overarching effects that social media has had on conflict as a whole, and make concise reference to three case studies: Israel's 2014 *Operation Protective Edge* against Hamas in Gaza; the conflict between Russia and Ukraine that continues to this day; and the battle against the Islamic State, also known as ISIS or ISIL.

Elements of this essay are drawn from my experiences covering the war between Russia and Ukraine throughout the majority of 2014, as well as my research into *Operation Protective Edge* and ISIS's use of social media.[2]

War on the ground, war online

I entered eastern Ukraine in the spring of 2014 and quickly realised that Twitter had more up-to-date information than either the BBC or CNN – individual people instead of institutions soon became my primary source of information. As spring turned to summer, two conflicts broke out in the Middle East. On 10 June, ISIS exploded into global headlines when it took Iraq's second-largest city Mosul. In July, Israel launched *Operation Protective Edge* and another Gaza war began.

I followed events closely in the region while continuing to report from Ukraine. It didn't matter that I was in Kiev or Donetsk: dozens of videos and photos from Gaza filled my Twitter and Facebook feeds each day. As ISIS continued its rampage across Iraq, horrific images were posted by bystanders, participants and state organisations alike. On YouTube and Twitter, Hamas entered into an online war of words with the Israel Defense Forces (IDF). On jihadist forums, ISIS members in Raqqa recruited teenagers from Birmingham to join them in their fight. It was clear that social media had opened up vital spaces of communication to the individual that had once been controlled exclusively by the state. War had never been so close, visceral or ubiquitous.

Personal experience in Ukraine and research into the other two conflicts indicated that two wars were being fought in each case: the first taking place on the ground with troops and weaponry; the second, an information war fought largely, though not exclusively, on social media. What was also clear was that, perhaps counter-intuitively, the latter's influence was arguably greater. It was, for example, clear that the Kremlin's information war against Kiev – just like those of the IDF and Hamas and ISIS – was largely aimed at a global audience as opposed to the traditional notion of the 'enemy' population.

The three conflicts displayed one striking quality: they all appeared to embody an enhanced version of the latest practices of 'hybrid war' – which the US Joint Forces Command defines as warfare that 'simultaneously and adaptively employs a tailored mix of conventional, irregular, terrorism and criminal means or activities in the operational battle space' – combined with an increase in both the speed and scope of traditional practices of conflict.[3] However, one aspect shone out above all others: the ability of social media to endow ordinary individuals – frequently non-combatants – with the power to change the course of both the physical battlefield and the discourse around it.

Everyone, it seemed, could now be an actor in war. The world was witnessing a form of virtual mass-enlistment. Ukrainians now used Facebook to raise money for their beleaguered army, while Russian citizens morphed into trolls to spread disinformation about Ukrainian 'fascists', and ISIS fanboys tweeted their support of the group. In December 2016, a seven-year-old Syrian girl, Bana Alabed, made global headlines by tweeting about the destruction that Syrian President Bashar al-Assad rained down on her home city of Aleppo. Her tweets, written in imperfect English, had more power to shape the argument surrounding Syria's civil war than the state's propaganda machine.[4]

The events of 2014 revealed three trends. The first is that power has shifted from institutions to individual citizens and networks of citizens. The second is that narrative wars are becoming arguably more important than physical ones – able to shape their scope, duration and intensity, but, perhaps more importantly, becoming the *reason* that some physical wars are now fought. The third and final trend is that the conflicts were not 'traditional' state-on-state wars: instead, they were either wars between state and non-state actors (as in the case of the Israel–Hamas war), more chaotic conflicts (such the rise of ISIS), or conflicts that seem to exist somewhere between the boundaries of war and peace, as in Ukraine. These, I argue, are trends that will only deepen.

Under what scholars would call the Clausewitzian paradigm (the ideas promulgated by the Prussian military theorist Carl von Clausewitz) that dominated twentieth-century thinking on conflict, war was thought of as something like a straight 'military' fight between sovereign states. The battleground was as clear as a boxing ring and the enemy was obvious. Military victory was easy to determine, and once victory had been achieved, the victor imposed a political settlement on the loser (the defeat of Germany in the First World War and the resulting Treaty of Versailles being an egregious example of this process).

This form of war still exists today. Emile Simpson, author of *War from the Ground Up: Twenty-First-Century Combat as Politics* and a former British soldier who served three tours in Afghanistan, cites the example of Sri Lanka, where the government militarily crushed its insurgent enemy the Tamil Tigers and forced them to the negotiating table.[5] The Tamils were an insurgent force, not a state actor, but the classic paradigm was still in clear evidence here. But from Ukraine to Gaza to Iraq, the gradual erosion of this type of war in favour of loose, more open-ended conflicts has been plain to see. Russian President Vladimir Putin had no interest in defeating Ukraine militarily (which he easily could have done) and forcing it to accept the annexation of eastern Ukraine. Rather, he sought to destabilise it. Israel had no intention of defeating Hamas militarily (which it could easily have done) and forcing it to finally accept Israel's existence. In Gaza, the violence, while horrific, had an almost perfunctory, almost balletic, quality to it. Hamas endlessly fired rockets at Israel that both it and the Israeli government knew would almost all be shot down by the IDF's Iron Dome missile-defence system. Instead, the social-media arm of the IDF Spokesperson's Unit flooded Twitter with information about Hamas's use of human shields and its rocket attacks on Israeli civilians. Its narrative was clear: 'we are a democratic state under terrorist attack'. In response, Hamas officials and ordinary Palestinians tweeted and posted photos of dead children killed in Israeli attacks. Its counter-narrative was equally clear: 'we are an oppressed people being slaughtered by an occupier'. As with the Ukraine conflict, for both sides, the goal was not a military victory but a narrative one.

Once this is understood, the great change in conflict that our age is witnessing becomes clear: war is becoming the physical manifestation of a clash of narratives – and the change could not be more profound.

Equally, unlike terror groups of the past, ISIS has no demands that can be met, short of Iraq and Syria (and then the rest of the Middle East and beyond) dismantling their states in order to be absorbed into the ISIS caliphate. Given that such demands are self-evidently impossible to compromise on, negotiation is therefore equally impossible. Without total victory (in this case requiring likely annihilation) by one side over the other, the conflict will not end.

The changing context of war

We live in a post-1945 security system that was designed to regulate war out of existence.[6] Following the atrocities of the Second World War, there was near-unanimous desire among the major powers to create an international order in which the use of force between major states was almost impossible. Organisations such as the European Union and United Nations were formed with this intention. The emergence of nuclear weapons also made it harder for states to use force to compel their enemy, for fear of possible escalation. The Cold War that followed the end of the Second World War was underpinned by a balance between the world's only two superpowers, the Soviet Union and the US, a balance that largely ensured – an admittedly uneasy – peace, or at least negated the threat of major war between multiple states.

The modern moment, however, has witnessed a dramatic shift not only in the way wars are fought, but also in the priorities and context of war, a shift driven by the information revolution. In the traditional conception of war, information operations support military action on the battlefield, but in Ukraine, Gaza and (to a degree) with ISIS, it became clear that military operations on the ground were supporting information operations on television and in cyberspace. The boundaries between politics and war have become blurred – and the boundaries between war and peace even more so. As Simpson notes, the goal of the coalition forces during his tours in Afghanistan changed from attempting to defeat the Taliban to convincing the local population not to join them. 'War as we understand it as [a] traditionally military fight distinct from peace still exists', he argues, 'however, the *general tendency*, driven by the information revolution, is away from that paradigm and towards open-ended, networked conflicts that occupy a "grey zone" between war and peace.'[7]

What has changed is not war itself – soldiers still fire on soldiers, tanks still fire on tanks – but the context in which it takes place. US Secretary of Defense James Mattis may have been right when he declared that 'Alex [sic] the Great would not be in the least bit perplexed by the enemy that we face right now in Iraq'.[8] But he failed to take into account the changing context in which war is now fought, which has been changed beyond all recognition by what Simpson describes as 'the impact of the information revolution and more broadly the speed and interconnectivity of contemporary globalization driven by the information revolution'.[9]

This development is critical because in an interconnected, globalised world, it is much easier to employ and amplify modes of coercive, non-military methods that bypass the battlefield. The financial sanctions imposed on Russia over its behaviour in Ukraine illustrate how the degree of modern global financial integration has enabled a rapid expansion in the capacity of conflict parties to wage war through non-military means. This breaking down of the boundaries between military and non-military methods – between war and politics – threatens international stability: if war has increasingly become the practice of politics (and its attendant economics), it can have no clear end, because politics never ends.

This state of affairs could well result in far more open-ended conflicts, and more open-ended conflicts have far greater potential to slip into outright war involving multiple states. The old world order, with its checks and balances against multi-state conflict, no longer exists. The globalised world that has replaced it has brought us so much, but it also offers challenges, especially in the sphere of conflict and conflict's relationship with social media.

The social-media revolution of warfare

According to the researchers Emerson T. Booker and P.W. Singer, around 3.4 billion people now use the internet. Each day they send roughly 500 million tweets and each second upload nearly seven hours of footage to YouTube in up to 76 different languages. Facebook has 1.7bn active accounts, giving it a larger 'population' than China, while Twitter and Facebook are the platforms from which the majority of Americans get their news; indeed, 59% of American Twitter users rely on the service to follow news events as they happen in real time.[10] And nowhere do news events happen as dramatically in real time as they do in times of crisis like war.

Web 2.0 has endowed people with two crucial abilities: firstly, to actively produce content; and secondly, through the use of social-media platforms, to form transnational networks. These abilities enable them to shape events, especially in times of civil strife and conflict. According to Alec Ross, drawing on his experience as senior advisor for innovation to then-secretary of state Hillary Clinton:

> Power is moving from hierarchies to citizens and networks, and connection technologies enable that shift in power (defining a hierarchy as the nation state, as a large media organisation, or other such things). And the kinds of capabilities that would have once been reserved for large media organisations or for nation states, have suddenly become available to networks of individuals.[11]

Recent history bears out his assessment. It is unthinkable that the Arab Spring uprisings of 2011 – which began when Mohamed Bouazizi, a Tunisian street vendor,

set himself on fire in response to harassment from Tunisian police on 4 January 2011
– could have happened without social media. The images, caught on camera phones
and uploaded to social-media platforms, sparked violent demonstrations that led
to the overthrow of then-president Zine al-Abidine Ben Ali just ten days later. They
then spread internationally, causing outrage among the population of neighbouring
Egypt, which rose up and overthrew the dictator Hosni Mubarak. Demonstrations
soon followed in Syria. The Arab Spring revealed the emergence of a new type of
hyper-empowered individual: networked, globally connected and more potent than
ever before – a uniquely twenty-first-century phenomenon of a type of individual I
term *Homo Digitalis*.[12]

From Ukraine to Gaza to Syria, the power of *Homo Digitalis* is plain to see, a
power that has irrevocably changed the relationship between the individual and
the state. The twentieth-century nation-state traditionally held primacy in two areas
from which it derived much of its power: its monopoly on the use of force and
its near-total control of information flows.[13] The emergence of social-media platforms has created new forums that allow people to communicate outside traditional
state hierarchies of communication such as state- or even privately owned but state-
permitted newspapers, radio and television. When this happens, new avenues of
power are created that empower the individual and challenge the nation-state.

This is especially dangerous for authoritarian states, since without near-monop-
olies on these information flows it is impossible for these states to project power
(especially in war or protest situations) in the way they once could. Because these
new forums are structurally more egalitarian, many see the internet – and specifically social media – as the ultimate tool against tyrants. However, this idea is what
the author Evgeny Morozov terms 'cyber-utopianism', or the belief that

the Internet favors the oppressed rather than the oppressor ... a naïve belief in
the emancipatory nature of online communication that rests on a stubborn refusal
to acknowledge its downside [by failing to take into account] how authoritarian
governments would respond to the Internet ... how useful it would prove for
propaganda purposes, how masterfully dictators would learn to use it for surveillance, and how sophisticated modern systems of Internet censorship would
become.[14]

The power of social media therefore cuts both ways: *Homo Digitalis* challenges the state, but the state will always fight back. While Ukrainians uploaded photos of Russian military hardware crossing the border, the Russian state used the same platforms to spread its counter-narrative of the post-Maidan government as a 'fascist junta' that wished to persecute ethnic Russians and stamp out the speaking of Russian in the country. New media has expanded the arena of conflict into the virtual world.

Because social-media platforms have created new venues that allow people to communicate outside traditional state hierarchies of communication, they have created a political reversal: a regression from centralised communicative modes to the more chaotic, network effects of an earlier, pre-twentieth-century nation-state age – and it is destabilising classic forms of war accordingly. The 'new wars' fought in Ukraine, Gaza and the battlefields of Syria and Iraq seem, in their fluidity and chaos, to be more like the wars of the early modern period – before states became as centralised and powerful as they are today – than the wars of the twentieth century.

Twitter and the Gaza conflict

Israel's 2014 war against Hamas is an archetypal twenty-first-century asymmetrical war, pitting a state against a non-state actor. Here, the power of *Homo Digitalis* to take on the power of a democratic state through the promulgation of powerful narratives is clear from the case of Farah Baker, a (then) 16-year-old girl living in Gaza who tweeted daily (and at the war's peak, more than hourly) about the horrors she was going through. Her tweets went viral, the international media picked up her story, and Farah – who should have been the epitome of weakness, being a civilian in a war, a female in a deeply patriarchal society and a child in a world of adults – turned into a significant actor in the conflict. She became a symbol of Palestinian suffering that caused Israel, the overwhelmingly dominant military power in the conflict, huge problems at the narrative level of war.

In this sense, Farah's story is more than just the tale of a young girl able to tweet her individual story of suffering; it is more than just a case of *Homo Digitalis* gone viral. What Farah's story illustrates is the new challenges *Homo Digitalis* brings to asymmetrical warfare, and critically the enhanced power she represents for smaller, less militarily powerful nations. Farah's ability to affect the narrative of the war

lay in her ability to use social media to amplify a narrative of Palestinian suffering that mobilised international outpourings of rage – often at the political level
– against Israel. In so doing she was able to affect the *discourse* surrounding the conflict. When the boundaries between war and politics have become so blurred as to be
almost indistinguishable, the importance of this cannot be overestimated – indeed,
it threatens the very idea that wars between state and non-state actors are asymmet-
ric. In a world where the battlefield is arguably no longer the most important arena
of conflict, the power embodied in Farah illustrates an almost entirely new development in warfare: states can win the physical battle on the ground but lose the war,
especially when the clash is between individual authenticity and institutional corpo-
ratism (represented in this case by the IDF's social-media unit's attempts to respond
in kind). In effect, when war becomes 'armed politics' and the Clausewitzian paradigm becomes almost redundant, the concept of a military victory but a political
defeat becomes possible.

Crowdsourcing armaments in Ukraine

Navid Hassanpour, associate professor at the National Research University Higher
School of Economics in Moscow, observes that 'social media can be used as a loud-
speaker or as a mobilization tool on the ground. Sometimes it happens that outsiders
get to know about an issue through Twitter or Facebook, and sometimes they are
mobilized to act on it. These are two distinct processes.'[15]

In Gaza, Farah used social media to amplify a message of suffering. In Ukraine,
another civilian, Anna Sandalova, used the second of these processes to great effect
through the use of a simple Facebook page to crowdsource funds for Ukraine's
badly undersupplied army. She sourced everything from uniforms to body armour
to night-vision goggles, as well as mobilising networks of people to donate money
or give their time to the cause. Once goods were bought or received (all through
the power of social media), Anna and volunteers (also largely sourced through
social media) physically transported them to the front-lines. Once again, a civilian,
morphed by the power of social media into *Homo Digitalis*, was able to make a tangible difference, this time on the physical battlefield.

And it is needed. Social media is tailor-made for the post-Soviet space where
institutions have atrophied from years of pervasive corruption. In Ukraine, the

ruling Yanukovych family, notably the president Victor (who was overthrown in the 2013–14 Euromaidan revolution) and his son, Oleksandr, became rich through effective manipulation of the arms of state, notably the judiciary and public prosecutor's office (appointments which Ukraine's president constitutionally controls), to target profitable businesses. Those that refused to pay were hit with tax investigations and other forms of government harassment – all of which were legal. The state became their personal fiefdom.

New media is allowing people such as Sandalova to act in place of the state in Ukraine: all you need is a laptop and a Facebook account and you can take action. People like Sandalova have become virtual government ministers, deciding which army divisions receive what equipment and when. New media is also providing sources of information outside traditional or government channels. Ukrainians find the most reliable military news not in the *Kyiv Post* or on the Ukrainian Ministry of Defence website but on the Facebook page of Information Resistance, an online analytical review that is widely read. The best source of information on government tenders was the Facebook page of the civil-society group Reanimation Package of Reforms. These different Facebook groups, each with their own quasi-governmental functions, have allied with each other to increase their cumulative influence – almost organically – to form, during the most intense years of the war, what can be described as an emerging virtual state in Ukraine, with *Homo Digitalis* at its heart.

Countering the ISIS virtual caliphate

It is important to understand that at its peak, ISIS existed on two planes. One was its physical manifestation: a statelet that straddled Syria and Iraq, an entity which might usefully be called the 'physical caliphate'. The other was its online manifestation, which encompassed the major social-media platforms (notably Twitter and YouTube), which might be called the 'virtual caliphate'. Indeed, so strongly is the latter idea embedded in the group's thinking that its many online followers still often refer to the online realm as *Wilayat Twitter* (the State of Twitter).[16]

The author Abdel Bari Atwan christened ISIS the 'digital caliphate' with good reason. Without social media, he argues, the group would never have been able to morph so quickly from a local Iraqi insurgent group to one of the most successful brands in modern history. Alberto Fernandez, the coordinator for strategic counter-terrorism communications (CSCC) at the US Department of State between 2012 and 2015, was charged with countering ISIS propaganda at the zenith of ISIS's power during late 2014 and 2015, and determined to challenge the jihadists directly online.[17] In essence, an arm of the world's most powerful government was going to war with *Homo Digitalis* – the outcome should have been a foregone conclusion.

Except it was not. The CSCC simply could not compete with networked individuals operating out of dilapidated buildings in war-torn Syria or teenagers sitting in their bedroom spreading and sharing content. Fernandez estimated that ISIS produced 1,800 videos from 2014 to late 2015. Not all were successful, but the sheer volume of the material and the number of people sharing them made ISIS seem ubiquitous. In contrast, from February 2011 to February 2015, the CSCC produced a total of around just 300 videos. Fernandez's staff of around 50 people were up against what he calculated to be around 90,000 pro-ISIS Twitter accounts across the world. The mismatch was startling. Again, the power of *Homo Digitalis* had been demonstrated in a state of affairs that would have been unthinkable just ten years earlier.

Fernandez repeatedly stated that the greatest problem he faced in countering ISIS propaganda was the fact that the CSCC was a US government organisation, which created two problems. The first was the bureaucracy, which is by nature slow and overly centralised. Moreover, bureaucracy is inherently reactive and perennially cautious; it can never compete with the freewheeling, networked nature of *Homo Digitalis*. The CSCC also operated under strictures which limited and censored its output. For example, government policy dictated that the CSCC could criticise Syrian President Bashar al-Assad but not Iraqi President Nuri al-Maliki, because Maliki was a US ally. Moreover, unlike Russian disinformation, the CSCC posted its social media as an identifiable US government body: it could not pretend to be something it was not. In this sense, the case of the CSCC also highlights the disadvantage democratic states have compared to authoritarian ones when fighting wars at the narrative level. Simply put, these states have to abide by a set of democratic norms, while their Chinese or Russian counterparts do not.

The second problem was one of credibility, which stands at the heart of the battle between institutions and *Homo Digitalis*. As Fernandez well knew, the US would be the last of all voices a disaffected young Muslim would listen to, given the US government's perceived litany of crimes in the Middle East, including the 2003 invasion of Iraq, its torture of prisoners at Abu Ghraib, detention without trial of those held in the Guantanamo Bay facility and its apparent indifference to the slaughter in Syria.

But there was a final, broader, problem. ISIS's overarching narrative can be defined as a form of 'active measures' (the name given to Soviet propaganda campaigns). This form of information operations seeks to use propaganda to shape the nature of the conflict and the battlefield. The strength of ISIS's propaganda is compounded by the fact that it focuses on a wide range of subjects and targets: some of it speaks to Sunni Muslim Arab populations, some is aimed at audiences in the Muslim diaspora, and some at Western populations and governments. All these strands are tied together by the overarching narrative that the ISIS caliphate offers its followers the chance to find meaning in their lives, as well as the opportunity to destroy its enemies. While the CSCC was focused on telling people *not* to do something, ISIS was urging them to take action: stay in Paris and drive a cab or come to Syria and be a warrior. There was only ever going to be one winner.

It is a narrative that chimes perfectly with the twenty-first-century 'Millennial' zeitgeist. Today's twenty-somethings have come of age in the aftermath of the global recession of 2008: job prospects are bleak and the future is uncertain. The turn of the century has also seen a loss of faith in the great institutions of the West, from politicians to the financial sector to the press. This has coincided perfectly with the emergence of social media, which has flattened the media space and given these various extremist actors greater ability to project power and to subvert Western institutions than ever before. *Homo Digitalis* – like social media – is a force for both good and ill. As Fernandez explains:

> People want to identify with something and it is hard to identify with discredited institutions. And then along comes a 'pristine' organization that is seen as sincere and authentic. The ISIS narrative provides certain cultural, emotional satisfactions, it releases endorphins, inspires in a certain way. If everything around you has been discredited you will have problems counteracting that. The lack of faith in Western culture prevents us from offering a positive alternative narrative. What moves us is evidently nothing – and you can't counteract them with nothing.

Social media is an inherently destabilising technology that has emerged to coincide with (and compound) a time of crisis in the West, which, as noted above, has since the beginning of the twenty-first century seen the systematic discrediting of its major institutions. Within this general miasma, demagogues and counter-cultural movements of all stripes now flourish. The alt-left and alt-right both take advantage of this climate: US President Donald Trump is the figure around which the alt-right has gathered, while Jeremy Corbyn, a figure from the hard left, leads the United Kingdom's main opposition party. Rebellion against establishment elites is strafing Europe and North America. The problem is therefore twofold: the boundaries between politics and warfare have never been so blurred; and the political landscape is increasingly volatile.

In the run-up to the First World War, none of the great powers wanted conflict but, through miscalculation and error, drifted into it. Everything I experienced in Ukraine and saw in Gaza and in the rise of ISIS made me believe that we may be heading in that direction once more, which makes it both urgent and imperative for politicians, policymakers and the general public to understand the ways in which conflict has changed. Twenty-first-century war requires a twenty-first-century response.

David Patrikarakos is the author of *War in 140 Characters: How Social Media is Reshaping Conflict in the Twenty-First Century*. He is a Poynter Fellow at Yale and a Non-Resident Fellow at the School of Iranian Studies, St Andrews University. He is also a Contributing Editor at the *Daily Beast* and a Contributing Writer at *Politico*.

Notes

[1] Andreas Kaplan and Michael Haelein, 'Users of the world, unite! The challenges and opportunities of Social Media', *Business Horizons*, vol. 53, no. 1, January–February 2010, p. 61, http://michaelhaenlein.eu/Publications/Kaplan,%20Andreas%20-%20Users%20of%20the%20world,%20unite.pdf.

[2] The essay is comprised of edited extracts from *War in 140 Characters: How Social Media Is Reshaping Conflict in the Twenty-First Century* by David Patrikarakos, © 2017. Reprinted by permission of Basic Books, an imprint of Hachette Book Group, Inc., and the author c/o Rogers, Coleridge & White Ltd., 20 Powis Mews, London W11 1JN.

[3] Brian P. Fleming, *Hybrid Threat Concept: Contemporary War, Military Planning and the Advent of Unrestricted Operational Art* (Fort Leavenworth, KS: United States Army Command and General Staff College, 2011).

4   See, for example, Juliet Samuel, 'Searching for the truth in the rubble of "Fake News" from Aleppo', *Telegraph*, 18 December 2016, http://www.telegraph.co.uk/news/2016/12/17/searching-truth-rubble-fake-news-aleppo/.

5   Emile Simpson, *War from the Ground Up: Twenty-First-Century Combat as Politics* (London: C Hurst & Co., 2012), p. 1.

6   Interview with David Betz, London, 23 March 2016.

7   Interview with Emile Simpson, 19 November 2014.

8   Geoffrey Ingersoll, 'General James "Mad Dog" Mattis Email about Being "Too Busy to Read" is a Must-Read', *Business Insider UK*, 9 May 2013, http://uk.businessinsider.com/viral-james-mattis-email-reading-marines-2013-5.

9   Interview with Emile Simpson, 19 November 2014.

10 Emerson T. Brooking and P.W. Singer, 'War Goes Viral: How Social Media Is Being Weaponized Across the World', *Atlantic*, November 2016, http://www.theatlantic.com/magazine/archive/2016/11/war-goes-viral/501125/.

11 Interview with Alec Ross, Baltimore, 26 June 2015.

12 This term has already been coined and some literature within technology circles exists on it. Indeed a book even carries its name (see Natasha Saxberg, *Homo Digitalis: How Human Needs Support Digital Behaviour for People, Organizations and Society* (Amazon Digital Services LLC, 22 July 2015). However, from what I can tell the term is not in widespread use and my settling upon the term was not derived from any previous literature and, to the best of my knowledge, I am the first to apply the concept to the field of war.

13 See, for example, Parag Khanna, 'Dismantling Empires through Devolution', *Atlantic*, 26 September 2014, http://www.theatlantic.com/international/archive/2014/09/stronger-than-democracy/380774/.

14 Evgeny Morozov, *The Net Delusion: How Not to Liberate the World* (London: Allen Lane, 2011), p. xiv.

15 Interview with Navid Hassanpour, 17 November 2014.

16 Alberto M. Fernandez, 'Why ISIS Flourishes in its Media Domain', *Defense Technology Program Brief*, September 2015, p. 6, http://www.afpc.org/files/getContentPostAttachment/247.

17 Quotes and comments from Alberto Fernandez come from three Skype interviews conducted variously on 28 March 2016, 31 October 2016 and 10 November 2016.

The Making of Peace: Processes and Agreements

Stefan Wolff

The term 'peace process' captures a wide range of different phenomena primarily related to the (mostly) international management of intra-state conflicts. As a label, it has been applied to processes at the end of which some form of peace had actually been achieved (such as in Northern Ireland), as well as to processes that are outright failures, including extreme cases like Rwanda where a peace agreement in 1993 became the precursor of a genocide in 1994. Between these extremes, however, a third type of peace process can be identified that would be better described as protracted, and which can take the form either of a serial failure to make a negotiated agreement last (such as the situation in South Sudan since late 2013), or of processes that are caught in more or less stable ceasefires without achieving a sustainable conflict settlement (such as Ukraine). This categorisation is admittedly crude: the great variety of actors involved, the relationships they have with each other and the types of agreements that they achieve (or not) speak to the uniqueness of each such process, but underneath the specifics of each situation, there are important commonalities that many peace processes share and that are worth exploring in an effort to understand the causes of both success and failure.

Broadly defined, a peace process might be understood as the process towards a non-military solution sought by the respective parties to a conflict, often supported by international involvement. Yet the local and international commitments that are necessary to achieve durable peace are not always sincere or sustained; they can be undermined by domestic and/or third parties; and they may suffer from unrealistic expectations that, if unfulfilled, cause peace processes to stall or collapse back into violent conflict. Given the human and material costs of conflict and its consequences often far beyond its immediate location, peace processes are worth-while efforts not only to engage in but also to study in order to attain a clear sense of what the 'ingredients' of a successful process are and how the risks of failure can be mitigated.

This essay will offer some insights into the general trends regarding the success or otherwise of contemporary peace processes and then focus on the centrality of the peace agreement to the peace process. The distinction between these two closely related but commonly confused dimensions of war-to-peace transitions is critical in gaining a better understanding of what accounts for their success or failure and which particular factors are receptive to mitigation – either to enhance the likeli-hood of success or to minimise the risk of failure. A third section provides three short empirical illustrations of the peace processes in Colombia, South Sudan and Ukraine. The essay will conclude with broader reflections on the management of peace processes.

Evaluating the success of peace processes

Existing scholarship on the success of peace processes is divided on whether they are useful approaches to managing the transition from intra-state war to peace. While it is not possible to cover this extensive debate here in much detail, it is never-theless helpful to remember that there is considerable disagreement on the wisdom of internationally managed peace processes. The opposite endpoints in this debate are exemplified by the positions of Edward Luttwak, who poignantly suggested to give war a chance by letting 'it serve its sole useful function: to bring peace', and Barbara F. Walter, who has asserted that '[o]nce adversaries agreed to negotiate, every case where a third-party stepped in to guarantee a treaty resulted in a success-ful settlement'.[1] There are 'softer' versions of both positions. For example, there is considerable evidence that military victories lead to more sustainable peace,[2] as well as that the overwhelming number of mediation efforts achieve at least some form of negotiated agreement.[3] Among the more recent analyses, there appears to be both consensus and evidence that the design of peace agreements (i.e., the provisions that they contain) matters; that implementation and its sequencing are important; and that international involvement more often than not is a feature of sustainable peace that flows from negotiated agreements.[4]

In evaluating the success of peace agreements, it is important to remember there are, of course, a considerable number of peace processes which terminate with the resumption of the war they were meant to end. The statistical evidence here varies quite significantly, in part due to the different statistical methods employed. An article published in 2007 demonstrated how one particularly influential figure – a near-50% chance of conflict recurrence within five years – could change quite significantly if different statistical methods were applied to the underlying data (the figure drops as low as just over 20% for an initial four-year period after the last conflict).[5] However, a study published in 2014 suggested that a peace agreement was preferable to no agreement, finding that while only about 22% of conflicts ended with a peace agreement, the risk of 'peace failure following a peace agreement is only 24.6% of the risk of failure following an indecisive outcome' (where fighting stops but neither does one side achieve a military victory nor do the sides negotiate any kind of agreement).[6]

These and other figures represent one dimension of the reality of contemporary intra-state conflicts: those that have a peace process leading to a negotiated agreement are relatively few (compared to the totality of conflicts), but a negotiated agreement, once achieved, still significantly increases the likelihood of durable peace. This is, of course, an intuitively logical finding: an agreement between warring parties is difficult to achieve, but once it has been concluded it tends to produce the desired outcome.

The role of peace agreements

Agreements are arguably the most critical element of the peace process. The success and failure of peace processes depend on more than just the agreement. Without genuine political will to make peace at the local level, or without political, financial and often also military support from the international community, agreements are unlikely to survive for long. Nonetheless, an actual peace agreement is a critical component of peace processes, and it would be difficult to imagine a successful peace process that does not include an agreement. While analytically distinct from each other, making peace agreements the focal point of peace processes also provides an opportunity to consider different stages of a peace process itself as it relates to the peace agreement that takes centre stage within it.

From this perspective, peace agreements normally involve three stages. Firstly, the conflict parties negotiate an agreement that they deem acceptable in the sense that it addresses their core concerns and demands, has the backing of their constituents and protects their future interests. This is followed by the implementation of the agreement – a period that is quite often fraught with difficulties stemming from both the 'constructive ambiguity' in the language of the agreement (which allows conflict parties to interpret potentially controversial provisions differently as they 'sell' the agreement to their constituencies) and the realisation of the costs and complexities of turning words and phrases into institutions that work on their own and in concert with others. It is during the implementation stage that peace agreements become institutionally embedded in the broader social and political environment. The third stage – the operation of the agreement – relates to the day-to-day functioning of the agreed and by now implemented institutions that reshape a post-war society and gradually, and hopefully sustainably, transform relationships between former conflict parties within it. During this stage, international involvement is often scaled down, if not abruptly ended.

The three stages of peace agreements comprise the benchmarks against which progress can be assessed. Consider Northern Ireland in this context, where internationally mediated negotiations took place between 1996 and 1998 and the Good Friday Agreement (also known as the Belfast Agreement) was concluded in April 1998. Despite endorsement in two parallel referendums north and south of the border, it took until December 1999 for the agreed institutions to be implemented in full; that is, for the devolution of power to the executive. The operation of the agreement, too, was beset with difficulties related to the decommissioning of paramilitary weapons, continuing terrorist activities by dissident splinter groups and disagreements over the reform of the police service. Three short suspensions of the institutions between 1999 and 2002 were unable to smooth out these problems, and 2002 saw the reintroduction of direct rule from London for five years. A new round of negotiations, following significant changes in the balance of power between the established parties which saw the hardliners of the Democratic Unionist Party (DUP) and Sinn Féin become the largest parties in their respective communities, eventually led to the St Andrews Agreement in 2006 that allowed for the restoration of the power-sharing institutions in Belfast in 2007. However, a decade later the executive collapsed again and has yet to be restored. Remarkably there has been no return to violence, and the original 1998 agreement (with its subsequent revisions) still stands. This illustrates a remarkable level of commitment to peace by local elites and their partners within and beyond the British Isles, as well as a high degree of flexibility and determination to find innovative political solutions to seemingly intractable problems and to persist in the search for solutions, sometimes against all odds. These characteristics are often absent from peace processes elsewhere (such as South Sudan, for example, where endless negotiation, precipitated by flawed agreements that local elites are unwilling and unable to implement, has become synonymous with a failed peace process since December 2013). The consequences of the United Kingdom's decision to leave the European Union (Brexit) now perhaps represents the gravest threat to the Good Friday Agreement's survival, rather than the internal political dynamics in Northern Ireland. It remains to be seen whether the skills, vision and determination that have prevented the collapse of the peace process to date will prevail again.

The Good Friday Agreement also illustrates that peace agreements are increasingly complex and multidimensional, including not only provisions on future governance arrangements but transitional justice issues, wealth sharing and the reform of educational and cultural institutions. This clearly reflects the complexity of issues on the ground: contemporary intra-state conflicts involve a multiplicity of local, regional and global actors, all of whom have their own agendas concerning the conflict which may not necessarily align. The complex governance structures often negotiated to accommodate local demands for power sharing, territorial self-governance, wealth management, judicial reform and so on tend to stretch the will and capacity of both local actors and their international partners, at times beyond breaking point. Moreover, as far as the regional and global levels are concerned, actors also have very different patterns of interaction across a range of arenas where their national interests align in equally complex and changing ways. Thus, while Russia and the West may share an interest in combatting international terrorism, such as in the fight against Islamic State, also known as ISIS or ISIL, they are at odds when it comes to the future of Syria or Ukraine.

International conflict management – the involvement of third-party states and/ or international and regional organisations – thus comes with its own problems, compounding those that arise from local dynamics. International assistance is often critical in getting conflict parties to the negotiation table, but what is then being negotiated also reflects outsiders' interests and often narrows the bargaining space that is available for finding an agreement that satisfies all parties.[7] Moreover, international priorities, such as preventing impunity for war crimes and gross human-rights violations, sit uneasily alongside the priorities of local elites, who are unlikely to negotiate a direct path for themselves to the International Criminal Court.

However, while international intervention may be problematic, the support offered by international parties can be crucial in sustaining the peace. While the 1995 Dayton Peace Agreement for Bosnia-Herzegovina is often cited as an example of a dysfunctional, internationally imposed peace agreement, it has been kept alive due to long-term international support (especially from the EU). The long-term viability of this approach has been questioned many times over the past two decades, but to date peace has been preserved in this highly volatile part of the western Balkans.[8] Bosnia-Herzegovina may not be a typical case of a successful peace process, or indeed offer a blueprint for ready replication, but it clearly underscores the importance of international involvement in all phases of a peace process – from negotiation, to implementation, to operation – and in particular the need for international (security) guarantees and long-term commitment of resources to making agreements 'stick'.

As has been emphasised elsewhere in the literature on peace processes, international guarantees have a vital role in helping peace processes succeed.[9] By reducing risks to negotiators and the constituencies they represent, they facilitate not only the conclusion of peace agreements but also their implementation and operation, especially when international involvement is directed towards monitoring and verification, dispute resolution and an international military and/or civilian presence. These guarantees may also often combine a mixture of incentives and pressure that ties good-faith implementation and operation of an agreement to specific rewards (such as development aid). This not only helps 'socialise' war-torn states into a new non-violent form of politics but also tangibly improves people's lives, further reducing the likelihood of a return to conflict. In this sense, guarantees in peace agreements, and international involvement more generally, are vital catalysts for the success of peace processes, but they cannot make up for flawed agreements that do not effectively address fundamental grievances of the conflict parties or fail to include the concerns of all relevant local and external parties and stakeholders in a conflict.

Three contemporary peace processes: Colombia, South Sudan and Ukraine

Northern Ireland and Bosnia-Herzegovina represent, with the caveats mentioned, examples of peace processes which have demonstrated some degree of success to date. The same can be said about Colombia, where an agreement was concluded between the government and FARC, one of the main rebel groups in the country, in September 2016 after four years of protracted negotiations. While the peace process was clearly driven domestically and remains the signature policy (and so far accomplishment) of incumbent President Juan Manuel Santos, who was awarded the Nobel Peace Prize for his efforts in 2016, it also benefited from significant international assistance by individual states, international organisations and civil-society actors. Initially hailed as a success, the agreement was rejected by a narrow margin in October that year in a referendum which witnessed a remarkably low turnout (37%). This triggered a complex renegotiation process involving separate talks between the government and the domestic opposition to the peace agreement, a shoring-up of the pro-peace camp (which included the Colombian government and various civil-society groups), and renewed talks between the government and FARC based on proposed amendments across 57 different areas. A revised agreement was achieved on 12 November after two rounds of negotiations in Havana and ratified by the Colombian Senate and House of Representatives on 29 and 30 November, respectively. However, the new agreement did not heal the rift between the opponents and advocates of the peace agreement (members of opposition parties abstained from the ratification votes in both houses of the Colombian Congress). With presidential and congressional elections looming in March and May 2018 respectively, the peace agreement is certain to remain a divisive issue. Despite the evident commitment of the current government and FARC leadership to the peace process, the progress made on the implementation of the agreement (especially concerning FARC disarmament and the implementation of key legislation required under the terms of the peace agreement, including a highly controversial amnesty law) has been limited. Another serious threat to peace in Colombia remains the unresolved conflict with a different rebel group, the National Liberation Army (ELN). A recent three-month ceasefire ended on 9 January 2018 with a rebel attack against an oil pipeline. Negotiations between the government and the ELN, scheduled to take place in Quito, Ecuador, are now in doubt again after Santos recalled his chief negotiator. Earlier efforts for a comprehensive peace agreement covering both FARC and the ELN failed because of the latter's insistence on a separate deal, and unless negotiations get back on track, there is a danger that the current opposition may emerge with a strengthened mandate to abandon the peace process altogether. Colombia thus highlights how peace agreements, which are initially negotiated among the leaders of conflict parties, require widespread public support for their ultimate success. This is particularly true in democratic countries, and can also lead to the rejection of an agreement, as demonstrated by Cyprus where a UN-proposed deal, based on local negotiations, was rejected in a referendum in 2004. Moreover, even where popular approval is widespread, there is no guarantee against violent elements at the fringes of society who will work to undermine peace processes at every stage as they hold out for maximalist demands that no longer have mainstream support, as has been the case with groups such as the Continuity IRA or the Real IRA in Northern Ireland.

In contrast to the optimism that might nonetheless prevail concerning the future of the Colombian peace process, the situation in both South Sudan and Ukraine is significantly less promising. While both cases exhibit a number of agreements concluded between the conflict parties in externally driven mediation processes, these agreements have been partially implemented at best, and at worst repeatedly broken down. Nonetheless, in the case of Ukraine a more or less stable ceasefire has emerged, whereas in South Sudan each agreement breakdown has resulted in a new bout of violence.

The latest incarnation in a long line of failed agreements in South Sudan was the Cessation of Hostilities Agreement on 21 December 2017, which has been repeatedly broken by both government and opposition forces in the form of actual exchanges of fire, attacks on civilians and movement of forces contrary to the terms of the agreement. The underlying complexity of the conflict may in part explain both the repeated infringements of the agreements and the accompanying violence. Civil war broke out in South Sudan in December 2013, triggered by a rivalry between factions within the ruling Sudan People's Liberation Movement (SPLM) led, respectively, by the country's president, Salva Kiir, and then-vice-president, Riek Machar. However, the subsequent dynamics of this multidimensional civil war – in which ethnic, political, regional, economic and cultural factors are the incongruently overlapping drivers of often intense violence – have their roots in a legacy of factors dating back to before South Sudan's independence in 2011.[10] The world's youngest country inherited a complex tribal, ethnic and religious demography physically disrupted by a new international boundary with the Republic of Sudan, from which it seceded under the terms of the Comprehensive Peace Agreement in 2005. The decades-old networks between political, religious and tribal leaders in South Sudan and across the border provided fertile ground for old conflicts to continue and new ones to emerge: the civil war between erstwhile allies within the SPLM is now but one of several conflicts that engulf the states of Central Equatoria, Unity, Upper Nile, Jonglei and Western Bahr el-Ghazal. Between them, the conflicts have killed tens of thousands of people, displaced almost half of South Sudan's nine million citizens (including about half as refugees across neighbouring countries) and led to the country being considered to be in famine between February and June 2017, with severe food shortages continuing to affect large parts of the population since.

Even in the face of such devastation, domestic elites have been unwilling to settle on a sustainable ceasefire, let alone a peace agreement, despite considerable international efforts, including from the United Nations (which has a now 17,000-strong mission in South Sudan), the African Union, the regional Intergovernmental Authority on Development (IGAD, which has taken the lead in the peace process, currently through the High Level Revitalization Forum) and the so-called Troika (Norway, the United Kingdom and the United States), as well as the EU and China. The first ceasefire, agreed in January 2014, broke down almost immediately, and talks meant to be held under IGAD auspices continued on and off for months against the background of intensifying violence targeted increasingly at civilians and pitting the country's two largest ethnic groups – Dinka and Nuer – against each other. A new ceasefire agreement was then signed in May 2014, followed by a separate agreement on the formation of a transitional unity government in June. However, fighting resumed in July, and the 10 August deadline for establishing a new unity government passed without any sign of it. A new ceasefire deal and agreement on steps to form a new government was then announced by IGAD at the end of August, yet opposition forces refused to sign up to it, paving the way for continuing violence despite the resumption of peace talks at the end of September. These peace talks were again suspended in November 2014 after the parties' renewed commitment to a ceasefire did not lead to any noticeable decrease in the levels of violence.

On–off negotiations between different conflict parties and increasingly fluid alliances of factions and splinter groups (mediated by Tanzania, China and IGAD) rendered no significant progress and the suspension of the main IGAD peace process in early March 2015 was followed by yet another increase in violence. By the end of May, the international community had managed to find common ground and announced the so-called IGAD+ format of the peace process, which brought together the hitherto separate tracks of intra-SPLM reconciliation and the existing IGAD mediation efforts. This new format produced a draft peace agreement proposed by the international community in July, which formed the basis of the Agreement on the Resolution of the Conflict in the Republic of South Sudan in August 2015. Following the conclusion of additional protocols, the implementation of the agreement finally began in December 2015, two years after the outbreak of civil war. In April 2016, former vice president Machar returned to the capital Juba and was sworn in as first vice-president under the terms of the agreement, but by June implementation had almost completely stalled and in July renewed fighting broke out in the capital, prompting Machar to flee and giving Kiir an opportunity to appoint a rival as new first vice president, claiming compliance with the agreement. Despite IGAD acquiescence to this and the (slow) deployment of a UN-mandated regional protection force, fighting escalated and engulfed five states by December 2016. At this point Kiir announced a national dialogue, which was eventually launched formally in May 2017, simultaneously with a unilateral government ceasefire. It then took another diplomatic push by IGAD and the Troika to reach an agreement to establish the High Level Revitalization Forum in December 2017, an effort to give the peace process renewed traction. The first round of negotiations was held in February 2018, with the second round scheduled for April. Nonetheless, fighting has continued ever since and progress in the peace process has remained elusive. This, too, underscores the importance of a viable agreement (i.e., one that actually has real prospects of implementation) and also highlights the critical role of local leadership commitments to peace. In the absence of those, no amount of international support can bring about an agreement or secure its implementation. Moreover, the case of South Sudan additionally highlights several serious dangers with protracted peace processes: they increase fragmentation among conflict parties, making comprehensive and inclusive agreements more difficult to achieve and implement; and that they prolong human suffering as violence continues and humanitarian relief becomes more difficult, which, in turn, puts future strains on the operation of peace agreements by (among other things) increasing the costs for post-conflict reconstruction.

As noted above, the situation in Ukraine somewhat resembles that in South Sudan, in that none of the internationally mediated agreements were ever fully implemented. However, there were far fewer agreements in the case of Ukraine (four in total between February 2014 and February 2015) and despite their incomplete and abortive implementation, a more or less stable ceasefire has remained in place since the so-called Minsk II agreement in February 2015. This assessment is, of course, a matter of relativity. The Organization for Security and Co-operation in Europe (OSCE) Special Monitoring Mission to Ukraine has recorded frequent violations of the ceasefire since March 2014, mostly in the form of mortar attacks and sniper fire across the ceasefire line. These violations resulted in 476 casualties in 2017 alone, including 86 people killed.[11]

In comparison to the intense fighting between the spring of 2014 and the winter of 2015 – which caused the death of close to 10,000 people and the internal displacement of around 1.8 million people plus an additional 700,000 refugees, primarily in Russia – the persistent ceasefire violations and their consequences indicate the overall degree of volatility and hostility between the sides in the period since the Minsk II agreement of February 2015, rather than an imminent return to the civil war that had previously engulfed the country. Yet while the consequences of the inconclusiveness of its peace process may be less dramatic than those in South Sudan, Ukraine is as far from a sustainable solution, albeit for very different reasons. While clearly reflecting many internal problems, Ukraine's descent into mass violence was externally instigated, triggered by the increasingly fierce competition over influence in the country between Russia and the West. Following a decision by then Ukrainian president Victor Yanukovych in late 2013 to suspend the country's association process with the EU, popular protests in Kiev in December and January quickly escalated into violence. International pressure, particularly from the EU and US, led to an agreement on a managed transition that included constitutional reform and early elections, but this agreement survived only three days before Yanukovych fled the country as protests against him continued. This left Russia, his main supporter, without a foothold in a strategically important country. Moscow moved quickly to annex Crimea (where its sole Black Sea naval base is located) and begin a proxy war in the Donbas region of Ukraine, while simultaneously engaging with the EU and key member states (especially France and Germany in the so-called Normandy Format) in a peace process meant to restore political stability to Ukraine.

Agreements reached in Geneva in April 2014 and thereafter in Minsk in September 2014 and February 2015, however, have remained largely unimplemented, especially with regard to constitutional reform and decentralisation. In consequence, over the course of a little more than 12 months, Ukraine became another Soviet successor state that has been territorially divided. Apart from Crimea, Russia has influence over another significant portion of Ukrainian territory comprised of parts of the regions of Donetsk and Luhansk that has formed another de facto state (not dissimilar to Transnistria in Moldova and South Ossetia and Abkhazia in Georgia, albeit much larger in terms of territorial and population size, as well as economic assets). While this new de facto state gives Russia significant leverage over Ukraine, its utility to Russia is somewhat more limited now that the Ukrainian government has increasingly turned towards a policy of isolating these currently occupied territories. This in turn has created a situation in which the status quo has become increasingly acceptable to all sides in the conflict (i.e., the local parties and their respective external backers), not because it is the most preferred state of affairs, but rather because their real preferences are unobtainable. Russia cannot, at the moment, achieve a government in Ukraine aligned to it in a similar way as the previous Yanukovych regime, nor can it force the current government to accept reintegration terms for the separatist areas that would allow Moscow to exercise an effective veto over major domestic and foreign-policy decisions in Kiev. The government in Kiev, meanwhile, has neither the political will nor the economic capacity to reintegrate the occupied territories on the terms 'on offer' in the Minsk II agreement, and neither does it have the military capabilities to impose its own reintegration terms. The separatists, finally, may well desire full annexation by Moscow, but in the absence of this being a viable option (i.e., as long as Moscow sees some utility in leveraging the ongoing crisis against Kiev and its Western backers), ruling over a de facto state represents far from a worst-case scenario,[12] not least because it has proven a rather viable alternative in several other conflicts in, and beyond, the post-Soviet space. The consequences of this for any peace process are obvious: the benefits of the status quo outweigh the costs of the compromises and concessions that would be necessary in the course of negotiating a peace agreement. Thus, the minimal existing commitments to avoiding escalation beyond the low-intensity violations of the existing ceasefire; the acceptance of the minimally effective but somewhat reassuring presence of the OSCE Special Monitoring Mission; and the on–off talks in the Trilateral Contact Group (comprised of Ukraine, Russia and the OSCE) are likely to substitute for any meaningful peace process aimed at achieving sustainable mutual accommodation in a peace agreement.

Key concepts for successful peace processes

This outline of some general trends and the few brief illustrations of contemporary peace processes above can only scratch the surface of an area of increasingly sophisticated scholarship and extensive and mostly well-meaning international practice. What should be clear from the foregoing discussion is that peace processes come in all shapes and sizes; that their specific nature and outcome is highly context-dependent; and that we cannot, and should not, aspire to finding a magic formula for an always-successful blueprint. Even on the basis of the limited empirical illustrations provided here, however, several insights can be gleaned which can be summarised under the headings of institutional design, diplomacy and leadership.

There should be no doubt that carefully crafted agreements that address conflict parties' grievances and demands in a balanced manner and pave the way towards viable new state structures without the pathologies that contributed to conflict in the first instance are an essential component of the ultimate success of peace processes. But such agreements are not negotiated, implemented or operated in a vacuum. Diplomacy, as a shorthand for international involvement in many of today's peace processes, is an equally crucial success factor. Negotiations often only take place following international pressure; they require international support – financially and politically – to sustain them, and they also tend to benefit from the substantive input that international mediators can offer into the designing of the provisions of a peace agreement. Beyond that, international support is necessary during implementation and operation to set up and fund institutional reform and economic reconstruction, to overcome implementation hurdles and to provide assurances to the former conflict parties against defections and spoilers. Yet without visionary, skilled and determined local leadership from the conflict parties themselves, without the genuine commitment to resolve their differences by peaceful means, no degree of institutional-design ingenuity and no level of international diplomatic commitment will bring a peace process to a successful conclusion.

Stefan Wolff is Professor of International Security at the University of Birmingham, England. An expert on ethnic conflict, he has published over 80 journal articles and book chapters, as well as 17 books, including *Ethnic Conflict: A Global Perspective* (Oxford University Press, 2007), *Ethnic Conflict: Causes, Consequences, and Responses* (Polity, 2009, with Karl Cordell), and *Conflict Management in Divided Societies: Theories and Practice* (Routledge, 2011, with Christalla Yakinthou).

Notes

1   Edward N. Luttwak, 'Give war a chance', *Foreign Affairs*, vol. 78, no. 4, July/August 1999, p. 44, https://www.foreignaffairs.com/articles/1999-07-01/give-war-chance; Barbara F. Walter, 'The critical barrier to civil war settlement', *International Organization*, vol. 51, no. 3, p. 349, https://www.cambridge.org/core/services/aop-cambridge-core/content/view/S0020818397440110.

2   Roy Licklider, 'The consequences of negotiated settlements in civil wars, 1945–1993', *American Political Science Review*, vol. 89, no. 3, September 1995, pp. 681–90, http://fas-polisci.rutgers.edu/licklider/publications/apsa%20article.pdf.

3   Karl DeRouen, Jacob Bercovitch and Paulina Pospieszna, 'Introducing the civil wars mediation (CWM) dataset', *Journal of Peace Research*, vol. 48, no. 5, pp. 663–72, https://www.researchgate.net/publication/227574768_Introducing_the_Civil_Wars_Mediation_CWM_Dataset.

4   See, for example, Lars-Erik Cederman, Simon Hug, Andreas Schädel and Julian Wucherpfennig, 'Territorial autonomy in the shadow of conflict: too Little, too late?', *American Political Science Review*, vol. 109, no. 2, May 2015, pp. 354–70; Madhav Joshi, Erik Melander and Jason Michael Quinn, 'Sequencing the peace: how the order of peace agreement implementation can reduce the destabilizing effects of post-accord elections', *Journal of Conflict Resolution*, vol. 61, no. 1, March 2015, pp. 4–28, https://pdfs.semanticscholar.org/01e1/0170b51aac437b5d5f748669b7494d0f6159.pdf?_ga=2.204446160.1558436065.1519824439-12949122.1519824439; Timothy D. Sisk, 'Peacebuilding as democratization: findings and recommendations', in Anna K. Jarstad and Timothy D. Sisk (eds), *From War to*

Democracy: Dilemmas of Peacebuilding (Cambridge: Cambridge University Press, 2008), pp. 239–59.

5   See Astri Suhrke and Ingrid Samset, 'What's in a figure? estimating recurrence of civil war', *International Peacekeeping*, vol. 14, no. 2, April 2007, pp. 195–203, https://www.tandfonline.com/doi/pdf/10.1080/135333106 01150776?needAccess=true.

6   Ramzi Badran, 'Intrastate peace agreements and the durability of peace', *Conflict Management and Peace Science,* vol. 31, no. 2, April 2014, pp. 193–217.

7   David E. Cunningham, 'Veto players and civil war duration', *American Journal of Political Science,* vol. 50, no. 4, October 2006, pp. 875–92.

8   Argyro Kartsonaki, 'Twenty years after Dayton: Bosnia-Herzegovina (still) stable and explosive', *Civil Wars*, vol. 18, no. 4, October 2016, pp. 488–516, https://research.birmingham.ac.uk/portal/files/40147735/

Kartsonaki_Twenty_years_after_Dayton_ Civil_Wars_2017_Published.pdf.

9   Stefan Wolff, 'From Paper to Peace: The role of guarantees in peace agreements', *World Politics Review,* 17 December 2013.

10 Stefan Wolff, 'South Sudan's Year One: Managing the challenges of building a new state', *RUSI Journal*, vol. 157, no. 5, October 2012, pp. 46–54, https://www.tandfonline.com/doi/pdf/10.1080/03071847.2012.733109? needAccess=true.

11 OSCE Special Monitoring Mission to Ukraine, 'Status Report as of 10 January 2018', http://www.osce.org/special-monitoring-mission-to-ukraine/366306.

12 Tatyana Malyarenko and Stefan Wolff, 'The logic of competitive influence-seeking: Russia, Ukraine, and the conflict in Donbas', *Post-Soviet Affairs*, 2018, https://www.tandfonline.com/doi/full/10.1080/106 0586X.2018.1425083?scroll=top&needAcces s=true.

Chapter Two

Maps, Graphics and Data

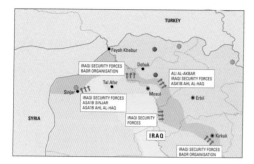

Territorial changes in northern Iraq   **82**

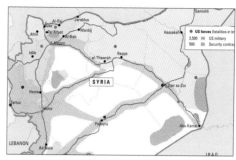

Foreign forces in Syria   **83**

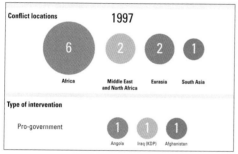

External interventions in
armed conflicts   **84**

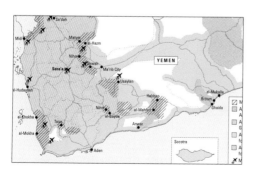

The changing Yemeni battlefield   **88**

Refugee totals in selected
non-Western countries   **86**

Territorial changes in northern Iraq

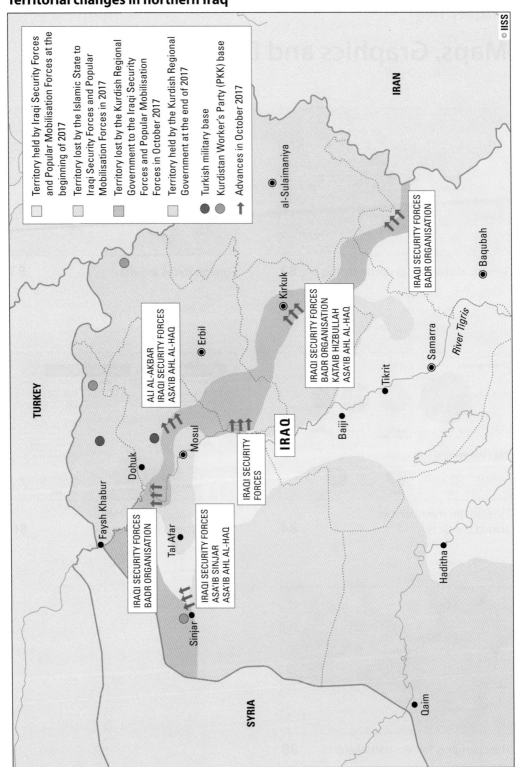

Sources: IISS; International Crisis Group; Institute for the Study of War; BBC

Foreign forces in Syria

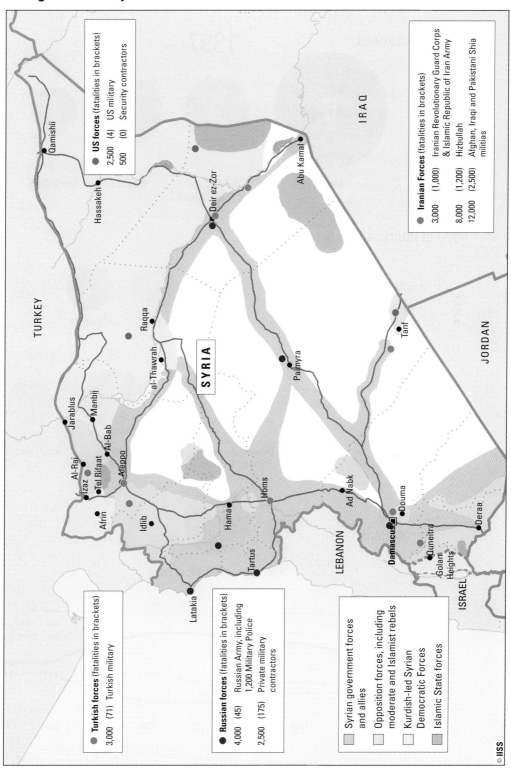

External interventions in armed conflicts

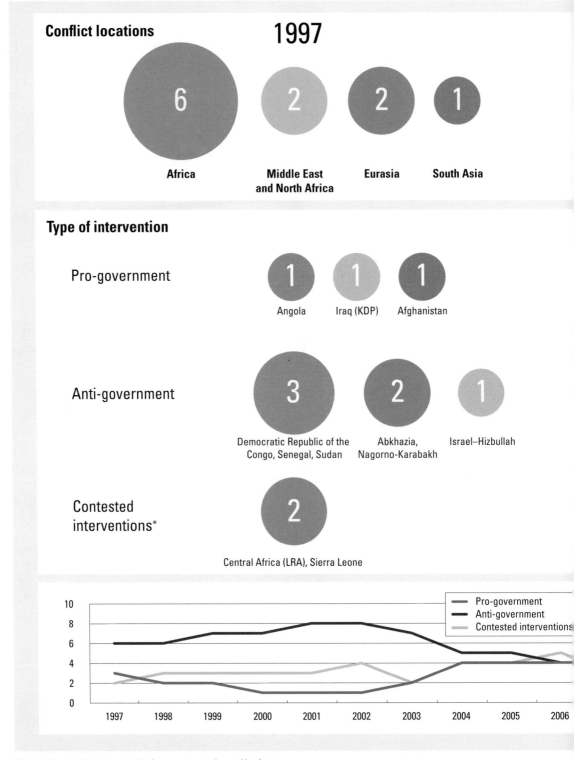

Conflict locations

1997

6
Africa

2
Middle East
and North Africa

2
Eurasia

1
South Asia

Type of intervention

Pro-government

1
Angola

1
Iraq (KDP)

1
Afghanistan

Anti-government

3
Democratic Republic of the
Congo, Senegal, Sudan

2
Abkhazia,
Nagorno-Karabakh

1
Israel–Hizbullah

Contested
interventions*

2

Central Africa (LRA), Sierra Leone

Legend:
— Pro-government
— Anti-government
— Contested interventions

*External intervention in support of both government and opposition forces

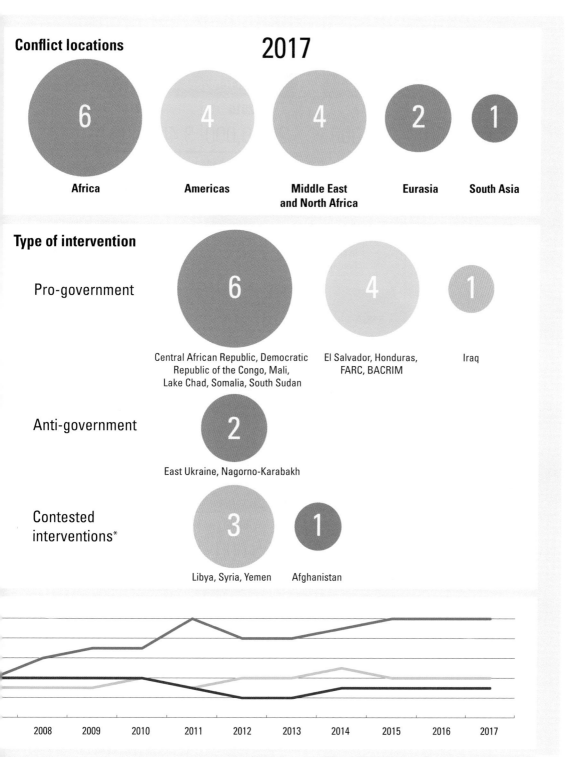

Conflict locations

2017

Africa	Americas	Middle East and North Africa	Eurasia	South Asia
6	4	4	2	1

Type of intervention

Pro-government

6 — Central African Republic, Democratic Republic of the Congo, Mali, Lake Chad, Somalia, South Sudan

4 — El Salvador, Honduras, FARC, BACRIM

1 — Iraq

Anti-government

2 — East Ukraine, Nagorno-Karabakh

Contested interventions*

3 — Libya, Syria, Yemen

1 — Afghanistan

2008   2009   2010   2011   2012   2013   2014   2015   2016   2017

© IISS

Refugee totals in selected non-Western countries

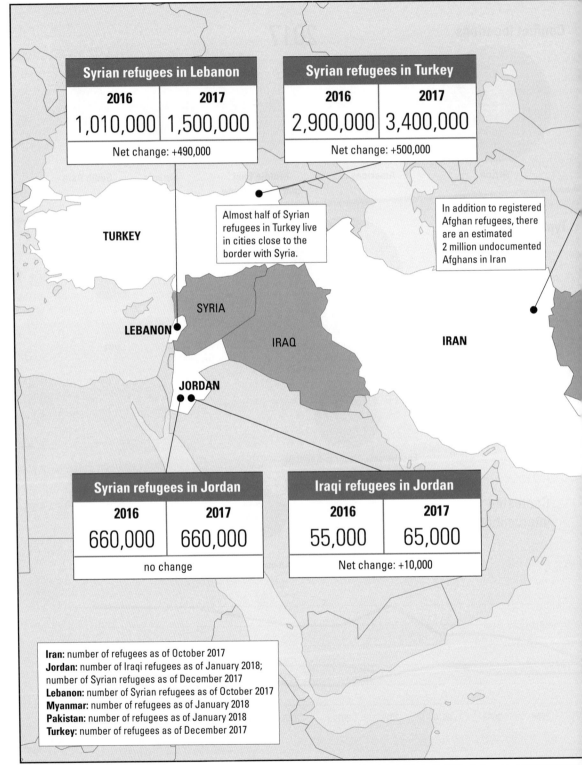

Syrian refugees in Lebanon

2016	2017
1,010,000	1,500,000

Net change: +490,000

Syrian refugees in Turkey

2016	2017
2,900,000	3,400,000

Net change: +500,000

Almost half of Syrian refugees in Turkey live in cities close to the border with Syria.

In addition to registered Afghan refugees, there are an estimated 2 million undocumented Afghans in Iran

TURKEY

SYRIA

LEBANON

IRAQ

JORDAN

IRAN

Syrian refugees in Jordan

2016	2017
660,000	660,000

no change

Iraqi refugees in Jordan

2016	2017
55,000	65,000

Net change: +10,000

Iran: number of refugees as of October 2017
Jordan: number of Iraqi refugees as of January 2018; number of Syrian refugees as of December 2017
Lebanon: number of Syrian refugees as of October 2017
Myanmar: number of refugees as of January 2018
Pakistan: number of refugees as of January 2018
Turkey: number of refugees as of December 2017

Sources: European Civil Protection and Humanitarian Aid Operations (European Commission); Government of Lebanon; International Organization for Migration (The UN Migration Agency); Iranian Bureau for Alien and Foreign Immigrant Affairs/BAFIA; Jordan INGO Forum; UNHCR

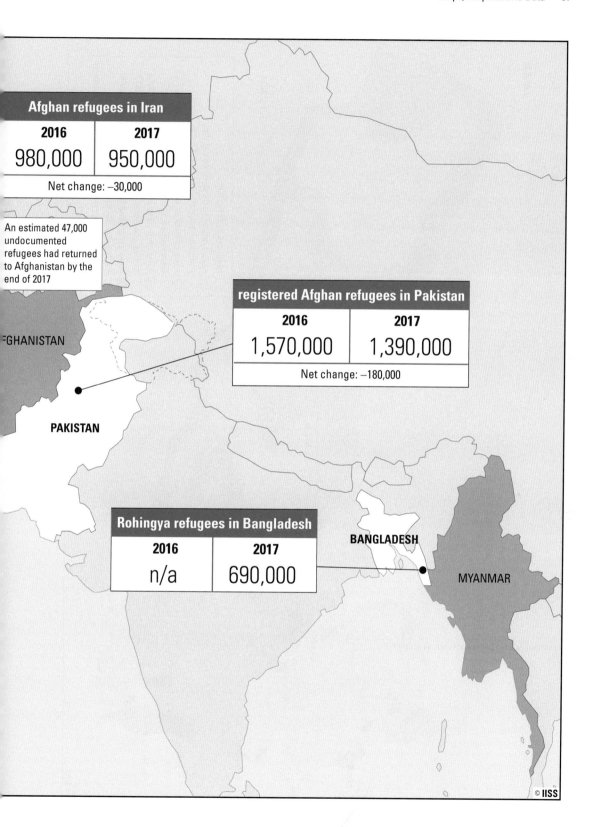

Afghan refugees in Iran

2016	2017
980,000	950,000

Net change: −30,000

An estimated 47,000 undocumented refugees had returned to Afghanistan by the end of 2017

registered Afghan refugees in Pakistan

2016	2017
1,570,000	1,390,000

Net change: −180,000

AFGHANISTAN

PAKISTAN

Rohingya refugees in Bangladesh

2016	2017
n/a	690,000

BANGLADESH

MYANMAR

© IISS

The changing Yemeni battlefield

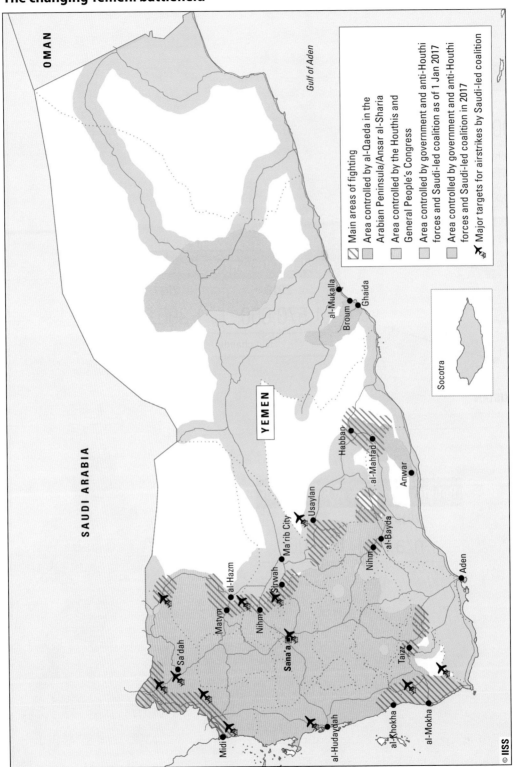

Chapter Three

Middle East

Egypt (Sinai)

Violence in North Sinai showed no
signs of abating in 2017, despite
heavy military deployment and
continuous operations. On 24
November, 311 people were killed in
an attack on a Sufi-affiliated mosque
in the region. No group claimed
responsibility for the attack, but many suspected the involvement of Wilayat Sinai

Key statistics	2016	2017
Type:	Internal	Internal
Fatalities:	1,750	1,500
New IDPs:	– [b]	3,800
New refugees:	– [b]	– [b]

(Sinai Province), the Sinai affiliate of the Islamic State, also known as ISIS or ISIL,
which is infamous for sectarian attacks against Sufis and Christians. Although
Wilayat Sinai dominated jihadi activity, there was a resurgence among other groups.
One example was Jund al-Islam, a group linked to al-Qaeda that condemned the
attack and announced its intention to repel 'the Kharijites of al-Baghdadi' (referring
to operatives from ISIS) from Sinai. Another group affiliated to al-Qaeda, Ansar al-
Islam, claimed an attack in the Western Desert, which emerged as a new front for
attacks against the security forces. In addition, Egypt faced smaller-scale attacks in
and around Cairo by groups such as Hassm. The various forms of violence were
politically expedient for the Egyptian government, which used security challenges
to stifle dissent and political opposition. While President Abdel Fattah Al-Sisi was
largely expected to run in – and win – the March 2018 election, opponents chal-

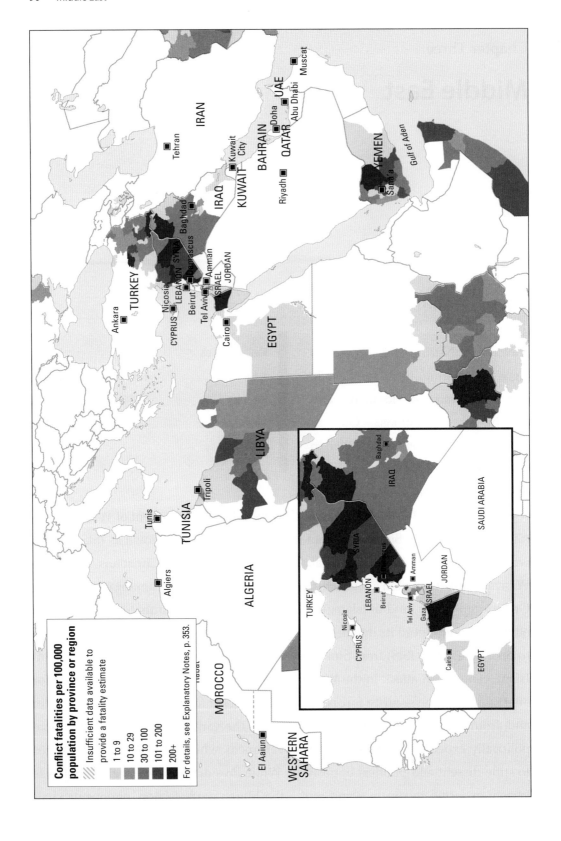

Conflict fatalities per 100,000 population by province or region

Insufficient data available to provide a fatality estimate

1 to 9
10 to 29
30 to 100
101 to 200
200+

For details, see Explanatory Notes, p. 353.

lenged him on key issues that negatively impacted his popularity, such as foreign policy (particularly the transfer of Tiran and Sanafir islands to Saudi Arabia) and Egypt's struggling economy.

Jihadi activity

Egypt witnessed its deadliest attack on 24 November, when gunmen killed 311 people during Friday prayers at a mosque in Al-Rawda village in Bir al-Abd, 40 kilometres west of Arish, the capital of North Sinai. The attack involved the use of improvised explosive devices (IEDs), followed by gunfire on civilians who were trying to flee, while assailants set parked cars on fire and shot at ambulances. The mosque is associated with a Sufi order in North Sinai, but it is not only visited by Sufis and in most cases there is no way to distinguish Sufis from other worshippers. For many, Sufism is simply an approach to the practice of Islam.

The attackers were reportedly brandishing the Islamic State's black flag, but the group did not claim the attack. Analysts have speculated that internal struggles – within Wilayat Sinai or between Wilayat Sinai and the Islamic State, which suffered significant territorial losses in 2017 – may explain why neither group claimed the attack. This is uncharacteristic for the Islamic State, which typically rushes to issue claims of responsibility, but the attack was in line with the group's focus on sectarian attacks in Egypt, reflecting a strategy it has used proficiently elsewhere. Wilayat Sinai previously targeted Sufi leaders in March, beheading two Sufis on video and accusing them of practising witchcraft. In February, ISIS released a video threatening Coptic Christians in North Sinai, after having killed numerous Christian civilians in the area. This led around 100 Christian families and 200 students to flee. The Islamic State also claimed large-scale attacks against Coptic Christians, including an attack in Minya province in May that killed 29 people.

The group's targeting of religious minorities and civilians may be undermining its popularity in North Sinai. In November, a rival jihadi group called Jund al-Islam claimed responsibility for an attack on Wilayat Sinai a month earlier, calling on the group to abandon ISIS leader Abu Bakr al-Baghdadi. Jund al-Islam, which is affiliated with al-Qaeda, is not new; it announced its formation in 2013 but was barely active. Its November statement suggests that it managed to capitalise on Wilayat Sinai's alienation and may have attracted disillusioned operatives from the group.

Wilayat Sinai also continued to clash heavily with the Egyptian security forces and tribal groups in North Sinai allied with the military. The group carried out multiple coordinated attacks against checkpoints, using vehicle-borne IEDs to kill dozens. It launched rocket attacks on southern Israel twice in January, but neither caused damage nor casualties. The group released photos of *Katyusha* rockets targeting what it described as 'Jewish settlements', and claimed to have killed three Israeli spies. It also released footage of its fighters carrying out religious policing in North Sinai, as well as photos of its operatives setting up checkpoints in Arish, as part of the overall effort to present itself as a state. Residents confirmed that fighters linked to Wilayat Sinai had indeed been roaming the city.

Shortly after the large attack on Al-Rawda mosque, Sisi ordered the army's chief of staff to restore security in Sinai within three months. The statement elicited concerns that Sisi was giving the military carte blanche to restore stability at any cost, even the use of brute force, which, as many have argued, can further drive residents into the arms of militant groups, thereby perpetuating a cycle of violence. While the military announced numerous victories against violent groups in Sinai in 2017, including the death of hundreds of operatives and leaders such as Wilayat Sinai's Abu Anas al-Ansari, it failed to bring an end to armed attacks.

The Egyptian security forces also faced increasing attacks in the Western Desert. An ambush in October that led to the death of at least 16 policemen was claimed by a group called Ansar al-Islam via Guardians of Sharia, a source affiliated with al-Qaeda. Egyptian officials tied the group to Hisham al-Ashmawi, a former military official turned jihadi who has operated from Libya and previously claimed several high-profile attacks. Ashmawi is known to be affiliated with al-Qaeda, rather than the Islamic State.

Violence and repression

The smaller 'revolutionary' and non-jihadi groups Hassm and Lewaa al-Thawra stepped up their attacks in Cairo against police forces, mostly relying on small arms and IEDs. These groups distanced themselves from sectarian attacks and attacks on civilians generally. Hassm, for example, released a statement in the aftermath of the attacks on Christians in Minya, denying involvement and reiterating that it does not target civilians. The group also released a statement in October after the United

States Embassy issued a warning to its nationals regarding possible attacks, stating that foreign nationals should fear Egyptian authorities instead and describing itself as a resistance and not a terrorist group. The US Embassy's statement followed an explosion at Myanmar's embassy in Cairo, which the group claimed was in retaliation for violence against Rohingya Muslims.

Both Hassm and Lewaa al-Thawra are thought to be comprised of former members of the Muslim Brotherhood, and they both describe the acts of violence they perpetrate as a response to state violence. The Muslim Brotherhood, which was outlawed after Sisi rose to power, witnessed its members killed, jailed, sentenced to death, forcibly disappeared or driven underground. Throughout 2017, Egypt regularly ordered the detention of individuals suspected of belonging to the Muslim Brotherhood. Human-rights groups believe that there are around 60,000 political prisoners in Egypt, of whom many are thought to be Islamists. Cairo continues to deny the presence of political prisoners; in a trip to Paris in October, Sisi reiterated that there are no political prisoners in Egypt.

Arrests were not restricted to Islamists. They included leftists and other political opponents, human-rights practitioners, journalists and members of the LGBTQ community. A lawyer who had been investigating the murder of Italian PhD student Giulio Regeni, widely thought to have been tortured and killed by the Egyptian security forces, was detained in September. This took place two weeks after Italy's foreign minister said the ambassador to Egypt would soon take up his position in the country, signalling the resumption of normal relations between the two states.

Meanwhile, Human Rights Watch released a report that described the institutionalised use of torture by the Egyptian security forces, which included beatings, electric shocks, stress positions and, at times, rape. The group argued that these acts constituted crimes against humanity under international law. The United Nations Committee Against Torture similarly stated that human-rights abuses such as torture were routine practice in Egypt. The government responded by taking the unprecedented step of blocking access to websites critical of the government, accusing them of supporting terrorism and spreading false news. Egypt also continued to prevent journalists from accessing conflict-affected areas, particularly Sinai (which requires entry and exit permits, and parts of which are considered closed military zones). The government concurrently targeted non-governmental organisations

(NGOs) by passing a law in May that severely undermined their work. Under the law, NGOs are restricted to carrying out development and social work, with the threat of up to five years' imprisonment for non-compliance.

The 2018 election

Egyptian presidential elections were scheduled to take place in the first half of 2018. Among the key figures who expressed interest in running in the election was Khaled Ali, a human-rights lawyer, member of the Coalition of Socialist Forces and director of the Egyptian Center for Economic and Social Rights. He co-founded the Front for the Defence of Egyptian Protesters, which provides legal support to non-violent protesters. Ali became well known for his protests against the maritime agreement between Egypt and Saudi Arabia, under which Egypt ceded the Red Sea islands of Tiran and Sanafir to Saudi Arabia. After legal challenges and protests, Sisi ratified the deal on 24 June, and by late October Saudi Arabia had announced a new megacity, Neom, which will include the two islands.

In addition to Ali, Ahmad Shafik, a former air-force chief and prime minister, announced his intention to run for president in the 2018 election. Shafik, who had been living in the United Arab Emirates since 2012, was deported to Cairo shortly afterwards, but it was not clear whether his deportation was carried out at Egypt's request. Shafik ran in the 2012 presidential election, narrowly losing to Muhammad Morsi. Due to Shafik's stature within the 'old guard' of the Egyptian government and the military, an arrest is unlikely to silence him.

Both candidates could capitalise on Egypt's shaky economic position. Ali previously won a case forcing the government to raise the monthly minimum wage to 1,200 Egyptian pounds (EGP) (US$68), while Shafik has strong connections to the Egyptian business elite, who perceive the military's intervention in the economy under Sisi as distorting markets. However, international financial institutions have been highly supportive of the government's policies, particularly the November 2016 decision to float the currency to qualify for a loan from the International Monetary Fund (IMF). The World Bank also disbursed US$1 billion in financial assistance to Egypt in March as part of a US$3bn programme. In 2017 Egypt's GDP expanded at the fastest pace recorded in seven years, and the IMF insisted that the economy was gathering strength. According to economists, the devaluation of the Egyptian pound and the subsequent high inflation rate made Egyptian exports 'competitive' abroad; however, combined with extremely low wages, it also exacerbated poverty for many Egyptians.

Egypt's economic situation is perceived as especially risky due to high rates of youth unemployment. After declaring that 2016 was the year of the youth, Sisi inaugurated an international World Youth Forum in November 2017, under the phrase 'We need to talk'. However, the conference faced similar critiques as many of his previous ones – that it was lavishly funded despite the narrative of belt-tightening and that it lacked opposing voices. It also quickly became apparent that the objective of the conference was to support the Sisi government's own political goals: in his opening speech, Sisi declared that 'combatting terrorism is a human right, a new right that I am adding to human rights in Egypt'.

Foreign policy

Egypt cemented its regional posture by participating in a Saudi-led drive to isolate Qatar over its alleged support for terrorist groups. Although Saudi Arabia is seen as the main architect of this policy, Egypt has long insisted that Qatar supports terrorist groups, especially the Muslim Brotherhood. The severing of relations in July 2017 was therefore seen as a continuation of Egypt's policy towards Qatar since 2013. The Egyptian state media has frequently demonised Qatar, and Muhammad Morsi was even sentenced to life in prison for espionage on behalf of Qatar.

While Egypt's political establishment made the eradication of the Brotherhood a main policy objective, relations with Palestinian group Hamas (considered an offshoot of the Brotherhood) improved significantly throughout 2017. In July, Hamas leader Ismail Haniyeh said the group had 'launched a new chapter with Egypt' following several rounds of talks between officials in Cairo. The rapprochement with Hamas was driven by greater security coordination in Sinai: there were reports of 'indirect cooperation' between Egypt, Hamas and Israel against the Islamic State, with Hamas arresting jihadis in Gaza and deploying the security forces along its border, where it was also reportedly building a buffer zone. Egypt may also be looking to benefit economically from Gaza's marginalised position, especially in sectors such as trade, health and construction. Haniyeh himself later visited Cairo to discuss intra-Palestinian reconciliation, a reconciliation which Egypt managed to broker in October. However, Egypt's actions were treated with suspicion given its continued support for Mohammed Dahlan, a rival to Palestinian President Mahmoud Abbas. Furthermore, reconciliation between Egypt and Hamas did not represent a break in Egypt's coordination with Israel, which remained a key ally of the Sisi government.

On the other hand, Egypt's relationship with the US in 2017 was tumultuous. Sisi visited the White House in April for a meeting with President Donald Trump, during which Trump praised Sisi and expressed strong support for him. In August, however, the US announced that it would withhold approximately US$95.7 million in aid to Egypt and delay a further US$195m. US officials attributed the decision to the aforementioned law regulating the work of NGOs, which was seen as a crackdown on political opposition. But some sources believed that the US administration's decision pertained to Egypt's relations with North Korea. A North Korean ship was seized off the coast of Egypt in October 2017 with a huge cache of rockets worth US$23m. The illicit deal was thwarted by US intelligence, and the UN argued that Egypt was defying international sanctions on North Korea. Egypt has enjoyed good relations with Pyongyang since the 1970s.

In a final ruling on 2 March, Egypt's Court of Cassation acquitted deposed president Hosni Mubarak of charges of ordering the killing of protesters during the 2011 uprising that ended his rule. Mubarak's return home, after six years of detention in a military hospital, symbolised the final step in the complete reversal of the 2011 revolution. There were few protests surrounding the exoneration, perhaps indicative of an overall atmosphere of disillusionment. Such disillusionment and the apathy it has resulted in also arguably defined the Egyptian population's reactions towards the March 2018 election, which they did not expect to be free and fair. Sisi did not officially declare whether he would run, but it was seen as likely that he would cite the 'will of the people' as a justification to seek another term and further cement his power. Sisi supporters had already started campaigning on his behalf, trying to stir up interest in the process and prevent the low turnout that had marred the parliamentary elections of 2015. As long as the election takes place in an environment where any political discussion continues to be perilous, the president's democratic legitimacy will remain in question.

Iraq

The government of Iraq declared the country liberated from the Islamic State, also known as ISIS or ISIL, on 9 December 2017, although inter-mittent fighting continued. The remaining ISIS fighters, number-ing fewer than 3,000, reverted to

Key statistics	2016	2017
Type:	Internationalised	Internationalised
Fatalities:	17,000	15,000
New IDPs:	660,000	1,380,000
New refugees:	50,000[a]	30,000[a]

guerrilla-style tactics, including suicide bombings and assassinations against both military and civilian targets. Some of the fighters who chose to flee began returning to their countries of origin, raising fear of further terror attacks outside the region: many were believed to have sought to join groups fighting in countries such as Egypt, Libya and Yemen, as well as Afghanistan, where the group competes with the Taliban for influence. In Iraq, there were fears that the government's declaration was premature and that ISIS could still stage a comeback. Further fragmentation between Shia, Sunni and Kurdish groups, supported by their state sponsors in the United States, Iran and Saudi Arabia, did little to alleviate the sense that the country has yet to see the end of violence.

A solid 'yes' vote in the independence referendum organised unilaterally by the Kurdish Regional Government (KRG) in the autonomous Kurdistan Region (KR) in September led to a federal military takeover of the disputed Kurdish-controlled Kirkuk governorate and the imposition of an international flight ban on the regional capital Erbil. Despite reconciliatory attempts by KR Prime Minister Nechirvan Barzani to reach a compromise, the ban was extended two months beyond its original end date until 28 February 2018. Fears resurfaced that the region would gradually regress into civil war – last seen among the Iraqi Kurds in the mid-1990s – as the financial crisis (now entering its fourth year) deepened, divisions between Kurdish political parties became more pronounced and low-level civil unrest swept over Kurdistan.

For the most part, Washington stood by while Tehran played the leading role, guiding its Shia ally to triumph over ISIS, shrink Kurdish territories and thwart secessionism. In an interesting turn of events, Saudi Arabia seemed keen to put

Iran's influence to the test by hosting Iraqi Prime Minister Haider al-Abadi and the radical Shia cleric Moqtada al-Sadr.

Last ISIS strongholds 'liberated'

In the course of 2017, ISIS lost its territorial gains made since June 2014 in the area between Aleppo in northern Syria and Diyala in Iraq. The town of Rawa in the Anbar governorate – the last ISIS stronghold in Iraq – was recaptured by the Iraqi Security Forces (ISF) on 17 November, leading to Abadi's declaration that the country was fully liberated on 9 December.

The operation to retake Mosul, the ISIS capital in Iraq for more than three years, witnessed the most intense and sustained fighting of the liberation campaign in 2017. Federal and Kurdish armed forces and counter-terror units, as well as the government-supported, Shia-dominated and largely Iranian-financed Popular Mobilisation Units (PMU), all participated in the operation to recapture the city, supported by the US-led coalition of 60 nations who contributed advisers and air-strikes. It was estimated that up to 120,000 Iraqi fighters participated in the operation in total, including up to 60,000 ISF, 40,000 Kurdish Peshmerga and 16,000 members of the PMU. Various smaller militant groups consisting of Kurds, Assyrians, Yezidi, Turkmen and others joined as well, such as the centre-left Kurdistan Freedom Party (PAK), the leftist insurgent group Kurdistan Worker's Party (PKK) and its affili-ates, and the Shammar Sunni tribe, which has worked with the US coalition since the early days of the Iraq War. The PKK's role in defending areas in Sinjar and the west of Mosul was strongly condemned by Turkey, despite the PKK's role being unrecognised officially, amid reports that Baghdad had been paying salaries to PKK militants through its funding to the PMU. A commander of the PKK-trained, Yezidi-dominated Shingal Protection Units (YBS) also stated that the group belonged to the PMU, an acknowledgement that signalled the blurring of the lines between the various non-state groups, the government and Iran.

Although initial rapid progress was made in the east of the city, the operation to liberate the western parts was more protracted. After eight months of heavy fight-ing, ISIS was eventually pushed into an enclave in the Old City, where it was trapped without supplies, running water or electricity. Thousands of civilians were trapped with them. By the end of the operation, more than 7,000 civilians were estimated to have been killed. Overall, the fighting displaced almost one million residents, out of a pre-war population of 2.5 million.

The city of Tal Afar was recaptured in August, and the town of Hawija in Kirkuk – the remaining ISIS urban bastion – in September. The last ISIS strongholds in the country – the towns of Qaim and Rawa in the western Anbar governorate bordering Syria – were liberated in November. However, the government was still attempting to regain control of the rest of the oil wells in November, many of which had been set ablaze by the retreating militants. Operations to catch the remaining ISIS militants continued, including a PMU operation to liberate 35 villages in the al-Jazeera Desert in Anbar province from ISIS in early December, and a large-scale operation west of Kirkuk that led to five ISIS operatives being killed and many tunnels and impro-vised explosive devices (IEDs) being destroyed. Sporadic confrontations between the ISF, the PMU and pockets of ISIS fighters continued through December in various parts of the country, as ISIS resorted to guerrilla tactics resembling those the group had adopted back in 2008 before its quick territorial expansion in Syria and Iraq. Towards the end of the year, the Meir Amit Intelligence and Terrorism Centre also reported signs of recovery in ISIS's media products – which had declined in quality over the previous two years – as ISIS increased its calls to its operatives both around the globe and in Syria and Iraq to persevere in the struggle.

According to an estimation based on a US Department of Defense (DoD) budget document, the US-trained Iraqi elite Counter-Terrorism Service (CTS) lost 40% of its overall strength in the Mosul operation alone, although the Iraqi government did not release official figures. Mass graves containing the remains of soldiers, cadets and civilians were uncovered in Nineveh, Salah al-Din, Kirkuk, Anbar and Fallujah governorates, including two mass graves found in Sinjar containing the bodies of 90 people, mostly Yezidi, and a new mass grave found in January at the infamous 2014 massacre site in Camp Speicher in Tikrit.

Following the declaration of victory, Abadi attempted to rein in the PMU by disarming and reintegrating it into the state forces (in accordance with the related law he had passed in 2016), as well as offering the PMU leaders the incentive of running for the general elections scheduled for May 2018. This initiative was sup-ported by the Shia cleric Ayatollah Ali al-Sistani, whose fatwa had provided the original impetus to form the units in June 2014. Most factions began demobilising in November and December, including the Iran-backed Badr Organisation. Some spectators, however, maintained that the PMU leaders would be unlikely to give up their influence over their fighters despite formally handing over their weapons, and that their successes or failures in the political arena might one day be manifested in a remobilisation of their militias, who would then be a part of the state armed forces.

In a separate affair, unverified rumours circulated in the Russian media of US collusion with ISIS to help their members and families escape Mosul in Iraq. In a peculiar social-media quarrel, the Russian Ministry of Defence (MoD) released what were largely identified by analysts as sham photographs intended as proof of these accusations, prompting the coalition spokesman Colonel Ryan Dillon on 14 November to call the Russian MoD's claims 'about as accurate as their air campaign'. The photographs were seemingly based on entirely unrelated older footage from Iraq, and on a video-game simulation.

Challenges facing the reconstruction of Mosul

The battle for Mosul resulted in widespread and extensive damage to the city's buildings, archaeological sites and key infrastructure, including the destruction of almost 90% of the Old City. Coalition airstrikes targeted bridges over the River Tigris which linked the east and west of the city in order to cut the supply routes of the militants. Water, sewage and electricity networks were also affected, and residents faced severe food shortages. While retreating from the city, ISIS militants sabotaged the governorate's key resources, such as its oil refineries and airport, and also blew up the 850-year-old Great Mosque of al-Nuri, where ISIS leader Abu Bakr al-Baghdadi had declared a caliphate in July 2014.

The United Nations estimated that more than US$1 billion was needed to rebuild the city's infrastructure and reopen its schools and hospitals. At least 40,000 homes had been destroyed, either completely or partially. Unexploded ordnance and booby traps hidden by ISIS would likely continue to affect construction sites and other areas for years to come, requiring decades of sustained investment to clear the area. The US began assisting contractors to locate explosives and asked its coalition members to declassify grid coordinates for bombs dropped on Iraq to facilitate clearance, but it was not certain whether the coalition members would be willing to do so. The UN Mine Action Service struggled with access and funds for Iraq: by the end of the year, the agency had received only 30% of the funds requested for 2017 and 2018 (mostly from European Union member states).

However, some Mosul residents did return to start rebuilding their own homes and shops. The government's promised assistance arrived slowly, however, meaning that many residents had to draw upon their own savings to clear the streets and buildings from rubble. A survey by the World Food Programme reported that insecurity and lack of capital were the main impediments to revitalising the city's markets. Despite this, however, barber, liquor, toy, shisha and smartphone shops (all banned under ISIS rule) reopened soon after liberation. Banned women's clothes also returned to the markets.

Aid to Iraq continued to be severely and chronically underfunded, a situation likely to be exacerbated by the Trump administration's promise of further cuts to UN funding. According to the UN Office for the Coordination of Humanitarian Affairs, 11m people in Iraq were in need of humanitarian assistance at the end of 2017, yet only 6.2m had been reached. Approximately 3m people remained displaced around the country as of November. The UN and many humanitarian organisations expressed concern over forced evictions and returns of families carried out by the government, repeatedly calling for the government to respect the right of voluntary return.

On 14 July, the UN Security Council extended the mandate of the United Nations Assistance Mission for Iraq (UNAMI) for another year, but requested the UN secretary-general to conduct an independent external assessment of UNAMI's structure and staffing.

Reconciliation efforts challenged by human-rights abuses

In the early months of the operation to liberate Mosul, the Iraqi forces had attempted to maintain a good image by casting themselves as the saviours of the civilian population. However, once ISIS was trapped in the Old City, civilians besieged with them began to be seen by the Iraqi forces as accomplices of ISIS. According to witness reports, rampant arbitrary killing, torture and rape of these civilians ensued. Both Amnesty International and Human Rights Watch (HRW) conducted investigations that attributed various killings, arbitrary arrests, vendetta attacks, looting, torture and other human-rights violations and war crimes to the KRG, the ISF and various militia groups – in particular the PMU and its members the Badr Organisation and the Sunni Hashd al-Asha'eri militia (sometimes referred to as the Sab'awi Tribal Mobilisation militia, this loose umbrella militia in fact comprises various tribes, many of them part of the original Sahwa (Awakening) tribal forces trained by the US between 2005 and 2008).

On 11 January, Iraq's highest criminal court found 47 PMU militants guilty of murder, kidnapping and arms possession, handing down sentences ranging from 15-year imprisonment to life imprisonment and death. Video evidence showing human-rights abuses perpetrated by the CTS and the PMU also prompted strong condemnation from the UN, finally leading Abadi to acknowledge these crimes on 17 August. On 21 September, the UN Security Council adopted Resolution 2379 urging accountability for crimes committed by ISIS in Iraq, and also established an investigative team for this purpose. Meanwhile, the Iraqi government and the KRG continued to prosecute ISIS suspects on counter-terrorism charges. HRW criticised these proceedings for various and serious legal shortcomings, including wrongfully identifying suspects and arbitrarily detaining them for extended periods of time, as well as not distinguishing between degrees of severity in the crimes. The organisation also criticised the inhumane conditions in which suspects were being held, the use of torture to gain confessions, failure to segregate children from adult detainees, as well as the issuance of arrest warrants for more than 15 lawyers who represented suspected ISIS militants. The group called for a fair trial of ISIS suspects and also for the government to consider alternatives, such as national truth-telling processes, to the prosecution of minor crimes.

In late 2016, HRW released a damning and detailed investigative report that documented a pattern of apparently discriminatory and unlawful demolitions of Sunni Arab homes and entire villages by the Kurdish forces – operations that had been conducted under US-led coalition air support between 2014 and 2016. However, despite the report, coalition members did not investigate their own role in enabling what might amount to war crimes. (The US-led coalition also received criticism from human-rights groups for having used white phosphorus in ISIS-held areas in Iraq and Syria.)

In May, a declassified audit of the US DoD from September 2016 found that the US military had failed to keep accurate records on arms and military equipment worth more than US$1bn that had been given to the ISF, the PMU and the Peshmerga under the Iraq Train and Equip Fund (ITEF) created in 2015. Reporting on the audit, Amnesty International said that it had previously documented poor record-keeping of weapons to Iraq, and warned that these arms have ended up in the hands of groups known to be carrying out atrocities, such as the PMU and Badr Organisation. In December, the independent research organisation Conflict Armament Research also released an extensive report on how ISIS had obtained a significant amount of the arms provided by the US to its allies in Iraq and Syria. The DoD audit was not the first time the US government has investigated this matter, as similar concerns were previously raised in another audit of the US arms supply to the Iraqi forces in July 2007.

Kurdistan independence referendum

After years of relative calm in the northern autonomous KR in Iraq, fears of a return to civil war were unleashed as a major crisis erupted in 2017, both between the Iraqi federal government and the KRG, and internally among Kurds themselves. Against Baghdad's orders, and despite enormous international and regional pressure to do otherwise, the KRG, under the leadership of President Masoud Barzani from the Kurdish Democratic Party (KDP), staged a non-binding independence referendum – with no outside scrutiny or oversight – that saw 93% of votes in favour of secession, with turnout at 72%. The opposition parties – the Patriotic Union of Kurdistan (PUK), the Gorran (Change) Movement and the Islamic party Komal – initially opposed the referendum as it was seen as premature in a situation of a deteriorating economy and an unresolved public-sector crisis: the latter was seen as protecting the ruling elite while leaving civil servants (especially those in the PUK-dominated Sulaimaniya governorate) unpaid for two years. The parties reversed their positions hours before the polls opened, possibly due to Barzani's threat that he would organise the elections in KDP-controlled areas anyway.

Immediately after the vote, Baghdad responded punitively in military, political and economic terms, imposing an international flight ban over the region's capital Erbil and sending troops (together with Iran-backed Shia militias) to retake the territories which the KRG had captured during the war against ISIS. The disputed Kirkuk changed hands with no resistance, which prompted some to accuse a faction in the PUK – known to have better relations with Baghdad and Iran – of treason. In the post-referendum aftermath, Barzani resigned (he had been due to step down on 1 November in any case) and handed over executive power to his nephew Nechirvan Barzani, who in turn proceeded to announce that the KRG would 'freeze' the implementation of the results. Abadi rejected the concession and demanded the result be pronounced void; during his declaration of victory over ISIS in December, Abadi avoided recognising the KRG's contribution to the operations.

The international community – including the UN, the US and Iran – had attempted to change Barzani's mind about staging the referendum, despite the fact that the Trump administration had said that the US would not be 'taking sides' in the dispute. Critics viewed the referendum as little more than a populist opinion poll aimed at consolidating the ruling parties' positions and popularity in a climate of general uncertainty, insecurity and economic turmoil. However, as an attempt to gain a stronger bargaining position against Baghdad over unresolved territorial and oil disputes, to many the referendum appeared counterproductive. Some blamed Barzani for having entertained a false sense of security and confidence gained after his cooperation with federal and international forces to fight ISIS, although he was probably also impelled by the popularity of the ongoing Kurdish state-building project in northern Syria. Overall, Barzani, and the KRG in general, came out of the affair considerably more isolated economically as well as politically, as evidenced by Baghdad's decision to cut the region's revenue share from 17% to 12.6%, and by oil exports, which more than halved.

The latter part of 2017 saw widespread civil unrest across the KR as the KRG cut civil-service salaries even further due to the economic fallout from Baghdad's blockade. Protests turned violent, in particular in the PUK-controlled Sulaimaniya governorate, which had to date been disproportionately affected by the cuts compared to Duhok and Erbil provinces, which are controlled by the ruling KDP party. The Kurdish parliament finally reopened after a two-year hiatus, but regional parliamentary and presidential elections were postponed from November until some point in mid-2018.

In the wider region, Iran reacted to the referendum by closing its land crossings with the KRG for three months (hurting its own local populations in doing so) and strengthening its troop positions along the border. Turkish President Recep Tayyip

Erdogan publicly condemned the referendum, but the punitive measures he took were half-hearted at best. Turkey went along with Baghdad's flight ban, organised a military exercise at the border and joined Iran's Supreme Leader Ayatollah Ali Khamenei in denouncing the referendum as a 'Zionist' scheme of Israel's intelligence agency Mossad. However, despite its bombastic threats, Turkey did not shut down the border or the oil trade, although it did open a second land crossing outside Kurdish control. Saudi Arabia called on the KRG to cancel the referendum, but its overall demeanour suggested that the kingdom hoped to position itself as a mediator between Baghdad and Erbil.

Political reform and diplomatic shifts

The government continued to struggle with political reform amid pressure to capture and prosecute the remaining ISIS militants swiftly. The support for Abadi, prime minister since 2014, waned in 2017 as his attempts to form a technocratic government faced opposition from those who benefited from the existing power-sharing arrangements. (Various former ministers, governors and officials had faced corruption allegations in the past.)

In January, the government filled its interior and defence positions that had remained vacant since 2015, seemingly in an effort to draw the country closer to Iran. The new interior minister – the Shi'ite Qasim Mohammad Jalal al-Araji from the Badr parliamentary bloc – was a vocal critic of the US and (according to some accounts) a friend of Major General Qassem Suleimani, the commander of Iran's Islamic Revolutionary Guard Corps' Quds Force. New Defence Minister Erfan al-Hayali, a Sunni, travelled to Tehran in July to sign a defence-cooperation agreement with Iran.

In February, protesters clashed with the security forces in Baghdad's Tahrir Square when demanding the reform of the Independent High Electoral Commission (IHEC). Several *Katyusha* rockets were fired into the Green Zone after the protesters (who included both secular groups and the followers of the radical cleric Moqtada al-Sadr) had left the area, but the rockets did not cause casualties. The Sadrists denied responsibility. A new electoral commission was announced the next day in response to the events. Protests continued in subsequent months, resulting in injuries from tear gas and rubber bullets. In October, the Sadrist Central Revolution

Committee threatened to storm the Iraqi parliament – a gesture commonly seen in Sadrist politics – if the IHEC's term was extended without reform.

The year witnessed important shifts among Shia political blocs that some interpreted as a nascent attempt at greater independence from Iran: Abadi moved closer to Riyadh at the expense of his already-weak relationship with Tehran, and King Salman bin Abdulaziz Al Saud proved more than accommodating. Abadi chose a cautious approach with Riyadh, however, and asserted neutrality during a diplomatic crisis that escalated between Qatar and Riyadh in June. Following Abadi's state visit to Riyadh, however, the kingdom announced the opening of consulates in Basra and the Shi'ite holy city Najaf, initiated a direct Baghdad–Riyadh flight route and started discussing security cooperation between the two countries. The cleric Sadr, also positioning himself against Iran's influence, followed suit and courted both Abu Dhabi and Riyadh, visiting the latter for the first time since 2006. The Trump administration expressed approval for these gestures towards Iraqi–Saudi rapprochement, prompting some to praise the US support as helping to counter against Iranian expansionism, and others to criticise it for undermining the progress made with Iran.

It remained to be seen whether the rapprochement with Riyadh would outlive Abadi's term, with challenges expected from the two most powerful pro-Iranian groups, the Sadrists and the Islamic Supreme Council of Iraq (ISCI), as well as influential Shia politicians who aim to position themselves somewhere between the pro-Iranian and the Saudi-receptive stances. On 24 July, Ammar al-Hakim resigned as the leader of the ISCI – the largest Shia political party in Iraq – reportedly taking a large amount of the party's funds with him and setting up the National Wisdom Movement as his new party, stating that he wished to 'get rid of sectarian and nationalist polarisation'. With Kurdish independence aspirations tempered for the time being, Abadi was free to focus on the parliamentary elections set for May 2018, although Nuri al-Maliki, Abadi's predecessor and likely opponent in the coming elections, tried to enlist Kurdish support in December by promising them a revenue increase and an end to the flight ban.

Despite liberating key cities from ISIS in 2017, the Iraqi government faced ongoing challenges in returning the country to a modicum of normality. The fair and transparent prosecution of ISIS militants for their crimes would be a litmus test for any genuine democratic reform in Iraq, but focusing only on ISIS crimes – and avoiding the prosecution of perpetrators from the PMU, Kurds and the ISF – threatened to hinder a sustainable reconciliation between sects and ethnic groups. At the end of the year, a comprehensive and inclusive national strategy for reconciliation, ISIS prosecutions and necessary military reforms was still lacking.

Israel–Palestine

Clashes between Israelis and Palestinians remained intermittent throughout the year, with a significant escalation in violence in December after the United States contentiously recognised Jerusalem as Israel's capital. The historical

Key statistics	2016	2017
Type:	Internal	Internal
Fatalities:	125	100
New IDPs:	1,500	700
New refugees:	– [b]	– [b]

drivers of the conflict – namely unchecked settlement construction in the West Bank, the annexation of East Jerusalem and the lack of peace negotiations – were reanimated, sparking widespread demonstrations across the West Bank, East Jerusalem and Gaza and threatening to destabilise the political situation.

Historic fault lines resurface

Despite the significant escalation in clashes in December, the number of overall casualties was lower than in the previous two years. According to the United Nations Office for the Coordination of Humanitarian Affairs (OCHA), 92 casualties were recorded – 77 Palestinians, 15 Israelis – compared to the 122 recorded in 2016. Furthermore, the number of Palestinians displaced because of Israel-led demolitions of Palestinian property was down by at least 55% compared to 2016. The pattern of violence remained the same throughout the year. Since October 2015, the conflict has been characterised by Palestinian lone-wolf knife, vehicle and gun attacks and Israeli settler violence against Palestinians, as well as heavy-handed Israeli security operations that often involved live ammunition.

The historic fault lines of the conflict continued to drive violence on the ground. Unchecked settlement expansion in the West Bank and East Jerusalem, the lack of a peace settlement and the disputed status of Jerusalem were reanimated by the US administration's alignment with Israeli interests and created a tense political environment. During the year, the Trump administration broke with previous US policies concerning the Israeli-Palestinian conflict. In February, Trump said that Israeli settlements were not an obstacle to peace and that the US had no preference concerning a two-state or one-state solution. The appointments of pro-Israel figures, such as David Friedman as ambassador to Israel and Jason Greenblatt and Jared Kushner as envoys to the Middle East peace process, presaged what followed in December, when Trump contentiously recognised Jerusalem as Israel's capital. Subsequently, he vowed to move the US Embassy from Tel Aviv to Jerusalem as a fulfilment of his presidential-campaign promise.

The announcements sparked mass demonstrations and riots on the ground that often turned violent across the West Bank, East Jerusalem and the Gaza Strip. Statistics released by the Shin Bet, Israel's security service, claimed that the number of security incidents in Israel and the West Bank tripled following Donald Trump's declaration. According to OCHA, at least 14 Palestinians were killed after the December announcement, and 4,549 were injured. Disconcertingly, the number of Palestinians injured in this period alone accounted for 56% of all injuries documented throughout 2017 (8,156, more than double OCHA's figure for 2016). Most of the casualties in December occurred in the Gaza Strip and marked a peak in violence in the enclave, which had remained relatively under control since the end of the Gaza conflict in 2014. Israel continued to target Hamas infrastructure in Gaza, particularly its vast tunnelling network, destroying two major tunnels. The biggest operation in October killed at least 12 Hamas and Palestinian Islamic Jihad (PIJ) operatives. Israel considers the tunnels to be a security threat and carried out the operations in response to a report issued by Israel's state comptroller in February which criticised the Israel Defense Forces' lack of preparedness in tackling Hamas tunnels during *Operation Protective Edge* in 2014.

Despite the United States' provocative Jerusalem announcement, the level of violence did not approach anything close to what many feared might be an intifada. Indeed, one reason for this was the restraint shown by both the Fatah-controlled

Palestinian Authority (PA) and Hamas, who stood to lose significantly in an all-out conflict. While both sides called for mass demonstrations and 'days of rage', they did not endorse all-out violence, which would be undesirable for the PA and unfeasible for Hamas. The former still saw a prospective route to peace through international forums, while the latter was still recovering from the heavy losses suffered in their previous 50-day war with Israel.

How long the conflict would remain contained was uncertain. Speaking in December, Palestinian President Mahmoud Abbas indicated that the trajectory of US–Israel policy could push vulnerable and desperate Palestinians who saw no hope for peace into the hands of opportunistic extremists. The deteriorating conditions in Gaza had already created the underlying conditions favourable to radicalisation, with youth unemployment peaking at 60%. In July, the UN Coordinator for Humanitarian Aid and Development Activities, Robert Piper, said the 'unliveability' threshold had already been reached, having initially estimated that Gaza would be uninhabitable by 2020.

Political uncertainties

Against this backdrop, there was an atmosphere of political uncertainty as both Palestinian and Israeli leaderships faced mounting calls to resign. While President Abbas and Israeli Prime Minister Benjamin Netanyahu both consolidated their hold on power last year, their longevity looked increasingly tenuous in 2017. Netanyahu faced mounting pressure to step down as prime minister after being embroiled in multiple corruption allegations relating to high-value gifts from businesses and favouring a news agency in exchange for biased news coverage. While Netanyahu denied the allegations, his tacit support for bills sponsored by his own party confidants that would effectively protect his office did little to reduce frequent Israeli demonstrations that called for his resignation. Not even the Jerusalem announcement discouraged the thousands who continued the weekly demonstrations.

Netanyahu's right-wing support base, who have backed some of the largest advances in settlement construction, stood firmly behind him, dismissing the allegations as politically motivated by elements of the left. However, this did not stop fellow coalition leader Naftali Bennett – leader of the right-wing religious Jewish Home party – from positioning himself as a capable successor should the 'age of

Netanyahu' come to an end. Other challengers, such as Netanyahu's former defence minister Moshe Ya'alon, also seized the opportunity to restate their candidacy. But Ya'alon may find it hard to convince the public that corruption, his present platform, poses a bigger threat to Israeli society than 'Iran, Hizbullah, Hamas or ISIS', as he claimed during one of the anti-corruption rallies.

For Abbas, the Jerusalem announcement was a major blow to his already dwindling popularity. In a poll published by the Palestinian Centre for Policy and Survey Research (PCPSR) a day after the announcement, 70% of Palestinians said they wanted Abbas to resign. Palestinians have been calling for an end to the age of Abbas for some time, and view his administration as systemically corrupt, untrustworthy and not acting in their best interests. In October, the octogenarian leader succeeded in forcing a historic reconciliation agreement between Hamas and Fatah, both of whom had remained at odds for the last decade. Heavy financial sanctions, which included cutting salaries to civil servants and electricity funding to the Gaza Strip, forced the militant group to relent and dismantle its shadow administrative committee and enter talks with the Fatah-controlled PA. After surprisingly successful negotiations, mediated by Egypt in Cairo, the group agreed to hand over control of the enclave with the key border crossings of Erez, Kerem Shalom and Rafah to a newly constituted unity government. The development flew in the face of a series of failed reconciliation agreements in the past, and many remained sceptical of the sustainability of the arrangement.

Abbas counted the agreement as a major victory, but will be unable to withstand the growing dissatisfaction with his administration if he fails to alleviate the humanitarian burden on Gaza and offer a plausible path to peace in line with Palestinian aspirations. Following the Jerusalem announcement, Abbas's only card left to play was to double down on leveraging international forums and pursuing other sponsors to replace the US as the sole mediator in the peace process. This will be a tall order, requiring significant pressure to be placed on Israel which has historically refused to engage in any negotiations without the US. Additionally, any attempts to pursue recourse through international bodies, such as the International Criminal Court, will be penalised by the US, as was demonstrated in November when the State Department threatened not to renew the permit of the Palestine Liberation Organization (PLO) mission in Washington DC.

The reconciliation between Hamas and Fatah further complicated matters, as both the US and Israel said they would not negotiate with a Palestinian government that included an armed Hamas. In May, Hamas revised its charter in a way that many interpreted as a softer stance. It accepted the possibility of a Palestinian state, in line with the PLO, along the 4 June 1967 borders, distanced itself from ties to the Muslim Brotherhood and said it was not interested in intervening in regional conflicts. In addressing the concerns of Egypt and some of the Gulf states, the revisions were no doubt aimed at garnering broader support from regional Arab allies. However, following reconciliation talks in October, Hamas's newly elected leader Yahya Sinwar made it clear that the group would not be disarmed.

US isolation and the end of the two-state solution

The incontrovertible alignment of US–Israel policy progressively isolated the US in the international community. Nowhere else was this more evident than within the United Nations. Following the December announcement, 14 of the 15 UN Security Council (UNSC) members (including strong US allies) condemned the move. The US vetoed the resolution but was unable to deter the UN General Assembly (UNGA) from overwhelmingly supporting a non-binding resolution calling on countries not to establish diplomatic missions in Jerusalem. In the lead-up to the emergency UN session the US adopted a belligerent tone, threatening to withdraw aid from countries that voted in favour of the resolution and saying it would still relocate the US Embassy to Jerusalem.

The muted regional Arab response to the Jerusalem announcement revealed the broad reassessment of Arab priorities and interests. While the Arab League condemned Trump's decision as illegal and said it undermined Arab confidence in the president, the league states did not rally behind the Palestinians in any other tangible way. While the UNSC resolution was proposed by Egypt, and the UNGA resolution by Yemen and Turkey, the wording of the documents took care not to name the United States directly. In short, it was evident that the question of Palestine was no longer at the top of Arab priorities. Following the Arab Spring, most Arab nations had been preoccupied with their own internal and external threats linked to developments in Iraq, Syria and Yemen. The reality facing them today is one in which Israel, once seen as an enemy, is now a pragmatic and useful buffer to Iran. In consequence, Palestinian public opinion has become deeply suspicious of regional Arab powers. A PCPSR poll in December revealed that more than three-quarters of Palestinians believed Palestine was no longer a 'first cause' for them, and a further 78% believed Arab powers would back a potential Trump peace plan – a plan that, if it materialised, would certainly prioritise Israeli demands.

In many respects, Trump's recognition of Jerusalem and the promise to move the US Embassy from Tel Aviv to Jerusalem closed the chapter on a year of opaque US diplomatic efforts to revive the Middle East peace process. Palestinian leadership remained cautiously optimistic in the early months of Trump's presidency as the president promised to achieve the 'ultimate deal'. Yet the move to 'take Jerusalem off the table' was a gross misreading of the historical significance of Jerusalem in any final settlement between the Israelis and the Palestinians. The failure to refer to Palestinian national aspirations or the claim they share over Jerusalem, the east of which would be the future capital of their state, marked what was quite possibly the end of the two-state solution. Angered, aggrieved and disillusioned, the Palestinian leadership declared that the US had deliberately undermined 'all efforts exerted to achieve peace', and thereby disqualified itself as a reliable sponsor of the peace process. Speaking in December, chief Palestinian peace negotiator Saeb Erekat said the time had come to focus all efforts on a one-state solution with equal rights for all Palestinians.

The toughest challenges for peace in the coming years will be in finding a new sponsor for the peace process and in shaping a domestic, regional and international consensus to back a one-state solution, while the international community (including the UN, the European Union and most of the Arab states) still view the two-state solution as the only viable path to peace. Emboldened by unwavering US support and the lack of an Arab response, Israel presently holds all the cards and may not see any incentive to enter peace talks in general. Against this backdrop, the historic fault lines of the long-standing conflict will be at the forefront of developments next year, and the evolution and stability of the conflict will depend on the new Palestinian unity government's ability to contain violence and establish a prospective path to peace.

Libya

The political stalemate in Libya became increasingly entrenched over the course of 2017. The failure of international actors to combine the disparate bodies which had been created by the December 2015 Skhirat Libyan Political Agreement

Key statistics	2016	2017
Type:	Internationalised	Internationalised
Fatalities:	2,000	1,500
New IDPs:	160,000	29,000
New refugees:	3,000	–[b]

into a consensual and functioning governing apparatus resulted in regional militias taking centre stage. With no national political system through which to channel local grievances and temper the ambitions of local forces, it was accordingly local dynamics which dictated how events unfurled over the year. Overall, 2017 was a year of consolidation for Libya's powerful militias, which took the opportunity to solidify control of their cities or regions and maximise the political and economic benefits therein. However, the exclusivist nature of Libya's civil war meant that this consolidation resulted in increasing numbers of disenfranchised groups, whose unresolved grievances in turn created a new driver for conflict and added a further layer of complexity to the process of achieving a durable political solution. Moreover, although each militia group may have increased its strength and control over its immediate environs, the limitations of a national security framework composed of a patchwork of uncooperative local groups became increasingly apparent. Large swathes of the country became overwhelmingly lawless and destitute, providing smugglers with the freedom to operate and terrorist groups such as the Islamic State, also known as ISIS or ISIL, the space to regroup, find new allies and plot future attacks. The relative freedom and economic opportunity afforded to those willing to fight for such groups also attracted foreign militants into the country, with non-governmental forces from Sudan and Chad finding Libya an increasingly hospitable operating base, either through working as mercenaries for Libyan factions or by seizing smuggling thoroughfares and extracting rents from those who use them. This cross-border activity indicates that Libya's destabilisation remains a potent threat to security in the wider region.

Profit not politics

One distinguishing characteristic of the civil war in Libya is the dominant role played by economic factors. Since the collapse of the formal economy in 2014, military actors have sought to profit from the 'prizes' of state assets – specifically the treasury and banking sector and control over seaports and airports. Since 2016, the United Nations-backed Government of National Accord (GNA) in Tripoli had been forced not only to legitimise the capital's main militias under the Ministry of Interior but also to turn a blind eye to these militias' exploitation of the state in order to ensure its own safety and the capital's security.

This relationship has had some political advantages for the GNA, as the pursuit by the Tripoli Revolutionaries Brigades (TRB) of monopolistic control over the state's financial sector necessitated the exclusion of other militias and their associated political factions. However, the TRB's attempt to assert control brought it into confrontation in early 2017 with the other main political power in the city. Since the GNA entered Tripoli in early 2016, it has competed with the Government of National Salvation (GNS), a rival government appointed by the rump General National Congress (GNC) after the GNC had been removed from power in the wake of the June 2014 elections. Khalifa al-Ghwell, president of the GNS, publicly denounced the GNA as illegitimate and sought to undermine them through sponsored media channels, while challenging them for effective control over ministries and state institutions. On 8 February 2017 a skirmish broke out between one of Tripoli's militias loyal to the GNA and a Misratan militia aligned to the GNS. Although the initial clash was related to an alleged disagreement over control of a bank, the conflict quickly escalated into a wider confrontation between the TRB and forces aligned with the GNS. By the end of March, the GNS had been removed from their offices in Tripoli, the television station representing them had been burned to the ground and their militias had been pushed back to the outskirts of the city. In May GNS-aligned militias launched the counter-offensive *Libyan Pride*, a name which in Arabic was a play on words similar to *Libyan Dawn*, the operation which had cemented their position in the capital in 2014. However, this offensive was far less successful and led to the complete removal of the GNS from Tripoli and the surrender of important real estate, such as the infamous Hadba prison where many key personnel from the Gadhafi era were being held. On 29 May Ghwell publicly announced that all of his fighters should withdraw from the capital.

Although the TRB fought the battle under the narrative of a war against Islamists and the GNS, the importance of state assets (and the lucrative rents which could be extracted from them) should not be overlooked when assessing the group's motivation. The confrontation in February tellingly started over control of a bank, and resulted in the TRB (under Haitham al-Tajouri) monopolising the security of the sector. The coercion levied upon the banking sector by this militia to issue letters of credit for the purchase of foreign goods at the central bank's exchange rate – which is considerably lower than the black-market exchange rates that goods and currency are traded at in the public marketplace – resulted in significant income for the TRB, with the racket involving letters of credit being most recently valued at US$5 billion per annum. The TRB's pursuit of control over key state assets also drove the conflict's continuation and expansion to the wider region long after the GNS had left Tripoli and surrendered its political power. After the withdrawal of Misratan militias from the capital, the TRB demanded that the Kani Brigade, a small, GNS-aligned militia from the nearby town of Tarhouna, surrender complete control of Tripoli airport to the group. Continuing its consolidation of the capital, the TRB overthrew a rival militia based at the Tripoli seaport in October.

However, over the last two months of the year there were signs that the consolidation of the capital by the TRB might come under threat in the near future. In November, powerful militias from Zintan engaged in a large conflict in the Nafusa Mountains of western Libya. Claiming they were combatting criminality, the militias defeated their long-standing enemies in the Amazigh city of Zuwara and the Warshefana district of Tripoli. A warning given in November by the head of the Warshefana Social Council al-Mabrouk Abu Amid that this operation was a precursor to a Zintani attack on Tripoli may well ring true in 2018. Militias from other Libyan cities may also be enviously eyeing the profitable position that the TRB has established over 2017 and could begin seeking their own share of the many revenue streams, both illicit and official, that the capital presents. An assault on the capital's only functioning airport, Mitiga, in December by the 33rd Infantry Brigade of Bashir al-Bugra from Tajoura, a militia based east of Tripoli, further suggested that clashes will continue in the capital until a national security framework can be agreed upon. Talks in Cairo in February were a positive first step towards this end, but it will take a more impartial body than the Egyptian government to conduct an inclusive security-unification programme effectively.

The growing power of grievance

General Khalifa Haftar and his Libyan National Army (LNA) also made attempts at consolidation in eastern Libya in 2017. With the help of Egypt and the United Arab Emirates, Haftar was able to announce his full control of Benghazi on 5 July after three years of fighting. However, skirmishes would continue until the end of the year and some outlying districts of the city (such as Sidi Akribesh) would not come under his control until early November.

Despite being labelled as a national Libyan army, Haftar's forces were a partisan group of tribal militias, ex-regime military personnel and neighbourhood youth who were recruited throughout the city as the front-lines reached their area. However, although the ambitions of each faction within Haftar's forces differed, they uniformly sought the removal of various elements of Benghazi's society. The ex-regime's military class saw the LNA as an opportunity to defeat eastern Libya's Islamist and jihadist factions, which had been in conflict with the ex-regime's forces since 2011. Eastern Libya's tribes sought to displace the urbanised merchant and technocratic class of Benghazi, many of whom had historic roots in Misrata, and to govern the city in its place. Mass punishment was often levied on entire extended families who were accused of having a member fighting against Haftar's forces, or on inhabitants of areas such as Ganfouda which saw particularly heavy fighting.

The number of people displaced from Benghazi since the start of Haftar's 2014 *Operation Dignity* has reached more than 90,000; many of the displaced sought revenge, or otherwise believed that a forceful re-entry was the only way to guarantee their homecoming. This resulted in the formation of the Benghazi Defence Brigades (BDB), which was comprised mainly of displaced Benghazi families who had sought refuge in Tripoli and Misrata, where they received training and support from groups who shared their animosity to Haftar. Despite the BDB's non-ideological ambition, its allies were drawn from across the Islamist spectrum, including groups aligned with the Grand Mufti Sadiq al-Ghariani and ex-members of the Libyan Islamic Fighting Group, as well as those with links to al-Qaeda in the Islamic Maghreb.

The BDB was repeatedly rebuffed by the LNA and Emirati air forces as it tried to move across the open Libyan hinterland in December and February. In early March, however, the BDB launched a surprise attack and overran key parts of the oil infrastructure concentrated in the area between Sirte and Ajdabiya known as the 'oil crescent'. The BDB was able to catch the LNA off guard by incorporating heavy armour and radar-jamming equipment into their expeditionary force, as well as by making a secret alliance with the tribal militias which provided Haftar's on-the-ground security but had subsequently grown disillusioned with his autocratic rule. Despite concerns that the BDB's operation would affect oil output, the BDB's commander Mustafa al-Sharksi stated that he would not remain in the oil crescent as his goal was solely to displace Haftar and return displaced families. He did unsuccessfully try to leverage his position to gain international support for his cause, but the past alliances made by the BDB with extremist groups made the movement toxic to the international community. By 14 March, the BDB had been forced to retreat to Misrata and Jufra due to heavy airstrikes followed by a ground assault led by Sudanese mercenaries employed by the LNA.

However, the BDB discovered another possible route to Benghazi by becoming embroiled in a conflict between the Misrata Third Force (an armed group from Misrata affiliated to the GNA) and the LNA's 12th Brigade in southern Libya. The Third Force had previously surrendered the Brak al-Shati air base to the LNA in an effort to placate LNA ambitions in the south, but the LNA then used the air base to launch offensives on Third Force checkpoints. This culminated in an assault on 5 April by the LNA on Tamanhint air base near Sebha as the LNA attempted to reinstate its air superiority following the embarrassing loss of the oil crescent to the BDB in March. The LNA assault failed and a ceasefire was declared, but on 19 May the ceasefire was broken as a joint operation by the Third Force, their Chadian mercenaries and the BDB, which collectively launched a surprise attack on Brak al-Shati air base (an attack allegedly sponsored by the GNA Minister of Defence Mahdi al-Barghathi). Brak al-Shati was at the time largely staffed by new recruits and quickly overrun, but a massacre then took place involving the execution of more than 120 LNA troops and non-combat personnel. The massacre caused a national outrage, leading to Barghathi being suspended pending an investigation and a complete withdrawal by the Third Force from its southern bases in Tamanhint, Sebha and

Jufra. Moreover, the BDB was largely expelled from Misrata city as a result of its role in the attack, with Misrata seeking to strengthen a recently adopted reconciliatory posture towards the city's enemies to the east and west. The LNA assumed complete control of the south, although acting as the sole power in the region may prove to be a difficult role for the group, given that it lacks the manpower to police the many inter-tribal conflicts over smuggling routes, as well as the presence of Chadian militias who have built a presence in the region since 2014.

Although the displaced people of Benghazi were the most strategically active group in 2017, they are not the only group that has been disenfranchised by the constant conflict in Libya since 2011. Those tribes and communities which supported Gadhafi during the 2011 revolution were similarly disenfranchised, subject to mass punishment and removed from any roles in the public sector. Much like the BDB, these groups began to see a violent return as their only route to addressing their grievances. In early October, a group named the Popular Front for the Liberation of Libya (PFLL) established a presence in the south of Tripoli. Once discovered, the PFLL were attacked by the TRB and pushed out of Tripoli into the Nafusa region, and the TRB continued its offensive until the PFLL had been completely defeated. On 15 October, the local PFLL commander Mabrouk Hneish and Imam Daoud – a leader of a Sudanese faction operating in Libya who was working alongside the PFLL – were arrested. This led to Hneish's tribe, the Megraha, shutting off the water supply to the capital in an attempt to pressure the TRB into releasing him. Although it was unsuccessful, the campaign of the PFLL is a further indicator that the many losers of Libya's revolutionary and post-revolutionary conflicts will need to be reconciled and their grievances addressed if Libya is to enjoy any kind of durable stability.

Terrorist threat

The remnants of ISIS and al-Qaeda in the Islamic Maghreb found it easier to establish transactional relationships with disenfranchised groups for safe haven or safe passage in 2017. Having been ousted from Sirte in December 2016, ISIS commanders sent emissaries to southern Libyan communities in Ubari, Temessa and Zweila to offer protection to their smuggling operations, an arrangement that would provide the group with a new source of long-term financing. ISIS was also reported to have made alliances with some members of the Debbabsha tribe based around Sabratha, using the tribe's involvement in human trafficking to move some of its operatives out of Libya. The group, however, remained active in the country, and the end of the year saw a rise in terrorist attacks. On 4 October Misrata's courthouse was attacked by three suicide bombers; two detonated their devices, killing four bystanders. In December a main pipeline feeding the Es-Sider oil terminal in eastern Libya was also destroyed – ISIS did not claim the attack, but the group was accused by the LNA of being the perpetrator.

As Libya enters the seventh year of its post-revolutionary descent to instability, it is clear that the original drivers of the conflict are strengthening on a yearly basis. The broken social contract Libya inherited from former leader Muammar Gadhafi (whereby only the state provides for the people), together with a collapsed legal and justice system that would prevent the predatory behaviour of militias on state assets, has created a destructive socio-economic system. Firstly, militias secure key state assets, be they banks, ports or distribution centres for subsidised goods; secondly, working with local politicians, the militias distribute these national assets on an exclusivist basis to their supporters, creating a violent zero-sum competition for state assets that drives conflict. Although in 2017 this resulted in consolidation in some areas (such as Tripoli and Benghazi) as militia collectives worked together to secure a common goal, the period between 2011 and 2014 highlights that these collectives are liable to fracture and fight among themselves once the initial goal has been secured. This pattern of collectivisation followed by atomisation can be seen in 2017 in the case of the BDB, which quickly rose and collapsed as it failed to reach its goal. Further conflict may be the only way of ensuring the stability and unity of these collectives, as Haftar may discover now that Benghazi has been won.

Moreover, the growing number of internally displaced people and disenfranchised communities who find themselves outside of Libya's new economic system has led to unresolved grievances becoming a growing driver towards further conflict. Without a political system through which to distribute state resources, nor a justice system to reconcile differences, violence is becoming the only way for people to assert their perceived rights or need for justice. This volatile mixture of vengeance and destitution is becoming increasingly potent as the number of conflicts across Libya continues to rise and the standard of living continues to fall. The year witnessed a massive price inflation in basic goods and a dearth of common services such as electricity and water supply, making day-to-day life increasingly untenable for the vast majority of Libyans who were not engaged in the civil war.

The only current momentum towards reversing this destructive cycle took the shape of the action plan announced by the new UN envoy Ghassan Salamé in September. The action plan was an attempt to re-instigate a mixture of top-down and bottom-up political dynamics to create a new political system for the country as well as an environment conducive to stability and cooperation. Salamé sought to repair the fractured transitional political system by coercing Libya's current political elite into agreeing a new unity government, which (if formed) will allow the international community to assist in some immediate governance and economic stability measures. Simultaneously, Salamé restarted talks between different factions, returning some fluidity to Libyan politics, which had been frozen since 2014, and also attempted to bring some public engagement to the constitutional process, which may drive it forward. Whether Salamé has the time and unified international support to complete this mission before another large-scale conflict erupts will be the defining issue of 2018.

Syria

The Syrian civil war continued unabated in 2017 and over the course of the year became ever more entwined with the different agendas of external powers – primarily those of Russia, Turkey and Iran. The military operations of the regime of

Key statistics	2016	2017
Type:	Internationalised	Internationalised
Fatalities:	50,000	40,000
New IDPs:	820,000	2,910,000
New refugees:	250,000	660,000

President Bashar al-Assad and the Turkish-backed opposition, along with the wider political process, were subordinated to these external interests and dependent upon these states for any resolution. The programme of talks organised by Russia, Turkey and Iran in Kazakhstan's capital Astana rendered United Nations-mediated talks between the regime and opposition in Geneva largely irrelevant. However, the ceasefire and de-escalation agreements made in Astana served only to stabilise fighting in certain areas, allowing the three states and their Syrian partners to focus on the pursuit of their strategic objectives in the country.

For the first time since its emergence, the Islamic State, also known as ISIS or ISIL, found itself the main target of both the regime's military efforts and those of the Kurdish-dominated Syrian Democratic Forces (SDF), backed by the United States. The SDF seized the territory that had been under ISIS control since 2014, establishing large areas of influence either side of the Euphrates River. By the end of the year, ISIS had lost almost all of its ground but threatened to linger as an insurgent threat for months and years to come. Moreover, as ISIS weakened, the al-Qaeda offshoot Hayat Tahrir al-Sham (HTS) – the latest iteration of Jabhat al-Nusra and Jabhat Fateh al-Sham – became the dominant force among the Islamist opposition.

Ceasefires and de-escalation

On 29 December 2016, the governments of Russia and Turkey brokered a new ceasefire between the regime, the Turkish-backed Free Syrian Army (FSA) in the north, and several of the Islamist factions based in Idlib, northwestern Hama and western Aleppo governorates. Although fighting quietened on several fronts, the regime continued with its offensive to the northwest of Damascus to capture Wadi Barada, purportedly with the intention of securing the capital's water supply. Despite the fact that the rebels offered to allow regime engineers to fix the water supply and observe the ceasefire, the regime continued its assault, using as a pretext the alleged presence in Wadi Barada of al-Qaeda offshoot Jabhat Fateh al-Sham which, as a terrorist group, was a non-signatory to the ceasefire. The regime's offensive in the area was successful, resulting in the outright capture of Wadi Barada on 29 January.

The ceasefire had been intended as a trust-building measure and precondition for opposition participation in talks with the regime in Astana. Convened for the first time in December 2016 by Russia and Turkey, and with the support of Iran, the Astana talks were pursued independently of the UN-led talks in Geneva. The two tracks continued in parallel throughout the year, with the Geneva process assuming responsibility for negotiations on an unlikely political settlement between the regime and opposition, and the Astana process assuming responsibility for negotiation on ceasefires and military de-escalation.

Talks in Astana in January and February focused on the establishment by Russia, Turkey and Iran of a joint monitoring mechanism for the ongoing, if only partially observed, ceasefire. When Russia reconvened the talks in March, and then in May, the opposition delegation refused to participate in protest at the regime's widespread infringement of both the nationwide ceasefire and the temporary ceasefire for Eastern Ghouta, a suburb of Damascus, which collapsed soon after it started on 6 March. Russia, Turkey and Iran continued with the talks irrespective of the opposition boycott and agreed in principle to the establishment of a number of so-called 'de-escalation zones' – areas under opposition control in which all the regime and opposition forces would agree to cease hostilities and permit entry of emergency relief for civilians.

Further talks in July on the details of these de-escalation zones were inconclusive, but the regional powers reached an agreement in September at the fifth round of talks in Astana on four de-escalation zones: one encompassing opposition-held territory in Idlib, western Aleppo and northeastern Latakia governorates; a second in the opposition-held area in the north of Homs governorate; a third in opposition-held Eastern Ghouta; and a fourth incorporating opposition-held territory in Daraa and Quneitra governorates. Russia, Turkey and Iran each committed to deploying military observers to the de-escalation zones, but given the frequent infringements of past ceasefires by Iranian-backed militias, Iran's role as an observer undermined opposition parties' confidence in the plan. The deployment of Turkish observers likewise riled the regime.

ISIS, HTS and other groups proscribed by the UN Security Council were excluded from the cessation of hostilities in each of the de-escalation zones, paving the way for the regime to continue its well-established pattern of attacking opposition-held areas on the pretext of targeting terrorist groups, in defiance of any ceasefire. Accordingly, heavy fighting continued in Eastern Ghouta with Russian airstrikes as well as strikes by the regime. Shelling and skirmishes persisted in Idlib and northwestern Hama governorates.

Having successfully advanced the idea of de-escalation zones, in October Moscow announced its intention of organising a Syrian national dialogue in Sochi, with a view to expanding its role in steering the peace process. Initially scheduled for November, the Sochi conference was postponed until January 2018. Opposition groups raised objections and reiterated that the UN-led Geneva talks would be the only legitimate forum for the political process, despite its failure to date. Staffan de Mistura, the UN special envoy to Syria, likewise expressed misgivings about a parallel process in Sochi.

The Geneva talks, however, did not result in a breakthrough. De Mistura organised five rounds of talks between the regime and opposition in Geneva throughout 2017, which – in line with all parties' low expectations – yielded no real progress. In the first round of talks, which took place between 23 February and 3 March (the fourth set of talks in Geneva since the beginning of the conflict), the parties agreed an agenda for future talks and on a set of principles. On this agenda were a new constitution, elections, governance and terrorism. However, in subsequent meetings – on 23 to 31 March, 16 to 19 May, 10 to 15 July and 29 November to 15 December – the regime delegation repeatedly refused to discuss any of the topics concerning political transition and rejected any direct talks with the opposition delegation. There was little hope of the regime delegation participating in the Geneva talks with any seriousness; Assad demonstrated complete disdain for the process, dismissing the talks as 'null' and 'merely a meeting for the media'.

In his only real achievement of the year, de Mistura succeeded in pushing for the main opposition representations – the Saudi Arabia-backed High Negotiations Committee (HNC) and the Russia-linked Cairo Platform and Moscow Platform – to form a united delegation ahead of the final round of talks. This prompted HNC leader Riyad Hijab and several other HNC members to resign in anticipation of a consequent weakening of the opposition delegation's stance on Assad's future. While nothing came of the November–December talks with this united delegation, the development paved the way for similar representation in future negotiations. The purpose of any such talks between the regime and opposition would only be to settle the details of the political process; control over ending the conflict itself had shifted conclusively away from the Syrian political and military factions to regional powers of Russia, Iran and Turkey, and to a lesser extent, the US and Gulf states.

Internationalised war

Both Russia and Turkey hoped to use the Astana process to further their respective goals in Syria – for Russia, a strategic victory over its rivals, a permanent military platform in the country and influence in Damascus and the region more widely; for Turkey, the containment of the perceived Kurdish threat, stability in Syria as a neighbouring country and a government in Damascus with which it can establish a pragmatic relationship. The two countries looked to prevent confrontation between their respective Syrian partners and sought to accommodate each other's objectives insofar as they posed no obstacle to their own.

In late 2016, Turkey had deployed a force comprising 3,000 Turkish soldiers and 5,000 Turkish-trained Syrian moderate rebels of the FSA to the northwest of Syria. The immediate aim was to oust ISIS from along the Turkish border. However, the intervention also served the wider Turkish objective of containing Kurdish forces, which had crossed the Euphrates River to combat ISIS and were coming close to capturing territory along the Turkey–Syria border. Turkey sought at the very least to force the advancing Kurdish-led SDF back east of the Euphrates, and ultimately looked to push the Kurds away from the full stretch of the border and cut them off from Kurdish-held territory in Iraq.

In February, Turkey and the FSA captured al-Bab from ISIS, giving them control of a 6,600-square-kilometre pocket of territory in the north of Aleppo governorate which successfully prevented Kurdish forces from linking their two areas of control. However, ISIS's retreat from al-Bab allowed regime forces to link up with the SDF, preventing Turkey from advancing any further without clashing with either the Russian-backed regime or the US-backed SDF. Ankara called the United States' bluff and announced an offensive to capture Manbij, held by the SDF. However, the SDF, the regime, Russia and the US cooperated on a number of deterrent measures and, following meetings between Russian, Turkish and US chiefs of staff in March, Ankara called off its attack. The Turkish offensive subsequently stalled. With no prospect for further advances without entering into conflict with either the Russian-backed regime or the US-backed SDF, Turkey and the FSA instead dug in. They worked to rebuild the region, trained civilian police forces, set up military facilities and prepared the ground for the opposition Syrian Interim Government to administer the territory. At the same time, they began to return Syrian refugees in Turkey to the region.

With several thousand Turkish troops on the ground in this pocket of territory, the regime, Russia and Iran likewise avoided confrontation in the north of Aleppo governorate for fear of escalation. For the time being, Turkey's operations in the northwest posed no threat to Russian objectives in Syria, even if they stood in the way of the regime's long-term aim of regaining control of the whole country and Iran's ambition of unrivalled influence. For Russia, the main objectives were to bolster Russian influence in Syria and the region; to maintain Russia's presence on the Mediterranean, with a naval fleet in Tartous and an air-force presence in Hmeimim in Latakia governorate; and to provide Russia with a strategic victory in Syria over the US and its allies to strengthen the country's standing on the international stage and in the eyes of its own population. In those terms, Turkey's confrontation with the US-backed SDF in fact worked in Russia's favour.

Russia continued its aerial campaign alongside the Syrian Arab Air Force in support of the regime's operations on the ground. Although publicly denied by Moscow, Russian paramilitaries or private military contractors (PMCs) also played a leading role both against ISIS (including the recapture of Palmyra from January to March and the regime's further successes in central Syria in subsequent months), and against Islamist rebels in Hama and Idlib governorates. Although Moscow announced in November that it would reduce Russia's military presence in Syria, it appeared to plug the gap with additional PMCs in order to maintain the regime's front-lines.

While Russia's intervention had been decisive in turning the tide of the war in the regime's favour, and Russia's support at the UN Security Council had protected the Assad regime from Western intervention, it was Iran's long-term support for Assad that had kept his regime afloat – militarily and financially – throughout the war. By contrast, Russia was less attached to Assad personally. Moreover, although both Iran and Russia sought to weaken US power in the region, the two countries were themselves competing for influence, and were building up rival power bases in Syria. Russia took a stronger role in training and working alongside the Syrian Arab Army (SAA), and supplemented the SAA's approximately 20,000 forces with Russian military advisers, mercenaries and counter-terrorism trainers. Iran meanwhile funded, trained and advised the Syrian paramilitary National Defence Forces (NDF), the Lebanese Shia militia Hizbullah and other Shia militias from Iraq and Afghanistan, totalling around 150,000 personnel.

These Iran-backed militias posed a multidimensional danger. Hizbullah and other Shia paramilitaries showed an alarming willingness to use indiscriminate violence to terrorise the civilian population of opposition-held areas: atrocities in Syria were regularly traceable to the NDF and paramilitary forces who acted with clear sectarian motivations. Moreover, the regime and the SAA had limited ability to rein in these militias, which looted, murdered residents and assumed warlord-like roles in the towns and cities that they had helped recapture from the opposition, extorting money at checkpoints and imposing other so-called taxes. Local civilian authorities and senior SAA officers were ignored, and tensions mounted between the population and militias.

The areas under the control of these militias in Syria linked together the territory in Iraq under the control of the Shia militias of the Popular Mobilisation Units and territory in south Lebanon under the control of Hizbullah, thereby bringing Iran closer to establishing a so-called bridge to the Mediterranean. At the national level, governments friendly to Iran looked safe in Baghdad and Damascus. But more importantly, Iran enjoyed immense influence on the ground throughout this continuous stretch of territory, causing alarm in Israel and the Gulf states.

In late 2017, Israel became increasingly active in Syria to address the threat posed by Hizbullah and other Iran-backed militias. Increasingly well equipped by Iran and with the experience of fighting for several years in Syria, the threat these militias posed to Israel – their sworn enemy – was growing. From September onwards, Israel undertook frequent operations against pro-regime targets in Syria, with strikes against weapons caches and military facilities – including one believed by the US to be used for manufacturing chemical weapons – and shooting down Iranian unmanned aerial vehicles (UAVs) operated by Iran's partners in the country. As with Turkey's activities in the country, Israel's ability to target Hizbullah and other pro-regime targets in Syria relied on a policy of mutual accommodation with Russia, although Russia nonetheless continued to supply the regime with anti-aircraft missiles that could easily be used against Israeli aircraft and pass into the hands of Hizbullah. Russian SA-5 missiles were fired in October, targeting a jet on a reconnaissance mission over Lebanon, and in November, targeting a jet involved in strikes on regime facilities in Homs governorate, although both attacks were unsuccessful. However, Syrian air defences reportedly had more success shooting down Israeli missiles in November and December.

The overt international support for the various conflict parties, in the areas delineated by the Astana de-escalation agreement, brought Syria to de facto partition.

However, questions remained over the fate of the Islamist-held Idlib governorate, Kurdish-held Afrin region and the opposition-controlled Daraa governorate, where there was no international force present on the ground to act as a deterrent to attack.

Islamists isolated

As the FSA, the SDF and pro-regime forces benefited from increased international assistance, support for Islamist groups dropped off. Islamist rebels became increasingly isolated through 2017 – both politically and territorially.

Following the regime's victory in Aleppo city at the end of 2016, the rebel groups involved in the two alliances or 'operations rooms' coordinating the fight against the regime in the region – Jaysh al-Fateh and Fateh Halab – redeployed to Idlib governorate. As the largest of the rebel groups and a Salafist jihadist organisation, Ahrar al-Sham posed a threat to the mission and *raison d'être* of al-Qaeda offshoot Jabhat Fateh al-Sham. Despite the long-standing close cooperation between the two groups, and the efforts made by Ahrar al-Sham to foster acceptance of Jabhat Fateh al-Sham among the wider Syrian opposition, tensions mounted. Compounding this rivalry, Jabhat Fateh al-Sham faced the additional concern that Turkey was encouraging and sponsoring other rebels to stage a 'counter-terrorism' offensive against it. In January 2017, Jabhat Fateh al-Sham moved to confront these perceived threats and assert itself as the dominant Islamist rebel faction.

Initially, Jabhat Fateh al-Sham attacked the smaller rebel groups in Idlib governorate suspected of cooperation with Turkey. The groups were faced with the choice of allying or merging with Jabhat Fateh al-Sham or battling against a group which significantly outnumbered them. Numerous rebel factions responded by seeking the protection of Ahrar al-Sham, bringing the two dominant Salafist jihadist rebel groups into direct confrontation. Others (Jaysh al-Sunna, Liwa al-Haqq, the Ansar al-Din Front and Nour al-Din al-Zinki) joined Jabhat Fateh al-Sham, and around 1,000 of Ahrar al-Sham's own members defected to the group, including the section responsible for manufacturing weapons. The newly strengthened al-Qaeda offshoot relaunched itself under the Hayat Tahrir al-Sham (HTS) name on 28 January with Ahrar al-Sham defector Hashem al-Sheikh (also known as 'Abu Jaber') as its emir and Abu Mohammed al-Golani, formerly the leader of Jabhat Fateh al-Sham and Jabhat al-Nusra before that, as its military commander.

After a lull in fighting between rebel groups in the region from March to May, HTS resumed its attacks. In June, HTS attacked the FSA-affiliated Free Army of Idlib and the Free Syrian Police. In July, HTS targeted Ahrar al-Sham, forcing it out of Idlib city completely and ousting it from the Bab al-Hawa crossing on the Syria–Turkey border. The offensive left Ahrar al-Sham significantly weakened and facing an internal split between a faction favouring close relations with HTS and a faction favouring strong relations with Turkey and FSA groups, which it sought to resolve with the appointment of Hassan Soufan as its new leader.

HTS's narrative and strategy attracted significant support. Framing the conflict as one between Sunnis and Shi'ites, refusing to negotiate with the regime and omitting much of its religious language about jihad, the group's rhetoric gained traction among some Syrians. Its unrestrained approach in fighting the regime also enjoyed greater military credibility in the eyes of many rebels than more moderate groups' strategies. However, its attacks on the wider opposition in Idlib reversed the concerted efforts of its predecessor groups, Jabhat Fateh al-Sham and Jabhat al-Nusra, to enhance their standing with other rebel factions and improve perceptions among the local population. Likewise, while its predecessors had largely refrained from interfering in local administration, HTS intervened extensively in local governance and undermined the independence of the local councils. This pervasive influence of HTS caused Western donors gradually to withdraw their support for the local administrations – including financial and material assistance and capacity building – to the cost of northwest Syria's civilian population.

The tumult in Idlib governorate risked externally trained fighters or their equipment being absorbed into HTS and caused international support for rebels in the area to fall away. The US Central Intelligence Agency promptly suspended its military aid to rebel groups in the area. Turkey – their largest remaining supporter – called on Ahrar al-Sham and its allies to extract heavy weaponry from Idlib governorate and redeploy in the north of Aleppo governorate alongside the Turkish-trained FSA. International actors increasingly abandoned Idlib to HTS.

The emergence of HTS affected the south of Syria as well, although the organisation adopted a less aggressive stance towards other rebel groups, recognising that the balance of power on the ground worked against it. HTS had a significant presence in Quneitra and Daraa governorates and fought alongside the FSA's Southern

Front. In Eastern Ghouta, HTS cooperated with Jaysh al-Islam and Faylaq al-Rahman to defend opposition-held territory from unrelenting offensives by the regime but also periodically clashed with both groups, typically resulting in significant casualties and causing outrage among the resident population. In late April, fighting between HTS and Faylaq al-Rahman on one side and Jaysh al-Islam on the other was so intense that it prompted protests involving up to 5,000 people.

The presence of HTS throughout opposition-held territory (excluding the Turkish-controlled northwest of Aleppo governorate and the SDF-controlled areas in north and northwest Syria) undermined the designation of any of these areas as a de-escalation zone: not only did the Astana agreement allow campaigns against al-Qaeda affiliates in de-escalation zones to continue, including against HTS, but HTS itself rejected the de-escalation zone and perpetuated the fighting. The result was the continuation of regime and Russian airstrikes on the Syrian population.

Regime consolidation

With complete victory throughout the country an unlikely prospect, the Assad regime sought through 2017 to ensure its political and military dominance on the ground and to carve out for itself a politically, militarily and economically viable territory. To this end, the regime worked to consolidate the territory under its control by eradicating the remaining pockets of resistance, and to secure key towns and cities, highways and border crossings. It had to achieve these aims as far as possible without direct confrontation with foreign forces deployed in the country.

In Damascus and the surrounding countryside of Rif Dimashq governorate, the regime looked to oust rebel forces from their remaining pockets of territory. In January, the regime enjoyed quick success in capturing Wadi Barada, to the northwest of the capital, and in April it ousted rebels from nearby Al-Zabadani. The main priority for the regime, however, was Eastern Ghouta – the towns, villages and farms to the east of Damascus which had been an opposition stronghold since the beginning of the civil war. To recapture Eastern Ghouta would constitute a major victory for the regime, giving it complete control of the capital and the surrounding countryside, comparable with its recapture of the cities of Homs and Aleppo. Again using the presence of HTS as a pretext for its operations, the regime attacked Eastern Ghouta throughout the year, despite a ceasefire supposedly in force there in March and international agreement on designating the area as a de-escalation zone in September. Over the course of four months from February to May, the regime captured the neighbourhoods of Barzeh, Qaboun and Tishreen, evacuating the remaining rebels and their families to Idlib governorate. However, the regime's subsequent offensive, from June until August, aimed at seizing the neighbouring district of Jobar, stalled as Faylaq al-Rahman mounted a successful defence. Fighting surged again in Jobar in October through to December, as well as in Ayn Tarma and Douma, with daily airstrikes and clashes on the ground.

In July and August, the regime launched a separate offensive to seize the opposition-held pocket of Qalamoun – to the north of the capital in the area of Rif Dimashq bordering Lebanon. SAA and Hizbullah forces attacked HTS and ISIS forces in the area from the north and west while Lebanese Armed Forces and Hizbullah attacked the groups across the border in Lebanon. The offensive brought quick success. The remaining HTS fighters were evacuated to Idlib and the remaining ISIS fighters sent to Al-Bukamal.

In the south, the regime's medium-term objective was to gain control of the two main border crossings to Jordan in Daraa governorate, as well as the highways running through Daraa city that led to the crossings. However, early in the year, fighters from the FSA's Southern Front and HTS launched their own offensive to capture Manshiyah district in Daraa and the section of the highway running through it. This marked the most intense fighting in the south of Syria since 2015. Through the Military Operations Centre (MOC) in Amman, Jordan, the Gulf states and the US had coordinated the Southern Front and managed to keep the region relatively calm and free of fighting. The MOC's attempts to rein in the attack on Manshiyah, however, were unsuccessful, and the regime pounded the city with around 2,000 airstrikes in the first six months of the year, according to war monitor the Syrian Observatory for Human Rights (SOHR). The rebel offensive was successful nonetheless, and the regime made no progress towards capturing the border crossings to Jordan.

Further east along Syria's southern border, the regime and Iranian-backed militias sought to capture opposition-held territory in the desert – the highway linking Damascus with Baghdad, the border crossing at al-Tanf, and the military base at the same location which hosted hundreds of US and United Kingdom special forces training the Southern Front's Revolutionary Commando Army and supporting them in offensives against ISIS in Deir ez-Zor governorate. Despite an agreement between the US and Russia on a so-called 'deconfliction zone' within a 55 km radius of the al-Tanf military base, pro-regime forces directed by Iranian advisers made repeated incursions into the zone, only to be forced back each time. The incursions brought the US into direct confrontation with the regime. In May, the US launched airstrikes at a convoy of pro-regime forces which had advanced to within just 25 km of al-Tanf, and in June, the US shot down two Iranian-made armed UAVs in the area.

In the northwest of Syria, the regime made only small advances against rebels. In Hama governorate, the regime captured strategic territory along the highway from Hama towards Aleppo city, taking the towns of Soran and Tayyibat al-Imam in April in the wake of an unsuccessful HTS offensive to reverse the regime's 2016 gains in the area. However, the main focus of regime operations in the northwest was to capture territory held by ISIS in Hama and the north of Aleppo governorate. It was not until December that the regime made any further significant advances against the rebels in the area, progressing towards Abu al-Duhur as they captured villages to the west of Khanasir and Ithriya. Regime airstrikes continued consistently throughout the year nonetheless. Regime warplanes twice deployed sarin-like toxic gas as a weapon – on Lataminah in Hama governorate on 30 March, and on Khan Sheikhoun in Idlib governorate on 4 April; although there were no fatalities in the former attack, the second caused approximately 100 deaths.

Demise of the Islamic State

In late 2016, ISIS had lost a series of towns and villages in Syria but nevertheless retained a large swathe of territory, from al-Bab in the northwest of the country, to al-Bukamal on the Iraq border, to Palmyra in the desert of Homs governorate. It was, however, under attack on several fronts and in 2017 the group ceded most of its territory in Syria, as well as in neighbouring Iraq.

At the beginning of the year, the regime, the SDF, and the FSA and Turkish forces all raced to seize ISIS's remaining territory in the north of Aleppo governorate. The FSA and Turkish forces were first to reach al-Bab. Upon the loss of the town, ISIS fighters rapidly withdrew from the surrounding villages and moved towards the southeast and the town of Deir Hafir. The SDF and the regime capitalised by seizing much of the vacated area and in the process drawing a new front-line between themselves and the FSA. The FSA and Turkish forces were left with no remaining front-lines with ISIS – their only option for further advances was to seize territory from either the SDF or the regime.

In early 2017, the SDF continued its offensive to capture the countryside around Raqqa from ISIS, in advance of an attempt to seize the city outright. In January, fighting centred around towns and villages northwest of Raqqa. Taking Tabqa Dam proved to be a major challenge for the SDF and US forces supporting it in the face of threats by ISIS to destroy the dam, an act that would cause an ecological and humanitarian disaster downstream. ISIS hinted at its willingness to take such drastic action by opening the dam's turbines, causing the waters of the Euphrates to rise and flood significant areas of land to the east. ISIS was also reported to be sheltering several of its leading figures inside the dam. ISIS repelled a first SDF raid on al-Tabqa city and Tabqa Dam in late January, prompting the SDF to withdraw temporarily from the surrounding area.

The SDF offensive against ISIS was, however, bolstered by a declaration of support by local Arab tribes, who encouraged residents to join the SDF's fight against the terrorist group. In February and March, the SDF made rapid advances to the east and northeast of Raqqa, capturing large swathes of territory, including ground in Deir ez-Zor governorate. By mid-March, the SDF had seized sections of the highway between ISIS's two remaining stronghold cities of Raqqa and Deir ez-Zor, cutting the group's supply lines. A separate operation saw SDF forces and US special-operations forces ferried by helicopter across Lake Assad, firstly to capture the Shurfa peninsula and then to lead an advance on Tabqa Dam from the southwest. The fight to take the dam itself was long and slow, lasting from 22 March until 10 May, when the SDF was able to announce that it had seized both the dam and al-Tabqa city, also known as al-Thawrah.

At the same time, the SDF had been making further advances to the north of Raqqa. From May onwards, having cut off ISIS's forces in Raqqa by capturing the Aleppo–Raqqa road and Tabqa Dam to the west and the Raqqa–Deir ez-Zor road to the east, they were able to begin the final stage of the Raqqa campaign, advancing on the city from the north, east and west. By 24 June the city was under total siege and the SDF, along with US special-operations forces, began to advance into the city itself. ISIS fought hard to maintain its Syrian capital. The SDF's progress was slow and lasted more than four months but on 17 October, the SDF announced its outright victory in the city, although it came at a significant humanitarian and material cost. ISIS used civilians as human shields; the SOHR reported the death of 1,333 non-combatants between the start of the attack on Raqqa in June and its capture in October. Most of the population had fled the city, which had suffered extensive damage in the battle. Both the SOHR and UN officials reported that approximately 80% of the city was uninhabitable due to the damage or destruction of buildings.

Further east, the SDF fought ISIS on a second front. Having captured the Raqqa–Deir ez-Zor highway in March, it advanced east along the north bank of the Euphrates, entering the industrial district to the north of Deir ez-Zor in September. The SDF stated that it would not challenge regime forces for control of Deir ez-Zor city itself, and instead directed its forces against ISIS further north, along the border between Deir ez-Zor and Hasakah governorates. On 8 November they captured the town of Markadah, establishing complete control of Hasakah governorate, and four days later seized nearby al-Busayrah.

The US played a major role in supporting the SDF offensive. The US Department of Defense acknowledged the presence of 2,400 US forces on the ground, training and operating alongside the fighters of the SDF (400 were withdrawn in November). The US also led an extensive coalition campaign of airstrikes against ISIS. However, the SOHR reported that these coalition airstrikes were the largest single cause of civilian deaths over the course of 2017, causing 2,423 deaths. The high civilian fatality count was in part due to the nature of any operation to retake a major urban centre like Raqqa and in part due to ISIS's use of civilians as human shields. However, whereas strikes prior to 2017 had reliably targeted ISIS with minimal impact on civilians, activists on the ground from the respected non-governmental organisation Raqqa is Being Slaughtered Silently reported a marked change in 2017 in the pattern of the coalition's airstrikes, with more and more causing non-combatant fatalities.

The regime continued its parallel offensive against ISIS on three fronts: firstly, along the highway running along the southern side of the Euphrates River; secondly, in Homs, around Palmyra and the surrounding desert towns and oil facilities; and thirdly, in Deir ez-Zor. In March, following the fall of al-Bab, regime forces made swift progress along the south side of the Euphrates, capturing the Khafsa water-treatment plant and the town of Deir Hafir. A difficult and lengthy operation lasting two months saw regime forces capture Jarrah air base in May, and over the following month they made further advances into the Maskanah plains, capturing the town of Maskanah itself in early June. From there they pushed further east – meeting the SDF at Wadi Shatnat al-Mityahah – and south, forcing ISIS towards the Ithriyah–Resafa road, which regime forces captured on 30 June.

In its remaining stretch of territory in the south of Raqqa governorate, ISIS came under attack by the regime from the south as well as the north as, from March onwards, the regime forces had made significant gains in Homs governorate and were pressing northwards. On 4 March, regime forces finally recaptured Palmyra (having captured it from ISIS previously in March 2016 and lost it again in December of the same year). From there, the regime rapidly gained ground, seizing the Arak oilfield in June and numerous other oilfields south of Raqqa in July – including the oilfields of Wahab, al-Fahd, Dbaysan, al-Qseer, Abu al-Qatat and Abu Qatash. In August, they captured the town of Sukhna and vast swathes of desert north of Palmyra. From there, the regime forced ISIS out of its remaining territory in the west of Homs governorate and east of Hama governorate – taking Uqayribat and other nearby towns – and advanced swiftly towards Deir ez-Zor along both the Raqqa–Deir ez-Zor highway skirting the Euphrates and the Palmyra–Deir ez-Zor highway further south.

Having lost Raqqa in October, as well as Mosul in Iraq in July, Deir ez-Zor was the last remaining major city under ISIS's control. In August it became clear that ISIS faced attacks on the city from the north by the SDF and from the south by the regime, prompting it to recruit forcibly all men between the ages of 20 and 30. However, ISIS was not only suffering from a shortage of fighters, but many high-ranking commanders had also been killed. On 5 September, regime forces broke the three-year siege imposed by ISIS on a government-controlled area of Deir ez-Zor city, and four days later they gained control of the city's military airport.

Regime forces then advanced further along the Euphrates. They seized the town of Mayadin from ISIS in October, and continued to al-Bukamal and the eponymous border crossing to Iraq. Al-Bukamal changed hands several times in November but was finally captured by the regime on 6 December.

The loss of almost all its territory across Syria and Iraq was a major blow to ISIS, forcing the group to abandon its preoccupation with territorial control and instead refocus on its core objective of dominating global jihad – establishing itself as the authority over all jihadists and jihadi groups. For ISIS, controlling territory had served as just one means of asserting its authority. Its other means – maintaining ideological authority and demonstrating an unrivalled ability to stage major attacks against 'unbelievers' – were also important to ISIS and were likely to become much more so in the wake of its territorial losses. ISIS's use of sleeper cells to retake the town of Qaryatayn, Homs governorate, behind the regime's lines in Homs governorate in October, albeit for just 20 days, was a demonstration of the organisation's ongoing ability to launch eye-catching attacks. The demise of ISIS as a territorial power in Syria raised the prospect of attacks against all and any enemies, and a growing competition with HTS and al-Qaeda for authority over jihad.

Assad's impunity

Forces of the Assad regime and pro-regime militias continued to employ tactics which caused immense human suffering. Regime airstrikes and artillery fire hit hospitals and medical facilities, markets and other civilian infrastructure, and in general were indiscriminate in their targeting. The regime continued to use sieges to induce opposition-held towns and districts to surrender. The main remaining area under siege was the heavily populated Damascus suburb of Eastern Ghouta, where almost 400,000 people were deprived of access to medical care and basic goods and services, and where humanitarian agencies were unable to gain access to deliver life-saving assistance.

The brutality of Assad and his regime continued to be the principal driver of the conflict and it was clear that Syria's opposition forces were determined to fight on against the regime for as long as Assad remained in power. However, having long refused to countenance Assad's continuation as president, in 2017 the US and its allies wavered in their stance. In March, US Ambassador to the United Nations Nikki Haley stated that the United States' priority was 'no longer to … focus on getting Assad out', and, in June, France's president, Emmanuel Macron, ominously stated that he saw no viable successor to Assad.

Despite equivocation on Assad's future, the US and its allies were however clear in their condemnation of the regime's war crimes. For the first time, the US enforced its so-called red line on the use of chemical weapons: in response to the attack on Khan Sheikhoun in April involving the use of sarin or a similar gas which killed approximately 100 people, the US launched a barrage of cruise missiles targeting the Shayrat air base, from which the planes which dropped the sarin had taken off. It was the first intentional direct strike on the Assad regime since the beginning of the conflict. The US reported in June that it had identified the regime making preparations for another such chemical attack and warned that it would 'pay a heavy price' for proceeding. No further chemical attacks were reported over the course of the year.

In 2017, as in 2016, the US and its allies also attempted to address the regime's use of chemical weapons and wider brutality at the UN Security Council; as in the previous year, Russia repeatedly used its veto to block resolutions. In February, Russia and China vetoed a resolution submitted by the US, UK and France which sought to ban the sale or transfer of helicopters to the Syrian regime in light of findings by the joint Organisation for the Prohibition of Chemical Weapons–United Nations Joint Investigative Mechanism (OPCW–UN JIM) inquiry that regime forces had used helicopters to release barrel bombs containing chlorine gas. In April, following the Khan Sheikhoun attack, Russia again vetoed a resolution that condemned the attack and reiterated support for the OPCW investigation of it. In October, Russia used its veto to prevent the renewal of the OPCW–UN JIM; and it used it again to prevent a second attempt to renew the mandate in November – the tenth time, in all, that Russia had used its veto on Security Council resolutions concerning the conflict in Syria to protect the Assad regime.

War-crimes prosecutor Carla Del Ponte said that the UN Independent International Commission of Inquiry on Syria had amassed sufficient evidence to prosecute Assad for war crimes but announced that she would resign from the body due to a lack of support from the UN Security Council, where Russia's veto prevented any referral of Assad's crimes to the International Criminal Court.

The continuing war exacted an immense humanitarian toll on Syria, particularly for the residents of besieged opposition-held territory. According to Siegewatch, approximately 736,000 people were trapped in areas besieged by the regime (estimated at 410,000 by the UN, which excludes certain areas counted by Siegewatch), with government forces blocking access to humanitarian aid and bombarding them with airstrikes and artillery fire. An additional 8,000 residents were besieged by the opposition in the regime-held towns of Kefraya and Foua, both in Idlib governorate. Operations to recapture territory from ISIS also caused enormous displacement, including around 320,000 from Raqqa governorate over the course of 2017. Any alleviation of this suffering remained a distant prospect.

The ongoing war had an increasingly destabilising effect on regional security. Despite their pronouncements on preventing Assad's continuation as Syria's leader, Western and Gulf states failed to prevent the regime's recovery and stood by as Hizbullah – a proscribed terrorist group – strengthened and as Iran's influence grew. However, with Turkey increasingly assertive, the opposition vowing to fight on, and relations between Russia and Iran strained, victory for Assad and his allies was not yet assured.

Turkey (PKK)

The conflict between the Turkish government and the Kurdistan Worker's Party (PKK) showed no signs of abating in 2017. The beginning of the year saw a period of lower-intensity clashes in the south-eastern provinces, but violence

Key statistics	2016	2017
Type:	Internal	Internal
Fatalities:	3,000	2,000
New IDPs:	200,000	– [b]
New refugees:	– [b]	– [b]

escalated again towards the end of the year (although by December fatalities had decreased once again, partly due to the winter period).

The PKK's relationship with its Syrian affiliate, the Democratic Union Party (PYD), and the People's Protection Units (YPG), the military wing of the PYD, continued to divide foreign powers, many of whom found themselves in a position of either risking antagonising Ankara if they continued their support for the PYD, or alienating and fragmenting the Kurds further. Much to the disappointment of Ankara, overall international support appeared to increase in favour of the self-determination of the Kurds, in part due to Ankara's brutal crackdown on the

Kurdish opposition following the failed coup attempt in 2016; the PYD's progress in developing a model of regional governance in the Kurdish-dominated northern Syrian region commonly known as Rojava; and, in Iraq, the Kurdistan Region's controversial independence referendum in September.

Largely due to these disagreements, the year witnessed a drastic deterioration of Turkey's relations with the European Union and the United States – not helped by the continued Greek-Turkish dispute over the status of Cyprus, or a crisis involving the arrest of two US consular officers in October that prompted the US to temporarily suspend its visa services across Turkey. President Recep Tayyip Erdogan responded in somewhat warmer terms once many European states attempted to adopt a more reconciliatory approach towards the end of the year. The EU's support for the United Nations resolution (co-sponsored by Turkey) in December which condemned the Trump administration's recognition of Jerusalem as the capital of Israel, as well as Germany's adoption of increasingly stringent measures against the PKK, may have also helped soothe relations – but only temporarily, as relations with the EU continued to be volatile.

Meanwhile, the atmosphere between Washington and Ankara remained cool, although on 23 August US Secretary of Defense James Mattis reassured Turkey over the United States' support to the YPG by pledging assistance to Turkey against the PKK in Qandil, the Iraq–Iran border and Sinjar in Iraq. There were also talks of upgrading the joint 'intelligence fusion centre' in Ankara and supporting Turkey to locate 'high-value targets' more effectively.

Anti-PKK crackdown in the southeast

Operations by the Turkish security forces against the PKK, including its affiliated youth organisations the Kurdistan Freedom Falcons (TAK) and the Patriotic Revolutionary Youth Movement (PRYM), continued throughout 2017. Clashes between January and July were of lower intensity than in late 2016 but deadly nevertheless, with casualties on both sides. The PKK claimed a number of sporadic attacks involving improvised explosive devices (IEDs), shoot-outs and 'assassination actions', including an attack on a referendum campaign bus of the president's own Justice and Development Party (AKP) on 15 April which took place in the Muradave district of Van province and resulted in the death of one village guard.

The TAK claimed two attacks in 2017: an attack on the Turkish police in front of a courthouse in Izmir on 5 January, and an explosion at the Tüpras Izmir oil refinery on 11 October that killed four contract workers and injured one, and which was reported in official sources as an accident. In May the TAK threatened renewed attacks on main cities and tourist sites, although no such attacks took place during the rest of 2017.

In November and December respectively, the Turkish security forces killed Hülya Eroglu (*nom de guerre* 'Gülbahar'), a senior member of the PKK's umbrella committee the Kurdistan Communities Union (KCK) and a commander in the movement's women's military wing YJA STAR, as well as Murat Dag (*nom de guerre* 'Ferhat Yilmaz'), another high-profile member; both fighters were on Turkey's wanted list. In December, the Turkish government reported a nationwide counter-terror sweep, with 1,323 operations held between 4 and 11 December that led to the death of two PKK members and 153 arrests of those accused of aiding and abetting the PKK. The operations also led to the arrest of 67 people linked with the Islamic State, also known as ISIS or ISIL, 699 people linked with the Hizmet movement dubbed by Ankara as the 'Gülenist Terror Group' (FETO) and four others linked to far-left groups. The authorities reportedly destroyed 22 PKK shelters and 34 hand-made explosives, as well as significant amounts of hashish and heroin, in 2,000 raids across 77 provinces. The PKK's ideological leader Abdullah Ocalan, who has been held in the Imralı Island Prison in the Marmara Sea since 1999, has not been allowed to meet with outside delegations since 5 April 2015, except for once with his brother Mehmet on 11 September 2015. The leader had not been heard in public since, and his supporters feared for his health and safety, including whether he was still alive.

In mid-December, the government ordered new curfews in the cities of Batman and Mardin, the village of Yaylak and the hamlets of Simetok, Derik and Licika Simo. Turkey has declared more than 250 curfews in the eastern and southeastern provinces since the peace process with the PKK collapsed in 2015, with an estimated 1.8 million residents affected by the curfews.

Displacement and destruction in the southeast

The southeastern areas of Turkey continued to suffer because of limited humanitarian access to the estimated 500,000 people displaced due to the fighting. Many non-governmental organisation (NGO) staff were also detained, international staff deported and permits revoked. In early March, the Turkish government revoked the licence of Mercy Corps to operate in Turkey. On 20 April, 15 staff members of the International Medical Corps were detained: four of them were later deported, allegedly due to lack of valid work permits. Overall, more than 370 NGOs have been shut down on terrorism charges since mid-November 2016.

Most of the attention and funding from the international and national humanitarian community was directed at the Syrian refugee crisis. There was very limited information and statistics available on the humanitarian situation affecting non-Syrians, especially in the southeast of the country, due to the government's regulatory framework which restricted independent needs assessments by non-governmental humanitarian actors. Populations affected by the fighting between the PKK and the Turkish government continued to suffer from lack of access to healthcare and shelter. The southeastern provinces were economically hit and unemployment increased, especially among the youth. School attendance rates – especially of girls – dropped among the internally displaced populations in southeastern Turkey, due to increased costs of transport, economic hardship and trauma. Curfews imposed by the government affected the opening hours of shops, while the construction of a wall between Turkey and Syria impacted on cross-border trade and livelihoods.

In April, the government resumed demolishing buildings in Sur and Diyarbakir with bulldozers, preventing many of the residents who were displaced during the fighting in early 2016 (numbering nearly 24,000) from returning. According to Amnesty International, at least 60% of the entire Sur district had been expropriated. By mid-2017, more than 7,000 people in the east of Sur were threatened by new evacuations as nearly 2,000 homes were set to be destroyed. Only 15–20% of Sirnak's 90,000 displaced residents have returned since November 2016, and families displaced or affected by the fighting have, according to various reports, received limited or no compensation or assistance from the Turkish government. There were also reports that military forces were preventing medical staff from entering health facilities.

In September, the minister of environment and urbanisation announced a US$3.4-billion plan to reconstruct urban areas affected by fighting in the southeast, to be completed within six months. The plan included six fortified police stations and the construction of 15-metre-wide streets to allow more space for patrolling armoured vehicles. The government also promised monetary compensation for the demolished buildings in line with a law passed in 2004 on the compensation of losses due to terrorism and counter-terrorism. The government had already processed hundreds of thousands of applications, but residents were reportedly not receiving their money's worth, being compensated less than a third of the value of their demolished house. It was expected that populations in these areas would be in need of assistance for some time while the reconstruction took place: the Turkish Red Crescent identified various districts in Mardin, Sirnak, Hakkari and Diyarbakır as in need of healthcare, shelter assistance and counselling.

Iraq: continued cross-border activities against the PKK

A major event in the wider region of Kurdistan was the non-binding independence referendum organised by President Masoud Barzani of the Kurdistan Democratic Party (KDP) on 25 September 2017, which saw 93% of votes favour secession from Baghdad. Albeit initially sceptical of the referendum – which was seen as largely advancing KDP interests – both the PKK and the Patriotic Union of Kurdistan (PUK), the main opposition party, eventually supported the initiative. Cemil Bayik, the co-leader of the KCK (which acted as the PKK's umbrella body), affirmed that the referendum was a 'democratic right' and should not be opposed. In August, however, the PKK claimed to have captured at least two high-ranking officials from the Turkish National Intelligence Organization (MIT) in Sulaimaniya, Kurdistan Region, Iraq, whom the group accused of having conspired to assassinate Bayik. Some unconfirmed reports discussed a total of 22 people, including four MIT personnel, being held by the PKK. Ankara has not provided any public statement on the issue.

Following the referendum in late 2017, the Kurdish Regional Government (KRG), in an attempt at rapprochement with Ankara, started planning the establishment of security zones along the Turkish border to prevent PKK militants from crossing into Turkey. The plans were designed to complement Ankara's construction efforts earlier in the year: in February Turkey had finished a 900 km wall on the Syrian–Turkish border, while in August news circulated of Ankara constructing a wall 144 km long, 2 m wide and 3 m high with portable blocks across Turkey's border with Iran.

Ankara also mounted several operations against the PKK in 2017. Turkish F-16 jets bombed the Qandil mountains located in northern Iraq – the PKK's symbolic home and key stronghold – on multiple occasions throughout the year, frightening villagers. However, no civilian casualties were reported this time, in contrast to the widely condemned attack on the village of Zergele in August 2015 which killed eight residents and injured another eight, including a child. A rocket attack against a PKK training centre on 6 December in the Makhmour refugee camp 65 km south of Erbil, the capital of the Kurdistan Region, killed five and wounded several, but the attack was not claimed by any party. Neither the Kurdish or Iraqi governments, nor the United Nations High Commissioner for Refugees, which provides assistance to the camp, investigated or even commented on the incident.

Throughout the year, reports surfaced of Erdogan discussing joint operations with Iran against the PKK in Qandil, as well as against the PKK's Iranian offshoot, the Kurdistan Free Life Party (PJAK), which was located in the eastern Zagros mountains. Iran also experienced attacks from PJAK's arch-rival, the Kurdistan Democratic Party of Iran (KDPI), which increased its operations in 2017 after a hiatus of several years by sending many of its fighters to the Iranian border, as well as openly discussing a change in tactics, including a surge of clandestine activities in Iran. Spring and summer saw sporadic clashes between Iranian border guards and KDPI guerrillas, and occasionally the PKK. In November, it was reported that Turkey, Iraq and Iran had launched joint operations against the PKK in northern Iraq's mountainous Asos region, 180 km south of the Turkish border and near the border with Iran: according to the Turkish general staff, 41 targets were destroyed, including tunnels and shelters. The attacks in Asos (which some reporters speculated may have also killed PJAK fighters) were believed to be the first in several years, and indicated that further joint attacks could take place in early 2018.

Operation Euphrates Shield, the military incursion in northern Syria initiated by Turkey on 24 August 2016 to ward off ISIS and the PYD from Turkey's border regions, officially ended on 29 March 2017 with the government announcing that it had secured areas around al-Bab and Jarablus, albeit at a cost of more than 70 military casualties. In October, Turkey also completed its military operation against the Nusra Front-led Tahrir al-Sham in Idlib, and soon set its sights on the PYD-controlled cantons of Afrin in Rojava, northern Syria, as well as Manbij, Tal Abyad,

Ras al-Ayn and Qamishli. The Turkish armed forces established bases around the area with a command centre on Sheikh Barakh Hill overlooking the Kurdish-majority city Afrin, east of which lies the strategically important supply route from Turkey to rebel-held eastern Aleppo, known as the 'Azaz corridor'.

While the Turkish presence in Afrin would have been unlikely to happen without the approval of Moscow, the Turkish troops refrained from immediate further action, in part due to the presence of Russian military personnel stationed there. The Russians had been among the many foreign states (in particular the US) training the Syrian Democratic Forces (SDF) and YPG personnel in the region. There were also unconfirmed reports concerning what may have been Moscow-sent paramilitary or mercenary personnel wearing YPG insignia.

In November, presidents Vladimir Putin and Donald Trump called for all parties (including the PYD) to participate in the Geneva talks, a development that unsettled Erdogan. Soon after, the Russian, Iranian and Turkish presidents met in Sochi to prepare for the Syrian National Dialogue Congress due to be held in 2018 (the congress has been postponed twice due to Turkey's objections). They jointly acknowledged that progress had been made on de-escalation zones in Syria, as agreed in the Astana talks held in May and September 2017. Uncertainty prevailed in December over whether Russia would invite the PYD to the congress, but reports later indicated that Putin had conceded to Erdogan's demands by offering that only non-PYD Kurds would participate. In response to Ankara's opposition to the PYD's participation, a PYD representative in December reportedly affirmed to Sputnik News the party's ideological relationship with the PKK as both being followers of Abdullah Ocalan, and announced that the PYD had no intention of breaking ties with the group. He also added that the PYD would be 'ready for talks with any party', including Ankara and Tehran.

Under the new Trump administration, the US had increased its arms deliveries to the YPG and the SDF to include armoured vehicles. However, Talal Silo, a Turkmen and former spokesperson for the SDF who defected to Turkey in late 2017, criticised the fact that US arms were being disproportionately handed over to the YPG – and by extension the PKK – with minimal oversight. In previous years the US had, by some accounts, attempted to sidestep the affiliation of the YPG with the PKK by rebranding the group as the SDF. In a rare public acknowledgement of this strategy, on 21 July at the Aspen Institute Security Forum General Raymond Thomas, the commander of the United States Special Operations Command (SOCOM), discussed the rationale behind this: the strategy, the general acknowledged in his talk, involved integrating non-Kurdish units into the SDF to make the forces appear more inclusive and balanced. While this was not news to analysts familiar with the YPG–PKK links, it was rare for a high-ranking US officer to admit to the rebranding strategy openly.

By the end of the year, speculation emerged that Moscow and Ankara would jointly stage an operation to push the YPG out of Afrin, with Ankara keen to set its eyes on the town of Manbij, some 20 km south of the border with Turkey, soon after that. It would have to be seen whether Russia would be ready to trade the goodwill of the Kurds – and by extension the US – to strengthen relations with Ankara and Damascus. This would also force the US to finally make a choice between either a rapprochement, or a possible military confrontation with the armed forces of Ankara, a NATO ally. The US had hoped to strike a delicate balance between the support it gave to the Kurds and the relations it had with Turkey, but a Russian-facilitated military operation in Afrin and Manbij would force the hand of the US. For the YPG, a loss of US support would strike a devastating blow to the movement, and potentially drastically reverse the gains made in the past year in Syria.

Purge continues amid coup speculation

The Turkish National Security Council extended the state of emergency, in place since the attempted coup on 15 July 2016, every three months throughout 2017. Prosecution of Kurdish parliamentarians on terrorism-related charges continued and the government dismissed thousands of police, civil servants and academics. Targeted individuals were mostly accused of links to either the Fethullah Gülen movement accused of orchestrating the coup, or the PKK. By late 2017 Ankara had not been able to prove conclusively that Fethullah Gülen planned the coup, leaving both the European Union Intelligence Analysis Centre and Bruno Kahl, chief of the German Federal Intelligence Service (BND), unconvinced.

By July 2017, the government had suspended or dismissed almost 150,000 civil servants, teachers, judges and police since the coup attempt; arrested more than 60,000 people; and dismissed almost 4,500 judges and prosecutors. In addition, more than 300 journalists had been arrested and 187 media outlets shut down. On 21 December, the Turkish constitutional court rejected the appeal of the People's Democratic Party (HDP) co-party leader Selahattin Demirtaş against his ongoing detention (Demirtaş had already been in prison for over a year). The government also cracked down on several international NGOs working with Syrian refugees.

A UN report released on 10 March condemned the human-rights violations by the security forces and the use of counter-terrorism legislation to pursue demo- cratically elected officials of the Kurdish HDP. International pressure led to some journalists being released in June, including Erol Onderoglu, a representative of Reporters Sans Frontières (RSF). However, the police detained ten human-rights activists in July, including Amnesty International's Turkey director and a German and a Swedish citizen, later released pending trial. In April, May and August respec- tively, the police detained an Italian and two French journalists, all accused of supporting the PKK or the YPG. According to the RSF, dozens of foreign journalists have been expelled from Turkey since the escalation in the southeast in July 2015. Human Rights Watch criticised the government for increased reports of torture and ill-treatment in police detention and for intimidation against lawyers and medical examiners. Prisons around the country continued to be severely overcrowded, exac- erbated by an emergency decree that increased the custody period from one day to 30 days.

Constitutional and military reform

Erdogan made a number of constitutional amendments in 2017, as well as propos- ing reforms to the security and defence sector which are scheduled to come into effect after the next general elections planned for November 2019. The constitu- tional amendments included the elimination of the position of prime minister and the expansion of the executive powers of the president, including increasing presi- dential and civilian control of the military and the national intelligence agency. The amendments were approved by the parliament on 21 January and a constitutional referendum held on 16 April affirmed the change. The referendum was widely criti- cised for being held in a climate of repression, intimidation and censorship that prevailed under the state of emergency, and there were strong allegations of elec- toral misconduct and vote-rigging.

Major structural changes to the security sector included limiting the power of the chief of general staff and increasing that of the president as commander-in-chief; involving more civilians in the Supreme Military Council; changing reporting lines from the chief of general staff to the Ministry of Defence; and subsuming the gendarmerie and coastguard under the Ministry of Interior. Ruling by decrees under the state of emergency, the government also purged the security services of thousands of personnel. In August, seven generals and admirals resigned, ostensibly to protest against the growing strength of Chief of General Staff General Hulusi Akar, a trusted ally of Erdogan and a commander of *Operation Euphrates Shield*.

A curiosity in the Turkish military reform was the move (publicised in late 2017) to increase the number of women soldiers in the army from 1% to 10%, likely a hearts-and-minds strategy responding to the international reputation of the women fighters in the PKK. The Turkish Gendarmerie Command set out to recruit 8,000 women younger than 26 and taller than 164 centimetres. (Headscarves were now also allowed.) After receiving commando training, many of the new women gendarmerie soldiers will be deployed to the southeast of the country to take part in anti-PKK operations. At the end of 2017, the gendarmerie had only 828 female personnel, of whom 52 were officers and the rest non-commissioned officers. Only 1,345 commissioned and 370 non-commissioned officers were female in the Turkish army, out of 723,741 total personnel.

Yemen

Civil war continued unabated in Yemen throughout 2017 as the humanitarian situation in the country deteriorated dramatically. The coalition of anti-Houthi forces, nominally supportive of President Abd Rabbo Mansour Hadi, made little headway

Key statistics	2016	2017
Type:	Internationalised	Internationalised
Fatalities:	7,000	17,000
New IDPs:	480,000	160,000
New refugees:	14,000	7,000

in its campaign to roll back the gains of the Houthis and their allies in the General

People's Congress (GPC). While front-lines barely moved, the movement of food, fuel and medicine was impeded by both sides' attempts to deprive each other of military resources and profit from the movement of goods – most markedly through the Saudi-imposed blockade of the country. The effort by the United Nations to mediate a political solution to the conflict failed in January, and the UN Special Envoy to Yemen Ismail Ould Cheikh Ahmed was unable to revive it for the rest of the year.

The prospects for a solution to the conflict appeared very distant by the end of 2017. In December, the tense alliance between the Houthis and former president Ali Abdullah Saleh's GPC came to a decisive end: hostilities broke out between them leading to the death of Saleh himself. This left neighbouring Saudi Arabia facing the unpalatable prospect of the Houthis as the dominant force in the north of Yemen. Meanwhile in the south, national and international support for Hadi fell away and a resurgent southern independence movement claimed the political and military initiative with Emirati support. By the end of 2017 Saudi Arabia and the United Arab Emirates were moving rapidly towards abandoning their ally Hadi, whose legitimacy inside Yemen was quickly disappearing. Instead, the Gulf states looked to an independent al-Islah to contest the Houthis in the north and to the southern independence movement as the political power of the future in the south.

Slow progress

In January 2017, as UN-mediated negotiations between Hadi's government and the Houthi–GPC alliance collapsed, anti-Houthi military forces and their international allies launched a major offensive in southwest Yemen under the name *Operation Golden Spear*. The operation sought in the first phase to capture the southwestern coast, secure the Bab El-Mandeb Strait and then advance eastwards to capture the main north–south highway linking Taizz and Hudaydah governorates, thereby cutting Houthi–GPC forces around Taizz city off from Hudaydah port. A second phase envisaged the forces moving northwards to take Hudaydah port itself, and ultimately also the ports of Al-Saleef and Ras Issa, in order to deprive the Houthi–GPC alliance of access to maritime supply lines and isolate their forces in the centre of the country.

The anti-Houthi coalition made quick progress at first. In February, it seized the port of Mokha with Sudanese as well as Emirati forces playing an important part in its capture. Through Mokha, the coalition was able to deliver tanks and reinforcements, and from there they advanced northwards along the coastal road to the outskirts of Khokha and eastwards along the Mokha–Taizz road. Their eastward advance came to a halt when it encountered strong resistance from the Houthi–GPC alliance at Khalid Ibn Al-Walid military camp – a major stronghold for the alliance and a strategic location just ahead of the main Taizz–Hudaydah highway. In July, after months of heavy fighting, the coalition managed to capture the base and the junction with the important north–south road.

The humanitarian implications of pressing the offensive further and attacking the port of Hudaydah caused consternation in the international community; serious consequences for the supply of food and fuel to Houthi-held areas and challenges for humanitarian access were anticipated. However, the collapse of the Houthi–GPC alliance in December presented the anti-Houthi coalition with an opportunity to advance towards Hudaydah while Houthi forces were focused elsewhere. Joined by the Tihamah militia, allies of the late Ali Abdullah Saleh, the coalition went ahead with the offensive, capturing Khokha and much of Hays district.

The end of the Houthi–GPC alliance also proved significant for the anti-Houthi forces' campaign inland. Through most of the year, fighting took place on four fronts with little territory changing hands. With Taizz under siege by the Houthi–GPC alliance, anti-Houthi forces fought unsuccessfully to gain control of the main road and supply route to the city from Lahij and Aden, and attempted to push the Houthis out of the suburbs of Taizz, from which they continued to shell the city remorselessly. To the east, anti-Houthi forces made frequent attempts to advance into Dhi Na'im district in Bayda governorate but failed to cut the supply lines from Sana'a and Dhamar to Houthi-controlled Bayda city. Along the border between Marib and Sana'a governorates, anti-Houthi forces looked to advance towards Sana'a, pushing Houthi–GPC forces westwards along the two Sana'a–Marib roads, with fighting focused around Sirwah on the southern road and in Nihm district on the northern route. Further north, the anti-Houthi coalition attempted to force the Houthis and GPC out of Al-Jawf governorate but enjoyed little success.

Al-Islah militias played a significant role in the anti-Houthi campaign on these front-lines. With its deep scepticism of al-Islah for its links to the Muslim Brotherhood, the UAE was reluctant to support the anti-Houthi forces in these areas. However, in December, al-Islah appeared to disavow the Brotherhood and reconcile with the UAE. With the subsequent support from the UAE-backed Southern Resistance Forces (SRF), the anti-Houthi alliance was able to take advantage of the collapse of the Houthi–GPC alliance and made several small but significant advances towards the end of the year. In Shabwa, it pushed Houthi–GPC fighters northwest out of Usaylan and Bayhan districts. From there, it advanced into the north of Bayda governorate, dislodging the Houthis from Numan and Nati districts. In the north, the coalition captured the road linking Saada and Al-Jawf governorates.

In support of the anti-Houthi ground operations, Saudi Arabia continued to wage its aerial bombing campaign. In addition to strikes along the front-lines, the Royal Saudi Air Force continued to target sites away from the front-line, including ballistic-missile launch sites in Saada and Sana'a governorates and perceived targets in residential areas. The civilian death toll from the bombing campaign remained high. The UN Panel of Experts on Yemen reported many strikes hitting civilian targets or killing disproportionate numbers in the vicinity of legitimate targets. Among the most grievous incidents were the bombing of a migrant boat in the Red Sea on 16 March, killing 42 civilians and injuring 34; the bombing of a motel in Arhab on 23 August, killing 33 and injuring 25; and the bombing of a night market in Saada on 1 November, killing 31 and injuring 26.

In contrast, Emirati forces played a decisive role on the ground, both through training and equipping large and effective anti-Houthi forces – including the Security Belt Forces (SBF, also known as Hizam), Hadrami Elite Forces (HEF) and Shabwari Elite Forces (SEF) – and through deploying its own special forces alongside them. However, Emirati forces (and forces trained by them) were implicated in arbitrary arrests and detentions in the Hadramaut and Shabwah governorates, with the UN Panel of Experts warning that detention by Emirati forces would amount to a breach of international human rights, as the UAE had no legal authority to make such arrests. Although the UAE denied any involvement, the arrests caused hostility towards the UAE and the UAE-backed forces in the two governorates.

Campaign against AQAP and the Islamic State

Al-Qaeda in the Arabian Peninsula (AQAP) sought to exploit this anger towards the UAE and UAE-backed forces in the south of Yemen, as well as the antipathy felt by many towards the Houthis in central Yemen. Having been ousted from their urban strongholds in 2016, AQAP was present at the beginning of the year primarily in the rural areas of Abyan, Bayda, Hadramaut and Shabwah governorates, from which they waged an insurgency campaign. In January and February, AQAP made notable gains from anti-Houthi forces in Abyan governorate and established itself as the dominant force in the north and centre of the governorate, despite directing less than a third of its operations against the anti-Houthi forces (more than two-thirds were against Houthi forces). The infighting and poor leadership among local anti-Houthi forces left them unable to provide an effective defence against AQAP.

However, from July onwards, the SBF assumed responsibility for the fight against AQAP in Abyan and launched an offensive to push the group out of the area and secure the main highway to Shabwah governorate. During this period more than half of AQAP clashes were with the anti-Houthi forces. At the same time, the newly trained and equipped UAE-backed SEF succeeded in ousting AQAP from Shabwah governorate, forcing its fighters to retreat in September into the territory still under its control in Abyan. By the end of the year, AQAP appeared markedly weaker; vulnerable to any uprising against it, AQAP issued a threat against any local tribes in Abyan tempted to join the mainstream anti-Houthi forces.

Although UAE-supported forces played the lead role in the campaign against AQAP in the south, the United States also played a very significant part. In 2017, the US carried out more than 120 strikes against AQAP and the Islamic State, also known as ISIS or ISIL, across Yemen, by aircraft, unmanned aerial vehicles (UAVs) and missiles – more than in any preceding year and up from just 30 strikes in 2016. US special forces also conducted a number of raids inside Yemen, including a notable operation on an AQAP base in Yakla in Bayda governorate to acquire computer material, which according to Yemeni officials resulted in the deaths of eight women and seven children, as well as around 15 militants and one US soldier.

Houthi resistance and the role of Iran

While the Houthi–GPC alliance's main military objective appeared to be the retention of its existing territorial gains, it also continued its offensive action against Saudi Arabia. The Houthis staged persistent cross-border attacks from Saada governorate into Saudi Arabia's Jizan, Asir and Najran provinces, variously involving the use of snipers, artillery fire, free-flight rockets and short-range ballistic missiles.

The Houthis also targeted the Saudis at sea, attacking the Saudi port of Jizan by boat in April and using remote-controlled vessels to direct improvised explosive devices at an Aramco fuel terminal. The Houthis also laid naval mines around the ports of Midi in the north and Mokha in the south.

In response to the cross-border attacks, Saudi-backed forces – including a contingent of the Sudanese Rapid Support Forces – launched their own cross-border offensive in Hajjah and Saada governorates, supported by Saudi airstrikes, with the intention of pushing Houthi forces away from the frontier. Although the coalition successfully seized Midi and Haradh in Hajjah governorate early in the year, it proved difficult for Saudi Arabia to control the mountainous border with Saada.

Houthi forces continued to be supported by Iran, with Iranian military advisers on the ground and Houthi forces making increasing use of Iranian-supplied technology. In addition to their own improvised naval mines, the Houthis laid identifiable Iranian naval mines around Mokha. Iranian UAVs were also used by the Houthis for reconnaissance and for carrying explosive devices. Most significantly, they made extensive use of Iranian short-range ballistic missiles, which were modified to increase their range. The UN Panel of Experts reported that the type of missile used by the Houthis was a modified Iranian *Qiam*-I missile, adapted and assembled by Houthi–GPC alliance engineers inside Yemen. Houthi leader Abdel Malik al-Houthi claimed in September that the adapted missile had a range of at least 2,000 kilometres and could reach Saudi Arabia. The Houthis deployed these extended-range missiles four times in 2017: on 19 May, landing in Riyadh province; on 22 July, landing in Yanbu port; on 4 November, directed at King Khaled International Airport in Riyadh; and on 19 December, intercepted in its flight towards Al-Yamama Palace in Riyadh.

The UN Panel of Experts issued a clear assessment that the Houthis' use of short-range ballistic missiles was non-compliant with international humanitarian law (IHL). The Houthis were also judged to have breached IHL with their indiscriminate shelling of territory under the control of the anti-Houthi coalition, especially in Taizz city.

Blockade and embargo

The ballistic-missile attack on King Khaled International Airport in Riyadh on 4 November prompted Saudi Arabia to force a complete closure of all ports of entry to Yemen – by land, sea and air. An arms embargo on Yemen had long been in force, involving inspection of all vessels entering the country by sea and strict border controls at the main border crossing from al-Maharah governorate into Oman. However, the Houthi–GPC alliance's continuing access to sophisticated Iranian weaponry (or the parts with which to assemble weapons), including ballistic-missile modules, naval mines and UAVs, highlighted the vulnerabilities in the embargo. (Despite this, there was a marked decline in the number of Houthi ballistic-missile attacks on Saudi Arabia between 2016 and 2017 – down by 64% according to the UN High Panel of Experts – perhaps reflecting that the embargo did pose a significant challenge to the Houthis' supply chain.)

Even before the total closure of ports in November, the humanitarian cost of the embargo had been severe. The UN, non-governmental organisations (NGOs) and journalists documented significant delays to the delivery of food, fuel and medicine due to the forced inspections of all vessels entering Yemeni ports, placing a serious strain on a country dependent on imports for 90% of its food. Saudi Arabia's imposition of a total blockade on Yemen therefore provoked a major outcry from the international community, including from the governments of the United States and United Kingdom. In response, Saudi Arabia announced on 22 November that it would partially lift the blockade, allowing humanitarian-aid deliveries into the country. However, as commercial shipments continued to be barred, the flow of fuel and food remained severely restricted. On 2 December, the heads of the World Health Organization (WHO), UN Development Programme, UN High Commissioner for Refugees, UN Children's Fund, World Food Programme, International Organization for Migration and the UN Office for the Coordination of Humanitarian Affairs issued a joint letter warning of widespread famine within months, with the likelihood of three million people facing starvation if commercial ships continued to be refused permission to berth in Red Sea ports.

Brink of famine

The humanitarian situation in Yemen was catastrophic throughout 2017. Although front-lines remained relatively constant through the year, approximately 160,000 more people were displaced internally by the fighting. Typically accommodated by relatives, internally displaced persons (IDPs) placed a severe strain on households in areas away from the front-lines, meaning humanitarian needs were significant across much of the country. Likewise, the continued flow of refugees into Yemen from the Horn of Africa still further increased the burden on the urban centres of Aden, Sana'a and Lahij which typically host them.

The obstacles to the movement of food, fuel and medicine placed enormous humanitarian pressure on the country. The limited supply, and therefore high cost, of fuel in Yemen posed problems both for transportation of food and other goods, and for electricity generation, affecting businesses, farming, hospitals and water-supply networks. Moreover, with government salaries unpaid for months at a time, households' ability to purchase food was increasingly limited. Overall, 17.8m people (61% of the population) faced some level of food insecurity, with severe food insecurity affecting 8.4m (29% of the population) as of November 2017 – up 24% from 6.8m in 2016. This particularly affected Taizz, Amran, Hajjah, Hudaydah, Saada and Sana'a governorates.

Rampant corruption within both the anti-Houthi administration and the Houthi–GPC alliance further slowed and increased the cost of essential supplies. Houthi–GPC forces taxed any imports into their territory and maintained an expensive black market in fuel. Likewise, the corruption of the anti-Houthi administration, led by Prime Minister Ahmed Obeid bin Daghr, prompted the governor of Aden to resign in protest in November, having only been appointed to the position by Hadi in May.

The gradual collapse of Yemen's health, water and sanitation systems under the strain of the war, blockade and corruption contributed to major outbreaks of disease in 2017. Although the cholera epidemic which occurred in late 2016 subsided early in the year, a critical 'second wave' epidemic broke out in late April 2017. The spread of cholera surged, with infections in excess of 180,000 per month in June and July, and high fatality rates of 0.7–0.8%. Yemen's hospitals were severely limited in their ability to respond due to a lack of equipment and medical supplies caused by the Saudi blockade.

Despite the difficult conditions, determined efforts by Yemeni health workers, the WHO and international NGOs brought the infection rate and fatality rates down. By the end of the year, the epidemic appeared to be subsiding, although cumulative cases had by then passed one million and cholera deaths passed 2,000. However, the cholera epidemic was followed by an outbreak of the deadlier diphtheria virus in mid-August, with around 450 cases and 45 deaths by the end of 2017. Treatment of the disease was again hindered by the Saudi blockade, according to the WHO, due to the delayed delivery of antitoxins.

Fragmentation of the anti-Houthi coalition

The failure of Hadi's government to provide aid or basic services, and its corruption under the leadership of Prime Minister bin Daghr, contributed to the destabilisation of Hadi's regime. Hadi's own continued exile in Riyadh compounded his illegitimacy in the eyes of those suffering inside Yemen. However, it was the strengthening southern secessionist movement, which built on this dissatisfaction with his government, and Hadi's response to that movement which drove the fragmentation of his coalition.

By early 2017, two power bases were already well established in the south of Yemen. On the one hand, Hadi continued to head a government based in Aden, backed by the Saudi government and with the support of loyal military units. On the other, a constellation of southern secessionist movements was strengthening with the support of the UAE: the SBF, the HEF and the SEF as the military arm of this constellation, and the Southern Movement as its civil-society arm. In February 2017, the two sides came into violent confrontation at Aden airport as the UAE and UAE-backed forces in control of the airport prevented Hadi's plane from landing. After being permitted to land on a second attempt, Hadi then ordered loyalist forces to lay siege to the airport, sparking clashes between the two sides. Although the situation calmed, the UAE-backed forces subsequently prevented Brigadier-General Muhran Qubati from landing at the airport, again triggering violence. As a result, President Hadi dismissed two pro-secession government figures – Governor of Aden Aidarus al-Zubaidi and Minister of State and SBF commander Hani bin Braik. The dismissals prompted large demonstrations in Aden with images of Hadi burned in protest.

In May, Zubaidi and bin Braik established the Southern Transitional Council (STC). Over subsequent months, the STC increasingly resembled a shadow government, building up its own capacity to govern with support from the UAE. Although Zubaidi publicly recognised the authority of Hadi's government, he warned that the STC would take over the role of providing public services if the government failed to perform it. With Hadrami leaders, socialist politicians, tribal elites and civil-society activists among the 26 STC members, the organisation had a strong base of support among the main southern factions. In November, the STC established a National Assembly for the south. Among its members were political figures who, until recently, had supported a unified Yemen and whose participation indicated the growing momentum behind the south's secession movement. As such, the STC was increasingly well established as the political arm of the wider assortment of southern separatist entities.

The UAE's support for the secessionists not only contributed to the fragmentation of the anti-Houthi coalition but also reflected the evolving Saudi-Emirati strategy for Yemen, pursued with the backing of the US and UK. In the first instance, Hadi's continuation as president served only to fulfil the requirements of the UN Security Council authorisation for the Gulf coalition's intervention; in reality, Hadi's credibility as Yemen's political leader had all but disappeared by the end of 2017. In the meantime, both Saudi Arabia and the UAE looked to strengthen viable alternatives to Hadi, with varying degrees of coordination. To this end, through 2017, Saudi Arabia looked to draw al-Islah away from the Muslim Brotherhood and thereby establish it as an alternative to Hadi which would be acceptable to the UAE. Additionally, in late 2017, the Saudi government appeared to open talks with Saleh to draw his GPC away from its alliance with the Houthis and into a coalition against their erstwhile partners. Meanwhile, the UAE's support for separatists in the south had the potential to bring about a referendum which could serve the UAE and Saudi ends as an ostensibly legitimate political process to move on from support for Hadi.

The overarching goals for Saudi Arabia and the UAE nevertheless remained the same: to make sufficient military gains to force the Houthis into a political settlement of the Gulf states' choice; secure the Saudi-Yemeni border; eliminate Iranian influence in the country; and influence or control Yemeni infrastructure (especially ports and pipelines) to serve their geo-economic interests.

Demise of the Saleh–Houthi alliance

Throughout 2017, tensions rose between the Houthis and Saleh's GPC. Their joint Supreme Political Council and the formation in October 2016 of a Houthi–GPC

National Salvation Government (NSG) failed to resolve or hide the gulf between their political outlooks and the clear disparity in the strength of the two factions.

Saleh and the GPC were frustrated by the Houthis' failure to dismantle the Revolutionary Committee which the Houthis had established in 2015 and which continued to interfere with and outmanoeuvre the NSG. Although Saleh was able to exercise a degree of power through his use of personal influence and accumulated wealth as a source of patronage, many within the GPC objected to the party's continued alliance with the Houthi movement, harbouring fears about the Houthis' political agenda and possible aspiration towards a revival of Yemen's imamate. In August, the GPC held a rally in Sana'a to celebrate its 35th anniversary and to advertise its political strength. In the lead-up to the rally, Saleh dismissed the Houthis as a militia and at the rally itself all colours of anti-Houthi residents of Sana'a joined with the GPC to demonstrate. Although tensions ran high, the Houthis and the GPC were restrained and only small-scale clashes followed the rally, with a GPC politician and three Houthi security personnel killed in two separate incidents.

For their part, many within the Houthi movement questioned their alliance with Saleh, whose regime had been their deadly enemy through six spells of conflict from 2004 to 2010, especially given the relative strength of Houthi forces. These doubts only strengthened following the GPC's August rally, and there were widespread suspicions that Saleh was secretly negotiating with the UAE and would join with them to turn on the Houthi movement.

Hostilities finally broke out in Sana'a on 29 November with a dispute between Houthi and GPC forces at Al-Saleh Mosque, resulting in the Houthis seizing control of the surrounding areas and raiding the homes of Saleh's brother Tarek and of GPC member and NSG Foreign Minister Ibrahim Sharaf. A brief attempt at mediation between the two sides failed on the same day. Five days of intense fighting ensued involving street fighting and artillery fire, with the Houthis seizing a series of GPC party buildings and military installations. The Houthis used reinforcements from outside Sana'a to cut off the GPC and successfully persuaded Saleh's tribal allies to withhold their support for him.

Saleh divorced the GPC from its alliance with the Houthis once and for all on 2 December with a public call for reconciliation with Saudi Arabia and the UAE. However, his hopes for this reconciliation were quickly extinguished; on 4

December, the Houthis overran Saleh's house, killing the former president along with GPC Secretary-General Arif al-Zouka. The Houthis proceeded to dismantle the GPC, executing its military commanders, imprisoning its politicians, threatening prominent individuals and suppressing opposition.

By the end of the year, in the wake of Saleh's death, the Houthi movement had established itself as the pre-eminent power in the north of Yemen. It remained unclear what opposition to the Houthis might emerge from the constellation of tribal actors in the north (the Bakil and Hashid confederations and the seven tribes of Sana'a) and whether Saleh's sons Ahmed Ali Abdullah Saleh and Khaled Ali Abdullah Saleh would attempt to continue the fight against the Houthis and keep alive his network of allies. Nevertheless, their father's death undoubtedly marked the end of an era in Yemen.

Chapter Four

Sub-Saharan Africa

Central African Republic

Central African Republic faced worsening violence and an unstable political situation in 2017, a state of affairs that was exacerbated by the plight of the United Nations' Multi-dimensional Integrated Stabilization Mission (MINUSCA), which strug-

Key statistics	2016	2017
Type:	Internationalised	Internationalised
Fatalities:	600	2,000
New IDPs:	46,000	540,000
New refugees:	40,000	150,000

gled with limited resources and ill-trained troops. President Faustin-Archange Touadéra, elected in early 2016, made little progress in cementing either his own authority or that of the fledgling state institutions. Support for him began to wane in light of the deteriorating security situation, while the slowness of his government to effect political reform strained relations with the UN mission. There was also no progress towards a wider settlement between the government and ex-Séléka factions to address the political marginalisation of Muslim communities and the secessionist aspirations of some militia leaders.

Although in the past fighting in Central African Republic had largely followed religious lines, in October 2016 a group of Muslim ex-Séléka and Christian and animist anti-balaka forces put sectarian differences aside. A coalition between them, led by the Popular Front for the Renaissance of Central African Republic (FPRC), instigated a campaign against a rival ex-Séléka group, the Union for Peace in

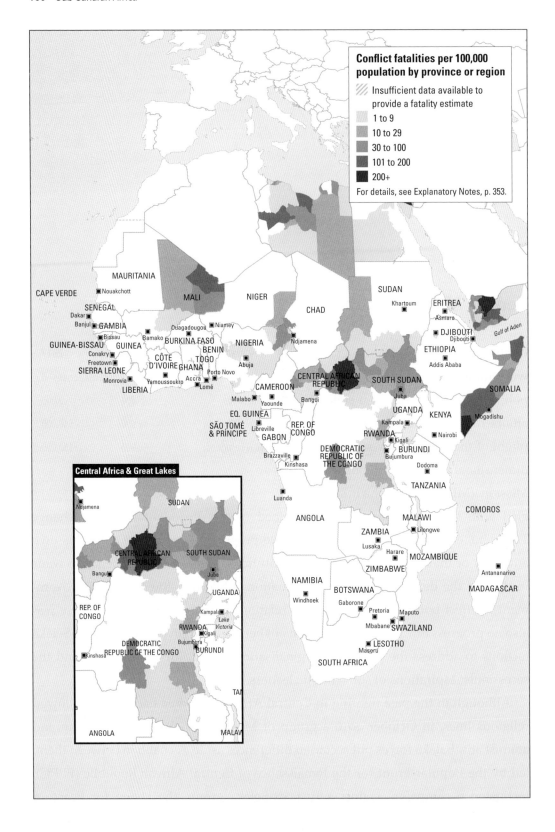

Conflict fatalities per 100,000
population by province or region

Insufficient data available to
provide a fatality estimate
1 to 9
10 to 29
30 to 100
101 to 200
200+

For details, see Explanatory Notes, p. 353.

Central Africa & Great Lakes

Central Africa (UPC), which had refused to participate in the proposed alliance. The fighting between these two factions continued in 2017, triggering a wave of intercommunal violence which saw hundreds of civilians killed and hundreds of thousands displaced. The fighting eventually forced the coalition, and the FPRC itself, to split along ethnic lines, reinforcing the ethnic pattern to the violence. From June onwards, the conflict was increasingly fought between Sahelian ethnic groups on one side and Savannah ethnic groups on the other.

Political inertia

President Faustin-Archange Touadéra was elected in early 2016 with high hopes that he would build a strong political power base and use it to negotiate with both ex-Séléka and anti-balaka militias to end sectarian violence. However, Touadéra and his government accomplished very little in 2017, failing to put in place almost any of the processes required to stabilise the country.

The government remained unable to project its authority much beyond Bangui and had no control of the security situation: it relied entirely on the limited peace-keeping forces of MINUSCA in Central African Republic to respond to the worsening violence. In August, President Touadéra appointed 16 new prefects to each of the country's prefectures but it remained to be seen whether they would be able to exer-cise any power in the regions. In Nana-Grébizi, the new prefect was for a period prevented from even entering his designated prefecture – and upon his eventual inauguration was the target of an unsuccessful grenade attack.

President Touadéra's main, and perhaps only, success in 2017 was the progress made in establishing the country's justice institutions. In January, legislation was passed to institute the Constitutional Court and the High Court of Justice. In subse-quent months, judges and prosecutors were appointed to both these courts and the Special Criminal Court, which had been established by law in 2015 and was respon-sible for prosecuting violations of human rights and international humanitarian law. There were, nevertheless, complaints that the courts were under-resourced and therefore were struggling to undertake the preparatory work required before they could begin hearing cases.

This small success did little to shore up Touadéra's position, and support for him, both among the political elites in Bangui and among the wider population, increasingly faded away over the course of the year. The president made little effort to build a coherent political support base: he neither brought together those political groups which had supported him in the second round of presidential elections nor strengthened his relations with the Kwa Na Kwa (the party of former president François Bozizé and the fifth largest in the current National Assembly). Instead, Touadéra increasingly concentrated power in the Office of the President, especially in the hands of presidential adviser Stanislas Moussa Kembe, at the expense of government ministers. Relations between the president and government deteriorated accordingly, and Touadéra relied on giving various political and military actors just enough stake in the government to keep himself afloat. In September, Touadéra carried out a cabinet reshuffle which saw the cabinet expand from 23 to 34 ministers. Touadéra brought in several new members with close links to major armed groups, to the dismay of civil society and international observers.

At the same time, both the president and the government faced worsening relations with the National Assembly. In May, the National Assembly threatened a motion of censure against Prime Minister Simplice Mathieu Sarandji for repeatedly failing to appear before the assembly to report on the government's work, although tensions were temporarily defused when Sarandji subsequently appeared alongside other ministers to answer the assembly's questions. In July, an ally of the president, Didacien Kossimatchi, stoked tensions with an allegation that the head of the National Assembly, Abdou Karim Méckassoua, was conspiring to conduct a coup. The situation looked likely to result in destabilising protests by Touadéra's supporters but was calmed thanks to the attorney general, who warned against any demonstrations but also promised to investigate the allegations.

Attempts at mediation

Mediation attempts continued in Central African Republic, both at the national and local levels. At both levels, a multiplicity of uncoordinated initiatives were led by the Central African Republic government, MINUSCA, various non-governmental organisations (NGOs), local mediation committees, local peace committees and religious actors.

There was some success at the local level. In December, the Centre for Humanitarian Dialogue, an NGO based in Geneva, facilitated discussions between the Return, Reclamation and Rehabilitation armed group (3R) and the anti-balaka group in Nana-Mambéré prefecture which led to a ceasefire agreement between the parties. In addition to a ceasefire, the agreement mandated the free movement of people and goods, free access to public services and the return of displaced people, as well as a prohibition on the movement of armed groups in the northwest of Central African Republic. In September, there was also a temporarily successful attempt to mediate an end to fighting between rival factions of the FPRC in Bria, Haute-Kotto prefecture. However, the mediation process in Bria highlighted the perverse rivalry between different local mediators: although religious mediators had brought the factions together, started negotiations and halted the violence in the city, a team of emissaries from Bangui and Birao subsequently forced the religious mediators out of the discussions. The competition between the different mediators and the absence of any strategy to tie local mediation into a wider national strategy reduced the chances of real success.

The situation was similar at the national level. The Community of Sant'Egidio, a Catholic NGO which had been active in Central African Republic for several years, brought together individuals from all the main armed factions, political parties and religious institutions to negotiate a ceasefire in Rome. The agreement committed all parties to cease military activity, to respect the country's territorial integrity, to recognise all politico-military groups and their role in reconstruction, and to respect the results of the 2016 presidential and legislative elections. However, fighting continued irrespective of the ceasefire: it was unclear whether the representatives of armed groups lacked the power to bring the agreement into effect on the ground in Central African Republic or whether their participation in Rome was simply insincere. The United Nations and MINUSCA were only permitted a negligible role in the negotiation of the agreement, despite the fact that enforcement of the ceasefire depended upon its peacekeepers.

The UN and MINUSCA were similarly sidelined in other mediation initiatives. In the wake of the signing of the ceasefire agreement in Rome, the African Union (AU), the Economic Community of Central African States (ECCAS), and the International Conference on the Great Lakes Region (ICGLR) reasserted their role in the peace process and set out a new Road Map for Peace and Reconciliation in Central African Republic, which assigned to the AU the responsibility for leading the peace negotiations. Unlike the previous African Initiative for Peace and Reconciliation, an agreement reached in 2016, the signatories to the new road map ruled out an amnesty and the return of former presidents Bozizé and Michel Djotodia. However, MINUSCA once again played no real role in the process, undermining the prospective enforcement of any agreements.

Meanwhile in Bangui, the government, with the support of the Centre for Humanitarian Dialogue, tried to advance the disarmament, demobilisation, reintegration and repatriation (DDRR) initiative. Having long rejected the process, the FPRC and the Maxim Mokom-led anti-balaka faction both agreed at the start of the year to limited participation in the DDRR Monitoring and Advisory Committee, and the committee convened with representatives of all 14 main armed factions for the first time in March. A subsequent meeting in April produced a national DDRR plan and – given a degree of additional impetus by the Rome agreement – a pilot phase began in August. However, as the FPRC became divided in the second half of the year and its coalition with the anti-balaka fell apart, both the FPRC and its close ally the Patriotic Movement for Central Africa (MPC) pulled out of the DDRR process.

Resurgent violence

In the last quarter of 2016, there was a marked escalation in fighting in Central African Republic which continued and worsened in 2017. This resurgence of violence was a result of the collapse of talks between ex-Séléka factions which had been convened by Noureddine Adam, the leader of the FPRC, with the aim both of creating a common strategy vis-à-vis the government and of sharing out territory to resolve competition over local resources. The UPC, an ex-Séléka group established to defend the Fulani population, refused to ally with groups that were attacking Fulani communities and declined to share its extensive control of economic resources. In response, the FPRC and its allies – MPC, the Patriotic Assembly for the Revival of Central Africa (RPRC) and the anti-balaka forces of Maxim Mokom – waged a new war against the UPC.

The confrontations between the two sides came to a head in Bambari in February 2017 when the FPRC-led alliance attacked the city of Bambari, the provincial capital of Ouaka prefecture in the centre of the country which had long been controlled by the UPC and had served as the group's headquarters since the establishment of the UPC in 2014. Tensions and violence increased as more fighters from the FPRC, anti-balaka groups and the MPC filtered into the city, essentially dividing the city in half, with the MINUSCA peacekeeping force separating UPC-controlled Fulani neighbourhoods and the FPRC-led alliance controlling Gula and Runga neighbourhoods. When a large convoy of FPRC fighters tried to move on the city, MINUSCA deployed attack helicopters to prevent their advance, killing the group's chief of staff, Joseph Zoundéko. Eventually MINUSCA forced the departure of both armed factions from Bambari, an outcome that represented a de facto defeat for the UPC as the group lost its headquarters in the city.

In the subsequent months, the two sides clashed sporadically in central and southeastern regions of the country. There were frequent attacks on civilians – both by the UPC on communities linked to anti-balaka groups and by anti-balaka groups on communities linked to the UPC. One of the worst attacks came in May when more than 500 anti-balaka fighters attacked Chadian Arab and Fulani residents of Bangassou, the provincial capital of Mbomou prefecture, at the MINUSCA base and in the Tokoyo district of the city. More than 115 people died in the attack and around 16,000 were forced to flee across the border to Ndu in the Democratic Republic of the Congo, while 2,000 others took shelter in Bangassou's Catholic seminary.

Ethnic divisions

The violence waged against Muslim communities by parts of the FPRC-led alliance, particularly against Chadian Arab communities, caused tensions within the MPC. The MPC had been established in 2015 with the express purpose of protecting Chadian Arab communities from militias linked to other ethnic groups – especially the Christian and animist anti-balaka. Although the alliance gave the MPC much-improved access to military equipment, the MPC found itself partnered with groups that were attacking its very own constituency. This caused rancour within the organisation, prompting a Bangui-based faction of the MPC, led by Mahamat Abdel Karim and Saleh Zabadi, to break away in protest in June.

The attacks on Chadian Arab communities caused similar tensions within the FPRC. A split within the group gradually emerged between the ethnic Runga members of the FPRC's leadership who sought to end the attacks on Muslim communities, most notably FPRC leader Noureddine Adam and chief of staff Abdoulaye Hissène, and the ethnic Gula members of the leadership, principally deputy chief of staff Azor Khalit. From July onwards, the Runga faction came repeatedly into conflict with the FPRC's anti-balaka allies, with clashes taking place across Haute-Kotto, Mbomou and Ouham prefectures. This escalated further in September when fighting broke out within the FPRC in Bria.

The FPRC–Runga faction and the MPC (returning to its mission of protecting the Chadian Arab community) sought to reconcile their differences with the UPC, and in October the groups signed up to an alliance with the FPRC's Abdoulaye Hissène as president and the UPC's Ali Darassa as vice-president. Meanwhile, the FPRC–Gula faction maintained its close ties to Maxim Mokom's anti-balaka faction and the newly established Republican Assembly (RDR) – an anti-balaka faction which had pledged to drive so-called foreign mercenaries out of the country, likely referring to the militias linked to Sahelian ethnic groups as well as fighters from Chad and Sudan which support them. The antagonism between the sides heralded intense fighting in November and December, first around Bria and the Ippy–Bria road, and then around Ippy and the nearby gold mines at Ndassima, where clashes lasted more than a week.

This realignment of rebel forces broadly reflected the Sahel–Savannah ethnic divisions which have long plagued the country (roughly corresponding to the division between peoples belonging the Nilo-Saharan ethnolinguistic group and the Fulani ethnic group on the one hand, and people belonging to the Niger-Congo or Bantu ethnolinguistic group on the other), with the latter contesting the indigeneity of Sahelian communities. These ethnic divisions were reflected in the RDR's anti-foreign-mercenary objective and Maxim Mokom's similar pledge that unless MINUSCA drove 'foreign mercenaries' out of Central African Republic, there would be fighting on a scale to match that of December 2013, when violence was at its worst in the country.

Violence along ethnic lines also flared up sporadically in the northwest of Central African Republic between Fulani herdsmen and sedentary farming communities. Sidiki Abass's 3R group, which formed in late 2015 purportedly to protect the Fulani community in the region, were often brutal in their reprisals for attacks on the Fulani and were frequently involved in intense clashes with local anti-balaka groups. The prefectures of Ouham-Pendé, Nana-Mambéré and Mambéré-Kadeï were all affected by this fighting. Two major flare-ups occurred in the year. In May, 3R laid siege to the town of Niem-Yéléwa, Nana-Mambéré prefecture, but withdrew when presented with an ultimatum by MINUSCA. In October, 3R joined with an MPC splinter group led by Hamed Bahar – the National Movement for the Liberation of Central Africa (MNLC) – and occupied the city of Bocaranga in Ouham-Pendé prefecture; on this occasion, the groups failed to respect a MINUSCA ultimatum for their withdrawal, prompting the UN force to launch a successful offensive to drive them out. The 3R subsequently signed a local ceasefire agreement with anti-balaka groups in Nana-Mambéré, but the MNLC continued its raids in Ouham-Pendé and Ouham prefectures, with violence surging around Paoua at the end of the year.

International support

The strengthening ethnic dimension to the conflict prompted Stephen O'Brien, then UN under-secretary-general for humanitarian affairs, to warn in August that Central African Republic was displaying the 'early warning signs of genocide', although a subsequent fact-finding mission by the UN special adviser on the prevention of genocide concluded that the country did not qualify as being in a pre-genocide situation.

Nevertheless, the UN recognised MINUSCA's failure to stem the escalating violence – a result both of having too few peacekeepers and of many of those peacekeepers being woefully undertrained and underprepared. In June the UN persuaded the Democratic Republic of the Congo to withdraw its troops from the mission, having failed to address their ill-discipline, corruption and human-rights abuses. Following a fact-finding mission to the country in August, UN Under-Secretary-General for Peacekeeping Operations Jean-Pierre Lacroix called for a small number of additional peacekeepers to bolster the MINUSCA force, and his request was subsequently seconded by UN Secretary-General António Guterres following Guterres's visit to Central African Republic. As a result, in November, the UN Security Council renewed MINUSCA's mandate and authorised up to 900 additional peacekeepers, a significant proportion of whom were expected to come from the more capable armed forces of Brazil.

However, MINUSCA faced a serious lack of trust among many in Central African Republic. Christian and animist communities alleged that MINUSCA's large contingents from Muslim-majority (and especially North African) countries were biased in favour of ex-Séléka armed groups, although there was no real evidence for the allegation. In July, thousands demonstrated in Bambari, Ouaka prefecture, calling for the withdrawal of Mauritanian peacekeepers, and in Bria, Haute-Kotto prefecture, thousands called for the departure of the Moroccan contingent. On the basis of the same allegation, anti-balaka groups repeatedly targeted MINUSCA patrols with ambushes. Over the course of the year, 15 MINUSCA personnel were killed.

The gradual reform and strengthening of the Central African Republic Armed Forces (FACA) continued with international support. In May, the government conducted an audit of all FACA units, requiring all officers and soldiers to report for inspection in order to root out 'ghost' soldiers and increase discipline. An estimated 25% of the army (approximately 2,500 men) failed to present themselves, and in June FACA began a series of measures to address the problem. At the same time, the European Union Training Mission proceeded with its work and by the end of 2017 had completed the training of two FACA battalions. President Touadéra called for the international community to support a more rapid expansion of FACA's military capacity but it was unclear how this could be done. In April, the government was forced to deploy FACA units to fill the security vacuum created in the southeast of the country by the withdrawal of the joint US–Ugandan task force which had been engaged against the Lord's Resistance Army (LRA). Contrary to the task force's claim that the group had been defeated, LRA raids and kidnappings had continued, necessitating the intervention of the FACA.

The UN Security Council renewed its arms embargo on the country, despite repeated calls by Central African Republic politicians for it to be lifted so that FACA units could be better armed. After months of lobbying by the Central African Republic government, Russia applied to the Security Council in December for an exemption to supply two FACA battalions with small arms, light weapons and precision-guided munitions, along with ammunition and training on relevant systems. The exemption was subsequently approved and shipments were due to arrive in Central African Republic in early 2018.

Fragile situation

At the end of 2017, there was a very real risk that the progress made to date in stabilising Central African Republic could be reversed. The political situation remained fragile with President Touadéra lacking a strong support base and so far failing to live up to domestic and international hopes for his presidency. Any political upheaval due to a lack of support for Touadéra or the current political settlement could undermine the tentative progress that has been made in establishing the new political institutions (especially those administering security and justice). Only with a stable government in Bangui can state authority be projected, gradually, beyond the capital. Moreover, although progress was made in the training of FACA over the year, it will take many more years to establish a force with an effective presence in all the main population centres of Central African Republic that can provide security and tackle the predation of armed groups.

The underlying drivers of Central African Republic's instability remained. In the absence of a political settlement, militia leaders had every incentive to continue violence in order to maintain both their personal importance and also the standing of their groups in the competition for local resources. Similarly, with no framework to resolve tensions between the nomadic Fulani and Central African Republic's settled communities, violent clashes between these two looked set to continue.

External threats to Central African Republic increased throughout 2017. There was a growing possibility that the situation in neighbouring Democratic Republic of the Congo could escalate into more widespread conflict and spill over into the country. Likewise, the constant potential for flows of fighters and weaponry across the border from South Sudan threatened to fuel the fighting in Central African Republic. While the country remains in a state of conflict with the drivers of instability unresolved, the potential of shocks from outside constitutes a significant threat to the political stability of Central African Republic.

Democratic Republic of the Congo

The year began with a sense of well-founded optimism that the political crises in the Democratic Republic of the Congo could be abated and the country would regain stability in 2017. However, President Joseph Kabila provoked political and armed

Key statistics	2016	2017
Type:	Internationalised	Internationalised
Fatalities:	1,500	2,500
New IDPs:	920,000	2,170,000
New refugees:	40,000	100,000

resistance as it became increasingly clear that the regime was undermining the 2016 Saint Sylvester Agreement by delaying the elections beyond 2017. The government reacted with repression and massive human-rights abuses. In addition, it purpose-fully fostered insecurity and escalated conflicts in order to further delay elections and make itself indispensable. While this tactic increased the suffering of the civilian population – the number of internally displaced persons (IDPs) rose to a staggering 4.1 million – it appeared to work for the regime: Kabila was not only able to cling on to power but also managed to consolidate his position through dismantling the opposition, weakening foreign observers and increasing his control over the secu-rity forces. Nevertheless, there remained a pronounced risk that Kabila could lose control of the situation, leaving the country in danger of reverting to full-blown civil war, which would have serious implications for the wider region.

Corrosion of the Saint Sylvester Agreement

The Congolese constitution specifies that presidents are limited to two terms, according to which Kabila should have stepped down in December 2016. However, instead of organising elections, the government has applied a strategy of adminis-trative delays, widely referred to as *glissement* (slippage). After increasing pressure, Kabila had somewhat surprisingly agreed to many of the opposition's demands in an agreement on 31 December 2016. This Saint Sylvester Agreement stipulated that elections were to take place in 2017 and that until then a transitional government would be formed. During this transition period, Kabila was to remain president but the prime minister was to be nominated by the opposition. After the transi-tion, Kabila was to respect the constitution and not attempt to run for a third term.

Under the leadership of veteran opposition leader Etienne Tshisekedi, the National Council for the Implementation of the Accord and the Electoral Process (CNSA) would supervise and monitor the process.

The implementation of the agreement, however, proved contentious, particularly regarding the division of ministries and the selection of the prime minister. While the presidential majority demanded that the opposition would provide a list of candidates for Kabila to make a choice, the opposition perceived this as an attempt to hand-pick the candidate. The sudden death of the 84-year-old Tshisekedi on 1 February seriously weakened the opposition and gave Kabila the opportunity to undermine the agreement. As the founder and president of the Union for Democracy and Social Progress (UDPS), the Democratic Republic of the Congo's first opposition party, Tshisekedi was an important figure in the country's democratisation process in the 1990s and possessed unique moral authority. Without him, the UDPS lost its capacity for mass mobilisation and ability to put the government under pressure. Factions quickly emerged as many of Tshisekedi's long-term companions disapproved of the appointment of Tshisekedi's son Felix as president of the UDPS and chair of the *Rassemblement* opposition coalition. In March deputy-secretary Bruno Tshibala was expelled from the party, among others, for having contested Felix's succession.

The government subsequently exacerbated and exploited this infighting by co-opting opposition members by offering them government posts. Kabila appointed Tshibala as the new prime minister on 7 April, a selection that formally fulfilled the criteria of the Saint Sylvester Agreement while also increasing the fragmentation of the opposition, as Tshibala no longer belonged to the UDPS and formed a *Rassemblement* splinter group. In a similar fashion, Kabila designated the *Rassemblement* dissident Joseph Olenghankoy as the president of the CNSA in July. As Olenghankoy was formally an opposition member but no longer represented the *Rassemblement*, his nomination further increased fragmentation of the opposition.

In parallel, Kabila's government continued its strategy of postponing the elections, primarily through withholding the election budget and delaying voter registration. On 15 February, Budget Minister Pierre Kangudia stated that the country could not readily afford the elections, estimated to cost US$1.8 billion, because the state's total budget was US$5.2bn. Meanwhile, insecurity disrupted voter registration and gave the government an excuse for further delays. At the beginning of the year, armed groups such as Mai-Mai Guidon and the Front for Patriotic Resistance in Ituri (FRPI) attacked registration centres across North Kivu, South Kivu and Ituri provinces, while the Kamuina Nsapu rebellion in the Kasai region became a major obstacle to elections as the year progressed. On 9 May, Corneille Nangaa, the president of the Independent National Electoral Commission (CENI), stated that violence in the Kasai region was delaying the election process after Kamuina Nsapu fighters allegedly looted six CENI offices and beheaded three election workers. On 7 July, Nangaa announced in Paris that given these security-related delays, elections could not be organised before the end of the year. On 10 October, Nangaa then announced that elections could not take place before April 2019, estimating that finalising voter registration would take another three months, with an additional 16 months to organise the polls. Many saw this as an exaggeration, and therefore as constituting a political move by the supposedly 'independent' Nangaa.

During a visit to the Democratic Republic of the Congo in October, US Ambassador to the United Nations Nikki Haley responded to these political manoeuvres by demanding that elections take place in 2018. Nine days later, CENI promptly published the overdue electoral calendar, setting the date for elections on 23 December 2018. Although the publication of the calendar could be seen as a concession to Haley's resolute demands, many observers criticised it for legiti-mising a delay beyond 2017 in violation of the Sylvester Agreement. There were also concerns that the new calendar would not be upheld and therefore would only serve to buy more time for the government to find a method of remaining in power. Opposition parties such as the UDPS, the Movement for the Liberation of the Congo (MLC) and the Union for the Congolese Nation (UNC) rejected the cal-endar and reiterated their demands that President Kabila must leave office by 31 December 2017, but international bodies such as the UN Security Council and the African Union accepted it, although they highlighted the importance of its timely implementation.

Government repression

In order to bolster its capacity to deal with mass demonstrations, the government 'professionalised' its security forces over the course of 2017 through better pay, training, management and equipment. Kabila ensured that he retained overall control by repeatedly reshuffling the army and police leadership. Among other elements, it was European training and equipment that allowed the security forces to repress demonstrations without necessarily resorting to lethal force. Throughout the year, the police and army obstructed demonstrations by blocking off streets and arresting leaders, while radio, internet and telephone services were suspended during critical periods to hinder communication and the organisational capacity of critics. In combination with the credible threat of lethal force, this combined approach proved successful in discouraging protesters.

No longer able to motivate people to risk their freedom and physical well-being, the opposition and members of civil society began organising general strikes – known as *villes mortes* (dead cities) – which were observed to varying degrees in the country's major cities throughout the year. When the extension period granted by the Sylvester Agreement expired without elections, the dynamics of protests changed yet again, with the Lay Coordination Committee (CLC) – a group associated with the Catholic Church – calling for nationwide protests on 31 December 2017. Despite heavy repression and open threats, protests after Sunday mass succeeded in mobilising tens of thousands of people for the first time since September 2016. The security forces fired tear gas and live ammunition at congregations, killing at least eight and arresting 123, including altar boys and priests. The resulting outrage revitalised the political debate and re-engaged international attention.

Escalating conflicts

Four major trends could be identified in the ongoing conflicts in the eastern provinces of Ituri, North Kivu, South Kivu and Tanganyika. Firstly, fighting often had an ethnic dimension, with self-proclaimed autochthonous tribes – such as Hunde, Kobo Nande and Nyanga – continuing to perpetuate cycles of retaliatory violence against perceived 'foreign invaders' of Rwandan origin in North Kivu. On 17 February, Mai-Mai Mazembe and Nduma Defence of Congo (NDC)–Guidon killed 27 Hutu civilians in Nyanzale, North Kivu. In Tanganyika province, the ethnic violence between the Luba and the Twa continued. On 4 August, a Twa militia attacked the village of Lambukilela in Tanganyika province, killing 55 people and injuring 30. By November, the ethnic violence between Luba and Twa communities had displaced more than 500,000 people since the start of the year, while only 5% of the required humanitarian funding had been raised.

Secondly, armed groups continued to splinter and proliferate. The Congo Research Group at New York University mapped more than 120 armed groups, representing an almost 50% increase since October 2015, in part due to greater military pressure and competition between and within groups. A prominent example was the split of the National Council for Renewal and Democracy (CNRD) from the Democratic Forces for the Liberation of Rwanda (FDLR) in 2016, which caused intra-ethnic fighting between different Hutu groups and furthered their fragmentation. Approximately 15 Hutu-based Nyatura militias took sides in the dispute, although increasingly aligning with the FDLR. On 26 April, clashes between the CNRD and Nyatura militias for control of Kivumbu and Mweso villages in Masisi territory killed 29 civilians in North Kivu province. On 20 December, Nyatura–FDDH (Force for the Defence of Human Rights) leader Kasongo Kalamo was killed during clashes with the FDLR, which also led to the displacement of several thousand people due to fear of retaliatory attacks.

Thirdly, armed groups became increasingly politicised due to the delay in elections and the government's growing illegitimacy, with their rhetoric shifting from the traditional focus against Rwanda to a much more pronounced anti-Kabila stance. Against the general trend of increasing fragmentation, armed groups also formed coalitions against the Kabila government. The most prominent of these was the National People's Coalition for the Sovereignty of the Congo (CNPSC) in South Kivu, a combination of at least 11 Mai-Mai groups under the leadership of William Yakutumba. From June to July, the group seized several towns from the government army. The mining company Banro suspended operations after 23 trucks from a gold mine near the town of Lulimba, Fizi territory, were briefly hijacked but subsequently released. In September, the CNPSC almost succeeded in taking the province's second largest town, Uvira – only decisive intervention by the United Nations Organization Stabilization Mission in the Democratic Republic of the Congo (MONUSCO) halted the advance.

Fourthly, there was a dramatic increase in the number of attacks against UN peacekeeping personnel, although the perpetrators of the attacks were not always known and their motivation was often unclear. Some of the attacks seemed to have been conducted because the UN was supporting (and often directly operating with) Congolese troops. However, the possibility remained that the government was also involved in the attacks in order to discourage MONUSCO from becoming too involved in sensitive matters. The unprecedented (and unresolved) killing in March 2017 of two UN experts in Central Kasai province (who had come to the region to investigate the violence and human-rights abuses), together with their translator and drivers, deeply unsettled international observers in the country and raised concerns about further attacks against civilian personnel. In an unrelated incident on 6 October, approximately 30 Mai-Mai Mazembe fighters attacked a MONUSCO base in Lubero, North Kivu, although in this instance the blue helmets were able to repel the attackers, killing five. More deadly were attacks by the Allied Democratic Forces (ADF) on peacekeepers. On 17 September, an attack (allegedly by the ADF) on a Congolese army position in Beni territory killed one Tanzanian peacekeeper. On 9 October, ADF elements allegedly attacked a MONUSCO base in Mamundioma 30 kilometres northeast of Beni, resulting in the deaths of two Tanzanian peacekeepers. However, the deadliest attack on blue helmets in the Democratic Republic of the Congo to date occurred on 7 December, when 15 Tanzanian peacekeepers were killed at Semuliki base. The UN and the Congolese government quickly blamed the ADF, although several factors cast doubt on the conclusion. The attack was, for instance, well organised and sustained with heavy weaponry – not the modus operandi of the ADF, whose fighters tend to operate in small groups armed with machetes and AK-47 rifles. The group has also been weakened by the recent *Operation Sokola I* conducted by the army and MONUSCO. Observers therefore assumed that if the perpetrators belonged to the ADF, they must have received support from third parties in the execution of these attacks. In a report published in September, the Congo Research Group uncovered that the ADF had cooperated with a myriad of other armed groups and the army between 2014 and 2016 in conducting massacres against civilians in Beni. It would therefore appear that the ADF collaborated with other armed groups, but also – and more damagingly for the UN – potentially with the army as well.

New violence in the Kasai region

In addition to the deteriorating security situation in the east, new areas of insecurity emerged in the formerly peaceful central and western areas of the Democratic

Republic of the Congo. Although the Kamuina Nsapu rebellion – named after the traditional leader who was killed by the government in a power dispute in Kasai-Central province – began in August 2016, the brunt of the fighting and its humanitarian consequences only developed throughout 2017. The rebellion continued to spread to Kasai, Kasai-Oriental, Lomami and Sankuru provinces through loosely connected militia groups, which heavily relied on the recruitment of children and disenfranchised youth.

During the first half of the year, Kamuina Nsapu elements stepped up their attacks against state agents. On 24 March, rebels ambushed a police convoy on the road between Tshikapa and Kananga and beheaded 42 of the officers. The security forces responded with military operations that were characterised by disproportionate force, including the summary execution of rebels and those associated with them. Between 9 and 13 February, Congolese soldiers killed at least 101 people, including 39 women, during operations against the Kamuina Nsapu militia in Dibaya territory, Kasai-Central province. Although the government denied these deeds, videos on social media provided evidence that Congolese soldiers had indiscriminately fired on unarmed civilians, drawing international attention to the excessive violence. The UN documented 87 mass graves in the course of the year, particularly in Kasai-Central and Kasai-Oriental provinces, apparently dug by the army and police to eliminate evidence of the operations.

The army also mobilised and equipped local ethnic minorities (the Pende, the Tetela and the Tshockwe) in the form of a militia called Bana Mura to fight the Kamuina Nsapu. Members of this militia not only operated with the utmost brutality (often mutilating their victims), but also increased the inter-ethnic dimension of the violence. While the authorities immediately blamed the Kamuina Nsapu militia for the killing of the two members of the UN group of experts in March, and subsequently hindered international investigations, Radio France Internationale (RFI) research later suggested government involvement.

In parallel to the strategy of excessive force, the government returned the remains of Kamuina Nsapu to his family in April, and recognised his successor, Jacques Kabeya Ntumba, as the customary chief. The government also tried to negotiate with the loosely connected militia leaders, but without direct connections or command-and-control structures, the decentralised groups continued fighting for several months. On 21 April, the UN Office for the Coordination of Humanitarian Affairs announced that more than one million civilians, including many women and children, had been displaced as a result of violence in the Kasai region. During 1–8 May alone, 100,000 people were displaced in the central region of the Democratic Republic of the Congo. From March onwards, up to 50,000 Congolese refugees fled to Angola, which prompted the Angolan government to pressure Kabila to stabilise the situation.

The government increasingly regained control of the Kasai provinces in the second half of the year. Schools and hospitals reopened, and MONUSCO deployments encouraged the return of refugees and IDPs. However, the return of IDPs sparked new tensions as villages had ethnically restructured during the conflict: in some areas, the lasting effect of the Kamuina Nsapu and Bana Mura militias compounded ethnic divisions and hampered the return of displaced people. In addition, the humanitarian crisis worsened further as villagers had been unable to access their fields for several months, with 2.8m people facing critical levels of food insecurity. In total, 1.5m people were displaced by the violence in the Kasai region, while the number of deaths was estimated at 1,400.

Limited foreign influence

International criticism of the Congolese government increased in 2017 due to concerns over the government's destabilising behaviour and the potential consequences for the country and wider region. On 15 June, former secretary-general of the UN Kofi Annan and a group of elder statesmen called for peaceful transition in the Democratic Republic of the Congo. However, as advocacy did not appear to have a major effect through the year, the international community resorted to sanctioning individuals responsible for repression and excessive violence, particularly in the Kasai area. On 29 May, the European Union imposed a travel ban and asset freeze on nine members of the government for 'obstruction of the electoral process and related human rights violations'. The US followed suit and imposed sanctions on Kabila's top military adviser, General François Olenga, on 1 June. When these sanctions failed to change the rationale of the regime, civil-society and human-rights organisations demanded that sanctions be widened to include people in Kabila's inner circle, who wield great influence despite not necessarily holding political office.

However, although the EU and US repeatedly alluded to further sanctions, they did not follow through. EU member states were divided on the issue of sanctions, reportedly because of French, Spanish and Italian business interests. Compared to the Obama administration, Donald Trump's government has, unsurprisingly, shown less interest in the Democratic Republic of the Congo and remained somewhat unsteady in its engagement. However, on 22 December the US did impose sanctions on the Israeli businessman Dan Gertler, a close friend of Kabila who is responsible for corrupt business deals which have cost the country at least US$1.3bn in revenues. Given that Gertler has provided Kabila with illicit funds since 2001, these sanctions could mean that Kabila might run into difficulties maintaining his war chest for the election challenge. It may be in this context that the government is revising its mineral taxes and royalties.

The government pushed back strongly against international interference in 2017 by stressing its right to national sovereignty, with former colonial power Belgium bearing the brunt of the government's intransigence. When Belgian Foreign Minister Didier Reynders stated on 8 April that the nomination of Bruno Tshibala as prime minister violated the letter and spirit of the Sylvester Agreement, the Congolese government responded by suspending its military cooperation with Belgium. While some of these measures had negative consequences for Congolese citizens, they also appear to have led Belgium to be more cautious in its approach. The Congolese government also engaged in clever diplomacy with its continental neighbours, who proved receptive to arguments of African solidarity and sovereignty, and tended to prefer constructive engagement over punitive sanctions. Kabila was also able to count on old supporters in key states, such as Angola, South Africa and Zimbabwe. On 20 August, during its 37th summit and under the leadership of South African President Jacob Zuma, the Southern African Development Community formally accepted delaying the elections beyond 2017.

The government also hindered the work of journalists and UN human-rights investigators by impeding their access to conflict areas, such as the Kasai region, as well as hospitals and morgues. It also expelled the most critical and competent international experts, such as Human Rights Watch's Central Africa Director Ida Sawyer, RFI's Kinshasa correspondent Sonja Rolley and Belgian Congo expert Kris Berwouts.

UN peacekeeping

MONUSCO had a particularly challenging year, encountering substantial resistance and intimidation from the Congolese government. The mission appeared reluctant to confront the government in the face of Congolese demands to reduce the troop ceiling and the looming threat of the government withdrawing host-nation consent. It was also difficult for the mission to cooperate with Congolese authorities given the latter's human-rights abuses: in many instances cooperation with military and police had to be reduced or cancelled, but without its Congolese partners, MONUSCO had little chance of undertaking its tasks and fulfilling its mandate.

The spread of violent conflicts and the emergence of new threats, including political violence, required the mission to do more while covering a wider area. Logistically, MONUSCO had to support the voter-registration process and redeploy to the Kasai region and Kinshasa. Instead of being supported to face these numerous challenges, MONUSCO suffered heavy cuts to its troop and budget, mainly due to the political priorities of the new US administration. With the renewal of its mandate at the end of March, MONUSCO's troop ceiling was cut from 19,815 to 16,215. As there were only in fact 16,893 troops deployed, the reduction was largely symbolic, but 600 troops still had to be cut, while a request to increase the number of trained police officers by 320 was denied. MONUSCO's new budget, agreed on at the UN General Assembly in July, also entailed cuts amounting to 8.5%, which contradicted the extensive tasks of the new mandate the mission was given by the UN Security Council. The mission responded by closing five bases in North Kivu and repatriating a full Indian battalion of 727 soldiers. Four additional companies (comprising 960 troops) were repatriated in October.

As mentioned above, the killing of the two UN experts in March and the attack in December that killed 15 Tanzanian peacekeepers deeply troubled MONUSCO. However, while both incidents were likely to make the UN even more careful and restrained, they also sparked a reflection on the performance and the use of violence by peacekeepers, culminating in the Cruz Report published at the end of the year. While these discussions are ongoing, the nomination of Leila Zerrougui as the head of mission on 27 December also raised hopes that the new leadership of MONUSCO would be able to achieve better results. Zerrougui – who previously served as deputy head of mission in the Democratic Republic of the Congo between 2008 and 2012 and special representative for children in armed conflict between 2012 and 2016 – had co-developed many of MONUSCO's protection tools and is widely respected for her experience and capacity.

The events of 2017 made it clear that the government was determined and willing to use any means necessary to retain power. Given the current situation, observers should recognise that a proper electoral process and the country's stability might not be attainable simultaneously. The large-scale demonstrations organised by the CLC on 31 December, however, provide a window of opportunity for decisive engagement by the international stakeholders. If this occasion is missed, the country's political crisis will be perpetuated at the expense of democracy, human rights and the country's population.

Lake Chad Basin

Boko Haram remained a major security concern in northeastern Nigeria and the wider Lake Chad basin in 2017, consistently proving that official statements regarding its 'defeat' were premature, although the Nigerian Army and a number of

Key statistics	2016	2017
Type:	Internationalised	Internationalised
Fatalities:	3,000	3,500
New IDPs:	790,000	420,000
New refugees:	80,000[a]	26,000[a]

other security actors did bring some semblance of stability to the region. The defining feature of the conflict in 2017 was the continuation of the shift in the tactics of Boko Haram towards suicide bombings and small, highly localised attacks, contrasting with the group's extensive territorial campaign in 2014 and early 2015. However, the Nigerian Army was partially responsible for the increased readiness of ground forces who managed to limit Boko Haram's cross-border activity. The government also sought to address the impact of the insurgency on internally displaced persons (IDPs) and the human-security challenge in general, working with international partners such as the United States and United Kingdom to stabilise the country. The army was also involved in a programme to reintegrate ex-Boko Haram fighters into their local communities.

Changing tactics

Whereas Boko Haram displayed less territorial ambition in 2017, the group demonstrated that it still remained a threat to military deployments. There were several incidents involving Boko Haram attacking military locations over the course of the year, including an attack at Buni Yadi, Borno State, in which at least five Nigerian Army soldiers and a captain were killed while repelling the insurgents. A spate of attacks by the group towards the end of the year contributed to the dismissal of Major-General Ibrahim Attahiru in December 2017; Attahiru had only held the post of theatre commander in northeast Nigeria since May 2017. Leading operations against Boko Haram remained one of the most difficult military appointments in Nigeria, with more than a half-dozen commanders dismissed or posted out from the role since military operations began in June 2011.

Maiduguri, the capital city of Borno State in northeast Nigeria, remained the epicentre of Boko Haram's activity: the city has witnessed more insurgency-related fatalities than any other location. Maiduguri's high fatality count is due in part to the record numbers of IDPs who have relocated to its makeshift humanitarian camps to escape Boko Haram. The group, however, has correspondingly broadened its attacks in Maiduguri and elsewhere to include vulnerable IDP camps along with markets, public centres and mosques. The IDP camps in Maiduguri were particularly vulnerable, being overcrowded and lacking sufficient security. Large urban centres such as Damaturu and Mubi in Yobe State and relatively well-populated rural townships such as Konduga and Magumeri in Borno State also suffered high numbers of Boko Haram attacks throughout 2017. Fatalities related to Boko Haram attacks were, however, lower in the neighbouring countries of Chad, Niger and Cameroon, which Boko Haram had previously targeted with great success.

Although statistically Boko Haram's attacks in 2017 leaned towards armed assaults – with 90 armed assaults compared to 59 suicide attacks – the year witnessed the intensification of the group's tendency to use suicide bombers. Although this may be due in part to the fact that suicide attacks tend to yield a higher fatality count, the decision may also have been driven by strategic necessity. In Maiduguri, where the Nigerian Army had its 7 Division Garrison and the highest concentration of forces in the country, Boko Haram was forced to increase dependence on suicide attacks (which are more difficult to guard against than armed assaults), leading to a higher ratio of suicide attacks in Maiduguri compared to elsewhere in northeast Nigeria. The group's attacks in bordering countries were also mostly suicide attacks.

Boko Haram increasingly used female suicide bombers for attacks. While the tactic itself was not new, it became more pronounced in 2017: within the space of a week in January, two attacks involving female bombers were recorded. Although the tactic might seem unexpected – Boko Haram's fighters are predominantly male and female suicide bombers tend to detonate their suicide vests less frequently – the relative ease with which female bombers could access even hardened locations offered a key advantage in executing attacks. This insight has even led to men dressing up as women in some suicide-bombing attempts. Females were not the only demographic which Boko Haram turned to for its suicide bombings, however, with the group also using child bombers. Children employed as suicide bombers appeared even more innocuous than women: even when Nigerian security forces identified the threat, this category of person-borne improvised explosive device (IED) continued to be more efficacious than adult bombers, male or female. The use of female and child suicide bombers was also particularly prominent in Cameroon's Far North region.

It was also likely that Boko Haram's technical proficiency in bomb-making improved over the year. On 21 November, a teenager mingling with worshippers at a mosque in Mubi, Adamawa State, detonated a suicide bomb during early-morning prayers that left 58 dead and several more injured. The incident marked the highest number of casualties resulting from a single suicide attack all year. The nature of the attack demonstrated Boko Haram's careful planning, exploitation of the youth element in its operations and proficiency in bomb-making.

In employing female suicide bombers in 2017, Boko Haram relied on a tactic that redressed the asymmetry between its conventional standing army and the forces of Nigeria and its allies. Throughout the year, suicide bombings rendered the army's extensive formations and capabilities largely ineffective, as well as making the counter-insurgency campaign highly cost-ineffective. Boko Haram's irregular threat therefore became the Nigerian Army's main preoccupation between 2016 and 2017 as part of a seemingly ever-expanding counter-insurgency campaign against it. The threat was made more complex by the continued activity of the Islamic State's West Africa Province (ISWAP) group – the faction of Boko Haram currently led by Abu Musab al-Barnawi which broke away from the group in 2016 and aligned itself with the Islamic State, also known as ISIS or ISIL – which carried out multiple attacks throughout the year. ISWAP demonstrated its resilience and continued to pose a potent threat nationally and regionally, even if 2017 did not see any significant internationalisation of the threat. The group remained focused largely on attacking military installations and bases, mostly avoiding civilian targets (reportedly due to ideological reasons).

Countering Boko Haram's insurgency

There were several developments in the command structure and deployments of security actors tasked with fighting Boko Haram in 2017. The presence of 8 Task Force Division – the new division created by the Nigerian Army in 2016 and head-quartered at Monguno, Borno State – relieved some administrative and operational tasks from 7 Division, which had been tasked with countering Boko Haram since 2013. The location of 8 Task Force Division further north in Borno enabled faster redeployment of outfield units to remote towns and communities, while its use of minesweeping vehicles, rapid-response units and the creation of several new task-force battalions indicated that the new task force had hit the ground running. The army also worked with international actors, with the UK the primary military train-ing partner to Nigeria in 2017, and the only Western country with a significant and ongoing assistance programme. (In total, around 22,000 Nigerian military personnel have been trained by British forces between 2015 and 2017.)

However, although the Nigerian Army was the spearhead of the counter-insurgency (COIN) operation against Boko Haram in 2017, other security actors also played an instrumental role in securing northeast Nigeria throughout the year. The Mobile Police (MOPOL) – the paramilitary section of the Nigeria Police Force (NPF) – played an increasingly front-line role throughout 2017, with units deployed in Damaturu (Yobe State) and Maiduguri and Bama (Borno State). Other civilian and paramilitary security groups also assisted the COIN effort throughout the year. On 4 June 2017, the Borno section of the Nigerian Security and Civil Defence Corps

(NSCDC) in Borno State announced that 600 of its security operatives had been deployed to protect areas of worship during the holy month of Ramadan.

The vigilante group the Civilian Joint Task Force (CJTF) was particularly prominent in the fight against Boko Haram. On 30 June 2017, the Borno chapter of the CJTF revealed that around 680 of its vigilantes had lost their lives in their contribution to the counter-insurgency effort against Boko Haram since 2012. The large number of lives lost by this actor – far more than any other group except the Nigerian Army and the NPF, and more than even MOPOL – was an indication of the importance of the role that the CJTF has played in helping secure northeast Nigeria from Boko Haram.

The Multinational Joint Task Force (MJTF) – a regional formation comprising troops from Benin, Cameroon, Chad, Niger and Nigeria – continued to be a major actor in the counterinsurgency efforts. Cameroonian forces participated in several joint clearance operations along the Nigeria–Cameroon border.

The human-security challenge

Aside from the constant military threat of Boko Haram attacks, a separate range of socio-economic issues contributed to the human-security challenge in northeast Nigeria in 2017. The household fishing economy that sustained the northeastern areas of the region adjoining Lake Chad remained under Boko Haram's control or influence in 2017, with taxation imposed by the group forcing many fishers – both men and women – to flee to IDP camps further inland. For the fourth consecutive year, farmers were unable to return to their local farming grounds for the planting season due to the conflict. This forced displacement of farmers and fishers served to erode food security further, with the reduced populations and deserted towns encouraging Boko Haram to make more daring raids and stake claims to the abandoned areas. Even within the IDP camps, however, displaced persons remained at risk, not only from starvation and disease but also from Boko Haram, which repeatedly attempted to carry out suicide bombings and gun attacks on resident IDPs and humanitarian workers at the camps. This combination of factors created a situation whereby IDPs were both insecure in-camp yet unable to return home due to a reduction in viable livelihoods as well as the persistent threat posed by Boko Haram.

Nevertheless, there was some progress regarding the numbers of IDPs in Borno between 2015 and 2017. With the number of new IDPs increasing at a much-reduced rate compared to the previous two years, the government's priority was to ensure that the existing 2.5 million IDPs (housed mainly in Borno State) had the healthcare, food and accommodation required to stabilise the IDP population in temporary camps, as the Nigerian Army tried in parallel to stabilise the communities from which these groups had been displaced. The plan is for these groups eventually to relocate to their homes once it is safe to do so. The practicalities of some IDPs returning home – something unthinkable when Boko Haram contested or controlled much larger tracts of territory between 2014 and 2015 – were also explored. Within the first week of the year, the Yobe State government began organising safety and awareness training for returning IDPs that enabled them to identify IEDs planted by Boko Haram. The increased hope of displacement reversals was made possible by the Nigerian Army's progress in stabilising some of the areas most affected by the insurgency in the country's northeast. In Borno State, the government earmarked NGN4 billion (US$13m) for road construction and reconstruction, particularly around Sambisa Forest and border communities that had been controlled by Boko Haram but were subsequently liberated by the army.

However, the success of the task of caring for this large IDP population – and eventually helping them return home – will depend not only on the Nigerian government but also on strategic partners such as international governmental and non-governmental organisations (NGOs). In 2017, the US Agency for International Development's Office of Transition Initiatives (USAID OTI) recognised Nigeria as one of the US government's most strategic allies in sub-Saharan Africa and launched the Nigeria Regional Transition Initiative to help communities return to their homes. Overall, the US remained one of the largest providers of non-military aid to Nigeria in 2017, but other non-US humanitarian programmes also made essential contributions to the human-security landscape in northeast Nigeria throughout the year. In April 2017, the UK launched the North East Transition to Development Programme (NENTAD), a five-year initiative run by the UK's Department for International Development. The policy's primary goal was to deliver an adequate response to those impacted in the North East geographic zone by providing humanitarian assistance (nutrition and food security), multi-sector support (health, water, shelter and livelihood), efficient crisis response and strengthened government planning. NENTAD also included various implementing organisations, such as the International Committee of the Red Cross and UNICEF. In 2017, Nigeria also became a pilot country for the Global Community Engagement and Resilience Fund, a global public–private partnership that supports local initiatives in strengthening resilience against violent-extremist agendas by combining security and development.

The Nigerian government in 2017 also took a more hands-on approach towards working with other international human-security programmes by establishing the Presidential Committee on the North East Initiative (PCNI) to address the human-security challenge of Boko Haram's insurgency. The PCNI laid the strategic framework for the rebuilding and recovery of the North East region through humanitarian relief, socio-economic stabilisation and the return and resettlement of IDPs. The policy also provided a guiding document – known as the Buhari Plan, named after President Muhammadu Buhari – for local or foreign interventions in the region by coordinating the activities of all stakeholders. Both NENTAD and the USAID OTI programme fall under the Buhari Plan.

The Nigerian Armed Forces also engaged in human-security initiatives. For instance, in June 2017, the Nigerian Air Force conducted a medical outreach programme for IDPs in Mainok, Benishek and Jakana, in Borno State, in which air-force personnel provided civilians and IDPs with free health screenings, medicine and eyewear. As part of the Nigerian Army's *Operation Safe Corridor*, repentant ex-Boko Haram fighters were taken through 16 weeks of a deradicalisation programme. The first stage of rehabilitation would consist of ex-fighters on the programme enrolling at a specialist centre in the northeastern state of Gombe. Following completion of deradicalisation at the centre, ex-fighters would receive the necessary vocational training to enable them to earn livelihoods upon reintroduction to society; some of the skills offered included soap-making and farming. The final step of the deradicalisation and reintegration programme would see ex-combatants handed over to the governments in their states of origin, with the aim of eventually having them reunite with their families while also having the skills to earn a livelihood rather than see insurgency as a viable means of economic sustenance. The first 254 fighters registered by the army began the programme in the final quarter of 2017 and were due to finish by mid-January 2018, whereupon they would be reintegrated into society.

The year 2017 demonstrated that the conflict in northeast Nigeria was at a stalemate. On the one hand, the Nigerian Army made considerable gains in stabilising the northeast and the government temporarily housed IDPs, while other actors such as the CJTF and NGOs all played roles in improving the region's humanitarian crisis. On the other hand, Boko Haram remained far from technically defeated, as President Buhari claimed in December 2015. Rather, Boko Haram – by shifting its tactics towards suicide bombing using women and children and focusing on fighting a bush war rather than hoping to control large swathes of territory – forced a permanent presence of Nigerian security forces in areas that could not be completely secured against the threat of suicide bombings and hit-and-run attacks.

Mali (The Sahel)

Mali saw a great coalescence of forces in 2017 which threatened more violence for the years to come. Both terrorist and counter-terrorist groups consolidated during the year: four influential terrorist organisations amalgamated to

Key statistics	2016	2017
Type:	Internationalised	Internationalised
Fatalities:	600	900
New IDPs:	6,500	35,000
New refugees:	12,000	– [b]

form Jamaat Nusrat al-Islam wal Muslimeen (JNIM) in March, and a transnational counter-terrorism task force began operations in October. The greater focus on these pressing issues, however, meant that related problems in the humanitarian and security spheres were insufficiently addressed by national and international governments. Most notably, the humanitarian crisis remained in stasis during the year and the lack of access for humanitarian actors indicated it was likely to get worse in the future. The United Nations demonstrated broad support for security-related measures in Mali and across the Sahel, but its mission in the country continued to lack sufficient resources to fully support its broad mandate. Though parts of the Algiers Accord were realised this year – most notably the installation of interim authorities and the creation of mixed joint patrols – progress was offset by serious security incidents and a lack of movement on key issues. Finally, state legitimacy and domestic politics stagnated in 2017, with no meaningful progress achieved in either building better governance across the country or guaranteeing safe and secure elections.

Joint Force of the G5 Sahel (FC-G5S)

Recognising the growing threat of terrorist activity in the area to peace and development efforts, the Sahel countries (Burkina Faso, Chad, Niger, Mali and Mauritania) announced in January their intention to form a regional coalition to combat transnational terrorism. The initiative received widespread support from across the globe, and the UN Security Council sanctioned the force on 21 June, passing a resolution unanimously. In the face of mobile terrorist forces, often operating out of highly remote, ungoverned areas of the desert, it was thought that a joint task force could provide additional resources to the fight against extremism. It would also allow greater flexibility for countermeasures, as the task force would not be beholden to international borders.

The joint task force, known as the Joint Force of the G5 Sahel (FC-G5S), was officially mandated to combat terrorism and drug trafficking; contribute to the restoration of state authority and the return of displaced persons and refugees; facilitate humanitarian operations and the delivery of aid to vulnerable populations as far as possible; and contribute to the implementation of development strategies in the Sahel. The primary focus of the force, however, was likely to be almost solely combatting terrorism and drug trafficking. The force consisted of 5,000 military and civilian personnel contributed from the G5, and its headquarters (located just outside of Mopti in central Mali) began operations in October.

While supporters of the FC-G5S, notably France, highlighted its usefulness in combatting terrorism and injecting further resources into unstable areas, the force may experience funding difficulties in the years to come. The United States and the United Kingdom blocked the force from gaining access to UN funds upon its inception. Instead, the joint force was emphasised as a Sahelian responsibility, despite the recognition of the far-reaching effects of instability in West and North Africa. Nevertheless, the G5 was able to source the required capital to fund the first full year of operations by early December.

The creation of the force and its subsequent reception demonstrated the emphasis both the region and the international community were putting on security issues in the Sahel, as well as their commitment to the cause. The establishment of the FC-G5S stemmed from the recognition that security issues in West Africa have a widespread effect and must be dealt with. Simultaneously, it was also a tacit recognition that existent counter-terrorism efforts, mostly undertaken by French forces in *Operation Barkhane* or by the UN Multidimensional Integrated Stabilization Mission in Mali (MINUSMA), had inadequate mandates and resources to effectively deal with the terrorism threats in the region. However, programmes such as the FC-G5S risk exacerbating the trend of prioritising security considerations over all other development and socio-economic factors. While funding and media attention are devoted to counter-terrorism, there can be little recognition of the issues that helped create security concerns in the first place.

Jamaat Nusrat al-Islam wal Muslimeen (JNIM)

In perhaps the most alarming development concerning the growing jihadist movement in Mali since 2013, four of the largest and most influential terrorist groups operating in the Sahel merged into one. Prior to the merger, Ansar Dine, the Macina Liberation Front (MLF), al-Mourabitoun and al-Qaeda in the Islamic Maghreb (AQIM) were separately responsible for more than 250 attacks across the Sahel region in 2016. Al-Mourabitoun was also responsible for the deadliest terrorist incident of 2017, in which a suicide bomber attacked a military base preparing for joint patrols with signatories of the Algiers Accord outside of Gao on 18 January. The attack killed approximately 60 people. With the formation of Jamaat Nusrat al-Islam wal Muslimeen in March, these disparate groups pooled their resources and influence over a far wider territory. As their constituent groups did before, JNIM officially pledged allegiance to al-Qaeda worldwide.

While in the past the component groups of JNIM funded themselves through a combination of looting and kidnapping, in December the Center on Sanctions and Illicit Finances identified the illegal drug trade as an increasingly important source of finance. Notably, the group tended to tax drug routes running through its territory, rather than participate in the sale of drugs directly. Consequently, a greater government and security-services presence (including, for example, an effective G5

Sahel Force) in regions with a large extremist element could help limit funding for JNIM and related jihadist groups.

JNIM conducted a number of bold and successful attacks throughout northern and central Mali in 2017. While the group appeared to target foreign personnel – one of its preferred methods was burying explosive devices to use on army or UN convoys, or even humanitarian actors – its consolidated influence, power and resources were used against targets in the Malian army viciously, often through the use of suicide bombers and armed assaults. JNIM also continued to attack high-profile international targets, including those within MINUSMA and places frequented by foreign civilians. The most well known of these attacks occurred in June, just outside Bamako, when a French-Malian resort popular with expats was attacked by gunmen, leaving five dead. JNIM's terror campaign undermined peace and development efforts, and consequently aid organisations were increasingly abandoning northern and central regions in the name of safety by the end of the year.

Humanitarian situation

The G5 Sahel Force, if effective in combatting drug trafficking and terrorism across the Sahel, may prove to be an excellent friend to the humanitarian community. At the close of 2017, international aid was increasingly under threat and organisations were either limited in the help they could provide to vulnerable populations or forced to pull out of regions entirely.

In 2017 there were double the number of attacks targeting humanitarian workers than in 2016. Between January and September 100 cases of aggression against humanitarian actors were registered, compared to 36 over the same period in the previous year. Of these incidents, 97 took place in northern and central Mali. Notably, 75% of incidents were related to robbery, carjacking and physical aggression, as opposed to ideological or extremist attacks. According to the UN Office for the Coordination of Humanitarian Affairs, humanitarian actors were primarily targeted for their vehicles and personal property, though incidents were becoming progressively more violent.

In light of the danger to personnel and resources, some aid organisations were closing operations in the north as well as central Mali. Many of these organisations provided necessary goods and services in areas where the government enjoyed little to no presence, and left a significant service void with their departure. This had serious consequences for vulnerable populations, but also put greater strain on the military and security forces in the region. The security services may be forced to mitigate the resultant shortfall, or contend with an increasingly desperate and distrustful local population. In areas such as Kidal, which saw significant armed clashes in 2017, humanitarian access was further limited because the airport had been out of service since 2016. Only MINUSMA could fly in and out of Kidal, putting the onus of any development or aid project on the overstretched UN mission.

The results of constricted humanitarian space were clear: despite consistent effort and continued funding since 2013, few meaningful gains had been won in improving the humanitarian and socio-economic situation for the vast majority of Malians. An estimated 20% of the population remained food insecure, and roughly 1.2 million required greater support for accessing clean water. The refugee crisis remained a destabilising force across the region but particularly in Mali – between 2013 and 2017, 498,000 internally displaced persons returned to their homes and 61,000 were repatriated. While this strained local and regional governance, challenges remained ahead. As of November 2017, 59,000 people were internally displaced, and roughly 142,000 Malians were living in refugee camps in neighbouring countries, particularly in Niger, Mauritania and Burkina Faso. If the security situation stabilises sufficiently for these refugees to return home, societal structures must be strengthened to support such an influx of vulnerable people.

Given the humanitarian challenges and the fact that international aid was likely to be strained further due to continuing instability, the limited funding provided by international organisations and governments was worrying. Only 38% of the funds requested by the Humanitarian Response Plan 2017 was received, out of a total request of US$305m. This ratio was consistent with a trend of steadily decreasing funds in the years after the height of the crisis in 2013, when US$265m was provided. In 2014, this dropped slightly to US$239m, but 2015 saw a further drop to US$132m. In 2016 funds remained steady at US$136m, but as of November 2017, only US$115m had been provided. Simultaneously, requests for funding have increased annually since 2013.

International engagement

The international community become more involved with affairs in Mali and throughout the Sahel in 2017. Early on in Secretary-General António Guterres's tenure, the UN agreed to sanction individuals and groups who were actively hindering the peace agreement. There was vocal support for the FC-G5S from the entirety of the Security Council, and representatives from UN headquarters as well as MINUSMA spoke on the links between instability in the Sahel and wars and extremism in Iraq and Syria.

Although members of the international community outwardly and vocally recognised the importance of securing the Sahel, this support only somewhat translated into action. The UN Security Council, based on the votes of the US and the UK, denied the FC-G5S UN resources. While the US and the UK were in support of the joint task force, it was considered to be a West African project and thus to be maintained and funded by the five countries of the Sahel. This approach risked the coalition not being able to sustain the required resources – Mauritania and Chad experienced fewer terrorism-related activities than Mali, Niger and Burkina Faso, and all five countries experienced differing humanitarian and governance challenges, so such an expensive task force may not always remain the priority for all of them. Nevertheless, the UN did vote to provide logistical support to the task force, namely supplies and evacuation support to missions occurring within Mali.

While providing this additional support may help the FC-G5S become more effective, it also risked overstretching MINUSMA even further. The mission lacks sufficient materiel and funding itself, and is put under further pressure by the absence of partner humanitarian organisations in highly unstable regions.

Implementing the Algiers Accord

There was progress in 2017 in realising a few conditions of the Algiers Accord, but the implementation of the peace agreement left much to be desired. Successes were finally achieved in installing interim authorities in northern regions, and in operationalising patrols comprised of fighters from all signatory groups to protect cities and towns against bandits and alleged terrorists. Nevertheless, the stalled disarmament, demobilisation and reintegration (DDR) process continued to create tensions between signatory rebel groups, the government and international actors.

Furthermore, the repatriation of refugees was a critical condition of supporting a proper and functional democracy, and the continued refugee crisis allowed opposition and rebel groups to cast doubt on the Malian government's legitimacy.

Any success towards implementing the peace agreement, however, was largely overshadowed by the widespread insecurity in the country. The installation of interim authorities, for example, was met with mass protest in some cities. As such, the achievement of the Algiers Accord's aims did not translate into a strong increase of belief in the peace process.

Most ominously, the peace process broke down over the summer due to the continued conflict between pro-government Platform and rebel Coordination of Movements for the Azawad (CMA) fighters in Kidal. Beginning in July, clashes killed dozens of fighters and civilians and injured more than 40 people. A two-week ceasefire was signed on 23 August and a peace and reconciliation agreement on 20 September, which brought the fighting to an official close. Though the breakdown of previous agreements indicated how divided signatories to the Algiers Accord were, the eventual return of rebel parties to the negotiating table also demonstrated that the political will for peace, though frail, still exists.

Given the growing focus on transnational counter-terrorism efforts and the influence and power of terrorist organisations in 2017, the exclusion of extremism and terrorism from all considerations in the Algiers Accord and in official negotiations seemed increasingly short-sighted. Over the summer, a meeting on the progress of the Accord saw all signatory rebel groups, including the pro-government Self-Defence Group of Imrad Tuareg and Allies (GATIA), express sincere concern about the viability of peace if the considerations of terrorist fighters were not included. Counter-terrorism strategies were designed to better secure the countryside and ensure tactics like DDR could be implemented without incident, but failed to take into account the popularity and influence of terrorist groups. Extremist fighters in Mali were entirely excluded from the peace process, despite their growing numbers, which was unlikely to quell their grievances or promote lasting unity and peace. Striking a balance between combatting the structural issues that promote radicalism and refusing to negotiate with terrorists was a challenging task, but needed to be recognised by the international community in Mali if the peace agreement was to survive in the long term.

Elections

At the close of 2017, national politics was gearing up for the 2018 national election. Incumbent president Ibrahim Boubacar Keïta (IBK) was widely expected to run for a second and last term, but his government experienced consistent challenges in 2017 which indicated discontent among both governing and opposition members of parliament and the people. Most notably, a constitutional referendum had been planned for 9 July which would both create new regions in the north as per the Algiers Accord and enhance the powers of the president. Multiple parties in coalition with IBK's Rally for Mali party requested delays, and the announcement of the referendum was met with mass protests in Bamako and across the country. The government responded by delaying the referendum indefinitely. IBK's administration and the Malian government more broadly continued to struggle with the eroding legitimacy of the state in 2017, as promises went unfulfilled and meaningful progress towards securing the north remained elusive.

Following the establishment of interim authorities in northern regions of Mali, municipal and communal elections were scheduled for December 2017. Due to insecurity across the country, particularly in northern and central regions, the vote was delayed until April 2018. The government expected terrorist activity and general insecurity that would threaten the safety of the candidates, the voters and the integrity of the democratic process. Though these aims were commendable, it was unclear how the Malian government would change its approach before running municipal elections in April, or if they expected the security environment to be markedly improved. The government's failure to protect municipal elections did not bode well for its ability to run inclusive, fair elections on the national scale, which was likely to be far more difficult.

The events of 2017 demonstrated a clear and widening interest, both nationally and internationally, in securing the Sahel and meeting the challenge of terrorism in the region. However, the task ahead remained significant. The birth of JNIM portended increased terrorist activity in Mali and surrounding countries, as well as a better financed, more centralised terror machine. While counter-terrorism is a laudable goal and a prerequisite for peace in Mali and the Sahel, it should not become the only goal. Task forces such as the FC-G5S Sahel command international attention and funding, but can come at the expense of other organisations. The humanitarian situation remained as dire as ever, and international non-governmental organisations were increasingly struggling due to limited funding and mounting danger to their projects and personnel. MINUSMA commanded a large presence in Mali, but its mandate was broad and it lacked sufficient materiel in 2017. The legitimacy of the Malian state continued to erode, as political promises went unfulfilled and discontent with the implementation of the Algiers Accord grew. Ultimately, security and development are not linear goals, but inextricably intertwined. One cannot be neglected for the sake of the other. While the security situation needed to stabilise to provide the best chance of success for Malian development efforts, real progress will depend on the effective marriage of priorities between combatting instability and addressing its root causes.

Nigeria (Farmer–Pastoralist Violence)

Armed conflicts between communities of pastoralists and farmers were one of the main national-security issues in Nigeria in 2017. These conflicts occurred in every zone of the federation but their scale and intensity varied, with different levels of

Key statistics	2016	2017
Type:	Internal	Internal
Fatalities:	– c	750
New IDPs:	– b	– b
New refugees:	– b	– b

violence between the 36 states. The most severe violence, with the highest numbers of fatalities recorded, occurred in some of the central and northern states. In general, these were mainly rural conflicts that affected large areas of territory. The main protagonists were pastoralists who rear cattle and sheep, and crop farmers whose production ranges from grains such as maize, millet, rice and sorghum to tubers such as yam and cassava, and dry-season irrigated cropping of vegetables. There is some overlap in activities as many herders are agro-pastoralists and some farmers also own livestock. Both agriculture and pastoralism are essential economic activities in Nigeria, engaging more than half the population directly or in related trade. As well as resulting in heavy loss of life, armed conflict between farmers and herders had a significant negative effect on agricultural and livestock production in the country.

Collapse of pastoralist infrastructure

Pastoralism refers to extensive livestock rearing, with herders moving their animals to areas of available grass and water for daily grazing. The movement of people and livestock between dry- and rainy-season pastures is called transhumance, and it can occur on a nomadic or semi-nomadic basis. Pastoralist systems have proved to be effective in utilising patchy resources, notably pasture and water, the location of which in the savannah and semi-arid environments varies seasonally and from year to year. Mobility increases the resilience of pastoralists to drought and fluctuations in rainfall, and when properly managed helps sustain the drylands by reducing overgrazing.

Historically, there was a symbiosis between pastoralists and farmers in Nigeria in the form of local arrangements whereby herdsmen grazed their cattle on crop residues after the harvest and on fallow land, with the manure on farmers' fields increasing crop yields. Pastoralists also brought money into local economies and exchanged livestock products, including meat and dairy, for other agricultural produce. In northern Nigeria there was also an organised system of livestock routes (*burti*) for pastoralists to move their animals along and designated grazing reserves linked by these routes. There were veterinary services for pastoralists, a system of nomadic education and a cattle tax known as *jangali*. This infrastructure, which supports and regulates pastoralism in Nigeria, was put in place during the colonial era and sustained in the first decades after independence in 1960.

However, the pastoralist infrastructure has since collapsed due to a weakening of state capacity in rural areas and increasing demographic pressure, with the Nigerian population more than quadrupling from 45 million at independence in 1960 to an estimated 190m in 2017. This demographic expansion resulted in a dramatic increase in the cultivated land area and a decrease in available grazing land, together with a breakdown in the relationship between herders and farmers over increasingly scarce resources. Pastoralists do not have secure land tenure in many places, meaning that farmers may move into what had previously been productive grazing areas without consideration for the traditional rights of the pastoralists.

Even grazing reserves, which were first protected by law in northern Nigeria in 1965, have not been protected, with most now cultivated or used for other purposes. Many livestock routes have also been blocked by farms or by fences erected by political elites who have seized land from local communities. At the same time, there has been a southwards movement of pastoralists from the semi-arid savannah zone into the sub-humid zone. Consequently, pastoralists are now distributed across the whole of Nigeria, whereas a generation ago they were overwhelmingly concentrated in the north. This southward spread of herders and their zebu cattle has happened due to changes in climate, prevention and veterinary treatments for trypanosomiasis (commonly known as sleeping sickness) – a disease carried by the tsetse fly – and, crucially, deforestation. Deforestation has altered the vegetation in much of southern Nigeria, changing the environment from tropical forest to derived savannah, which is more suitable for cattle and which has concurrently reduced the area of tsetse-fly infestation. Pastoral livelihoods are, however, under threat throughout Nigeria.

Even with these constraints, the number of livestock in Nigeria is thought to have increased, exacerbating the competition for resources. No accurate data exists due to the fact that the last livestock survey was done in the early 1990s, but based on projections from earlier surveys the official figure for 2017 was that there were some 20m cattle in Nigeria. Most of these were either herded or owned by Fulani pastoralists, the largest pastoralist group in Nigeria and in West and Central Africa.

Ethno-religious violence

Armed conflicts have increased over the past decade due to the constraints and extension of pastoralism and the continued expansion of farming, resulting in competition for land and water between herders and farmers. Ethnic and religious divisions are also important factors: conflicts are often triggered by disputes between herders and farmers but then escalate into armed conflicts along communal, ethnic or religious lines. Conversely, violence recently spilt out from areas of urban rioting between Muslims and Christians into surrounding rural areas and triggered what became protracted armed conflicts between farmers and pastoralists in those locations. That was the case with deadly riots in the cities of Jos in 2001, 2008 and 2010 and Kaduna in 2011, which triggered ethno-religious violence between farmers and herders in nearby rural areas in the respective states of Plateau and Kaduna. These conflicts persisted or resurfaced in 2017 in both states, claiming hundreds of lives and displacing people from the affected areas as villages and pastoralist camps were destroyed in violence.

This linking of farmer–herder conflicts to identity politics and wider regional, ethno-religious tensions was especially prevalent in the Middle Belt and in southern Nigeria. The Middle Belt refers geographically to a zone extending laterally across central Nigeria, but its boundaries are ambivalent. It is equally a political idea, dating to the late 1940s and 1950s, when mainly Christian elites from minority groups within what was then the Northern Region began a struggle for autonomy from the Hausa–Fulani political class in the north and sought to carve out a separate region. A Middle Belt region was never created, but Middle Belt discourse has persisted and it is in that context that the present violence is being interpreted by different ethnic groups in central Nigeria, influencing the public narrative of the present violence. The main protagonists of the conflict in the Middle Belt region are Fulani pastoralists (who are predominantly Muslim) and farming communities of diverse ethnic groups and religious backgrounds (but with Christians in the majority). The Fulani lived peaceably among diverse farming communities in the Middle Belt for decades, and until the 1990s armed conflicts between them were rare. However, violent conflicts have been increasing in scale and frequency since the beginning of the millennium and are now widespread, with numerous cases of mass violence recorded in 2017. The Middle Belt zone suffered higher levels of violence between farmers and pastoralists than the rest of Nigeria combined in 2017. Much of the violence occurred in places with a past record of collective violence along inter-ethnic and inter-religious lines, in parts of Adamawa, Benue, Kaduna, Nasarawa, Plateau and Taraba states.

The framing of the conflict tended to lack partiality in political and media discourse, with the pastoralists portrayed as the aggressors. There were numerous reports of herdsmen driving their livestock onto farms and attacking individual farmers or villages, and such cases were often accompanied by allegations of sexual assault and rape. These attacks mostly took place in parts of southern Nigeria and in parts of the Middle Belt, and were partially due to changed herding practices, in which herds of cattle were given to young men to take on transhumance without any supervision from the wider pastoralist community or elders. These herders are distinct from longer-established pastoralist communities in the affected areas: some are hired (they are not looking after their own cattle), while others are criminals who are also involved in cattle rustling, armed robbery and kidnapping for ransom. There is also a problem of drug abuse among some of the young herders. This has led to internal conflicts within the pastoral Fulani, who in some states have vigilantes to confront these issues.

In contrast, violence against herders, or against pastoralist communities more widely, was under-reported, even though it frequently did occur. In some cases, it was prior violence or attacks on livestock that elicited retaliatory attacks by herdsmen. The single deadliest conflict event in Nigeria in 2017 was perpetrated against a Fulani population, not by it. In June militants from the local Mambilla ethnic group launched a coordinated series of attacks on dozens of Fulani settlements on the Mambilla Plateau in Taraba State in the northeastern region of Nigeria, near the border with Cameroon. The motivation for the attacks was to kill and displace the Fulani population and seize their land. It was allegedly orchestrated by local political elites in Taraba State who then gave impunity to the perpetrators.

Anti-pastoralist legislation

In 2017, Benue, Edo and Taraba states passed laws banning pastoralism, or what they called 'open grazing'. (Ekiti State passed its anti-open-grazing law in 2016.) The laws were enacted because of increasing violence between herders and crop farmers, but political gains were also anticipated for the governors who introduced the bans as more people in those states were linked to farming than pastoralism, giving the anti-open-grazing laws a level of popular support. No viable alternative was created for the pastoralists. In Benue State the enforcement of the law began in November, with Livestock Guards, a quasi-militia, employed by the state government to expel pastoralists. In some instances the Livestock Guards seized the cattle of the pastoralists, inciting violent clashes that resulted in fatalities. Pastoralists who left Benue mainly moved into neighbouring Taraba and Nasarawa states, increasing pressures there. Taraba State, which is more important for pastoralism than Benue and is home to long-established Fulani communities, enacted its law but did not start enforcing it in 2017. There were nonetheless violent clashes between pastoralists and farmers interspersed across Taraba.

The anti-open-grazing laws were populist policies indicative of growing hostility to pastoralists in the states that adopted them, and a failure by states to effectively mediate between communities and manage rural resources. The conflicts were compounded by the phenomenon of rural banditry which increased in parts of central and northern Nigeria in 2017. This affected both pastoralists and farmers and was linked to the weakening of governance in rural areas and the pressures on pastoralism. The areas worst affected by banditry in 2017 were southern Zamfara State and bordering Birnin Gwari in northern Kaduna State, where mass violence resulted in the deaths of dozens of people. The lawlessness and political sponsorship of ethnically based vigilante action against the bandits fuelled continued conflicts between mainly Hausa farmers and Fulani pastoralists in affected areas of Zamfara State.

Supporters and opponents of Nigerian President Muhammadu Buhari added a particular resonance to the politicisation of conflicts involving Fulani herders in 2017. Buhari is Fulani by ethnicity, from Katsina State in northwest Nigeria, though he is not from a pastoralist background and he speaks Hausa rather than Fulfulde as his primary language. The escalation in violence between pastoralist and farming communities during Buhari's presidency was interpreted in public and political discourse in different ways, but two dominant interpretations stood out. A widespread perception in the Middle Belt and southern Nigeria, particularly but not only among Christians, was that Fulani herdsmen felt emboldened to attack villages and invade farmland because their kinsman was the president. A more extreme variant of this interpretation was that the president himself was in support of the violence. It should be emphasised that there was no evidence for these claims against Buhari: they can be dismissed, and there are facts to suggest the opposite. In reality, attempts by the federal government to introduce policies on pastoralism and livestock were blocked within the federal system at the state level or by the national assembly. The deployment of the military to some of the affected areas became the main federal response to the crisis; although this did not resolve the conflicts, it did help reduce the escalation of violence in some areas. The political impasse in implementing policy solutions to the conflicts that would be acceptable to different constituencies adversely affected farmers, pastoralists and the wider population. A second interpretation of the crisis was that President Buhari's opponents were aggravating the farmer–herder conflicts by whipping up anti-Fulani sentiments as a way of expressing and consolidating opposition to the federal government. This trend may increase in the lead-up to the 2019 elections, political campaigning for which began in 2017.

Somalia

The year began with a mixture of anticipation and apprehension when the presidential elections, which had been due to take place in the new year, were postponed for a fourth time due to security threats, a rise in violence, widespread accounts

Key statistics	2016	2017
Type:	Internationalised	Internationalised
Fatalities:	3,500	5,500
New IDPs:	110,000	390,000
New refugees:	9,000[a]	9,000[a]

of voter fraud and a lack of organisational capacity. The election was, however, eventually held on 8 February, and a palpable air of optimism greeted the result as former prime minister Mohamed Abdullahi Mohamed was elected president, unseating the incumbent Hassan Sheikh Mohamud. The transition of power was peaceful, and Somalis worldwide looked forward to new prospects for security and economic development in the year ahead.

The new administration, however, struggled to maintain this optimism. The public's confidence in the new government was eroded by the expanding presence of United States military forces in Somalia, which recalled the poorly conceived and heavy-handed US military intervention of the 1990s, while the Qatar crisis aggravated internal tensions between Somalia's federal and member-state governments. The militant Islamist group al-Shabaab proved its continued ability to carry out complex attacks against both civilian and government positions in the capital Mogadishu and around the country, despite initial impressions that it had been weakened by the new president's hardline approach to securing the capital in the first half of the year. In October, Somalia experienced what has been widely described as the worst attack in its history when a suicide truck bomb detonated in the nation's capital, which was estimated to have killed more than 500 people.

New leadership and high expectations

The constitutional framework of the presidential elections – initially scheduled for September 2016 but postponed multiple times due to political infighting, clan disputes, security threats and institutional unpreparedness – underwent a key change before the election was finally held on 8 February 2017. The popular electoral process was abandoned early on by Somalia's electoral commission, which cited regional instability as the primary reason; instead, it was decided that the president would be elected by members of Somalia's upper and lower houses of parliament. The members of the houses were elected by a select constituency that was representative of Somalia's clan structure, with the members of the constituency chosen in turn by a group of 146 clan elders.

On the day of the election, 330 parliamentarians gathered at Mogadishu's heavily guarded Aden Adde International Airport to cast their votes in what turned into a three-round voting process, resulting in victory for Mohamed. The surprising turn of events incited nationwide celebration as many Somalis took to the streets to rejoice at the promise of a new era of leadership.

Mohamed, fondly known as 'Farmajo', was elected on a platform of strong national unity and anti-corruption, and also promised a renewal of the struggle against al-Shabaab. However, these pledges promised to be challenging to accomplish given the lack of reconciliation between Somalia and Somaliland and the inter-state tensions that have frequently led to low-intensity confrontations. The national fighting force was also under-resourced and disjointed, with soldiers owed more than a year's salary due to financial malfeasance by the former government, making counter-terrorism operations more problematic.

The first part of the year saw the president focus on national security, which he supplemented in April with the offer of a two-month amnesty to militants who were willing to disarm and defect. A specialised operation referred to as the Mogadishu Stabilisation Mission was launched in June to prevent al-Shabaab from carrying out attacks in the capital during the month of Ramadan. While the mission was effective in preventing an upsurge in violence (which had characteristically occurred during the holy month in previous years), it also resulted in the detention of hundreds of suspects who were often arrested during large-scale raids and detained on questionable grounds. The operation also achieved the voluntary disarmament of politicians, civilians and non-state security personnel, but it also exacerbated inter-communal tensions, with the mission accused of extending immunity to specific politicians based on clan allegiances.

Increasing foreign intervention and deteriorating security

The development of Somalia's security architecture was an urgent priority for the government in order to facilitate the planned transition of responsibilities from the African Union Mission in Somalia (AMISOM) to local authorities. AMISOM conducted a number of capacity-building training events over the course of 2017 and transitioned certain military assets and command posts to the Somali authorities in advance of the mission's drawdown of forces, which was set to begin in December 2017. International scepticism about the ability of the security forces to assume their responsibilities comprehensively remained an issue and in November the US Department of State announced through a local news channel that they did not support the withdrawal of AMISOM forces at that time based on a demonstrated lack of capacity on the part of national forces.

In May, the national leadership met with international partners in London for the multi-day London Somalia Conference to discuss ongoing challenges and possible solutions to achieve progress in Somalia. Items on the agenda included the high-priority topic of security-sector reform, the humanitarian crisis and economic development, while the functions and responsibilities of various federal and state-level security actors were also clarified in advance of the planned exit of AMISOM from Somalia by 2020. International partners pledged their support and reaffirmed their commitment to assist Somalia to achieve its security and development goals.

Despite the diplomatic progress abroad, however, the situation in Somalia witnessed an increase in military intervention by foreign actors. US President Donald Trump's decision in March to loosen restrictions on US counter-terrorism activities empowered US Africa Command (AFRICOM) commanders to initiate offensive airstrikes and ground operations more rapidly and with less oversight. While this decision initially bolstered the capability of the Somali National Army (SNA) to identify and target enemy positions supported by US airpower, it also led to an increasingly visible and unconstrained presence of US forces in Somalia: the US independently claimed 28 airstrikes in 2017 (compared to 13 in 2016 and only five in 2015), with local reports of airstrikes being conducted against civilian assets.

Trump's announcement and the subsequent US military engagement in-country predictably fuelled resentment among the civilian population. This tension culminated in a night raid conducted by US and Somali forces in Barire which left ten civilians dead on 25 August. (Local reports later revealed that US forces had been falsely alerted to the presence of al-Shabaab militants in a local farming village by a rival clan.) In the aftermath of the attack, clan elders initiated a large-scale protest by transporting the bodies of the deceased to Mogadishu and refusing to carry out a burial until the government accepted accountability for wrongdoing. Six days later, Somali government officials announced that compensation would be paid to the families. AFRICOM admitted the presence of US troops and announced that it would conduct an independent investigation into allegations of civilian casualties.

The military operation in Barire gave fodder to extremist elements, who leveraged the unlawful killing of civilians to motivate a foot soldier to carry out the bombing attack on the Zobe intersection in Mogadishu on 14 October, which resulted in more than 500 deaths. While al-Shabaab did not publicly claim responsibility for the explosion, analysts believed that no other group had the planning or technical capabilities to carry out an attack of such magnitude. The Zobe attack renewed concerns about the group's strength in Somalia, despite earlier indications to the contrary when former al-Shabaab official Sheikh Mukhtar Robow publicly defected to the government in August. While Robow had parted from the group years ago, his official defection highlighted internal fragmentation within al-Shabaab and hinted that the group's current remit may not be enough to maintain the loyalty of key leaders.

Impact of the Qatar crisis

Building on its election pledge to improve national unity, cooperation and reconciliation, the new administration prioritised the progression of Somalia's federalist project in the first half of the year. Unfortunately, efforts to achieve cohesion between federal and state administrations suffered considerable setbacks in the third quarter of 2017, beginning with the president's decision to extradite a former commander of the Ogaden National Liberation Front (ONLF) to Ethiopia on 28 August after he was arrested in Galkayo on 23 August. (Designated as a terrorist group by the Ethiopian authorities, the ONLF has pushed for self-determination of the Ogaden region in Ethiopia, which is historically considered part of greater Somalia.) The president's decision offended key Somali nationalist leaders and undermined the administration's pro-nationalist position.

The Qatar crisis, which began in June, also had a divisive effect on relationships between Somalia's federal and state governments. After Saudi Arabia, Bahrain, Egypt and the United Arab Emirates severed relations with Qatar following a hacking scandal in May and on the basis of Qatar's positive relations with Iran and alleged support for international terrorism, the government in Riyadh began pressuring its Horn of Africa partners to follow suit. Somalia is of strategic significance to Saudi Arabia, and Riyadh has previously leveraged its relationships in the Horn to serve its political aims elsewhere, namely in the political proxy war against Iran.

The federal government immediately took an official position of neutrality, seemingly to prevent the meddling of foreign powers in Somalia's internal and external affairs, which proved toxic in the past. After Saudi Arabia's attempts to persuade the federal government to take a different position failed, members of the Saudi-led coalition leveraged their existing relationships with a number of state governments in Somalia in an effort to change federal policy. Internally, Somalia's announcement angered a number of state authorities who viewed the federal government's decision as a direct threat to their economic and strategic interests. The decision caused great discontent among many who viewed maintaining relationships with Riyadh and Abu Dhabi as bringing significantly more economic return than maintaining relationships with Doha.

Puntland State was the first to vocalise opposition because the state had secured a deal with a Dubai-based company to operate in the state's main port earlier in the year. The Puntland government's siding with Saudi Arabia and its allies was mirrored by the administrations of Galmudug and South West states shortly thereafter in September. All three state authorities challenged the federal government's position on the premise that federal member states had not been consulted in the initial decision to remain neutral. The situation quickly spiralled when Ahmed Duale Haaf, the president of Galmudug State, was illegally voted out of office, although the decision was reversed on the basis that it was unconstitutional. Ali Abdullahi Osoble, the president of Hirshabelle State, was also subsequently removed from office after announcing his anti-government position on the Qatar issue, fuelling allegations of federal government interference in state-government affairs and highlighting a need to expedite a long-overdue constitutional review. President Mohamed's decision to dig in proved alienating, despite his intent, and motivated state authorities to negotiate independently with the Gulf states.

The political discord resulting from the Qatar crisis in 2017 reinforced an unfortunate national narrative of a weak central government unable to protect itself from predatory international interests. Historically, these internal divisions have empowered extremist elements in Somalia to take advantage of any opportunity to paint the government as a foreign-backed anti-Islamic weak state to enhance recruitment and undermine the government's legitimacy.

Prolonged humanitarian crisis

Widespread drought, food insecurity and the prevalence of acute malnutrition in vulnerable populations was a major concern for the international community at the start of 2017, who were desperate to avoid a repeat of the deadly 2011 famine. A strategic call for support by UN actors in February reinforced existing humanitarian interventions with funding and resources, staving off a prospective famine and humanitarian emergency. However, a lack of rainfall throughout the year resulted in ongoing drought-related displacement and high levels of food insecurity. Internally displaced populations, displaced by drought and conflict, constituted a significant portion of the 6.2 million people who remained in need of assistance at the end of 2017. The coordinated response to the impending humanitarian crisis by national and international actors at the start of the year was overshadowed by a large-scale increase in the number of people living with emergency levels of food insecurity at the end of the year. Gains were made by the government in terms of disaster-risk reduction and the development of relevant state infrastructure to mitigate and respond to future emergency, but unfortunate environmental conditions and the continuation of armed conflict in rural areas caused an overall deterioration in the humanitarian environment in 2017.

Growing threat of al-Shabaab

The year 2016 saw a resurgence of Somalia's main militant group al-Shabaab after the withdrawal of Ethiopian troops from Gedo region and other areas enabled the group to re-establish an operational presence in key areas outside of the capital. In 2017 the group proved its ability to execute high-profile complex attacks in Mogadishu and elsewhere. While the president's campaign to combat al-Shabaab achieved certain notable victories – namely key defections – al-Shabaab was able to flex its muscles in strongholds in South-Central region and in Puntland State. A US-led campaign of airstrikes targeted and killed a number of the group's leaders, but this did not seem to negatively affect the group's ability to launch effective attacks against government positions and civilian targets in and outside of Mogadishu. The group orchestrated an attack on a military base in Af Urur in Puntland State in June resulting in the deaths of at least 59 soldiers and civilians.

Throughout the year the group claimed responsibility for high-casualty attacks in Mogadishu as well as notably carrying out two complex suicide attacks on hotels in the capital. One in January left 28 people dead while a similar event in October left 23 people dead and 30 others injured. In addition to a number of high-profile attacks, al-Shabaab continued to execute political assassinations and smaller-scale attacks on police and military checkpoints throughout the country.

While the group did not achieve major territorial gains in 2017, it was clear that the SNA's lack of projection power outside of the capital created an enabling environment in which al-Shabaab could assert relatively unchecked influence in places such as Jilib in Kismayo, areas in and around Baidoa, Bay region, Beledweyne, Hirshabelle region and much of Galgudud. A lack of effective governance in rural areas and nominal military projection power outside of regional capitals contributed to the group's ability to grow and maintain support bases outside of Mogadishu. While al-Shabaab control in these areas was not necessarily overt, Somali forces often proved inadequately trained and equipped to do more than temporarily clear al-Shabaab militants from a given area. The Somali National Army's questionable record combatting al-Shabaab and allegations of corruption led the US to suspend military aid to Somalia at the end of the year. These events indicated that despite some progress in early 2017, the Somali National Armed Forces still lacked the capacity and training to secure contested areas outside of the capital.

The year ended with a heightened threat environment as AFRICOM released the outcome of its investigation into the Barire raid in November. AFRICOM's findings claimed that only combatants were killed in the raid despite ground accounts and visual evidence to the contrary. This announcement has the potential to undermine the public's confidence in the new government even further, with the government running the risk of being perceived as a proxy for foreign-military interests. Past administrations have suffered considerably when foreign intervention has undermined public confidence, and President Mohamed's government will have to navigate this potential hazard carefully in order to avoid losing credibility with the Somali public, who can recall the disastrous consequences of US mission creep in Somalia in the 1990s.

South Sudan

The conflict in South Sudan became more intractable and geographically widespread in 2017. The multiplicity of opposition movements and military groups fed into localised conflicts resulting from numerous community grievances, many

Key statistics	2016	2017
Type:	Internationalised	Internationalised
Fatalities:	3,000	4,000
New IDPs:	280,000	860,000
New refugees:	1,070,000	560,000

of which were tied to the mismanaged federalist model that President Salva Kiir Mayardit installed when he expanded the ten states to 28 in late 2015, before adding four more in January 2017.

Intercommunal fighting and increased levels of violence hardened political positions on all sides. The war strategies of all actors were characterised by widespread human-rights violations, the targeting of civilians on political and ethnic grounds, 'scorched-earth' policies, forced dislocation, the denial of humanitarian aid and the use of starvation as a weapon of war, all of which contributed to a crippling financial crisis and a devastating humanitarian emergency. After almost a year of inaction and contradictory bilateral responses, the regional Intergovernmental Authority on Development (IGAD) initiated a process to revitalise the Agreement on the Resolution of the Conflict in South Sudan (ARCISS).

Fragmentation and proliferation of actors

The three main political and military groupings – the ruling Sudan People's Liberation Movement–In Government (SPLM–IG) and two factions of the SPLM–In Opposition (SPLM–IO), led by Taban Deng Gai and Riek Machar respectively – all faced internal dissent and fracturing. Several alliances emerged and armed groups proliferated while these three main actors struggled to maintain the veneer of representing broader interests than their narrow constituencies.

The government faced a serious rift after Paul Malong Awan, the powerful army chief, was removed and put under house arrest in May. This action not only divided the government's military front but also disrupted Dinka ethnic unity in the Bahr el-Ghazal region. Military officers close to Malong called for an uprising to topple the Juba government, particularly after Malong was released in November. Meanwhile, the rift among the Dinka elites became layered: between the Dinka of Bahr el-Ghazal and Jonglei; between the Dinka Bor and Dinka Renk; within the Renk sections of Warrap (Aguok, Apuk, Twic, Nyok and Awan); and the Bor sections, who were divided at the leadership level. Fighting between the Aguok and Apuk clans was fuelled by politicians in Juba, with each clan having their respective militias (Machar Anyaar and Titweng) – the Apuk appeared to be pushing for their own separate state. A state of emergency was declared in Gogrial, Aweil East, Tonj and Wau in July, as communal fighting revealed the political fragility of military alliances Juba had established locally in its strongholds; in Aweil East, a new group emerged called the South Sudan Patriotic Army (SSPA) commanded by Agany Ayii Akol. Fighting in Western Lakes State between sections of Agaar and some clans of Gok State led key Dinka politicians in December to request that a state of emergency also be declared in Western Lakes and a military division be deployed immediately.

Despite the disruption, the security apparatus became increasingly dominated by Dinka in 2017. (Efforts to entrench the Dinka military and political stranglehold of the state and the security apparatus have, among other policies, been thought to drive the creation of the 32 states.) Several high-profile resignations in February revealed the level of frustration with 'tribal' politics, including General Thomas

Cirillo Swaka, the most high-profile Equatorian in the government's Sudan People's Liberation Army (SPLA). Brigadier-General Henry Oyay Nyago – a Shilluk and director for military justice in the SPLA – also resigned, accusing President Kiir of obstructing accountability and investigations into crimes committed by the SPLA. Colonel Khalid Ono Loki (head of military courts) and Brigadier-General Kamila Otwari Aleardo (a former commander of the Logistics Support Brigade) followed suit. In March, General Khalid Butrus Bora, the Murle commander of the Juba-aligned South Sudan Democratic Movement/Army (SSDM/A), joined the rebellion. Grievances over Dinka hegemony and the subjugation of other communities added to zero-sum calculations of several warring factions.

The SPLM–IO's resilience continued despite recent military losses and the absence of its leader Riek Machar, who remained under house arrest in South Africa. The movement appeared to have transitioned from a hierarchical structure to decentral-ised units of command that acted autonomously. This reorganisation may allow the SPLM–IO to keep fighting for a long time, but it will create difficulties for mediation efforts and implementation of the revitalised ARCISS. The Equatorian front suffered from internal fragmentation after SPLM–IO commanders defected to the National Salvation Front (NAS), the rebel group founded by Cirillo in March following his resignation from the SPLA. Despite this, the SPLM–IO remained the most organised and cohesive front in the Greater Equatoria region, while the Chollo front in Upper Nile also became more cohesive. Following intra-ethnic fighting between General Johnson Olony and Lam Akol's forces in January, the Shilluk king organised a meeting to reunify the groups. The forces attached to General Yoanes Okij (who was killed in battle) were integrated under Olony and remained allied to Machar.

The creation of the NAS triggered, as mentioned above, several SPLM–IO defec-tions and also saw an alignment of rebel groups once affiliated to the SPLM–IO. The NAS, however, lacked military capacity. By taking on a national rather than an Equatorian cause, Cirillo failed to rally the large groups of fighters that were already mobilised in Equatoria as community self-defence groups. Three key Equatorian leaders (Cirillo, Joseph Bakosoro and Clement Wani Konga) were thought to have been able to unite, but this eventuality did not materialise. As a result, Greater Equatoria lacked a unified command and a visible leader who could lay claim to the aspirations and grievances of the region.

Overall, there were 47 political and smaller armed groups in South Sudan in 2017. These can be considered in terms of five categories, although there were alliances between groups from different categories. Firstly, there were groups that held national agendas directed at regime change, the largest of which was the SPLM–IO faction commanded by Riek Machar. As mentioned above, the SPLM–IO (Machar) maintained an alliance with the Shilluk insurgency under Olony, along with several Equatorian communities under the command of ethnic Zande, Bari and Lotuko commanders (among others), and with Fertit and Balanda commanders in Bahr el-Ghazal. The NAS was the second of such groups that formed an alliance with under-represented communities and minorities.

Secondly, there were political groups with no armed wing that focused on pro-posing negotiated and political solutions, such as the SPLM Leaders, also known as the SPLM–Former Detainees (FD). The FD possessed a critical mass of leader-ship but lost traction with different communities and international partners over the course of the past two years, despite representing a very diverse group of elites from all of the three greater regions of South Sudan (Bahr el-Ghazal, Equatoria and Greater Upper Nile).

Thirdly, there were groups affiliated to particular leaders who, despite their appeals for national reforms, held mostly ethnic agendas. These groups included the Federal Democratic Party (FDP), led by Gabriel Changson and Peter Gadet and representing a section of the Nuer; Lam Akol's National Democratic Movement (NDM), representing a portion of the Shilluk; Hakim Dario Moi's People's Democratic Movement (PDM), from the Didinga; and Bakosoro's South Sudan National Movement for Change (SSNMC), representing a portion of the Zande. Some of these possessed armed wings while others were solely political.

Fourthly, there were militia groups that were local in nature but deployed across the country to serve the narrow interests of political elites in Juba. (The Matiang Anyoor militia was the most prominent of these groups.) Fifthly, there were local militias that mobilised around local and community issues and were considered as non-elite groups, the most well known being the White Army in Jonglei and the Arrow Boys in Western Equatoria; within this category were also the community self-defence groups spread throughout the country.

This proliferation of armed groups, led by both elites and non-elites, increased the difficulty of securing a negotiated settlement. The political landscape became ever more complex due to the different needs, interests and purposes of the groups, whose political agendas frequently lacked ideology, common standing and purpose, and concrete political programmes to implement reforms. However, several of the elite-driven groups showed an ability to act in coordination and with convergence of purpose. Six groups – including SPLM–IO, the NAS and the FD – signed a press release on 17 April drawing attention to the unfolding genocide in the country.

Military offenses and a complex humanitarian emergency

Large-scale military campaigns gave the SPLA a military advantage throughout the three greater regions of Upper Nile, Bahr el-Ghazal and Equatoria, although in many areas the government controlled only the main towns, not the surrounding countryside. Government offensives continued to include tribal militias that jointly conducted scorched-earth policies that contributed to mass displacement, instrumentalised starvation and atrocities against civilians. New politico-military groups emerged partly as a response to escalating local and national tensions, the polarisation of identities and the need for self-defence. The Ceasefire and Transitional Security Arrangements Monitoring Mechanism (CTSAMM) – the body monitoring the ARCISS ceasefire – was largely unable to conduct the much-needed monitoring and investigation of such military campaigns. The United Nations Mission in South Sudan (UNMISS) tried to reach Parjok in Eastern Equatoria – the site of atrocities against civilians in early April – but was stopped at a government checkpoint and prevented from proceeding. There were many similar incidents, indicating that the ceasefire agreement signed in December 2017 will likely be plagued by similar monitoring, enforcement and accountability issues.

Fighting in Upper Nile escalated in January with clashes intensifying near the Paloch oilfields in Renk and Malakal. The bombing of Wau Shilluk by the SPLA left the area in Upper Nile almost deserted, which was deemed by the Shilluk king as evidence of targeted ethnic cleansing. (UNMISS reported that the fighting had displaced more than 30,000 inhabitants from the area.) The SPLA capture of two strategic areas held by the SPLM–IO – Pagak, their headquarters, in July and Yuai in Jonglei in March – were significant defeats for Riek Machar's movement. The loss of Pagak sent several refugees and armed elements into Ethiopia, which caused concern in Addis Ababa; the Gambella in Ethiopia currently hosts an estimated 290,000 Nuer refugees. Under the command of General Ochan, SPLM–IO's 5th Division attempted to retake Pagak, causing concern in Ethiopia over the proximity of operations to its border. Elsewhere, the Fertit Lions of Western Bahr el-Ghazal continued to wage a rebellion against Juba. Fighting in and around the city of Wau gradually escalated from the middle of the year, pitting Dinka and Fertit communities against each other. More than 150,000 people were displaced as a result, leaving Wau mostly deserted.

The war in the Greater Equatoria region continued to escalate. In late March the SPLM–IO took Kajo Keji county in Yei River State, a significant military victory that further weakened the government's presence in Equatoria. The Torit–Juba and Torit–Nimule roads, both strategic trade and transport arteries, witnessed a higher level of fighting. The increased level of refugee movement out of the Equatorias allowed for several other communities to move into different areas; Dinka communities moved into and occupied land around Yei and Kajo Keji.

On 20 February, a famine was declared in South Sudan and the wider region. Pockets of Unity State were most affected, yet officials also reported famine in different parts of the country. The famine was averted by a mass humanitarian response, but more than six million people continued to face serious food insecurity, with more than one million children under the age of five acutely malnourished. The United Nations, the United Kingdom and other countries defined the famine as a 'man-made' crisis, rather than a result of drought (as in other parts of the Horn of Africa). Over 50% of harvests had been lost because of the war, exposing new populations to food insecurity and aid dependence, while nearly 71% of all counties were contaminated by explosive remnants of war, rendering more than 300 schools and 30 clinics unsafe for use. The UN reported 103 humanitarian-access incidents in November 2017 alone, compared to more than 831 incidents in the whole of 2016. Many of the areas denied access by relief operations were under control of the opposition, and in January eight international organisations were directed by the government to cancel operations in areas of Upper Nile controlled by the SPLM–IO. In addition, there were several violations of the Status of Forces agreement with the UNMISS, undermining UNMISS's ability to patrol, move and monitor developments.

Regionally, the conflict in South Sudan increased the volatility of the region. Mass flows of refugees into Uganda, and to a lesser extent Ethiopia and Sudan, also led to military activity crossing into these countries. The SPLA was thought to have staged several incursions into northern Uganda aimed at eliminating key rebel leaders and disarming refugees, although Uganda warned against such activities. The increasing presence of SPLM–IO and Equatorian opposition forces in the Democratic Republic of the Congo added another regional dimension. The situation was complicated by the location of the SPLM–IO's headquarters in Lasu (near the Democratic Republic of the Congo border) and the movement of armed fighters from other groups (such as the Arrow Boys) across the border into the refugee camps. There was added concern that more than 700 of the best-trained elements of the SPLM–IO (the Tiger battalion defectors) and Machar's bodyguards were in the Dungu and Munigi camps in the Democratic Republic of the Congo and had not undergone any disarmament, demobilisation and reintegration. Authorities in the Democratic Republic of the Congo claimed that the SPLA did not control a single area along the 628-kilometre-long border and that rebel groups controlled the area. Recruitment of transnational fighters occurred in the southern borders, creating a very difficult feedback loop of instability, particularly in Central African Republic, the Democratic Republic of the Congo and Uganda.

Attempt to revitalise ARCISS

Policies of containment were prioritised over coordinated efforts to stop the conflict in 2017; an array of competing regional and bilateral initiatives were attempted that were neither complementary nor coordinated. The international response was deficient on many fronts, exacerbating the conflict in many ways and creating space for the parties to pursue their narrow zero-sum agendas. Attempts to impose an arms embargo and wide-ranging sanctions failed. The UN Security Council remained divided on South Sudan: while there was agreement that the situation required a political solution, members lacked a unified strategy to exert leverage on all sides of the conflict. In July, a revitalisation forum for the ARCISS peace agreement was established at the IGAD heads of state summit, aimed at reviving the agreement to address the current political realities. The forum agreed to discuss concrete measures to restore a permanent ceasefire; to fully implement ARCISS; and to develop a realistic timeline for the transitional period to end in elections. The US stated that the IGAD revitalisation forum was the 'last chance' for peace in South Sudan and warned that if this initiative failed, other alternatives would be considered on how to 'individually and collectively do more to end the conflict'. In September, the US Treasury imposed sanctions on Information Minister Michael Makuei, Deputy Chief of Defence Malek Reuben and former army chief of staff Paul Malong Awan, saying that the three had engaged in actions or policies that threatened the peace and stability of South Sudan.

The Kenyan process that saw President Uhuru Kenyatta appoint two diplomats (Senator Amos Wako and Ambassador Monica Juma) stalled in 2017, mostly due to the domestic situation in Kenya. Attempts by Nairobi in October to unify opposition parties achieved some level of success but the strategy was not aligned with other initiatives. Authorities in Kenya came under pressure to explain their role in the 'rendition' cases of exiled and refugee SPLM–IO elements in their country. Following the deportation of SPLM–IO spokesperson James Gatdet in 2016, two other SPLM–IO activists (human-rights lawyer Dong Samuel Luak and writer Aggrey Idri Ezibou) disappeared on 22 February and are reportedly being held by the National Security Services in Juba.

The Ugandan initiative taken by President Yoweri Museveni to reactivate the Arusha process and reunify the SPLM also stalled. In July, three factions of the SPLM (IG, IO–Taban and FD) signed the Entebbe Declaration to implement the reunification process. While there was some momentum created, the absence of the SPLM–IO faction led by Machar was a fundamental problem. Although Machar was invited, he declined to participate and rejected the format, calling instead for a new political process. Another general concern was the overall objective, which remained unclear given that the conflict had expanded beyond the confines of an intra-SPLM dispute and a return to the status quo would fail as a mitigating strategy. Egypt's involvement in South Sudan added to the conflict's intractability, along with embedding proxy dynamics. The recent diplomatic drive by Juba towards Cairo resulted in military support and in relief aid, but the motivations for Egypt's involvement were tied to its interests in the Nile and countering Ethiopia's drive to continue building the Grand Ethiopian Renaissance Dam. These regional dynamics brought IGAD's credibility as an impartial arbiter into question.

The IGAD-led ARCISS High Level Revitalization Forum (HLRF) also had a slow start. Two extraordinary summits and a two-day meeting were convened in July and August respectively to discuss the specific requirements for revitalising the 2015 agreement, with the process being led by Ismael Wais, the IGAD special envoy to South Sudan. The HLRF was arranged with four levels of consultation: 1) the parties to the Transitional Government of National Unity (TGNU) including the SPLM–IG, FD (Deng Alor and John Luk), SPLM–IO for Peace (Taban), other parties represented by Martin Lumoro and parties in the National Alliance led by Agriculture Minister Onyoti Adigo Nyikwec; 2) stakeholders outside of the TGNU including Riek Machar, Pagan Amum (FD), Lam Akol (NDM), Bakosoro (SSNMC), Cirillo (NSF), Gabriel Changson (FDPSS) and Costello Garang Ring Lual (SSPA); 3) eminent personalities outside the TGNU, including Rebeca Nyandeng, Peter Gadet, General Bapiny Montuil and General Johnson Olony, among others; 4) civil society, youth, women, faith-based leaders and business associations. In a reversal of the policy of excluding Machar from any future political process, IGAD ministers from Ethiopia and Kenya reached out to the South African presidency in September to bring Machar on board.

The forum released a pre-consultation report in November that the government met with numerous reservations and objections. Juba's main concern was to avoid the process resulting in regime change and a return of Riek Machar to the TGNU. The pre-consultation report revealed many divergent approaches to key political and military aspects of the conflict, including the form of a future transitional government, state restructuring, composition of the executive, judiciary and parliament, the timing of elections, and the reform and composition of the security sector, among others. Coupled with the questionable political will to implement the agreement, reconciling these differing views will remain key difficulties for the peacemaking process.

On 24 December, a cessation of hostilities agreement (CoHA) was signed, constituting the first step in the ARCISS HLRF process. However, the CoHA was criticised for failing to alter the structural impediments of ARCISS and the seven previous CoHAs signed since January 2016, as well as failing to improve the monitoring body to investigate violations and establish robust mechanisms to de-escalate situations and enforce the ceasefire. In addition, it was not clear that the design, time frame and format of the HLRF process would resolve the inadequacies of ARCISS. The obvious problem with the process was that it was based on a selection of leaders and groups with military organisation, rather than political and armed groups that had community representation and who have taken up arms since August 2015. Equatoria, with all its diversity, was not properly represented, while the Fertit and Murle were left without representation. The parties may not have the organisational capacity to implement what they agree if they are unable to bring on board the constituencies they purport to represent. The ARCISS HLRF remained a forum of powerful individuals that was personality-based and excluded large portions of the armed community groups (including many from Equatoria and Bahr el-Ghazal), yet there were also no guarantees that the government delegation would be cohesive and represent all the conflicting interests in the SPLM–IG itself. Should the implementation of ARCISS continue to be delayed, then the suspension of international financial aid – as intimated on 21 July by the Troika (the United Kingdom, Norway and the United States) and the European Union – will become another stumbling block as financial commitment by IGAD countries will not be forthcoming.

Following the July 2016 crisis that saw the near collapse of the peace agreement and led to the exile of Riek Machar, the UN mandated that a regional force be established to add a layer of security around the capital, although this was a too-little, too-late measure. A portion of the 4,000-strong Regional Protection Force (RPF) was deployed in 2017. The first batch of 150 troops from Rwanda arrived in Juba in early August, and the force stood at 850 with the addition of an Ethiopian advanced company deployed in October. However, the government requested a revision of the RPF's mandate, accusing the RPF of 'creating havoc in Juba by carrying guns'. There was also disagreement over the RPF taking over security of the Juba International Airport as mandated. Despite the tensions with Juba, the overall effect of the RPF was not significant: with more than 12,000 UN personnel in the country, the presence of a handful of RPF troops under a similar mandate did not increase security or accountability.

The National Dialogue (ND) appeared to be moving forward but faced some difficulties, as expected; the declaration of a state of emergency in five different areas in the country was perceived by some as a way to hinder the work of the ND. Despite this, the body's steering committee has managed to engage key players inside and outside the country, as well as key international stakeholders. Several opposition leaders who previously rejected the process showed interest in joining the ND, including Lam Akol, Joseph Bakosoro and Thomas Cirillo. In April, a new decree appointed more than 100 members to join the Secretariat and steering committee. However, President Kiir remained the main patron of the ND despite having stated that he would hand over the position to the chairperson, feeding the perception that the ND was politically motivated and not a neutral exercise.

With the conflict due to enter its fifth year in 2018, signs of any effective strategy of peacemaking and stabilisation remained elusive. The challenges for the coming year appeared insurmountable, with political fragmentation haunting all sides, a collapsed domestic economy and flailing war economy that put at risk key containment strategies of the government, as well as a continued humanitarian crisis. The configuration of the crisis indicated that it would most likely remain a long war, with recurring waves of asymmetry and proxy involvement of regional powers. The conflict's intractability was likely to deepen as polarised perceptions of enmity continued to elicit violent responses at all levels, while irreconcilable issues of identity and sovereignty fed demands on all sides, made worse by the fragmentation of alliances and groups. The entrenched geopolitical situation could hamper any effective intervention, with South Sudan remaining low on the international agenda, key countries in the region buffering any robust intervention, and IGAD experiencing a crisis of legitimacy due to its late and inadequate peacemaking efforts.

Sudan (Blue Nile, Darfur and South Kordofan)

Following the de facto defeat of several major rebel groups in 2016, violent conflict in Blue Nile, Darfur and South Kordofan states continued to evolve in character throughout 2017. With international actors failing to sway Khartoum's

Key statistics	2016	2017
Type:	Internal	Internal
Fatalities:	3,500	1,250
New IDPs:	95,000	17,000
New refugees:	24,000[a]	22,000[a]

behaviour, the humanitarian situation threatened to deteriorate while the peace process remained stagnant. In an attempt to restore security in the region, Sudanese authorities launched a campaign to collect weapons and ammunition, but the policy encountered fierce resistance and also came under scrutiny for the heavy-handed tactics employed by the Rapid Support Forces (RSF). There were also numerous demonstrations throughout Sudan against the highly punitive 2018 national budget, which pre-emptively led to price increases of up to 300% for some basic commodities.

Regional violence

Different regions within Darfur experienced varying levels of violence over the course of 2017, although relatively little of it involved traditional combat between rebel groups on the one hand and either the Sudanese Armed Forces (SAF) or the RSF on the other. The military triumph of the RSF in Jebel Marra in 2016 seemed to deny the forces of the Sudan Liberation Army led by Abdel Wahid al-Nur (SLA–AW) – the last cohesive element of the rebel groups – its final redoubt, and there was little evident truth to Abdel Wahid's claim that the rebellion remained fully active in 2017. Although weapons continued to pour into the Sahel region, including North Darfur, from post-Gadhafi Libya, the RSF was too entrenched for any of the major remaining rebel groups to do more than conduct minor operations. Over the course of the year it became increasingly apparent that the SLA–AW, the Sudan Liberation Army led by Minni Minawi (SLA–MM) and the once-formidable Justice and Equality Movement (JEM) were no longer significant military actors. The Sudan People's Liberation Movement–North (SPLM–N) continued to occupy areas in the south of the country, but divisions within the SPLM–N leadership fractured the movement and made the idea of a united, armed, Sudan-wide Sudan Revolutionary Front (SRF) seem highly unlikely. Tensions within the two main elements of the SPLM–N have long been festering, and the apparent collusion between SPLM–N Secretary-General Yasir Arman and Malik Agar (former governor of Blue Nile) on the question of self-determination for the Nuba Mountains brought about a decisive rift, as well as significant fighting between SPLM–N forces in South Kordofan and Blue Nile (primarily in Blue Nile).

However, the Darfur region still experienced a high level of violence in 2017. Violence was largely concentrated around issues of land and the continuing plight of those living in camps. One consequence of the intra-Arab tribal conflict that has waxed and waned over the past 15 years has been the permanent disruption to the traditional seasonal arrangements for the migration of livestock (both camels and cattle). In 2017 there was an especially early (and hence much more destructive) movement of livestock through remaining cultivated African farmlands, destroying many crops in a region with a high level of food insecurity. In some areas the passage occurred three months before the historical window. Even more disruptively, a substantial amount of the farmland belonging to non-Arab African tribal groups in Darfur was violently expropriated and subsequently converted to foraging ground for the camels and cattle of nomadic and semi-nomadic Arab tribal groups.

Sexual violence was a continuing feature of life in and around camp areas, and was an extremely serious threat to women and girls attempting to work their farmlands or tend their livestock. In rural areas and on farms near enough to IDP camps to be worked by their owners, rape, beatings and murders were a constant, although these incidents were no longer reported by the United Nations or the United Nations Mission in Darfur (UNAMID). Instead, information about the violence was transmitted exclusively through the extraordinary network of contacts on the ground that has been fashioned by Radio Dabanga in Darfur. (There is no independent human-rights-assessment presence in Darfur, nor does Khartoum allow any independent news reporting from Darfur.)

Lifting of sanctions and new priorities

As a consequence of the success of the military campaign against rebel groups in 2016, the government's focus in 2017 began to pivot from confronting organised (if fractious) well-armed and -supplied rebel groups to two tasks: firstly, disarmament, and secondly, the dismantling of IDP camps. However, the government's regional disarmament campaign in Darfur, initiated in July, quickly ran into difficulty. As a result of intercommunal disputes over water and pasture land, tribal militias refused to hand over their weapons, with tribal chief and former Janjaweed leader Musa Hilal even threatening to fight the SAF and RSF personnel involved in the disarmament process. There were also allegations that the disarmament campaign, which became compulsory in September 2017, gave the heavily deployed RSF an additional pretext to assault, arrest and even murder individuals, especially in the IDP camps.

The decision to begin dismantling the IDP camps was triggered by a diplomatic shift by the United States towards Sudan. In January 2017, in the last week of the Obama administration, the US provisionally lifted sanctions on Sudan – a state of affairs that was later made permanent by the Trump administration in October 2017. However, the lifting of sanctions, together with the all-but-certain removal of Sudan from the US State Department's annual list of state sponsors of terrorism, was not necessarily a reflection of progress on the ground, and also diminished the United States' leverage over Khartoum. Improvements in humanitarian access and an end to aerial attacks on civilian targets were the only meaningful benchmarks set by the two US administrations, but while bombing largely ceased in July 2016 (at the beginning of the Obama administration's 'trial period'), there was no real improvement on the ground in humanitarian access, either in Darfur or South Kordofan and Blue Nile, where a near-total humanitarian embargo continued in areas controlled by the SPLM–N.

No longer constrained by US diplomatic pressure, the government decided to move forward with its long-promised dismantling of the camps, despite the fact that camp leaders repeatedly made it clear that the idea was intolerable, given the extreme insecurity in all five Darfur states. The racial/ethnic divide that has defined the conflict since it began in late 2002 has endured, most conspicuously in the targeting of ongoing pervasive violence, both sexual and otherwise. Virtually all the tens of thousands of girls and women who have been raped over the past 15 years have been non-Arab African, while the overwhelming number of destroyed villages and seized farmlands belonged to non-Arab African Darfuris.

In addition to protecting IDPs from dangers in the region, the camps also provided the only practicable means for humanitarian organisations to supply and distribute resources, including food and medicine. If the camps disappear, so too will the (still very large) international humanitarian presence. Although the roughly 2.7 million Darfuris who are presently internally displaced live in a variety of settings, including ad hoc settlements and with host families, the census for the camps as a whole – which collectively number some 100 locations – was more than 2.2m. If the inhabitants are forced from the camps, or if the camps are violently dismantled, they will have nowhere to go safely – and they will be largely beyond the reach of even the most intrepid international non-governmental organisations (INGOs).

The government, however, remained fixed on ending both the existence of the camps (which Khartoum considered embarrassing evidence that almost half the pre-war population of Darfur remained displaced, especially as the IDPs were conspicuously and overwhelmingly non-Arab African) and also the international humanitarian presence in Darfur. The hostility of the regime to INGOs has long been obvious and has frequently led to harsh actions, even against such organi-sations as the International Committee of the Red Cross and the various national sections of Médecins Sans Frontières. However, despite insisting that the camps must be closed and dismantled (although the actual time frame remained unclear), Khartoum showed no inclination to take on the exceedingly difficult problem of land restoration: an essential task given that the main reason people remain in the camps is that they have no way to reclaim their lands. Many Arab groups regard the land they have violently seized for pasturage as payment for military services rendered to Khartoum and the SAF, and disorganised irregular Arab militia forces were regularly reported to be attacking non-Arab African civilians, especially if they sought to return to or work their farmland. Moreover, many of the more irregular Arab militia groups are not from Darfur, but from Chad, Niger and Mali. Having migrated to Darfur – often with Khartoum's assistance – they will not leave quietly.

Ineffectiveness of UNAMID

The volatility of the situation was likely to be compounded if Khartoum secured its other primary desideratum from the international community: the complete removal of UNAMID, the badly failing UN–African Union (AU) hybrid peacekeep-ing mission in Darfur. In June 2017, the UN Security Council largely acceded to Khartoum's wishes when it renewed UNAMID's mandate, agreeing to a 44% reduc-tion of UNAMID's military personnel and a 30% reduction of its police personnel. From October, UNAMID started to scale down, handing over the Eid Al Fursan, Tulus and Forobaranga team sites to the Sudanese government. UNAMID will only become weaker in the near future, and is likely to be reduced further with the UN Security Council's next reauthorisation of the mission (due in June 2018). The RSF is now the overwhelmingly predominant force on the ground in Darfur.

The problems behind UNAMID are long-standing. From the mission's inception Khartoum has dictated terms, and UNAMID has had to operate with very little support from the international community, lacking critically important aircraft and helicopters in particular. It relied overwhelmingly on AU troop-contributing countries in an operation unprecedented since the creation of the AU Peace and Security Council (AUPSC), but there has been almost no 'inter-operability' (the term military planners use to describe the shared communications, planning and intelligence-gathering of discrete military units working in concert within a given theatre of operations). In 2017 UNAMID did virtually nothing to provide protection for civilians and humanitarians. It reported some atrocities to the UN secretary-general, but only a very small percentage of what had been reported to UNAMID as needing investigation. In some locations it acted as a deterrent force, but often gave way, even in positions of strength, before the demands of the SAF and militia forces.

One notable consequence of UNAMID's ongoing deployment out of Darfur will be the highly restricted flight ability of the UN Humanitarian Air Service (UNHAS), which requires a military presence to land its aircraft in Darfur. With a diminished capacity and an extreme concentration of the remaining forces, there will be a great many locations where UNHAS will no longer be able to fly.

Failing peace process

The peace process made no tangible progress in 2017. In early July, Sudanese President Omar al-Bashir extended a unilateral ceasefire in the Darfur region, as well as in Blue Nile and South Kordofan states, for another four months. Around one month later, the SPLM–N faction led by Abdel Aziz al-Hilu declared a six-month unilateral ceasefire in Blue Nile and South Kordofan states. In spite of this, fighting – while much abated – continued in areas along the front-lines. Moreover, the split within the SPLM–N leadership led to fighting between the two factions: Khartoum was content to see its military adversaries fight one another, although South Kordofan remained a serious long-term concern for the regime.

The history of the various peace agreements indicates an ongoing lack of diplomatic initiative. Notable attempts include the Abuja (Nigeria) Darfur Peace Agreement in May 2006; the ill-conceived Roadmap for Darfur, promulgated by Thabo Mbeki as head of the African Union High-Level Panel on Darfur (now re-designated as the AU High-Level Panel for Implementation, but without any clear indication of what exactly is being implemented); and the Doha Document for Peace in Darfur (DDPD) in July 2011, which failed to represent the views and demands of either the consequential rebel groups or Darfuri civil society.

The decision to cling to the DDPD – still the diplomatic posture of most European countries in 2017 – reflected largely a lack of willingness to invest real diplomatic resources in ending the conflict. Indeed, European countries appeared far more interested in rapprochement with Khartoum, nominally in the interest of securing assistance from the regime in stanching the flow of African migration to the European continent. Confronting Khartoum over the lack of any movement on the peace process was simply not a European priority, given European anxiety about what was widely perceived as an African refugee crisis. The US State Department privately acknowledged that the DDPD was a 'diplomatic dead letter', but refused to say as much publicly and explicitly. A public admission would reveal the expediency of past support for the DDPD – which was largely dictated by the views of a former Obama administration special envoy for Sudan, Air Force Major-General (Retd) Scott Gration – as well as the complete absence of a back-up plan or new diplomatic initiative.

The AUPSC long ago decided that the best strategy in Darfur was simply to declare UNAMID successful. Indeed, at one point before the offensives in East Jebel Marra, the AUPSC referred to UNAMID as a peacekeeping operation that could serve as a model 'worthy of emulation' for future such operations. Certainly there has never been a strong appetite in the AUPSC for a confrontation with Khartoum.

Darfur in 2017 appeared to be mired in a grim, violent status quo, which neither the international community nor the Khartoum regime seemed willing to address in any meaningful way. Sexual violence remained at epidemic proportions; humanitarian assistance was increasingly attenuated and deeply threatened by the prospect of camp dismantlings; assaults on non-Arab African populations, by both the RSF and irregular Arab militia groups, continued; and land seizures were ongoing and increasingly rendered permanent by the prevailing insecurity. Very few of the roughly three million people who remain displaced as IDPs or refugees had any real prospect of returning to their homes and lands.

Chapter Five

South Asia

Afghanistan

No side in the conflict in Afghanistan made a decisive breakthrough in 2017. The Afghan National Security Forces (ANSF), with assistance from the United States and NATO's *Operation Resolute Support*, prevented the Taliban from seizing control of a

Key statistics	2016	2017
Type:	Internationalised	Internationalised
Fatalities:	16,000	15,000
New IDPs:	650,000	470,000
New refugees:	500,000[a]	400,000[a]

single provincial capital. However, by the end of 2017, the insurgents remained in control of 14 districts and were openly present in 263 others, thereby threatening at least 70% of the country. Both the Taliban and Khorasan Province (ISIS–KP), an affiliate of the Islamic State, also known as ISIS or ISIL, carried out a number of mass-casualty terrorist attacks in the capital Kabul that had political repercussions for the National Unity Government (NUG). Meanwhile, the peace and reconciliation process with the Taliban saw little real progress.

No progress on peace

As the Afghan peace process remained moribund, Moscow hosted a series of talks apparently designed to give itself a stronger role in Afghanistan. Neither Kabul nor the Taliban were likely to view a peace process without the participation of the US as credible, however, and even Kabul was only invited to the fourth iteration

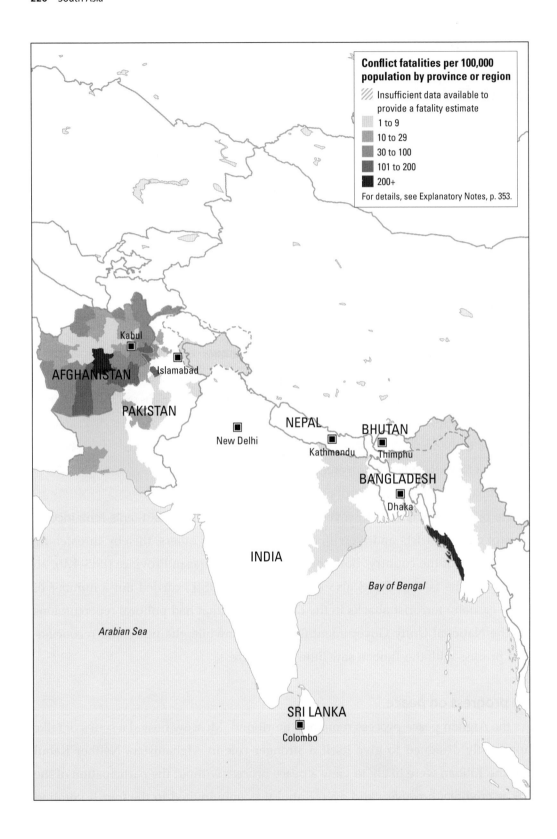

Conflict fatalities per 100,000
population by province or region

▨ Insufficient data available to
   provide a fatality estimate
☐ 1 to 9
☐ 10 to 29
☐ 30 to 100
☐ 101 to 200
■ 200+

For details, see Explanatory Notes, p. 353.

AFGHANISTAN

Kabul

Islamabad

PAKISTAN

NEPAL

New Delhi

Kathmandu

BHUTAN

Thimphu

BANGLADESH

Dhaka

INDIA

Bay of Bengal

Arabian Sea

SRI LANKA

Colombo

of Russian-led talks, in February. This was followed by an 11-country conference in April which produced a joint statement of little significance, although Russia's increasingly forward-leaning policy on Afghanistan did lead to an increase in tensions with the US that mirrored the wider nature of the relationship. General Curtis Scaparrotti, NATO's Supreme Allied Commander Europe, accused Russia of having 'increased influence in terms of association and perhaps even supply to the Taliban'. Scaparrotti's claim was the third time in a few months that a high-ranking US military official had publicly expressed concern about Moscow's ties with the Taliban. Russia and the Taliban both denied the allegations, although Moscow has admitted on several previous occasions that it has contact with the Taliban in order to protect Russian interests in Afghanistan and to help the group fight ISIS–KP.

Russia's intervention in the peace process contrasted with China's quieter approach, of which few details were publicly available, although Pakistani media reported on 7 March that a Taliban delegation had visited China in February. Beijing also denied reports that its forces patrolled inside Afghanistan.

With international efforts not bearing fruit, Afghan President Ashraf Ghani launched the Kabul Process on 6 June in an attempt to reinvigorate the peace process and to improve relations with Pakistan, given that Islamabad's involvement is crucial to any agreement. Ghani said this was the Taliban's 'last chance'; the group replied that 'peace negotiations will mean nothing' as long as foreign troops remain in Afghanistan. The Kabul Process initiative was followed by a meeting between Ghani and Pakistan's then-prime minister Nawaz Sharif on the sidelines of the Shanghai Cooperation Organisation summit in Astana on 10 June, during which they agreed to revive the Quadrilateral Coordination Group (QCG) peace-talks mechanism (which had held five previous rounds of talks, with the last being held in 2016) and to use bilateral channels to deal with actions against terrorist groups. Chinese Foreign Minister Wang Yi visited both countries at the end of the month as part of his mediation efforts and brokered a trilateral agreement to launch a crisis-management mechanism and dialogue between foreign ministers. After a hiatus of more than a year, in October Oman hosted the sixth round of QCG talks.

The High Peace Council announced on 6 December that the body was prepared to offer the Taliban an office in Kabul if the group was ready to enter into dialogue and negotiate an end to the conflict. The Taliban was unlikely to accept an office in enemy territory, however, and replied that only its political office in Qatar would engage in peace talks. By the end of the year, the peace process appeared to have progressed very little.

Political rifts widen

The government was confronted by greater political challenges at the end of the year than at the beginning. Former Northern Alliance leaders, unhappy with their level of influence in Kabul, formed the Coalition for the Rescue of Afghanistan in June. This included leading figures of the Jamaat-e-Islami and Junbish-e Milli-ye Islami parties – both important blocs during the civil war, with the former predominantly representing Sunni Tajiks and the latter Sunni Uzbeks. The creation of the coalition followed the unofficial exile to Turkey of Junbish leader and First Vice-President Abdul Rashid Dostum after sexual-assault allegations. Several high-profile terrorist attacks in Kabul – at least one of which targeted Jamaat leaders – also played a part in the formation of the coalition as Jamaat leaders met with Dostum in Turkey to launch the alliance.

The long-serving and influential governor of Balkh province, Jamaat's Atta Mohammad Noor, then declared himself a presidential candidate on 29 October, saying that the current situation was worse than it was under the Taliban and that the NUG's incompetence was causing rampant insecurity and corruption. On 18 December, President Ghani attempted to force Noor out by announcing that he had accepted Noor's resignation and naming his successor as Mohammad Dawood, also a Jamaat member. Noor said he had indeed offered a resignation, but only under certain preconditions which had not been met, and he therefore had refused to step down. The head of the United Nations Assistance Mission in Afghanistan (UNAMA), Tadamichi Yamamoto, said the emergence of political fault lines largely based on ethnicity posed a particular risk to the country's stability, and added that 'without changes in governance practices we are likely to face future crises that might be more difficult to contain'.

Governance reform appeared a distant hope, however. On 22 June the Independent Election Commission (IEC) announced that parliamentary and district-council elections would be held on 7 July 2018 – almost three years after the current parliament's term was supposed to have ended. Ghani dismissed both the chief secretary and head of the IEC in October and November respectively, citing 'corruption and poor performance'. The dismissals undermined already-low expectations for a transparent and well-run election in July 2018.

The Taliban also experienced political infighting in 2017. Taliban leader Mullah Haibatullah Akhundzada attempted to consolidate his leadership in the face of ongoing internal opposition. In January, he replaced 16 of his 34 provincial 'shadow' governors. Infighting between the main group under Akhundzada and that of a rival, Mullah Mohammed Rasool, continued sporadically, but the small size of Rasool's group meant it was unlikely to pose a serious military challenge to Akhundzada. Economically, however, the Taliban appeared to be secure. The group's finances were likely strengthened by an estimated 87% year-on-year rise in opium production across Afghanistan, according to the United Nations Office on Drugs and Crime. However, although the narcotics business was the group's main source of income, it was far from the only one: Helmand province officials said in January that the Taliban earns around US$4.8 million annually from the Kajaki Dam hydroelectric power plant in the province, equating to about 90% of the income generated by the dam.

Trump's Afghanistan policy

After several delays, the Trump administration's Afghanistan policy was announced in August. President Donald Trump stated on 21 August that he would deploy between 3,500 and 4,000 additional troops who would be primarily focused on training Afghan forces. The figure was later clarified to be 3,800, which would bring the total number of US troops in Afghanistan to around 15,000, given that the Pentagon revealed on 31 August that there were already 11,000 troops in-country, rather than the previously reported 8,400 (the Pentagon claimed that the lower figure had excluded counter-terrorism forces). Trump's speech included a blunt declaration that the US would place greater pressure on Pakistan to end Islamabad's alleged support for the Afghan Taliban. The new US strategy also involved loosening restraints on the use of airpower to support the Afghan security forces – something that had begun well before Trump's announcement. A US Air Force report published on 13 September showed more bombs were dropped on al-Qaeda, ISIS–KP and Taliban positions in August 2017 than in any month since 2012.

Stalemate on the ground

The Taliban's spring offensive, dubbed *Operation Mansouri* after the group's previous leader Mullah Mansour, was officially launched on 28 April. The Taliban declared that the operation would have a 'twin-tracked political and military approach' and focus on 'foreign forces, their military and intelligence infrastructure and in eliminating their internal mercenary apparatus'. According to the group, the operation would include the use of 'conventional attacks, guerrilla warfare, complex martyrdom attacks, insider attacks, and use of IEDs [improvised explosive devices]'. The stated geographical focus was on the provinces of Farah, Faryab, Helmand, Kunduz, Sar-e Pul and Uruzgan, and there were to be attempts to overrun their respective provincial capitals. Both the tactics and locations represented a continuation of the Taliban's 2016 efforts as the group sought to conquer rural districts and selected district centres, while also undermining the legitimacy of the NUG by conducting high-profile attacks in the centre of Kabul.

Although the operation was announced at the end of April, its principles were clear long before then in the pattern of attacks the Taliban carried out from the start of the year. On 10 January, a Taliban suicide bomber detonated his explosives near the parliament in Kabul before a car bomb exploded nearby. The attacks killed 38 people and injured more than 70 others. However, the killing of five diplomats from the United Arab Emirates (UAE) and senior Afghan officials in a bomb attack at a government guesthouse in Kandahar city on the same day went unexplained. Kabul blamed the Taliban, which denied responsibility. The UAE was one of only three states that recognised the Taliban government, and had diplomatic links with the group. If the Taliban was indeed responsible, the main target was likely Kandahar police chief General Abdul Razik.

As serious clashes continued across Helmand into February, and in anticipation of the spring offensive, Brigadier-General Douglas Sims of *Resolute Support* announced on 29 January that the Afghan National Army (ANA) would deploy an additional 600 soldiers to the province. The additional personnel would double the ANA's combat capacity in the province, with the additional troops centred on the provincial capital Lashkar Gah and other strategic locations. This followed earlier announcements by US officials that around 300 marines would be deployed to Helmand in the spring as advisers (replacing an army unit), and that NATO would deploy 200 soldiers to Farah province in western Afghanistan in a train-and-advise capacity.

The Afghan government's Chief Executive Abdullah Abdullah visited Lashkar Gah on 1 February, where he vowed that the city would not fall. He also said that Sangin district, where fighting was ongoing, would soon be cleared of insurgents. Meanwhile, the Taliban commander in Kunduz province, Mullah Abdul Salam Akhund, was killed in an unmanned aerial vehicle (UAV) strike in Dasht-e Archi district on 26 February. On the same day, Afghan forces killed the Taliban shadow governor of Uruzgan province. In western Afghanistan, the governor of Khak-e Safed district, Farah province, was killed in an IED explosion on 7 February.

March was a poor month for the ANSF as a series of assaults in Kabul once again showed its inability to secure the capital from terror attacks. On 1 March, there were three coordinated Taliban attacks in Kabul on a police station, an army recruitment centre and a National Directorate for Security (NDS) office, which in total killed 23 people (including 20 civilians) and injured 106 others. At least six suicide attackers were killed. On 7 March, one person was killed by a bomb attached to a government vehicle in Kabul, while about 100 people were killed in an attack on the Sardar Daud Khan military hospital by suspected Taliban or Haqqani network militants on 8 March. ISIS–KP claimed responsibility for the attack on the hospital but eyewitnesses said the militants seemed to shout a Taliban slogan, and two floors housing injured insurgents were untouched. There were also two incidents on 13 March, including a suicide car-bomb attack that targeted employees of a telecoms company and left three people dead and 19 injured.

The situation in southern Afghanistan also took a turn for the worse as the Taliban conquered the strategic district of Sangin in Helmand on 23 March, less than two months after Abdullah had pledged that it would be cleared of militants. The loss of the strategically located district put further pressure on the provincial capital Lashkar Gah – more or less surrounded since 2016 – and increased the threat to neighbouring Kandahar province, the birthplace of the Taliban. Insurgents carried out deadly attacks on ANSF bases in both Kandahar and Uruzgan. A Taliban attack on an army base outside Mazar-e Sharif on 21 April, which killed at least 140 soldiers and injured some 160 others, led Defence Minister Abdullah Khan Habibi and Qadam Shah Shahim, army chief of staff, to resign as *Operation Mansouri* began.

The Taliban's offensive in the south was sustained and widespread. Helmand remained a hotspot, although much of the province was already in the Taliban's hands. The Taliban's attack on Ghazni's provincial capital on 20 May resembled previous attempts to seize Kunduz city, with the Taliban first establishing a presence in surrounding districts before attacking from three directions. The assault was pushed back. In Kandahar, the Taliban attacked three army bases over four days, killing at least 38 ANSF personnel. An assault on Kunduz city also failed, and government forces retook the Zaybak district of Badakhshan province (which had fallen to the Taliban at the end of April) on 11 May.

May saw another two major suicide attacks in Kabul. On 31 May, a massive suicide car bomb exploded outside Kabul's Wazir Akbar Khan neighbourhood, home to many embassies. At least 92 civilians were killed and 491 others injured in the deadliest single attack in Kabul over the past two decades. The Taliban condemned the attack and authorities blamed the Haqqani network. An ISIS–KP suicide bombing on 3 May targeted a US military convoy in the city, killing eight civilians and wounding 25 others. Three US soldiers were also injured.

The Taliban suffered setbacks in Helmand in June and July, however. Its provincial military commission leader, Mullah Abdul Bari, was killed in a UAV strike in Nad-e Ali district on 11 June, and air and ground operations in Marjah and Nad-e Ali killed dozens of insurgents. The Taliban killed 34 people and injured more than 60 others in a suicide car-bomb attack on 22 June, which targeted people queuing outside the New Kabul Bank branch in Lashkar Gah. Most of the victims were reportedly members of the Afghan police force. A joint Afghan–US campaign in the Nawah-e Barakzai district, southwest of Lashkar Gah, led to the district being recaptured on 17 July after it had been in insurgent hands for about nine months. However, the Taliban continued attacking ANSF bases in Kandahar, reportedly killing more than 100 personnel in July. At least 24 civilians were killed and 42 others injured when a Taliban suicide bomber detonated his car bomb near a bus carrying government employees in Kabul on 24 July.

In August, the insurgents redoubled their efforts in Helmand, carrying out several major attacks on ANSF outposts in an attempt to capture or at least isolate Lashkar Gah. This included a major operation to capture the city of Gereshk, located between Sangin and Lashkar Gah, which ultimately failed. The Taliban conducted more major operations in Helmand than in any other part of Afghanistan as part of its drive to capture or contest most, if not all, of the province by the end of the fighting season.

The Taliban also continued in its attempts to encircle Kunduz city, launching attacks in the Dasht-e Archi, Aliabad, Qala-e Zal and Khanabad districts, but night raids, airstrikes and other tactics weakened the insurgents. The Taliban's second-in-command for Kunduz province was killed in an airstrike on 17 July, along with three other insurgents.

The group did capture several districts elsewhere in the country, although it was only able to retain control of one of them. The ANSF retook Jani Khel district, in Paktia province, on 4 August, only for it to fall to the Taliban again five days later. Afghan special-operations forces recaptured the district on 25 August; by the end of the month, it remained contested. This pattern of district capture, loss and recapture was also evident in seven other provinces across the country. Usually, the force that retook a district or repelled the Taliban relied heavily on Afghan special-operations personnel, who have proven effective but were overstretched due to their relatively small numbers. President Ghani announced on 20 August that the government would establish a new corps of special-operations troops, raising the number of such personnel from 13,000 to 30,000.

On 3 September, Ghani announced a four-year, US$6 billion investment in the Afghan Air Force (AAF) to expand its capabilities. This included plans to expand Afghanistan's UAV capabilities with the construction of UAV bases in Herat, Kandahar and Nangarhar provinces, and to augment existing bases in Helmand and Balkh. The AAF also announced on 16 September plans to procure 150 *Black Hawk* helicopters as part of a multi-year purchase from the US. In a move similar to the 2010 creation of the Afghan Local Police, the defence ministry said on 15 September that it was examining plans to develop 'regional forces' composed of former soldiers to augment the ANSF in rural areas. The announcement was supported by the US government but was criticised by human-rights groups, which said that the force would pose a threat to civilians.

The Taliban carried out at least five attacks on foreign forces in September, killing one soldier and one civilian, and injuring 11 others. On 27 September, Taliban fighters launched rockets at Kabul International Airport to coincide with a visit to the capital by US Secretary of Defense James Mattis and NATO Secretary-General Jens Stoltenberg.

The Taliban briefly gained control of three districts during October – Andar in Ghazni, Shib Koh in Farah and Siyah Gird in Parwan – although the ANSF retook the areas within a few days. The insurgents carried out other successful operations, however. On 19 October the Taliban attacked an ANA base in Maiwand district, Kandahar, using car bombs and suicide vests. The attackers killed at least 43 soldiers, wounded nine others and captured six, and also destroyed the base. A similar attack two days earlier in Gardez, Paktia province, killed around 40 people. On 21 October, a suicide bombing against military cadets at the entrance to a military academy in Kabul killed 15 and wounded four others. The previous day a suspected Taliban suicide bomber attacked a Sunni mosque in Dolina district, Ghor province. The target of the attack – a local Jamaat commander – was killed along with 30 civilians.

The first contingent of the additional troops promised by Trump, numbering some 3,000 personnel, were deployed to Afghanistan by mid-November as the stalemate continued. The US Air Force expanded its targeting to Taliban-linked narcotics-processing and -storage facilities in Helmand. At least eight facilities were destroyed in northern Helmand, and another nine sites were destroyed and as many as 44 Taliban fighters killed in the border town of Baramcha, Dishu district.

In December, the ANSF, with foreign military support, launched large-scale, multi-day operations in multiple locations across Afghanistan. The government announced that the ANSF would maintain a high operational tempo in the winter in order to 'clear' unstable regions of the country of insurgent groups. Similar plans in previous years have ended up having little discernible effect once the snow melts, however, and by the end of the month, there had been no evident change in the overall situation.

ISIS–KP and al-Qaeda

ISIS–KP proved resilient in the face of leadership attrition, continued airstrikes, ground operations and clashes with the Taliban, although these challenges did weaken the group. On 6 April a spokesman for *Resolute Support* said that the coalition had reduced the amount of territory controlled by ISIS–KP by two-thirds and killed some 75% of the group's fighters. The group had also been targeted by the largest non-nuclear bomb ever used in combat by the US, when the US Air Force dropped a Massive Ordnance Air Blast bomb on an ISIS–KP cave network in Achin district, Nangarhar, on 13 April. On 27 April, ISIS–KP leader Abdul Haseeb was killed along with 35 militants in a joint US–Afghan raid in Achin district. (Two US soldiers were killed and another injured during the operation.) Abu Saeed, a Pakistani, was appointed as ISIS–KP's new leader in June. He was reported to have been killed in a UAV strike on 11 July, although the group denied this and did not appoint a new leader. The US said on 20 May that 750 ISIS–KP militants had been killed since March and that the group would be defeated in 2017.

However, ISIS–KP defied US predictions by increasing its influence outside its Nangarhar province stronghold in 2017. The group strengthened its foothold in northern Jawzjan province – first gained in late 2015 when a local Taliban commander, Qari Hikmatullah, swore allegiance to Abu Bakr al-Baghdadi – and claimed responsibility for the killing of at least six employees of the International Committee of the Red Cross in Qush Tepa district on 8 February. The day before, an ISIS–KP suicide bomber had targeted employees of the Supreme Court in Kabul, killing at least 22 people and injuring another 41. The group carried out another attack on 24 February on a mosque in Jawzjan's Darzab district where police officers were attending a service; ten officers and a civilian were killed. More than 3,000 families reportedly fled ISIS–KP's increasing influence in Darzab and Qush Tepa in December: Darzab residents and the province's human-rights commission reported that hundreds of children were being indoctrinated and trained by the group.

ISIS–KP also expanded into Nuristan province, attacking a police post there, and, after clashes with the Taliban on 8 and 13 June, briefly seized control of parts of Tora Bora, the mountain stronghold in Nangarhar province once famous as the base of Osama bin Laden. The security forces reacted swiftly with ground and air operations, as the group would have been very difficult to dislodge if allowed to settle in the stronghold. Acting Defence Minister Tariq Shah Bahrami said on 17 June that the area had been recaptured.

On 31 July, four ISIS–KP militants attacked the Iraqi embassy in Kabul. They failed to kill or take hostage any embassy personnel, but this was the first time an attack by the group appeared to be directly linked to the parent group's fight in

Iraq and Syria. ISIS statements and social-media accounts celebrated the attack as revenge for the loss of the Iraqi city of Mosul.

ISIS–KP's sectarian terror campaign continued, with 87 people killed and 111 others injured in attacks on predominantly Shia targets in Kabul from September to November. Meanwhile, joint ANSF–US operations in Nangarhar's Achin and Khogyani districts continued into late December, with the defence ministry claiming large casualty counts for ISIS–KP fighters and saying they had freed many parts of the districts. However, these claims were undermined by further ISIS–KP attacks in Kabul and Jalalabad. The Kabul attack against a Shia cultural centre on 28 December killed at least 50 and wounded another 90, while the attack in Jalalabad on 31 December killed at least 15.

A number of al-Qaeda members were reported killed in southern Afghanistan in 2017. The most significant incident occurred in early December, when the NDS announced that 81 al-Qaeda fighters and facilitators, including Omar Khattab, the organisation's highest-ranking leader inside Afghanistan, had been killed in a special-forces operation by the ANSF and foreign forces across three provinces. While there is little reliable data publicly available, al-Qaeda rebuilt some of its capabilities in Afghanistan in 2017, with one example being the formation of al-Qaeda in the Indian Subcontinent (AQIS).

Human security

The dire situation of Afghan civilians continued in 2017 as the high-intensity conflict remained mired in strategic stalemate: thousands of people were killed or displaced by fighting in the course of the year. With limited access to food, healthcare, sanitation and other services, an estimated one-third of Afghanistan's population required assistance in 2017. The International Criminal Court considered opening formal investigations into potential war crimes committed in Afghanistan by all parties to the conflict, but postponed this in July.

As of 31 December 2016, there were 1,553,000 internally displaced persons (IDPs) in Afghanistan. According to the Internal Displacement Monitoring Centre, a total of 653,000 people were newly internally displaced in 2016. Adding to this number in 2017 were returning refugees from mainly Pakistan and Iran – more than one million between March 2016 and March 2017, according to the Ministry of Refugees and Repatriation. This was mainly a result of Pakistan's policy of forcibly repatriating Afghan refugees, ostensibly over security concerns despite the fact that many of the refugees had lived across the border for decades.

The United Nations reported an estimated total of 10,453 civilian casualties – 3,438 people killed and 7,015 injured – in Afghanistan in 2017. This was a decrease of about 9% from 2016, but still at the historically high levels seen in recent years. Anti-government elements were responsible for 65% of the casualties: the Taliban 42%, ISIS–KP 10%, and undetermined and other anti-government elements 13%. Many of these casualties were caused by indiscriminate terror attacks by both the Taliban and ISIS–KP, though the groups' other activities also threatened civilians. ISIS–KP claimed responsibility for the abduction and massacre of dozens of Shia civilians in the village of Mirza Olang, Sar-e Pul province, in August. Although the Taliban condemned the attacks, local officials and the UN stated that the group had participated in the violence. In December, Taliban forces in Badghis province forced the closure of eight healthcare clinics as punishment for the locals' purported support for the Afghan government, thereby denying medical access to as many as 100,000 civilians.

In February 2018 UNAMA released a report which concluded that pro-government forces caused 20% of the civilian casualties in 2017, with 16% attributed to the ANSF, 2% to international military forces, and 1% each to pro-government armed groups and undetermined pro-government forces. The report stated that many of these were caused by airstrikes – there were an estimated 631 civilian casualties (295 deaths and 336 injured) caused by aerial operations, a 7% increase from 2016. On 28 August, a US airstrike on a suspected Taliban command centre in Shindand district, Herat province, resulted in the deaths of at least 15 civilians, according to a preliminary investigation by UNAMA. The Mission also concluded that a US airstrike near Pul-e Alam, in Logar province, two days later resulted in the deaths of at least 13 civilians. International forces and the Afghan government launched investigations into the incidents. *Resolute Support* commander General John Nicholson travelled to Kunduz on 28 November and publicly apologised for a similar incident in which ten civilians were killed in an airstrike in Chahar Dara district on 4 November.

The stalemate that developed in 2017 was likely to continue into 2018, with Afghanistan facing another challenging year ahead. The Taliban failed to conquer any provincial capitals, but remained strong in rural areas. Militarily, the increase in US troops with loosened rules of engagement strengthened counter-insurgency operations, but was unlikely to prove a game-changer on the ground. There is a risk that politics will be further divided along ethnic and sectarian lines, something that groups such as the Taliban and ISIS-KP will attempt to encourage and exploit. Key challenges for Kabul and the international community include jumpstarting a moribund peace process and implementing political reforms to strengthen the embattled Afghan government's legitimacy.

India (Assam)

Key statistics	2016	2017
Type:	Internal	Internal
Fatalities:	100	30
New IDPs:	— [b]	— [b]
New refugees:	— [b]	— [b]

Assam witnessed one of its most peaceful years since the onset of insurgency in the late 1980s, with an estimated 33 conflict-related fatalities in comparison to 96 in 2016, 63 in 2015 and 305 in 2014. This led Assam's Chief Minister Sarbananda Sonowal to proclaim that Assam had now transitioned into a peaceful state and was no longer severely affected by insurgency. However, key developments in 2017 demonstrated that the underlying conditions for potential civil unrest and insurgency remained present. The continuing operational activity of non-ceasefire signatory armed groups such as the United Liberation Front of Asom–Independent (ULFA–I) and the National Democratic Front of Bodoland–Saoraigwra (NDFB–S), along with the slow progress in the peace processes with ceasefire-signatory groups, demonstrated that insurgency was not yet at an end in the state. Crucially, growing frustrations in Assam's political scene pertaining to the state's fragile identity politics and anti-migrant sentiments meant that the root causes of unrest remained unresolved.

Insurgents 'down but not out'

Anti-talks armed groups in Assam continued to sustain losses and were increasingly confined to outlying areas, but nonetheless remained active in conducting recruitment, extortion and limited armed clashes with the security forces. NDFB–S sustained 15 casualties during 2017. This statistic, almost half of the state's total conflict-related fatalities, was reflective of Assam's continued and sustained counter-insurgency operations since it launched *Operation All Out* in December 2014. Reports that further senior members of the organisation had left the group in June to form their own organisation, National Freedom Fighters of Bodoland, pointed to the impact of counter-insurgency operations on the NDFB–S's internal cohesion.

The ULFA–I, historically the most powerful armed group in Assam, sustained nine fatalities during 2017, but continued to demonstrate its ability to adapt and survive in adverse circumstances. Three ULFA–I militants were killed in Nagaland's Mon district in June during a clash with Territorial Army personnel, which also led to the deaths of one army major and a civilian. The group's presence in Mon district, the traditional stronghold of Naga armed group and United National Liberation Front of Western South East Asia (UNLFWESEA) ally, the National Socialist Council of Nagalim–Khaplang (NSCN–K), reflected the ULFA–I's growing reliance on cooperation with regional allies in a bid to sustain its military capacities, an assessment that was confirmed by Assam Director General of Police Mukesh Sahay on 16 May. Similarly, members of the group operated as part of a joint team with Manipur-based Coordination Committee (CorCom) militants at Jairampur, near the Assam–Arunachal Pradesh border, on 22 January, engaging in a clash with Assam Rifles personnel that led to the deaths of two Assam Rifles troopers and two of the ULFA–I/CorCom party. The geographical extent of the group's operations, although limited in comparison to its earlier capabilities, cast doubt on estimates that the group had little more than 100 active militants. Further doubt was cast on these figures on 27 August when an interrogated ULFA–I militant suggested that the group's shared camps in Myanmar held up to 500 ULFA–I militants, far above previous estimates made by the security forces. India's frustration with Myanmar's lacklustre approach towards the armed camps dotting the international border became evident on 3 April, when India cut its foreign-aid budget to Myanmar from INR400 billion (US\$6.1bn) to INR225bn (around US\$3.4bn). The move sought to pressure Nyapyidaw into cracking down on groups such as the ULFA–I that were exploiting sanctuary across the international border and thereby preventing Indian counter-insurgency forces from achieving complete victory.

Slow progress in peace talks

While the peace processes between the government and the pro-talks factions of the ULFA and the NDFB continued throughout 2017, little tangible progress was made. The year nonetheless began with the renewal of ceasefires with the pro-talks armed groups on 10 January, ensuring that peace talks would continue. Furthermore, moves towards ceasefires and peace talks with smaller groups ensured that the number of armed groups continued to decrease. On 28 January, the state government suspended counter-insurgency operations against the Karbi People's Liberation Tigers, while the commander-in-chief of the National Socialist Council of Adivasi surrendered to the police on 7 February. In May, the United People's Revolutionary Front declared a six-month unilateral ceasefire, while police sources hinted that surrenders were expected from two local armed groups based in Hailakandi and Karimganj districts – the Bru Liberation Army Union and the United Democratic Liberation Army – suggesting that an increasing number of armed groups sought a return to mainstream political life.

However, 2017 marked a slow year for peace talks with the major armed factions: NDFB–Progressive (NDFB–P), NDFB–Ranjan Daimary (NDFB–R) and ULFA–Pro-Talks Faction (ULFA–PTF). On 6 April, ULFA–PTF questioned what it perceived as the central government's 'apathetic' attitude towards talks. Indeed, after P.C. Haldar's term as the government interlocutor for peace talks in Assam expired in December 2016, it was not until June 2017 that the new interlocutor, former Intelligence Bureau director Dineshwar Sharma, was appointed to the role. The appointment was welcomed by the ULFA–PTF as an attempt to build momentum in the peace process. However, despite Sharma's chairing of a series of meetings with the ULFA–PTF and the two pro-talks NDFB factions, NDFB–P and NDFB–R, and a statement from Union Minister of State for Home Affairs Kiren Rijiju on 9 June which suggested that peace agreements with all three groups were likely to be signed soon, little noticeable progress was made in the talks. On 6 November, NDFB–P conveyed its frustration with the peace process by holding a three-hour demonstration in conjunction with Bodo civil-society organisations across the Bodo-inhabited areas of Assam, urging the central government to expedite the peace process. The group had expressed optimism in October that it could successfully negotiate the creation of a separate Bodoland State within the Indian Union, but the protest implied that little progress had been made in navigating this issue.

Unresolved political questions

The decades-long political turbulence that has fuelled insurgency and armed conflict in Assam has been dominated by the issue of illegal migration into the state and the perceived demographic threat to local identities. While the 2016 state elections saw the accession of Sonowal of the Bharatiya Janata Party (BJP) on a decisively anti-migrant platform, the BJP's national policies put Assamese political sentiment on a collision course with the incumbent government. While Sonowal, a former activist of the Assam Agitation (1979–85), urged that the international border be sealed immediately in August and continued to adopt anti-migrant rhetoric, his counterparts in New Delhi threatened to contradict the political climate in Assam. The central government's plans to push through a proposed Citizenship (Amendment) Bill, intended to grant citizenship rights to Hindus and other minority communities from Afghanistan, Bangladesh and Pakistan, drew the ire of civil-society organisations with connections to the agitation. On 14 December, for example, an organisation consisting of the family members of Assam Agitation martyrs said that the bill would fundamentally disrespect the 855 protesters who died during the agitation, while peasant organisations such as the Krishak Mukti Sangram Samiti threatened to conduct protests if the bill was passed.

The process of updating the National Register of Citizens (NRC), which would effectively determine the number of illegal migrants in the state and provide the grounds for their deportation, risked both alienating those seeking the prevention of illegal migration and the state's significant indigenous Muslim population. On 15 October Muslim civil-society organisations recommended that indigenous Muslims be included in the pre-1951 citizens list to ensure their status as fully fledged citizens in the state; however, other groups, such as Jamiat Ulema-e-Hind, warned that Assam would 'burn' if the state's Muslims were excluded from the register, revealing multifaceted tensions associated with the register's publication. On 6 August, official sources suggested that the release of the NRC would be delayed beyond the anticipated deadline of 31 December. By the end of the year, however, it became clear that the state government would meet the deadline, and December saw the deployment of an estimated 45,000–60,000 extra paramilitaries to deal with potential unrest associated with the release of the register.

Although there was a dramatic reduction in violence in 2017, the conditions that sustained unrest and insurgency remained ultimately unresolved. This had significant implications for civilians, reflected in the deaths of eight civilians during the year. Extortion, kidnappings and threats to businesses remained endemic in areas where insurgent groups continued to operate. The central government's policy of demonetisation undertaken in 2016 pushed groups such as the ULFA–I and the NDFB–S further into intensified extortion campaigns. On 25 February, ULFA–I militants fired on a tea estate in relation to an unpaid extortion demand in Tinsukia district, whereas in June a tea-garden manager and his assistant were abducted during a journey between two plantations in Goalpara and Kokrajhar districts. On 28 September, ULFA–I militants kidnapped another tea-garden worker in Tinsukia district, demonstrating the continued ground-level conditions of uncertainty and insecurity for those residing in rural Assam.

India (CPI–Maoist)

The Naxalite insurgency posed a serious security challenge to the Indian government during 2017. The Communist Party of India–Maoist (CPI–Maoist) remained, by far, the insurgency's largest and best-armed organisation. It conducted numer-

Key statistics	2016	2017
Type:	Internal	Internal
Fatalities:	400	300
New IDPs:	–[b]	–[b]
New refugees:	–[b]	–[b]

ous attacks on the Indian security forces and civilians, primarily in the rural regions of Andhra Pradesh, Chhattisgarh, Jharkhand, Maharashtra and Odisha states. Though CPI–Maoist used violence to both control 'liberated' territory in the hinterlands and contest the government's hold on other areas, it suffered from a series of government-inflicted setbacks. In keeping with previous years, the central government deployed paramilitary law-enforcement units, primarily the Central Armed Police Force (CRPF), to reinforce the state-level security forces. This security build-up was coordinated with investments in economic-development and infrastructure projects throughout the 'Red Corridor' (the term commonly used to refer to areas under Naxalite influence). There were several indications that these measures helped government forces to consolidate gains made against the insurgency in previous years: many Maoist leaders surrendered, local communities showed further signs of estrangement from the insurgents and the security forces inflicted high numbers of fatalities on CPI–Maoist. Though the insurgency showed clear signs of distress (possibly even its eventual unravelling), it also made efforts to learn from its setbacks and adapt to the government's strategy. However, a resurgence appeared unlikely by the end of the year.

Violence in the Red Corridor

Naxalite-related violence was dispersed across India's central and eastern regions in 2017, with an estimated 314 fatalities from combat or assassinations observed in 52 different districts spread over eight separate states. The violence was fiercest, however, in southern Chhattisgarh State, which witnessed the majority (around 53%) of the year's fatalities. Southern Chhattisgarh's Bastar region, comprising eight different districts (including the eponymous Bastar district), has been Naxalism's greatest stronghold since the movement's resurgence in the 1990s, and contains most of CPI–Maoist's remaining 'liberated zones', or territories in which the group holds a near monopoly on the use of violence. Of the 147 deaths that occurred outside Chhattisgarh, nearly all happened (along a roughly even distribution) in Andhra Pradesh (48), Odisha (30), Jharkhand (24), Bihar (22) and Maharashtra (21) states. Non-combatants suffered most from the violence, as a clear majority of fatalities (around 66%) were deemed to be civilians. CPI–Maoist militants were responsible for each one of these victims, most of whom were assassinated for allegedly passing information to police. In a rare instance of mass violence, Maoists derailed a passenger train in January, killing 40 passengers. Unlike in previous years, no substantiated reports of government-perpetrated extra-judicial or accidental killings of civilians emerged, though several incidents remained under investigation at the end of the year.

Fighting between Naxalites and government forces occurred regularly during 2017, and generally took the form of brief gunfights and improvised explosive device (IED) ambushes. Government forces, comprised mainly of well-armed paramilitary law-enforcement units, launched numerous short-range and long-range patrols to find and engage militants at their temporary and (more rarely) permanent encampments. Naxalites, on the other hand, attempted to avoid pitched battles, and relied primarily on IEDs to ambush the security forces. These actions culminated in the deaths of 141 Naxalites and 67 federal or state law-enforcement officers. Put differently, slightly more than two Naxalites died in fighting for every law-enforcement officer killed, indicating that the security forces were outfighting the insurgents. Indeed, there was evidence to suggest that the security forces were launching more sophisticated operations with greater precision than ever before. In late June, for instance, the Chhattisgarh security forces launched *Operation Prahar*, a 48-hour raid on the headquarters of CPI–Maoist's heavily armed '1 Battalion'. Though *Prahar* culminated in little more than a large skirmish (as many as 20 Maoists may have been killed), its scale (it mobilised approximately 1,500 personnel) was unprecedented, and government forces had never before penetrated so deeply (albeit briefly) into a Maoist-liberated zone.

The security forces also achieved notable successes against the People's Liberation Front of India (PLFI), a small CPI–Maoist splinter group. Several Chhattisgarh-based PLFI commanders surrendered to the authorities in July, weakening the group's influence there. Later in September, Simdega district police (Jharkhand State) succeeded in ambushing the PLFI's leader, Dinesh Gope, as he travelled with a contingent of militants. Gope escaped capture, but may have been wounded during the encounter. Several days later, police in Sundargarh district, Odisha State, also succeeded in ambushing a PLFI unit and captured a member of the PLFI's Odisha–Jharkhand Zonal Committee. Police claimed that both operations were planned and conducted using information gleaned from intelligence assets. This suggests that during 2017 the PLFI's top commanders could no longer conceal their movements from government forces, and that they may have been unable to depend on the loyalty of their subordinates.

CPI–Maoist, despite setbacks, frequently attempted to ambush the security forces with IEDs. On two occasions, Maoists managed to detonate IEDs under vehicles transporting security personnel: one attack in February killed eight Odisha-state police officers on a training exercise in Koraput district, while another attack in March killed 12 CRPF commandos in Sukma district, Chhattisgarh. In a much more intensive operation in April, CPI–Maoist forces ambushed two CRPF companies as they patrolled a road (connecting Injiram and Bheji villages) under construction in Sukma district, Chhattisgarh. The attack, which killed 25 CRPF troopers, was the single most lethal incident for the security forces since 2010, and prompted India's minister of home affairs to call for a review of the national anti-Naxalite strategy. Despite the success of these ambushes, the security forces reported in December that their countermeasures were effectively neutralising remotely detonated IEDs, forcing Maoists to use pressure-activated mines, which are less reliable and more dangerous to bomb-makers.

Economic and infrastructure development

Since 2012, the Indian government has coupled its security operations in the Red Corridor with economic and infrastructure development projects. This strategy, which is designed to attract the support of civilian communities that might other-wise aid insurgents, continued in 2017. The chief minister of Chhattisgarh restated this strategy during a speech in December when he observed that 'Change can't be brought at gunpoint. It will need dialogue and development.' He promised to bring peace to the Red Corridor by expanding economic opportunities for Chhattisgarh communities. India's vice-president, Venkaiah Naidu, made a similar statement during a September speech in which he asked local communities in Naxalite-affected areas to abandon or rebuff the insurgency. By helping the government to defeat the Maoists, the vice-president argued, civilians could remove the largest impediment to future prosperity: 'Peace is required for development', he said.

The government moved to realise its 'peace through development' rhetoric by implementing several programmes and a diverse array of individual projects. The security forces in Visakhapatnam district in Andhra Pradesh, for example, began providing local communities with an ambulance service. They also built and maintained free weigh-stations for local farmers, who had complained that local merchants were cheating them with skewed, privately owned scales. Road construc-tion continued to be one of the government's highest priorities, as it is considered to both provide economic development and increase the mobility of the security forces. The government estimated in August that 25% of road-construction projects planned since 2011 had been completed. CPI–Maoist often extorted the firms con-tracted to build these roads, and raided construction sites either to demand further payments or to resist the projects outright. In April, CPI–Maoist attacked two CRPF companies guarding the Injiram–Bheji road project, the most lethal assault on the security forces since 2010. Despite CPI–Maoist's resistance, the government completed the Injiram–Bheji road in September, suggesting the Maoists could only delay road construction, not prevent it indefinitely. In fact, the pace of road construction may accelerate in the future, since completed roads increase the mobility of the security forces, which facilitates, in turn, subsequent road construction.

Not all communities in the Red Corridor welcomed road-construction projects, however. Members of the Dongria Kondh tribe in Rayagada district, Odisha, demanded that the government significantly restrict road-building efforts in the area. To build rapport with this community, the local CPI–Maoist unit acknowledged the demand, and cited it as the reason for subsequent raids on a nearby road-construction camp. In addition to road construction, some local communities also resisted government-backed mining projects. In January, more than 70 village bodies in the Surjagad hills of Gadchiroli district in Maharashtra formed Visthapan Virodhi Jan Vikas Andolan (VVJA) ('Agitation Against Displacement') and declared their opposition to mining, saying that it had damaged local agriculture and religious sites. As in Rayagada district, the local CPI–Maoist unit appeared to support the VVJA's goal by regularly raiding Surjagad mining operations, which kept the mines inactive for long periods. Other state governments implemented development projects to compensate or mitigate the negative effects of mineral extraction. Jharkhand's government, for instance, announced in May that it would invest INR150 million (around US$2.3m) to supply mining-affected communities with drinking water. However, the Maharashtra government planned no similar projects for the Surjagad area.

Counter-insurgency strategy progress

By several measures, the government's counter-insurgency strategy – which combines a security build-up with economic development – achieved meaningful progress in 2017. In terms of fatalities, slightly more than twice as many CPI–Maoist militants died in fighting (at least 141) compared with security-forces personnel (67). Though this ratio is nearly identical to that observed in 2015 (when 101 Maoists and 46 security personnel died), it points to a decline in the security forces' battlefield effectiveness compared to 2016, when more than three militants died for every member of the security forces. It is important to note, however, that no decline would have been detected if CRPF forces guarding the Injiram–Bheji road in Sukma district, Chhattisgarh, had evaded a deadly ambush by CPI–Maoist militants in April, an attack that left 25 troopers dead. A similarly sized detachment of CRPF forces easily fended off a similar ambush by Maoists in Gadchiroli district, Maharashtra, in November. A comparison of these two ambushes suggests that government forces have the tactical competence to handle the largest and most well-organised Maoist attacks, but that any unit caught unawares could be punished severely by the Maoists.

The government's investment in economic development may have contributed to CPI–Maoist's relatively high death toll. This strategy is designed to win the loyalty of civilians, thereby depriving Maoists of the local support they need to conceal their movements from government forces. Anecdotal evidence suggests that the strategy has met with some success. In April, for instance, a strategically important bridge over the Shabri River, connecting Chhattisgarh's Sukma district with Odisha's Malkangiri district, was completed. The project had been scheduled to begin in 2006 but, by intimidating construction workers, CPI–Maoist had prevented work beginning until 2013. Local communities contributed to its completion in 2017 by volunteering labour and materials, despite the Maoists' continued opposition. In another example, tribal communities in Gadchiroli district, Maharashtra, refused to honour CPI–Maoist's 'Martyr's Week', an annual occasion on which Maoists attempt to rally public support and recruit more militants. Both instances illustrate how communities became more willing to thwart Maoists' instructions during 2017, despite the risk of violent retaliation. This suggests two possibilities: the legitimacy of the Indian state grew in the Red Corridor, or civilians valued the benefits of state-sponsored development more than they feared Maoist retaliation. Either would indicate a decline in CPI–Maoist's influence and a commensurate increase in the effort needed to evade government forces.

Persistent surrenders from CPI–Maoist's ranks also suggested a weakened insurgency. Militant surrenders occurred throughout the year, no doubt encouraged by the government's offer of amnesty and rehabilitation assistance (often including financial aid). Asked why his brother left CPI–Maoist to surrender, a villager from the Ayodha hills region explained to the *Times of India* in July that 'Every former Maoist now earns handsomely. My brother wanted to avail [himself] of the opportunity.' In all, 584 militants (or self-proclaimed militants) surrendered to the authorities between 1 January and 31 October. This constitutes a reduction of around 57% in surrenders compared to the same ten-month period of 2016, but police have claimed, with good reason, that this drop was due to a declining pool of active militants eligible for surrender rather than improved morale on the part of CPI–Maoist.

More than twice as many Maoist commanders also surrendered to the government in 2017 (45) as did during 2016 (18). Once the group's overall losses are taken into account, this increase in surrenders is even more significant than the absolute number suggests. The stature of these surrendered commanders should also be considered: among them were several high-ranking leaders, including the commander of CPI–Maoist's Bihar regional zone and a member of CPI–Maoist's Central Committee, the organisation's highest decision-making body. If CPI–Maoist's highest echelons grappled with poor morale, the lower ranks almost certainly did as well.

Evidence of the insurgency's decline could also be found in the Maoists' own rhetoric. For instance, a squad in Bihar's Gaya district conducted a recruiting drive in November asking potential recruits to help 'revive' Maoism, a term suggesting that the Maoists themselves did not believe their movement was thriving. The Maoists' Central Committee certainly appeared aware of setbacks to the movement, and continued in its attempts to adapt to the counter-insurgency effort. These attempts at adaptation included structural reorganisation. In January, for instance, CPI–Maoist's Andhra–Odisha Border Special Zonal Committee announced the creation of a new institution for rebel governance, the Janatana Sarkar, and instructed civilians to send their children to its education centres. CPI–Maoist also split up at least one of its 'divisions' (a first-order administrative unit) as part of a plan to redistribute its resources and efforts.

Aside from reorganising itself, CPI–Maoist also continued its efforts to mobilise new communities as sources of recruits and materiel. To do this, the Maoists attempted to forge links with communities aggrieved by government policies. In June, CPI–Maoist's Pratap Area Committee spread pamphlets to express solidarity with farmers protesting government policies in Jharkhand's Kanker district. Efforts to bring new communities under Maoist influence succeeded on at least one occasion, as when a tribal community living along the border of Kerala and Tamil Nadu states were convinced to resettle out of the government's reach in the remote Agali forest of Kerala's Palakkad district. It is difficult to gauge the overall success of this strategy, however, as militants conceal the collaboration of newly co-opted communities. However, at least some attempts to expand into new areas encountered major setbacks. In September, Uttarakhand state police arrested a high-ranking Maoist commander sent to establish links with villages expected to be displaced by a planned hydroelectric project on the Mahakali River. The setbacks were more severe in Telangana State, where eight high-ranking commanders, mostly from Bhadradri-Kothagudem district, surrendered to police during the third quarter of the year.

The government's counter-insurgency policy appeared to weaken support for the insurgency among local populations, an outcome that was perhaps related to the heavy losses inflicted on CPI–Maoist's militant forces by the government's paramilitary units. These setbacks likely accounted for the surrender of many Maoist fighters and high-ranking leaders. CPI–Maoist attempted to adapt and devise new strategies to help it withstand India's counter-insurgency efforts, but few signs of a resurgent Maoist influence could be found. Overall, an eventual collapse of CPI–Maoist appeared more likely at the end of the 2017 than it did at the beginning of the year.

India (Manipur)

Manipur remained one of northeast India's most violent states during 2017, witnessing an estimated 58 conflict-related fatalities, as political and social life continued to be beset by insurgent activity both in the Meitei-dominated Imphal Valley and the Kuki- and Naga-dominated hill areas. Changes in the government following the

Key statistics	2016	2017
Type:	Internal	Internal
Fatalities:	45	60
New IDPs:	–[b]	–[b]
New refugees:	–[b]	–[b]

spring state-assembly elections brought a new sense of optimism that the political gridlock – characterised by a 139-day economic blockade and political opposition to a peace process that would integrate Nagas living in the state into a larger Naga territorial entity – might be addressed. Despite this initial optimism, little progress was made in addressing the underlying tensions within the peace talks, while the new Bharatiya Janata Party (BJP)-led government failed to allay widespread fears that Manipur's territorial integrity could be bargained away by its counterparts in New Delhi.

BJP victory in Imphal: false dawn?

The state-assembly elections in March 2017 took place in a highly charged political environment. The then Congress Party-led state government under Okram Ibobi Singh had adopted an antagonistic stance towards the United Naga Council's (UNC) economic blockade of Manipur, which began in November 2016 as an act of protest against the government's creation of seven new administrative districts that bifurcated Naga ancestral lands. The creation of the districts was perceived by the UNC and Naga armed groups, such as the National Socialist Council of Nagalim–Isak Muivah (NSCN–IM), as a deliberate attempt to undermine the rights of Nagas within Manipur, in the context of the broader valley-based Meitei population's opposition to any peace process that might give away Naga-inhabited areas of the state. Singh had also questioned the central government's commitment to the territorial integrity of Manipur on 19 February, demanding that Prime Minister Narendra Modi disclose the details of the Framework Agreement signed between the NSCN–IM and New Delhi in August 2015.

Despite the presence of around 37,800 security-forces personnel at the onset of the elections, a number of violent incidents took place across the state during the first and second rounds of polling as armed groups sought to impose themselves and influence the results in their areas. This mainly took the form of internecine violence within and between non-state armed groups. On 6 March, for example, the general secretary of the United Tribal Liberation Army (UTLA) was killed by militants of the group in Kangpokpi district over a reported disagreement concerning the UTLA's involvement in the state-assembly elections. On the same day, rival Kuki armed groups the Kuki Revolutionary Army–Unification (KRA–U) and the Kuki National Front clashed in Khengjang, Kangpokpi district, resulting in the death of one KRA–U militant. In another incident, a polling official died on 8 March after succumbing to injuries caused by an improvised explosive device (IED) blast in Kamjong district a day earlier, while nine were injured following an IED blast in Imphal West district on 8 March. Reports circulated that groups such as the NSCN–IM had forced villagers to sign 'surety bonds' to ensure favourable votes in the elections, while on 9 March Congress Party and BJP workers clashed during polling, leading to nine injuries. This reflected the charged environment prevalent in the state.

While the Congress Party won 28 seats compared to the BJP's 21, the BJP successfully negotiated the support of a number of key parties such as the Naga People's Front, leading N. Biren Singh to form a government on 15 March. The victory also led to alignment between the state government and the BJP government in New Delhi, which promised to mend centre–state relations and allow for a coherent government approach to the peace process with the NSCN–IM. Indeed, four days after the BJP-led government was formed, the UNC lifted its economic blockade and proceeded to enter into substantive talks with the central and state governments. However, little progress was made throughout the year, as it increasingly became evident that efforts to reverse the creation of the seven new administrative districts would be resisted by those that benefited from their creation, such as the Kuki community. On 27 June, the UNC accused the government of employing 'delaying tactics', while on 13 July it accused one of the parties of deliberately attempting to undermine the process. By 29 September, the group issued an ultimatum asking both parties to clarify their negotiating positions, but little further progress was made throughout the year, demonstrating the continued complexity of communal politics in Manipur.

A similar trajectory occurred in relation to the formal Naga peace process. While addressing a Naga crowd in Senapati district on 22 May, Chief Minister N. Biren Singh declared his support for the peace process and asked for forgiveness from the Naga people. Despite this initial optimism, the state government faced the competing political pressures of maintaining Manipur's territorial integrity while supporting the peace process. This was made more complex by statements repeated by NSCN–IM spokespersons in March and October that the central government had recognised the Nagas' right to territorial integration. The political sensitivity of such statements in Manipur compelled both the state and central governments to persistently reaffirm their commitment to Manipur's territorial integrity. However, the continued reluctance of the central government to disclose the details of the 2015

Framework Agreement meant that political anxieties remained. These were reflected in a state-assembly resolution passed on 21 December demanding that New Delhi disclose the agreement's details, citing concerns over Manipur's territorial integrity.

Stabilising violence levels

Conflict-related fatalities remained high at 58 during 2017 but did not constitute a major change from 47 in 2016 and 55 in 2014, pointing towards a gradual stabilisation in violence levels. Nine of these fatalities were incurred by the security forces and came as the result of armed clashes with multiple armed groups. On 8 May in Lokchao, Tengnoupal district, two Territorial Army personnel were killed after an IED was detonated by United National Liberation Front militants. On 15 November one Assam Rifles trooper was killed during a clash with People's Liberation Army militants in Chamol, Chandel district. Two days before the clash, in nearby Maha Mani village, two Assam Rifles troopers had been killed in an IED explosion.

Civilian fatalities accounted for 26 of the total, highlighting the pronounced degree of insecurity faced by both influential and vulnerable civilians in the state. January saw a spike in civilian fatalities, with seven deaths. On 8 January, a village chief and a local religious leader were kidnapped from Nomgkham Gammom, Tengnoupal district, and killed by unidentified militants. On 28 January, an excavator driver and a labourer were kidnapped by an armed gang in Molsohoi, Ukhrul district. An attempt to rescue the civilians was made by Kuki National Organisation militants, but the two were nonetheless killed in the crossfire. Groups also attempted to mete out their own forms of justice; in two separate incidents on 28 July and 8 August, suspected sexual offenders were killed by militants in Imphal West district. In addition to conflict-related fatalities, business establishments and civilians continued to face extortion attempts and the use of grenades and IEDs as tools to issue threats against them, highlighting that the state of insecurity felt by many civilians in Manipur remained far more pervasive than the fatality statistics suggest.

The remainder of conflict-related fatalities were militants, a result of counter-insurgency operations and inter- and intra-faction armed clashes. On 4 June, army personnel clashed with NSCN–Khaplang (NSCN–K) militants in Noney district, leading to the death of one militant. Fatalities as a result of counter-insurgency operations even included members of ceasefire signatory organisations such as the

NSCN–IM; on 23 February, an armed clash led to the deaths of one NSCN–IM militant and a civilian in Khoupum Valley, Noney district, demonstrating the fragile nature of bilateral ceasefires in a highly militarised environment. That Imphal's East and West districts saw the arrest of 216 militants throughout 2017 demonstrated the considerable challenges of conducting law-enforcement and counter-insurgency operations in such an environment.

However, clashes between state forces and non-state armed groups were responsible for a minority of fatalities, highlighting the fragmented nature of non-state armed-group relations in Manipur. In one significant armed clash in September, NSCN–IM militants killed five People's Liberation Army militants in Makan, Kamjong district. The NSCN–IM also clashed with rival Naga armed group the Zeliangrong United Front (ZUF) on multiple occasions throughout the year. On 12 January, for example, NSCN–IM militants killed one ZUF militant in Padanpung, Noney district. United Tribal Liberation Army–SK Thadou (UTLA–SK) faction militants clashed with UTLA–Poukhai militants on 16 September in Mukhtohal, Tamenglong district, leading to the deaths of two UTLA–SK militants and one civilian. In a particularly violent case of intra-group violence, the bodies of four Hmar People's Convention–Democratic militants were recovered from various locations on the Barak River on 27 and 28 June, reportedly in a case of internal punishment after the deceased militants had conducted an armed robbery at a health centre in Pherzawl on 21 June.

Despite the overall stabilisation of fatality levels in the state since 2014, there was no significant improvement in the political climate or the day-to-day human security of civilians in 2017. While the state saw a substantial political shift as the BJP won power in the March assembly elections, the underlying tensions between constituencies in the valley and the hills continued to permeate everyday politics and the Naga peace process. This meant that the initial optimism of the BJP's victory was ultimately unfounded as the state's long-standing political tensions proved resilient throughout 2017.

India (Nagaland)

Although 2017 marked the second anniversary of the signing of the Framework Agreement between the Indian central government and the National Socialist Council of Nagalim–Isak Muivah (NSCN–IM), a conclusive peace accord to

Key statistics	2016	2017
Type:	Internal	Internal
Fatalities:	20	15
New IDPs:	–[b]	–[b]
New refugees:	–[b]	–[b]

build on and finalise the contents of the Framework Agreement remained elusive, despite assurances from both the central government and NSCN–IM sources. This fuelled continued anxieties that a final accord would threaten the territorial integrity of neighbouring states with significant Naga populations. However, a number of the disparate breakaway Naga armed factions were brought into a separate dialogue process by the close of the year, signalling important progress in the government's efforts to bring together a range of stakeholders to settle on a solution to the conflict. This was reflected by a further reduction in conflict-related fatalities, despite continued hostilities between government forces and the NSCN–IM's rival faction, NSCN–Khaplang (NSCN–K), highlighting the NSCN–K's increasingly isolated position as the only Naga armed group not engaged in dialogue with the central government.

Political instability

The year was characterised by political instability in the state government, beginning with the downfall of the T.R. Zeliang administration in Kohima following a series of protests against the proposed Urban Local Body elections. The opposition to the elections, organised by the Dimapur-based Joint Coordination Committee (JCC) and the Kohima-based Nagaland Tribes Action Committee (NTAC), concerned clauses in the Nagaland Municipal Act, but primarily rallied against the quota for 33% female representation that was due to be implemented in the elections process. Zeliang had demanded on 29 January that the elections go ahead 'at all costs' but increasingly intense protests prompted the state government to cut mobile internet services the following day. The death of two civilians as a result of police gunfire on 31 January in Dimapur district and the death of another civilian on 5 February led to the immediate suspension of the elections. Continued JCC and NTAC protests in February ultimately forced the hand of legislators within the ruling Naga People's Front (NPF), who rebelled and ousted Zeliang on 16 February. By 22 February Shurhozelie Liezietsu had been sworn in as chief minister, ending Zeliang's three-year tenure. Liezietsu's term in office was short-lived, however. By 19 July, the state's governor, P.B. Acharya, had requested that he step down after a rebellion instigated by Zeliang deprived him of his legislative majority, revealing deep divisions within the NPF ahead of the 2018 state-assembly elections.

Continued peace parleys

Although both the Zeliang and Liezietsu governments expressed their commitment to the peace process with the NSCN–IM, developments tended to highlight the continued importance of outstanding issues such as the status of Naga-inhabited areas in the neighbouring states of Arunachal Pradesh, Assam and Manipur. On 21 March, NSCN–IM leader Thuingaleng Muivah hinted that the central government had in fact recognised the group's demand to integrate Naga-inhabited areas in these states into the proposed 'Greater Nagalim', provoking protests from politicians and non-Naga sections of civil society in Arunachal Pradesh, Assam and Manipur. This forced New Delhi to deny decisively that any such agreement had been made. Similarly, on 6 October, the convenor of the NSCN–IM's steering committee, Rh Raising, suggested that the 3 August 2015 Framework Agreement recognised the principle of territorial integration. This was rejected by the government's interlocutor, R.N. Ravi, on 15 October after rumours circulated that areas of Assam would be parcelled off as part of the peace process.

Further anxieties were raised on 18 August when NSCN–IM sources suggested that the group would not decommission its arms after a peace agreement, but would instead recommission its current armed units into a regular military force to police the borders of its proposed Nagalim. Four days later, the group reportedly demanded the drafting of a separate Naga constitution, but this was flatly rejected by the government on 29 August. Seemingly in despair, the group suggested on 24 September that it was seeking 'divine intervention' to secure a successful conclusion to the process.

Considerable progress was nonetheless made with the factions of the Working Committee, an umbrella organisation consisting of a conglomeration of armed groups: NSCN–Reformation (NSCN–R), NSCN–Kitovi Neokpao (NSCN–KN, also known as NSCN–Unification and Government of the People's Republic of Nagaland/ NSCN), National People's Government of Nagaland/Naga National Council–Non-Accord (NPGN/NNC–NA), Government of the Democratic Republic of Nagaland/ NNC–NA (GDRN/NNC–NA), Federal Government of Nagaland (FGN) and NNC–Parent Body. On 27 September, the Working Committee met R.N. Ravi, marking the formal initiation of peace talks with the central government despite all of the groups already being signatories to ceasefire agreements with New Delhi. On 17 November the central government signed a framework agreement with the umbrella organi-sation. This, combined with efforts (albeit unsuccessful) to appeal to the NSCN–K to return to the peace process, ultimately highlighted the government's efforts to include a wider range of stakeholders in the peace process rather than dealing uni-laterally with the NSCN–IM.

Incremental reductions in violence

The incorporation of a broader range of groups into the peace process was accom-panied by an overall reduction in fatalities related to political violence in 2017, with 16 confirmed conflict-related fatalities taking place during the year, compared with 20 during 2016 and 100 during 2015. Indeed, on 3 June, Union Home Minister Rajnath Singh suggested that insurgency-related violence in the region had reached a 20-year low.

Despite the death of the NSCN–K's founding member and leader, S.S. Khaplang, in Myanmar on 9 June, the group continued its broader strategy of leveraging regional alliances with insurgent groups such as the United Liberation Front of Asom–Independent (ULFA–I) to attack Indian security-forces personnel. This was primarily done using entry corridors from the group's bases in Myanmar into the eastern border areas adjoining Arunachal Pradesh, northeast Assam and eastern Nagaland. Consequently, Arunachal Pradesh accounted for six of the 16 overall fatalities related to the Naga conflict throughout 2017. On 6 June, a significant armed clash took place in Nagaland's Mon district between Territorial Army personnel and ULFA–I militants, leading to the deaths of three militants, one army major and one civilian. That the clash took place in Mon, traditionally an NSCN–K stronghold, was reflective of the NSCN–K's overall strategy.

However, the Mon district clash marked the only conflict-related fatality for the security forces in 2017; armed clashes consistently produced higher casualty rates for the NSCN–K than for the Indian security forces. Army personnel, for example, killed one NSCN–K militant in Longding district on 2 February. Assam Rifles personnel killed one NSCN–K militant in Tirap district on 1 March and another NSCN–K militant during a clash in Wakka, Longding district, on 6 May. Two further clashes on 1 and 4 September in Longding district resulted in the deaths of two more NSCN–K militants. Reports circulated that army personnel had engaged in a massive armed clash with the NSCN–K close to the Indo-Myanmar border in Arunachal Pradesh on 27 September, although accounts of heavy NSCN–K casualties ultimately remained unsubstantiated.

Despite the presence of numerous armed groups in Nagaland, no fatalities resulted from inter-factional violence in 2017. The only militant casualty not inflicted on the NSCN–K by the security forces was that of one NSCN–R militant, who was killed by fellow NSCN–R militants in Dimapur district in an apparent internal disciplinary issue on 15 May. Civilians accounted for seven of the year's 16 fatalities. Three civilians died as a result of the civil unrest during January and February in clashes with police personnel; these deaths played a significant role in bringing down the T.R. Zeliang government in February. A further four civilians died in a series of violent incidents. On 29 May an improvised explosive device killed one civilian in New Market, Dimapur district, while NSCN–K militants killed a taxi driver on 2 September. The remaining two civilian deaths resulted from cross-fire and mistaken-identity incidents as the security forces pursued the NSCN–K and its allies, demonstrating the continued risk for civilians living and working in what remained a highly militarised environment.

The continuing reduction in conflict-related fatalities, notwithstanding ongoing clashes between NSCN–K and security-forces personnel and incidents of violence against civilians, reflected gradual improvements in the security situation in Nagaland and the Naga-inhabited areas of neighbouring states. The signing of a framework agreement with the Working Group in November provided grounds for optimism in bringing together the various stakeholders in the peace process.

However, the continued lack of a conclusive peace agreement with the most powerful armed group, the NSCN–IM, seemingly as a result of the apparent deadlock with regards to the status of a potential Greater Nagalim, precluded opportunities to consolidate the reductions in violence and developments with other groups. Apparent frustration with the progress made during 2017 was apparent on 27 November, when civil-society organisations expressed hope that a peace accord would be finalised before the 2018 state-assembly elections. These sentiments were echoed by state legislators in Nagaland on 7 December, who urged the central government to hold elections only after an 'honourable and acceptable' solution to the conflict was reached.

India–Pakistan (Kashmir)

The conflict in Indian-administered Kashmir intensified in 2017, particularly in the second half of the year after the Indian army announced *Operation All Out* against militant groups in June. By the end of the year, the Indian security forces had

Key statistics	2016	2017
Type:	International	International
Fatalities:	400	400
New IDPs:	450,000	120,000
New refugees:	– [b]	– [b]

killed more than 200 militants, a marked increase compared to previous years. Although *Operation All Out* was presented as a success, particularly due to the reduction in the number of civilian casualties, a closer look revealed that the results of the operation were mixed. Civil resistance against Indian rule continued throughout the year, with one of the largest student protests taking place in April.

Military operations and domestic diplomacy

In July 2016, widespread anti-India protests had erupted in Kashmir, which were quelled by the government through disproportionate force. The massive state repression consequently incited many young men to pick up arms, surging the ranks of militant organisations. *Operation All Out* was devised in the wake of the uprising:

after intelligence-gathering and a district-wise survey of militant hideouts, about 258 active militants (130 local and 128 foreign) were identified as potential targets. The operation officially started in June 2017, while Sabzar Ahmad Bhat, a top rebel commander, was killed a month before on 27 May 2017.

By the end of 2017, *All Out* appeared to have achieved its objectives. Armed groups in Kashmir had suffered heavy losses, including the deaths of their top leaders in quick succession: Bashir Lashkari (July), Abu Dujana and Yasin Itoo (August), and Abu Ismail and Qayoom Najar (September). Although the security forces were successful in eliminating more militants, the killings also renewed support for the insurgency. Large-scale funeral processions of militants killed in combat functioned as effective recruitment propaganda for militant groups and young men from Kashmir continued to join. According to the security agencies, 117 local youth had become militants by the end of November 2017, compared to 88 in 2016.

The increase in militant fatalities did not necessarily indicate an enhanced counter-insurgency strategy either. That the number of militants killed has increased nearly every year since 2012 could also signify the growing presence of militants in the state. Indeed, the dynamics of the conflict in Kashmir appeared to be changing in radical ways, with groups such as Ansar Ghazwat ul-Hind (an al-Qaeda affiliate) and the Islamic State, also known as ISIS or ISIL, attempting to establish themselves in Jammu and Kashmir. The conditions in the state could give these groups the opportunity to make an impact if they were to introduce violent tactics such as suicide bombing. Moreover, groups such as these can exploit the vast pool of Kashmiri youth who have complex grievances, have experienced genuine or perceived harassment by the security forces, and have access to either radical ideology or people who are involved in radical or violent networks.

As the military approach reached its limitations, New Delhi began to mull over a political approach in Kashmir. A clear hint was given by Indian Prime Minister Narendra Modi during his Independence Day speech on 15 August 2017 when he claimed that 'bullets and abuses' would not solve the Kashmir issue, but 'embracing' Kashmiris would. The statement appeared to mark a shift in the rhetoric of the ruling Bharatiya Janata Party (BJP) in relation to the Kashmir situation: in the past, the BJP has maintained a hardline approach on Kashmir, to the extent that some of its affiliates have suggested effecting 'demographic change' in Kashmir by removing Article 35A from the Constitution of India, which gives the Jammu and Kashmir legislature exceptional powers to determine access to employment and welfare, as well as property rights. A month after Modi's speech, the Indian security establishment seemed to concur with the notion of a non-military approach when Major-General B.S. Raju, commander of the counter-insurgency unit Victor Force in south Kashmir, said that 'the situation [in Kashmir] has been brought to a level where political initiative can be started'.

In October, New Delhi appointed Dineshwar Sharma, the former chief of India's Intelligence Bureau, as the special representative for Jammu and Kashmir with a mandate to talk with all stakeholders in the Kashmir conflict, including the All Parties Hurriyat Conference (APHC), the broad alliance of oppositional parties in the state who demand the right to self-determination. The Kashmir press responded cautiously to the appointment, citing the Indian government's failure or reluctance to implement the recommendations of the previous interlocutors. Even the former chief minister of Jammu and Kashmir, Farooq Abdullah, gave a lukewarm response, saying that he had low expectations of the negotiations. However, Sharma's appointment was a significant political development for the ruling Jammu and Kashmir People's Democratic Party (PDP) as it provided its ministers with a positive development and consequently political space to reconnect with their constituency. (Since the uprising in 2016, pro-Union parties, especially the PDP, have felt unable to visit their constituencies; admittedly, their political space had shrunk in the wake of the youth-led summer uprising.)

Some commentators interpreted Sharma's appointment as a tactical response to the regional security scenario in South Asia, where Washington was considering a new policy for Afghanistan. India has been wary of such policy developments in the past, especially in cases where the United States had indicated its willingness to mediate on the Kashmir conflict. Previously, in 2009, when the Obama administration appointed Richard Holbrooke as a special envoy to Afghanistan and Pakistan, the Indian lobby in Washington pushed to remove Kashmir from Holbrooke's South Asia mission.

Sharma, however, failed to convince the APHC to engage in talks during his two visits to the state in November and December. Although some parties within the APHC had previously held talks with the Indian government, on this occasion the alliance presented a united front and refused to meet Sharma. In a press statement on 5 November, the APHC said that it 'rejects the facade of talks initiated to kill time' and reiterated 'that no forum or party from Hurriyat camp will become part of the process'. The current leadership of the APHC – Syed Ali Geelani, Mirwaiz Umar Farooq and Yasin Malik (collectively referred to in the media as the 'Joint Resistance Leadership') – must unanimously approve any dialogue process. While Yasin Malik and Mirwaiz Umar may be amenable to talks, Geelani, who wields considerable power within the APHC, is staunchly opposed to dialogue for historical reasons – he has claimed that the previous 150 rounds of negotiations have failed due to lack of Indian sincerity. Among the most senior leaders of the APHC, only Professor Abdul Gani Bhat showed a willingness to meet the special representative, stating that not only the future of Jammu and Kashmir 'but the future of the entire South Asian region is at stake'. On 10 December, however, it was reported that Bhat had been removed as the president of the Muslim Conference (a constituent party of the APHC) due to a 'secret meeting' with Sharma.

Some observers attributed the failure of the special representative to the delayed timing of the political initiative itself, claiming that it should have begun in 2016 as a political response to the uprising. However, the alternate view was that the Indian government had purposely delayed the dialogue process in order to improve its negotiating position, as launching a dialogue during the 2016 uprising would have sent the wrong signal to the APHC. To this end, in June 2017 the Indian administration not only initiated *Operation All Out* but also began pursuing APHC members and their affiliates through the National Investigation Agency (NIA) by opening old cases, raiding their residences, interrogating them and summoning some of them and their relatives to the headquarters of the NIA in New Delhi for questioning. Geelani's son-in-law and six other APHC activists were arrested by the NIA on 24 July on charges of 'criminal conspiracy' and 'waging war against state', while the NIA also arrested an influential Kashmiri businessman, Zahoor Watali, on 17 August for his alleged involvement in transferring foreign funds to the APHC. These relentless NIA raids were seen by APHC leaders as pressure tactics to force them to the negotiating table and undercut their mobilising capabilities. In any case, Sharma's mission in Kashmir yielded little in 2017, but that was as expected: despite its apparent shift in rhetoric, the substance of New Delhi's approach to negotiation had not fundamentally changed. As many unionist politicians in Kashmir stress repeatedly, unless Pakistan is included in the dialogue process, change on the ground is unlikely.

The APHC's role in any future dialogue process is also likely to face challenges from the Kashmiri youth-driven insurgency, which gained considerable public support after the death of the militant leader Burhan Wani in 2016. While the APHC remained a relevant party in the conflict, the balance of power in the region appeared to have shifted to the militants. The APHC must therefore take along the militant leadership in order to reach a consensus in any future dialogue process, a task that looks likely to be more difficult in light of the recent fragmentation in the militant ranks and the radical political alignments of the new groups. In mid-May 2017, the 26-year-old Zakir Musa, a Kashmiri militant (and close associate of Burhan Wani) with an Islamist stance, split from the largest indigenous militant group Hizbul Mujahideen (HM) due to an ideological clash. In an unprecedented move, Musa openly criticised not only the APHC leadership but also the Pakistan establishment. In July the media reported that Musa had launched a rival group called Ansar Ghazwat ul-Hind.

Student revolt and by-election violence

On 15 April 2017, personnel from the Jammu and Kashmir Police (JKP) and paramilitary Central Reserve Police Force (CRPF) raided the premises of a government college in the town of Pulwama about 30 kilometres south of the capital city Srinagar. According to various news reports, around 55 college students received injures during the police action. At least 12 female students passed out due to tear-gas inhalation. Two days later, in solidarity with their peers from Pulwama college, students from different schools and colleges around the Kashmir Valley protested against Indian rule by chanting popular pro-independence and anti-India slogans. Armed with smartphones and high-speed internet, the tech-savvy Kashmiri youth broadcast these protests on social media, thereby garnering worldwide attention.

In many places, students clashed with the JKP and the CRPF by throwing stones, a common mode of protest among Kashmiri youth. At south Kashmir's Kulgam college, around 32 students were injured in police action, including three women. In Srinagar, students from the prestigious Government Women's College protested on the streets.

Iqra Sidiq, an undergraduate student, suffered a skull fracture after she was hit by a stone (allegedly thrown from a paramilitary bunker). She remained unconscious for several days in the city's main hospital. At around 3pm on 17 April, the state government shut down 3G and 4G internet services in the Kashmir Valley to stop the spread of rumours, although some protesters believed that it was done to block the circulation of videos and photographs of the student revolt. Coming within a year of the 2016 uprising, the April 2017 student revolt once again put Kashmir on alert and the government was caught in a dilemma about how to tackle the protests without inciting more. To curb further student protests, the authorities made several arrests and suspended college classes, and on government orders, all educational institutions in the Kashmir Valley remained closed for a fortnight. On 24 April, the police arrested at least six students from Srinagar's Sri Pratap Higher Secondary School.

The Kashmiri youth has remained at the forefront of anti-India protests since 2010. According to the 2011 census, the youth represents over 30% of the population in Kashmir. For the Indian government, this 'youth bulge' in Kashmir presented a security challenge. Accordingly, it devised schemes – including sports activities and the Udaan and Himayat initiatives focused on driving private-sector job placements – to discourage Kashmiri youth from joining the anti-India movement. On Special Representative Sharma's recommendation, in late November 2017 the state government announced an amnesty for more than 4,000 Kashmiri youth against whom police cases were registered for stone-throwing.

The by-election for the parliamentary seat of Budgam–Srinagar constituency also became a focal point for civil protests in 2017. The seat had become vacant after Tariq Hameed Karra, a senior parliamentarian and founding member of PDP, resigned in September 2016 in protest against civilian killings and repression in Kashmir. The by-election was held on 9 April 2017 but quickly descended into violence: protesters attacked polling stations, resulting in clashes with the police and paramilitary forces in which eight civilians were killed by government forces. As election results confirmed a low voter turnout – 88,951, or 7% of the constituency total – the Election Commission of India ordered a re-poll in 38 selected polling stations within days. However, in response to the call of the APHC, people boycotted the re-poll on 13 April: election officials confirmed that 'only 709 of the 34,169 voters [2%] exercised their franchise across all the 38 polling stations by the time the polling ended at

4pm'. This was the lowest voter turnout in the state's history, and came as an embarrassment to the Indian government, which has been using encouraging election results in Kashmir to demonstrate the acceptance of Indian rule by Kashmiris to an international audience. Nevertheless, despite losing political legitimacy, the by-election result was still accepted by the winning National Conference candidate, former chief minister Farooq Abdullah, who defeated the ruling PDP's candidate by a margin of more than 10,000 votes.

The year of CASO

After an interval of 15 years, in May 2017 the Indian army reintroduced door-to-door searches – known as Cordon and Search Operations (CASOs) – in the Kashmir Valley. Such searches had been frequently conducted in the 1990s, when they had often been a source of resentment among Kashmiris. Unlike in the 1990s, however, when residents were taken outside and paraded before a masked informer, the renewed CASOs were carried out on the basis of specific intelligence – people were asked to come out of their houses while searches and the frisking of civilians were carried out. Despite these modifications, the local population was still concerned by the resumption and frequency of the CASOs due to the attendant risk of gunfights breaking out. During gunfights with militants, government forces would usually attack the houses with mortars and improvised explosive devices to kill militants inside, leaving the legitimate owners of the buildings without shelter. In December 2017 a gunfight in Batmurran village, Shopian district, left 34 people homeless.

The increased use of CASOs appeared to be part of a larger strategy to drive militants out of south Kashmir, which had emerged as a bastion of the new armed militancy in the wake of the death of HM commander Burhan Wani. Reports in June 2017 suggested that around 200 militants were active in Kashmir, of which 110 were local youth, most of them drawn to militancy in the second quarter of the year. Nearly 90 of the local youth were from south Kashmir. The challenge facing the Indian army was exacerbated by the fact that militants were evading arrest with the help of local people: during some gunfights, young men – and sometimes women – tried to help militants escape military cordons by throwing stones at the government forces. In 2017, at least 19 people, including five women, were killed when government forces targeted civilians in the vicinity of such clashes.

Most CASOs were carried out in Pulwama district, but the largest CASO was conducted on 4 May in Shopian district, 52 km south of Srinagar, after a spate of militant attacks and bank robberies. Aided by unmanned aerial vehicles and helicopters, around 30,000 members of the Indian government forces (comprising armed police, CRPF and army personnel) marched through 20 villages in search of hiding militants. The CASO did not yield any success, with every militant managing to escape the combing operation. However, a local taxi driver was killed while ferrying personnel of the 62 Rashtriya Rifles Battalion when militants ambushed his vehicle.

International diplomacy

Global diplomacy made little headway on the issue of Kashmir in 2017, although there were two significant developments. Firstly, in May 2017, Turkey's President Recep Tayyip Erdogan called for 'multilateral dialogue' to solve the Kashmir dispute. While welcomed by Pakistan and the APHC, the suggestion was dismissed by India, which preferred bilateral engagement with Pakistan. Although Erdogan's statement was a diplomatic success for Pakistan, Islamabad was not able enlist broad international support regarding the Kashmir dispute aside from the Organisation of Islamic Cooperation (which remains the only international forum that supports the right of self-determination for the people in Jammu and Kashmir).

Secondly, in what Indian security journal *Force* called 'extraordinary news', Yao Wen, the political counsellor of the Department of Asian Affairs (part of China's Ministry of Foreign Affairs), was quoted as saying that 'China considers the Kashmir conflict as a top priority along with the Korean peninsula, the South China Sea dispute and instability in Afghanistan'. Yao's statement suggested that Kashmir had become a diplomatic weapon for China to offset both the growing US–India alliance in the South China Sea and also India's position in the Doklam border area, which had witnessed a 73-day stand-off between India and China in summer 2017. Pakistan may well turn this situation in its favour in the coming years as part of its effort to bring India to the negotiating table over the Kashmir dispute.

For India, diplomatic success came on 26 June when the US Department of State designated the new leader of HM, Mohammed Yusuf Shah (also known as Syed Salahuddin), as a 'Specially Designated Global Terrorist'. The announcement came soon after Modi's meeting with US Secretary of Defense James Mattis and then secretary of state Rex Tillerson. In response to the US decision, Pakistan said that 'the designation of individuals supporting the Kashmiri right to self-determination as terrorists is completely unjustified'. On 16 August, the US also designated HM as a foreign terrorist organisation. Without a UN Security Council endorsement, however, such designations were only of symbolic importance: Pakistan was not legally bound to act against HM or Salahuddin, who is based in Pakistan-administered Kashmir. Moreover, to balance its relationship with Pakistan (whose cooperation in Afghanistan is vital for the US), a State Department spokesperson reiterated that 'our policy on Kashmir has not changed … the pace, scope, and character of any discussions on Kashmir is for the two sides to determine'.

Relations between India and Pakistan remained cold and tense. On 5 January 2017, Pakistan's then-prime minister Nawaz Sharif said that Kashmir was 'an integral part' of Pakistan's identity and that the 'martyrdom of vibrant and charismatic Kashmiri leader Burhan Wani has given a new turn to the Kashmiri movement'. On 20 January, he raised the Kashmir issue with the UN Secretary-General António Guterres at the 2017 World Economic Forum at Davos. In early March, at the 34th Session of the Human Rights Council, the Indian representative responded to Pakistan's accusation of human-rights violations in Indian Kashmir by saying that 'the fundamental reason for disturbances in parts of Jammu and Kashmir is cross-border terrorism aided and abetted by Pakistan'. Nevertheless, on 20 March, a ten-member Indian delegation took part in the two-day meeting of the Permanent Indus Commission in Islamabad in relation to water-sharing agreements between the two countries.

There was a sharp rise in cross-border skirmishes in 2017, from 93 in 2016 to 205 in 2017. Both countries suffered casualties: according to Indian media reports, 138 Pakistani soldiers were killed in tactical operations and retaliatory shootings across the Line of Control (LoC) in 2017. In addition to 26 Indian soldiers, 13 civilians also lost their lives due to exchanges of gunfire and shelling at the LoC. The reports further claimed that in targeted retaliatory sniper shootings, Pakistan lost 27 soldiers in 2017 while India lost seven. (The Indian army did not officially confirm the reports.)

Overall, 2017 witnessed an escalation of the armed conflict in Kashmir. Contrary to statements that the situation had been brought under control, the year saw the reintroduction of emergency military operations such as CASOs, together with a surge in the recruitment of local militants and the large-scale cross-LoC infiltration of trained insurgents (around 310 in 2017 compared to 152 in 2015). These developments all indicated that militant groups continued to pose a challenge to the security situation in Kashmir.

Pakistan

Uncertainty and insecurity continued to challenge Pakistan throughout 2017. Although the number of attacks by militants declined compared to previous years, there were still multiple incidents of violence involving terrorist tactics against minorities

Key statistics	2016	2017
Type:	Internal	Internal
Fatalities:	1,250	1,250
New IDPs:	2,500	7,000
New refugees:	— [b]	— [b]

and security personnel, as well as on places of worship and in commercial areas. The two regions most affected by violence were Balochistan and the Federally Administered Tribal Areas (FATA), with the majority of the attacks being carried out by the Islamist groups Tehrik-e-Taliban Pakistan (TTP), Jamaat-ul-Ahrar, Islamic State, also known as ISIS or ISIL, and its affiliates including the Sunni militant group Lashkar-e-Jhangvi al-Alami (LEJ–A), an offshoot of Lashkar-e-Jhangvi. In addition, Pakistan saw growing religious intolerance on university campuses, the most tragic manifestation of which was the murder of the student Mashal Khan.

Counter-terrorism, military operations and security

Pakistan continued to implement its counter-terrorism policy, the National Action Plan (NAP), in 2017, albeit with mixed results. In order to monitor the progress of NAP, the government had mandated frequent meetings of federal and apex committees involving political and military leaders. The provincial apex-committee meetings had begun with great fervour in 2015, with provincial governors, chief ministers, inspectors general of police, directors general of the Pakistani Rangers and members of intelligence agencies all in attendance, but by 2017 the number of such apex-committee meetings appeared to have declined. For instance, in Sindh province, where apex committees were overseeing the targeted operation against militants and criminals in Karachi, only three committee meetings were held in 2017 compared to at least six in 2016. This decline in the number of meetings may imply a decreasing interest in Pakistan's counter-terrorism policy, although there was also some evidence for the policy's success in the shape of a report released by the Ministry of Interior that commended the results of NAP, stating that 2,127 terrorists had been killed in Pakistan and 5,884 arrested since 2015. These findings were given further weight by a report by the Pakistan Institute of Peace Studies, an Islamabad-based think tank, which stated that there had been a 16% decline in the number of violent attacks in Pakistan since 2016.

The government also explored other counter-terrorism initiatives in addition to NAP. To counter the threat of terrorism in the cyber sphere, the National Counter Terrorism Authority (NACTA) launched an online portal for citizens to report extremist content, and suggested that it would also be developing mobile-phone applications for monitoring suspicious online activity. The government also tasked NACTA with reformulating the National Internal Security Policy (NISP), which had remained unimplemented and largely overlooked since its conception in 2013, with NAP being prioritised in the wake of the attack on the Army Public School in Peshawar in December 2014. NISP was, however, the more detailed and comprehensive policy, including in its remit the changing of national narratives on extremism, sectarianism, terrorism and militancy, as well as laying down the responsibilities of counter-terrorism departments and the national internal-security apparatus. Due to come into effect in 2018, NISP (if implemented in full) could aid Pakistan's long-term efforts in countering terrorism and extremism. The federal government also tasked National Security Advisor Lieutenant-General (Retd) Nasser Khan Janjua to prepare a National Security Policy (NSP), also due to launch in 2018.

In February 2017, Pakistan began *Operation Radd-ul-Fasaad* ('Elimination of Discord') in response to attacks in the first two months of the year that killed more than 130 people. In July, the Pakistan army also launched *Operation Khyber IV* in Khyber Agency, FATA, to target militant groups such as the TTP, Lashkar-e-Islam, Jamaat-ul-Ahrar and ISIS. Militants from these groups have been suspected of operating in northwest Pakistan. In November, the armed forces began an offensive in South Waziristan that resulted in the displacement of 500 families who had to relocate to camps for internally displaced persons (IDPs) in Khyber Pakhtunkhwa. In what was viewed as a success for the army's ongoing operations, Ehsanullah Ehsan, the leader of Jamaat-ul-Ahrar, surrendered to the Pakistani security forces in April. The Pakistan army announced Ehsan's surrender through its media arm, the Inter-Services Public Relations, with Major-General Asif Ghafoor, its director general, commending Ehsan's surrender as a 'success of the state', although it remained unclear where and when the surrender took place, and under what conditions. A few days later, the army released Ehsan's confessional statement in which he criticised the Pakistani Taliban for 'misleading' their recruits in the name of Islam. Ehsan further claimed that leaders of the Pakistani Taliban were in touch with the Indian intelligence agency in Afghanistan, which provided them with financial support. He also blamed the Indian and Afghanistan intelligence agencies for furthering terrorism in Pakistan.

The main threats of violence in 2017 came from the TTP, ISIS, LEJ–A and Jamaat-ul-Ahrar, along with Ansar-ul-Sharia Pakistan, a new group that emerged in Karachi. In February, the TTP claimed two attacks: an improvised explosive device (IED) attack on three personnel of the paramilitary Frontier Corps force in South Waziristan, and an attack on a local news-channel cameraman in Karachi. In April, a TTP suicide attack in Lahore targeted an army census team, killing eight people. In July, a TTP suicide bomber attacked a police checkpoint in Lahore, claiming as many as 26 lives, with the majority being police personnel. In December, the TTP claimed responsibility for the attack on the Agricultural Training Institute of Peshawar, Khyber Pakhtunkhwa, in which at least nine people were killed.

ISIS claimed the highest number of attacks after the TTP in 2017. According to the 2017 security report released by the Pakistan Institute for Peace Studies, the ISIS presence increased in Balochistan and northern Sindh: in February, ISIS claimed the attack on the Lal Shahbaz Qalandar shrine in Sehwan, Sindh, in which at least 88 people were killed. Additionally, ISIS continued to attract young, educated urban radicals in Pakistan. In February, a woman named Noreen Leghari, a medical student from Hyderabad, Sindh, was reported missing. She contacted her brother several weeks later, claiming that she had reached Syria. This information turned out to be false and Leghari was arrested by the security forces in Lahore. In her widely publicised confessional statement, Leghari revealed that she was inspired by ISIS through social media and intended to join the group. She further admitted that she and her husband, Ali (who was killed in a shoot-out with the security forces), were planning suicide attacks on the Christian community during Easter.

Although it did not participate in as many attacks as ISIS, LEJ–A – a sectarian militant group believed to be close to ISIS – asserted that it was responsible for two. In January, it claimed responsibility for an attack on a vegetable market in Parachinar, FATA, which killed at least 25 people. In February, LEJ-A claimed an attack in Quetta, Balochistan, in which two police officers, including a bomb-disposal officer, were killed.

Jamaat-ul-Ahrar, an offshoot of TTP, was, however, more active in 2017. In February, the group carried out a suicide bombing on Mall Road in Lahore in which 18 people were killed, including senior police officials. The same day, Jamaat-ul-Ahrar announced the launch of *Operation Ghazi*, in which it threatened to attack military, intelligence and law-enforcement officials, as well as non-governmental organisations (NGOs) and civil-society organisations. In March, Jamaat-ul-Ahrar purportedly carried out an attack on an imambargah (a Shia shrine) in Parachinar. In June, the group said that it was responsible for a suicide car bombing in Quetta, in which 14 people, including seven police officers, were killed. However, ISIS also claimed responsibility for the attack. It remained unclear whether such dual claims were the result of operational alliances made between militant groups in Pakistan or attempts by ISIS to further its own propaganda in the region, but Jamaat-ul-Ahrar has been recognised as a local affiliate of ISIS in Pakistan.

The emergence of Ansar-ul-Sharia in mid-2017 was a significant development in the security sphere. The group claimed at least five attacks in Karachi alone, target-ing primarily law-enforcement officials. In June, it targeted and killed four on-duty police officials in the city; in pamphlets left at the site, Ansar-ul-Sharia declared that it had been formed by defectors from ISIS and other militant organisations in Pakistan, and was ideologically aligned with Osama bin Laden and Ayman al-Zawahiri, thereby furthering concerns of the presence of al-Qaeda in Pakistan. Law-enforcement agencies identified one of the members of Ansar-ul-Sharia as being a student of NED University of Engineering and Technology, highlighting the potential pathways to extremism on university campuses. In subsequent raids, law-enforcement officials arrested the group's spokesperson, who revealed that would-be militants had travelled to Afghanistan for military training and joined al-Qaeda, but had formed Ansar-ul-Sharia upon returning to Pakistan. Given that Ansar-ul-Sharia was not only founded but also able to operate during ongoing military and intelligence-based operations in Pakistan, it is possible that similar groups may emerge in the foreseeable future, thereby increasing the need for more comprehensive and strategic counter-terrorism and counter-extremism policies in Pakistan.

FATA and Khyber Pakhtunkhwa

Although no practical steps were taken in 2017 towards finalising the long-anticipated merger of FATA and Khyber Pakhtunkhwa, the year ended on a positive note for northwest Pakistan when government sources revealed that a decision on the merger would be taken soon. If the merger is successful, FATA will be able to elect 23 members to the Khyber Pakhtunkhwa Assembly in the 2018 elections. The merger will also give FATA an improved constitutional status by bringing it in line with the other regions of Pakistan, as well as allowing FATA access to a reforms package that will be economically beneficial for the development of the tribal areas. The reforms package may also repeal the Frontier Crimes Regulation, a piece of colonial-era legislation that denies residents of FATA the right to legal representation and the right to appeal in any court to challenge convictions.

Some analysts suggested that the delays in finalising this merger may be a result of opposition by Jamiat Ulema-e-Islam and Pakhtunkhwa Milli Awami Party, which are allied with the ruling government, the Pakistan Muslim League–Nawaz (PMLN). Following the ousting of then-prime minister Nawaz Sharif, the PMLN may have attempted to retain the support of these allies and the prospect of the FATA merger may have been compromised as a result. In late December, however, Imran Khan, the leader of opposition party Pakistan Tehreek-e-Insaf (PTI), announced that the PTI planned to launch a movement to pressurise the federal government into finalising the merger and implementing the FATA reforms package. Towards the end of the year, the federal government approved the formation of a National Implementation Committee to oversee the merger and the future implementation of the FATA reforms package.

In terms of security, the northwest remained volatile and vulnerable to terrorists in 2017, with both the security forces and citizens being targeted by attacks
perpetrated by the TTP, Jamaat-ul-Ahrar, LEJ–A and ISIS. The Pakistan Air Force
carried out aerial strikes in North Waziristan as part of the ongoing *Operation Radd-
ul-Fasaad* in February, and a suspected US unmanned aerial vehicle strike in North
Waziristan targeted seven TTP militants in April. There was a slight rise in violence
in FATA compared to 2016, but the level of violence remained lower than in 2014
when *Operation Zarb-e-Azb* began. However, there was a considerable increase in the
number of civilian casualties in 2017 (760) compared to 2016 (164), as per a report by
the FATA Research Centre.

Kurram Agency – one of FATA's seven agencies, and which borders Afghanistan's
Nangarhar province – was one of the most affected regions in terms of civilian casualties, particularly in the predominantly Shia town of Parachinar. As the largest
city in FATA – and one that has long resisted succumbing to pressure from the
Pakistani Taliban – Parachinar remained vulnerable to sectarian attacks orchestrated
by militants from other areas of Pakistan, as well as from across the border with
Afghanistan. At least three attacks took place in Parachinar in the first six months
of 2017. On 21 January, Shia Muslims – a minority in Pakistan – were targeted in
Parachinar by a bomb blast that killed 25 civilians. On 31 March, another bomb
blast killed 23 people. On 23 June, twin bombings targeted the Shia community
once again, killing more than 80 people and injuring at least 225. The first blast took
place in Parachinar's Turi Bazaar on the last Friday of Ramadan before Eid-al-Fitr,
when marketplaces were particularly busy with shoppers. The second blast targeted
the rescue teams and workers who had arrived at the site of the blast to help the
injured victims. The Sunni militant group LEJ–A claimed responsibility for these
twin bombings.

In Khyber Pakhtunkhwa, the provincial capital Peshawar once again came under
attack, bringing back memories of the assault on the Army Public School in 2014.
On 1 December, gunmen affiliated with the TTP attacked an Agricultural Training
Institute hostel in Peshawar. More than a dozen people were killed. The attack came
a week after a suicide bomber attacked the vehicle of Additional Inspector General of
Police Ashraf Noor in Hayatabad, Peshawar, killing him and his guard. (The attack
was claimed by ISIS.) In the Mardan district of Khyber Pakhtunkhwa, the lynching

of the student Mashal Khan by a mob at the Abdul Wali Khan University in April was recorded on mobile phones. Within hours, the videos were circulated across social media and created an intense uproar in the country. Khan had been falsely accused of posting blasphemous content on his social-media profiles, highlighting the lack of religious tolerance on university campuses in Pakistan and furthering debates on how to curb extremism at academic institutions. Khan's death also raised questions about the problematic blasphemy laws in Pakistan: following the rise of the religious–political group Tehrik-e-Labaik Pakistan (TLP) – which vehemently supports the pre-existing laws – it has become evident that Pakistan's political and social landscape is unprepared for changing such legislation. In other words, allegations of blasphemy may continue being abused and compromise the security of individuals in Pakistan.

Balochistan: militant landscape

Although the number of people killed in Balochistan fell in 2017, and the number of bomb blasts reduced as well, there were still more than 160 violent incidents reported in Balochistan. The primary threats in this province came from ISIS, LEJ–A, Jamaar-ul-Ahrar and the Pakistani Taliban. Although these groups differed in terms of their organisational structure and command, they were believed to cooperate logistically in areas such as Balochistan.

In May, ISIS claimed responsibility for an attack on a senior politician, Senate Deputy Chairman Abdul Ghafoor Haideri, in Quetta. Although Haideri survived the attack, 25 others were killed. In October, ISIS claimed responsibility for the suicide bombing that targeted Pir Rakhel Shah shrine in Jhal Magsi, central Balochistan. At least 18 people were killed, and more than two dozen were injured. In December, the Bethel Memorial Church in Quetta was attacked, and at least nine people were killed, with ISIS again claiming responsibility.

In June, the Pakistani armed forces carried out a three-day operation in Mastung, allegedly killing some of the top ISIS leadership. However, the operation did not eliminate the threat of ISIS; a day after the Mastung operation, ISIS announced through its Amaq news agency that it had killed two Chinese nationals whom the group had abducted in May in Quetta: the couple had been in Balochistan to teach Mandarin and learn Urdu when they were kidnapped by ISIS militants dressed in police uniforms. (The couple were not part of the China–Pakistan Economic Corridor (CPEC) project, which explained why they did not have sufficient security, which is otherwise provided to Chinese nationals in Balochistan by Pakistani armed forces.) In October, Pakistan's foreign office confirmed and condemned the death of the two Chinese citizens.

Despite the protection offered by the Pakistani armed forces, CPEC workers also remained vulnerable to attacks. In May 2017, ten labourers were killed in Gwadar where China is developing a port, with the Baloch Liberation Army (BLA) claiming responsibility for the attack. A few days later, three labourers were killed in Turbat, with initial reports suggesting that they may have been targeted by outlawed Baloch separatist groups. These incidents confirmed that nationalist insurgent and separatist groups in Balochistan – namely the BLA and Balochistan Liberation Front (BLF) – continued to remain active in 2017. In October, the BLF reprimanded local journalists for spreading propaganda in favour of the Pakistan army in Balochistan and threatened to 'take strict action' against them. The BLF also claimed responsibility for an IED attack that killed three soldiers on 16 February.

Aside from workers associated with CPEC, law-enforcement officials and ethnic Hazara Shia continued to be targeted by militants in Balochistan. In August, Frontier Corps and military personnel were attacked in different areas of Balochistan. On 9 November, a roadside bomb killed a senior police officer, Deputy Inspector General Hamid Shakil.

Political turmoil

The PMLN suffered a significant setback following a Supreme Court judgment on the Panama Papers that led to the disqualification of then-prime minister Nawaz Sharif on corruption charges (making this his third incomplete tenure as prime minister). The decision came after a joint investigation team revealed irregularities in the financial earnings of Sharif and his family and was based on a controversial clause in the constitution of Pakistan that demands elected members of parliament (but not military leaders or judges) be 'honest and righteous'. Shahid Khaqan Abbasi was elected as prime minister in Sharif's place in August: he is known to be loyal to the PMLN and a close ally of the former prime minister. (Abbasi will hold office until the general election scheduled for August 2018, when it is expected that Nawaz

Sharif's brother Shahbaz, the chief minister of Punjab, will run for office.) Ahead of the 2018 elections, the state also carried out its first population census in almost two decades, the results of which will determine the delimitation of constituencies and the numbers of national- and provincial-assembly seats. However, the preliminary results of the census were criticised for not considering IDPs or Afghan refugees residing in urban centres such as Karachi, Peshawar and Quetta.

The political landscape also saw the arrival of the Milli Muslim League (MML) in August 2017, a new political party launched by a previously banned religious group Jamaat-ud-Dawa, the charity and political arm of the terrorist group Lashkar-e-Taiba which was founded by Hafiz Saeed. The MML contested a by-election in Lahore, Punjab, challenging a PMLN candidate. Saifullah Khalid, the MML chief who had been a central figure in Jamaat-ud-Dawa, was its nominated candidate. However, in October 2017, the Election Commission of Pakistan rejected MML's registration as a political party, stating that its charities were affiliated with Lashkar-e-Taiba.

The year also saw the emergence of another new political group, the TLP. The TLP was founded in 2017 by Khadim Hussain Rizvi with the intention of opposing changes to the country's existing blasphemy laws; establishing sharia law in Pakistan; and representing Barelvis, the Sunni Muslim majority in the country. The new political party posed a significant challenge to the PMLN, as the TLP's more conservative Islamist agenda appealed to the PMLN's traditional Barelvi vote-bank in Punjab. In September, the TLP contested the above-mentioned by-election in Lahore, coming third after the PMLN and the PTI. In November, members of the TLP staged a three-week-long sit-in in Faizabad, near Islamabad, contesting changes to the existing election laws that altered the declaration of religious beliefs by members of parliament. The Islamabad High Court ordered the government to act against the demonstrators, who retaliated by using force against the police (who were outnumbered by TLP supporters). The violent clash between TLP and the police claimed six lives and ended after the armed forces intervened and negotiated with the TLP. This eventually led to a deal between the government and the TLP in which most of the latter's demands were met, including the resignation of Zahid Hamid, the minister of law and justice.

Meanwhile, Pakistan's foreign policy continued to be dominated by tense relations with the United States. In August, US President Donald Trump requested

India to provide economic assistance in Afghanistan while reprimanding Islamabad for not taking enough action against terrorists despite receiving financial assistance from Washington. This was viewed by Pakistani analysts as a measure that could increase the Indian presence in Afghanistan, which is not only likely to encourage the Pakistani military – which plays the lead role in foreign policies pertaining to India and Afghanistan – to be more aggressive in its involvement in Afghanistan, but also likely to hurt Islamabad's relations with the US president. Pakistan's National Security Committee – comprising military and civilian officials – rejected Trump's allegations, claiming that they were 'hurtful' and 'humiliating'. In November, a Pakistani court released Hafiz Saeed, who had been under house arrest under anti-terrorism laws since January 2017 in relation to his role in masterminding the 2008 attacks in Mumbai, India. The decision was viewed as a form of defiance towards the US: as well as designating Saeed as a 'terrorist', the US had also placed a US$10 million bounty for his arrest and conviction. In December 2017, the Pentagon released a report that criticised the Pakistani state for supporting the extremist Haqqani network and the Afghan Taliban, and for providing them with safe havens.

Relations with Afghanistan also remained disturbed throughout 2017. In February 2017, Pakistan closed the Torkham and Chaman border crossings with Afghanistan in response to the deadly attack on the Lal Shahbaz Qalandar shrine in Sehwan, Sindh, on the basis that the attackers had been given sanctuary inside Afghanistan. Following the closure, the Pakistan army launched strikes on militant bases in Afghanistan's Nangarhar province; reports from Afghanistan suggested that several people were killed and others displaced due to the shelling. The borders were temporarily reopened in March to allow Afghans back into Afghanistan, but in May 2017, Pakistan claimed that the Afghan security forces had opened fire on Pakistani troops that were protecting the population-census teams, resulting in an exchange of fire. The clash resulted in the closure of Chaman border crossing once again and increased tensions between the two neighbours.

The case of Kulbhushan Jadhav continued to dominate relations between India and Pakistan in 2017. Jadhav was arrested in Balochistan in 2016 while crossing the border with Iran, and tried by a military court in Pakistan for 'espionage and sabo-tage activities against Pakistan'. In January, Jadhav told the Pakistan media that he was a commissioned officer of the Indian Navy and subsequently worked for the

Indian intelligence agency, the Research and Analysis Wing. In April, Jadhav was sentenced to death but in May the International Court of Justice stayed Jadhav's execution, and in December Jadhav's family was allowed to visit him in Pakistan on humanitarian grounds.

Human rights and civil liberties

Civil society in Pakistan saw increasing restrictions and curbs on its civil liberties in 2017. Journalists, activists, and development and aid workers bore the brunt of state policies, which were defended by the government as being necessary for national security and countering terrorism. The year began with the abduction of five social activists in January, when the security forces allegedly took Samar Abbas, Waqas Goraya, Salman Haider, Ahmed Raza Naseer and Aasim Saeed into custody: these activists had all been vocal in their criticism of religious extremism and state-security policies. There was no clarity on where the activists were kept, and in what conditions, during their detention. Four of these activists were subsequently reunited with their families, with at least two leaving the country following their release. However, Samar Abbas's whereabouts remained uncertain in 2017.

Government authorities also tried to curb the activities of NGOs and international NGOs (INGOs) by implementing a 'Regulation of INGO in Pakistan' policy. (Pakistan has grown increasingly suspicious of the activities of foreign aid and development workers since the disclosures that the CIA had used a vaccination campaign to gather intelligence on the whereabouts of Osama bin Laden, leading to the raid by US Navy Seals in Abbottabad in May 2011.) In a blow to humanitarian work, the Ministry of Interior gave 27 NGOs – including ActionAid, Open Society Foundations and Oxfam – a 90-day ultimatum to conclude their operations in the country. The ministry justified this move on the grounds that these NGOs were operating outside of their defined mandates.

In another example of the restriction of civil liberties in the name of counter-terrorism, in March parliament passed a constitutional amendment that allowed for the continuation of military courts for another two years after the sunset clause included in the original legal provisions had expired in January 2017. Those opposing the military courts continued to argue that the cases tried in them had no transparency, the suspects were unknown and the charges against them unclear.

The status of refugees in Pakistan – including an estimated 1.4m registered and 700,000 undocumented Afghan refugees – remained uncertain. Civil-society activists urged the Pakistani government to extend the stay of Afghan refugees in Pakistan beyond the initial extension given in March, which ended in December. More than 50,000 registered Afghan refugees were estimated to have returned to Afghanistan in the first three-quarters of the year, a considerable decline from 2016 when at least 370,000 refugees were repatriated. Human Rights Watch called Pakistan's voluntary repatriation process – which is facilitated by the UN High Commissioner for Refugees – 'coercive' and in 'violation of international law'. Furthermore, no efforts were undertaken to improve the living conditions of Rohingya Muslims in Pakistan, which hosts the second-highest concentration of Rohingya after Bangladesh. Approximately 55,000 Rohingya were known to be officially registered in Pakistan, a majority of whom lived in Karachi. Although Pakistan registered an official protest with the Myanmar government for violence perpetrated against the Rohingya, journalists and activists called upon the Pakistani state to grant citizenship to Rohingya refugees, many of whom have lived in Pakistan since the 1960s. Due to the lack of legal identification provided to them, the Rohingya remained 'stateless', rendering them vulnerable to abuse and harassment by the security forces.

Overall, the mainstreaming of radical groups such as the TLP and MML looked likely to exacerbate sectarian tensions, while the country remained at risk from militant groups connected to ISIS. With the Khyber Pakhtunkhwa–FATA merger still stalled, no headway was made for converting the FATA reforms bill into law. The implementation of NAP slowed in 2017, casting increasing importance on the need to implement NISP and NSP, both of which may provide long-term visions for stability and security in Pakistan and the region. Relations with Afghanistan, India and the US remained strained and the state of human rights in Pakistan continued to be poor, particularly for activists, journalists, religious minorities and refugees.

Chapter Six

Asia-Pacific

Myanmar (ARSA)

Decade-old tensions exploded in Rakhine State in 2017 as the Tatmadaw (the Myanmar armed forces) initiated a disproportionate military response to a series of attacks carried out on 25 August by the Arakan Rohingya Salvation

Key statistics	2016	2017
Type:	Internal	Internal
Fatalities:	– c	12,000
New IDPs:	25,000	35,000
New refugees:	– b	690,000

Army (ARSA), formerly known as Harakah al-Yaqin. The fighting and subsequent 'clearance operations' of the Tatmadaw sent up to 690,000 Rohingya Muslims fleeing into neighbouring Bangladesh, with the crisis seriously impacting Myanmar's international relations as well as domestic stability and security.

In the months prior to the outbreak of violence in August, tensions grew in the volatile townships of Buthidaung, Maungdaw and Rathedaung in Rakhine State, indicating that some sort of ARSA attack was imminent. The likelihood of communal violence between the Rakhine Buddhist population and Rohingya Muslims led the Tatmadaw to expand its activities in the area in order to observe the increasing ARSA activity and protect ethnic Rakhine Buddhists who felt threatened. The international community's closer scrutiny of the situation resulted in significantly heightened pressure on the government to address the violations against Rohingya Muslims that were being reported from Rakhine State (the

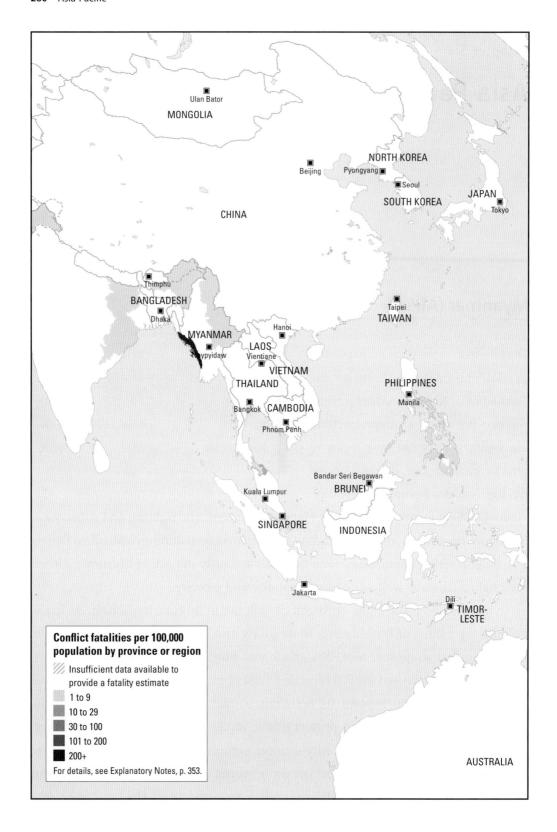

Ulan Bator

MONGOLIA

NORTH KOREA

Beijing

Pyongyang

Seoul

JAPAN

SOUTH KOREA

Tokyo

CHINA

Thimphu

Taipei

BANGLADESH

TAIWAN

Dhaka

Hanoi

MYANMAR

LAOS

Naypyidaw

Vientiane

VIETNAM

THAILAND

PHILIPPINES

Bangkok

CAMBODIA

Manila

Phnom Penh

Bandar Seri Begawan

Kuala Lumpur

BRUNEI

SINGAPORE

INDONESIA

Jakarta

Dili

TIMOR-
LESTE

**Conflict fatalities per 100,000
population by province or region**

Insufficient data available to
provide a fatality estimate

1 to 9

10 to 29

30 to 100

101 to 200

200+

For details, see Explanatory Notes, p. 353.

AUSTRALIA

government consistently denied all charges of human-rights abuses). In March, UN Special Rapporteur Yanghee Lee called for a commission of inquiry to investigate the 'systematic, structural, and institutional discrimination in policy, law and practice, as well as long-standing persecution, against the Rohingya and other minorities in Rakhine State'. On 24 March, a week after China and Russia blocked the UN Security Council from issuing a statement on the situation in the state, the UN Human Rights Council agreed to send an international fact-finding mission to investigate the alleged abuses. The mission was never allowed entry into the country, which prompted serious critique from the UN, the international community and human-rights organisations. In December Lee was permanently banned from entering the country.

On 1 July the national security adviser on Rakhine State said in a statement that the military had observed increased activities of militants in the Mayu mountains of Buthidaung and Maungdaw townships. The security forces in Maungdaw township were put on high alert after six civilians were murdered, two were abducted and up to 200 Rakhine Buddhists fled their villages during late June and early July. On 9 July two militants were killed by the security forces in Buthidaung township, and the next day the Rakhine State Hluttaw legislature approved a proposal to increase security and protection measures for the ethnic Rakhine population in the townships of Buthidaung, Maungdaw and Rathedaung. The tension continued to rise as a community leader was attacked by masked men carrying swords. In response, the local population of Rakhine ethnic origin in Kayukphyu township established the Rakhine State Security Support Committee on 8 August and asked the government to mandate the formation of a people's militia. This call was taken up more broadly and public demonstrations demanding the establishment of people's militias were held in 15 townships across the state. On 15 August, San Shwe Kyaw, the NLD Sittway township chairman, said that the government was planning to provide military training to people of ethnic Rakhine origin. However, this was rejected by a government spokesperson the following day, who said it was not government policy to support paramilitary forces. Instead, the Tatmadaw continued counter-insurgency operations and on 11 August deployed the 33rd Light Infantry Division into Maungdaw township, but towards the end of August, local tensions had reached new heights.

On 24 August the Advisory Commission on Rakhine State, headed by former UN secretary-general Kofi Annan, published the final report on challenges and policy recommendations for Rakhine State. On 25 August, up to 30 police outposts in the townships of Buthidaung, Maungdaw and Rathedaung, as well as a camp of the 552 Light Infantry regiment at Khamara, were attacked by the ARSA – 77 militants and 12 members of the security forces were killed in the initial clashes. In the following days communal violence broke out, making it nearly impossible to verify the competing claims from government and ARSA sources concerning the killing of civilians. On 31 August the Tatmadaw claimed that 370 ARSA fighters (essentially local Rohingya villagers mobilised and poorly armed by the ARSA) had been killed between 25 and 30 August in 90 clashes in northern Rakhine State. In the following days (and throughout the rest of the year) vast numbers of Rohingya Muslims fled Rakhine State to Bangladesh, bringing reports of the burning of villages, rape and extrajudicial killings committed by the Myanmar security forces and local militias. According to a survey released in December by Médecins Sans Frontières, at least 6,700 Rohingya Muslims had been killed since the outbreak of violence and up to 655,000 Rohingya Muslims had fled to Bangladesh, where they formed the world's largest refugee camp. Subsequent reports and estimates, including by the UN, pushed refugee and fatality estimates higher.

The attacks by the ARSA on 25 August set in motion a wide range of political and security-related developments with implications for local, regional and international dynamics. On the domestic scene, the Tatmadaw continued to present a narrative that portrayed the ARSA as terrorists with ties to transnational networks, while also claiming that local Rohingya Muslims burned their own villages in an attempt to frame the central authorities. A few days after the attacks, Lieutenant-General Kyaw Swe, minister of home affairs, said that the ARSA was trying to capture territory and 'establish an Islamic state' in the three townships. This narrative was picked up and repeated by influential Buddhist monks: Sitagu Sayadaw, a highly respected member of the monkhood, provided religious justification for the mass killings of non-Buddhists during a sermon for army officers in Kayin State in October.

Meanwhile, the Myanmar authorities continuously condemned the international community for blindly siding with the 'terrorists' and interfering in

Myanmar's internal affairs. This narrative appeared to have been accepted by a majority of the population, especially those in major city centres who on several occasions demonstrated their support for the government and the army. As a result, the extreme Buddhist nationalist sentiment in the country was reinforced together with an anti-Western, anti-UN movement. On a domestic level it appeared likely that systematic discrimination against non-Buddhists would continue, with a risk that the new nationalist sentiment could potentially be channelled towards other minorities.

The crisis could also give rise to new security threats towards the country and its population. In the wake of the violence against the Rohingya, several extreme Islamist transnational terrorist networks called for attacks against the central authorities in Myanmar and military support to militant Muslims, although any such attack would further fuel anti-Muslim sentiment across the country and heighten the risk of communal violence. The crisis could also precipitate tensions with countries bordering Myanmar. By driving out the Rohingya Muslim population, the Tatmadaw effectively undermined the insurgency tactic adopted by the ARSA of operating under the cover of the civilian population. This could potentially result in the ARSA adopting new tactics based on cross-border safe havens and raids, which in a worst-case scenario could contribute to a deteriorating relationship with neighbouring countries such as Bangladesh.

The crisis also significantly impacted Myanmar's international relations. Following the outbreak of large-scale violence, the UN consistently denounced the conduct of the Myanmar central authorities: as early as 5 September, UN Secretary-General António Guterres announced that he had written officially to the president of the UN Security Council with proposals to end the violence in Rakhine State. However, Myanmar continued to be shielded by China and Russia in the Security Council as they consistently vetoed substantial resolutions. UN High Commissioner for Human Rights Zeid Ra'ad al-Hussein said that the situation resembled a textbook example of ethnic cleansing, a description that was later repeated by then-US secretary of state Rex Tillerson. The official denouncements were followed by some concrete actions. Speaking at the UN General Assembly in New York on 19 September, British Prime Minister Theresa May said that the United Kingdom would suspend all military cooperation with the Tatmadaw – a measure also adopted by the United States, which also implemented travel bans on certain military leaders and discussed possibilities for reinstating sanctions. The European Union Council of Foreign Ministers also announced a close review of military cooperation and the possibility of the adoption of sanctions.

On 23 November, Myanmar and Bangladesh signed an agreement on the repatriation of Rohingya refugees. However, the agreement has been widely criticised for not involving the UN High Commissioner for Refugees and for being premature, as the security situation on the ground does not allow for safe returns, thereby discouraging the majority of refugees from commencing the process.

In the short term it appeared unlikely that international pressure would have any real influence on the position of the central authorities or gain traction with a significant proportion of the population. These dynamics could result in a mutual rejection between primarily Western governments and the authorities in Myanmar, thereby undermining the much-improved relationships which have been observed since the country set out on a path of political transition. This potentially could impede economic and democratic development as trade, investment and tourism fade, setting the country on a course of isolation and renewed dependency on China.

Myanmar (EAOs)

The Nationwide Ceasefire Agreement (NCA) encountered serious challenges in 2017 as several powerful Ethnic Armed Organisations (EAOs), based primarily in northern parts of the country, gathered under a new alli-

Key statistics	2016	2017
Type:	Internal	Internal
Fatalities:	300	125
New IDPs:	10,000	10,000
New refugees:	– [b]	– [b]

ance and actively sought to derail the adopted framework for peace and political negotiations. Armed clashes between the Tatmadaw (the Myanmar armed forces) and the Kachin Independence Army (KIA), the Ta'ang National Liberation Army

(TNLA), the United League of Arekan/Arakan Army (ULA/AA), the Shan State Progress Party/Shan State Army–North (SSPP/SSA–N) and the Myanmar National Democratic Alliance Army (MNDAA) continued throughout the year, affecting the possibility of securing a political settlement and durable peace in the country.

New challenges to the peace process

On 22–24 February, the powerful United Wa State Party (UWSP) hosted a summit at its headquarters in Pangsang on the Chinese border. Seven northern-based EAOs (all non-signatories to the NCA) participated, including the four groups belonging to the Northern Alliance–Burma (NA–B), which was involved in heavy fighting against the army from November 2016 and was branded as a 'terrorist organisation' by the Shan State legislature in December 2016. In a joint statement released after the February conference, the seven groups denounced the current NCA and called for a completely new ceasefire agreement to be negotiated between the Myanmar authorities and EAOs. The group also demanded equal participation in the political dialogue on the future state structure for all EAOs (the current framework dictates that only signatories to the NCA can partake in discussions). Finally, they called for China and the United Nations to mediate the peace process and encouraged Myanmar's involvement in China's Belt and Road Initiative.

A follow-up meeting was held on 15–19 April between the same groups to consolidate their agreements. After the meeting, the participating EAOs announced the creation of their new alliance, named the Federal Political Negotiation and Consultative Committee (FPNCC), and declared their joint support for a peace-policy document drafted by the UWSP and released by the FPNCC on 19 April. The document outlined a putative governance structure that emphasised a high degree of autonomy for national states and a very limited role for the central government, declaring that each state should have independent power over legislation and the right to interact autonomously with foreign investors and control natural resources. In terms of foreign relations, national states should have the power to establish agreements and diplomatic ties with neighbouring countries with little involvement from the central government, and also be free to control border crossings. Furthermore, the text prescribed that the 25% of seats in parliament held by the Tatmadaw should be reallocated to ethnic minorities and that the army should not be allowed to retain its current and constitutionally protected political powers. The FPNCC also stated that other groups accepting the terms of the new alliance were welcome to join and that future peace negotiations with the government would only be conducted under the FPNCC umbrella.

The political consensus reached between the groups of the FPNCC during the summits represented a clear break with the government- and military-led peace process: the demands of the FPNCC were in direct conflict with the decades-old mission statement of the Tatmadaw that enshrines the principles of non-disintegration of the union, non-disintegration of national solidarity and the perpetuation of sovereignty. In the short term, these developments will most likely contribute to a deteriorating security situation in geographical areas under the control of FPNCC members as the Tatmadaw continues to deploy coercive measures in the face of stalled negotiations. As seen previously, violent clashes will probably occur around geographical points of tactical importance and close to areas of economic importance to EAOs, such as along transportation roads as well as illegal logging and mining sites. The local population in these areas will continue to suffer under the infamous 'four cuts' strategy of the Tatmadaw, which includes the tactic of isolating EAOs from local support bases in order to deny opponents access to vital intelligence and resources in the field.

If the Myanmar authorities continue to reject the legitimacy of the FPNCC and refuses to engage in any dialogue with the group, and if the ethnic bloc continues to maintain its demand for a high degree of autonomy for ethnic national states, national reconciliation and a genuine peace seems a distant prospect. At the same time, these developments also raise the question of whether achieving peace really represents the desired end state for the parties to the conflict, or if prolonged indecision and the continued lack of national law enforcement is the true objective.

Diminishing relevance of the UNFC

The creation of the new ethnic coalition significantly contributed to further fragmentation of the United Nationalities Federal Council (UNFC) – the previously dominant non-signatory bloc. The UNFC lost some of its most powerful members to the new FPNCC alliance over the course of 2017: on 29 April the Kachin Independent Organisation (KIO) resigned from the group and joined the FPNCC, followed by the smaller Wa National Organisation (WNO). On 12 August the SSPP/SSA–N also left the bloc to join the FPNCC. After the defections, the UNFC included only four members, down from its original 11 when the coalition was formed in 2011. The departure of those groups – who were mainly involved in armed struggle with the Tatmadaw – was a significant blow to the UNFC, as only two of its remaining members were active militarily and commanded troops in the field.

The UNFC, as opposed to the FPNCC, accepts the current format for the peace process and the NCA in principle. However, in order for the bloc to sign the NCA, compromises need to be negotiated with the Myanmar authorities on nine points. Specifically, these negotiations revolve around the UNFC's desire to obtain a commitment from the central authorities to establish a federal union, and to allow international ceasefire monitoring and the creation of an independent body to mediate disputes. Throughout the year these negotiations continued and some progress was made, although the process also witnessed false starts and frustration. On 30 March – coinciding with the first anniversary of the government – it was officially announced that the UNFC members would sign the NCA. However, the following day the groups said that they had no intention of signing the agreement and that they had not received advance notice of the government's announcement. While embarrassing for the government, the incident nevertheless demonstrated the eagerness of the administration, led by Aung San Suu Kyi's National League of Democracy (NLD), to secure a breakthrough in the peace process. On 12 December, Mai Aung Ma Nge, the deputy leader of the UNFC Delegation for Political Negotiation (DPN), said that the bloc had requested direct consultation with the highest level of authority in the country to finalise the NCA signature negotiations, which had by then already been in progress for some 17 months.

In the short term it seemed likely that the Myanmar authorities would continue to prioritise NCA signature negotiations with the UNFC. Should these negotiations succeed, the bloc would be granted access to the political dialogue conducted at Union Peace Conferences and gain influence in the development of a new governance structure. This would mean that all major EAOs in the southeast would have agreed to the NCA, a situation which potentially could lead to greater isolation of the FPNCC bloc.

The Second 21st Century Panglong Conference

In an effort to progress negotiations, the Myanmar authorities chose to invite all non-signatories of the NCA to attend the Second 21st Century Panglong Conference on 24–29 May as 'specially invited guests', despite the fact that according to the NCA only signatories can participate in the political dialogue at the peace conferences (meaning that only eight of 21 EAOs were in fact eligible to attend). However, the Myanmar authorities still excluded three groups – the ULA/AA, the TNLA and MNDAA – due to the continuing conflict with these groups, while the EAOs participating as guests were allowed to submit papers but were not permitted to address the conference.

This led most non-signatories to decline their invitations and on 23 May the UNFC bloc decided not to participate. As the three EAOs that did not receive an invitation to the conference were all members of the FPNCC, it seemed unlikely that the northern bloc would participate despite its public statement on 17 May that indicated its willingness to attend. However, as a result of diplomatic efforts between the Myanmar authorities and China, representatives from the FPNCC joined the conference in Naypyidaw on 23 May. As such, 15 EAOs participated when the conference started: the eight NCA signatories and the seven FPNCC members. However, the absence of the UNFC and guest status of the seven FPNCC members compromised the overarching function of the conference and highlighted the growing gap between the Myanmar authorities and groups opposed to the format of the peace process. In his opening remarks at the conference, Tatmadaw Commander-in-Chief Ming Aung Hlaing reiterated that the current process would remain unchanged, stating that the NCA text encompassed all demands put forward by EAOs and that the agreement would serve as a springboard for building 'a democratic federal Union'.

Despite the controversy over the attendees, the conference did produce limited results. Before the conference, 41 'basic federal principles' had been proposed by NCA signatories and approved by the Union Peace Dialogue Joint Committee (UPDJC), chaired by State Counsellor Suu Kyi, for inclusion on the conference agenda. These 41 principles were grouped into political, economic, social and land/ environment-related matters in an attempt to guide the creation of a new federal governance system. (Security-related issues were absent from the negotiations as no agreement had been reached during processing in the UPDJC.) During the conference, the 41 principles served as the basis for negotiations. Intense debate arose between the political principle of the right to self-determination of ethnic groups (including, for example, the right of ethnic states to write their own constitutions) and Myanmar authorities insistence on the principle that no ethnic state could ever secede from the union. Eventually it became clear that the Myanmar authorities saw the two as interrelated, meaning that in order for the principle of self-determination to be adopted, the principle of non-secession should be adopted as well. The conference did not produce any final agreement with regards to these and other important points, but 37 principles were agreed and adopted by the participants, bolstering the view of the central authorities that the current process was suitable. However, given that NCA signatories as well as non-signatories have continued to criticise the framework throughout the year, it remained unlikely that the process would produce substantial results in the short term.

Philippines (ASG)

The dynamics of the conflict in the Philippines involving the Abu Sayyaf Group (ASG) evolved significantly during 2017. The powerful Basilan-based faction of the ASG led by Isnilon Hapilon played a leading role in the five-month siege of the

Key statistics	2016	2017
Type:	Internal	Internal
Fatalities:	250	1,250
New IDPs:	– [b]	350,000
New refugees:	– [b]	– [b]

city of Marawi, which began in May, alongside the ISIS-aligned Maute group, although the ASG's operational capabilities were significantly damaged after Hapilon's cohort of fighters were defeated by the Armed Forces of the Philippines (AFP) in late October. Hapilon was killed during a gun battle with AFP troops in the final days of the siege, effectively rendering the ASG leaderless.

The threat from the ASG's piracy operations and kidnapping-for-ransom activities in the Sulu Sea also decreased during 2017 due to enhanced maritime-security measures involving closer regional cooperation between Indonesia, Malaysia and the Philippines. However, the ASG continued to pose a substantial threat on land by launching ambushes against the state's security forces and staging deliberate attacks on civilians in their primary areas of operation. In the aftermath of the Marawi siege, President Rodrigo Duterte and the AFP's newly appointed Chief of Staff General Rey Leonardo Guerrero vowed to take on the ASG's remaining factions in their remote island strongholds.

The siege of Marawi

In the early months of 2017, reports suggested that Hapilon's Basilan-based faction of the ASG had relocated from its island base to Mindanao's mainland and joined forces with the ISIS-aligned Maute group, led by brothers Abdullah and Omar Maute. In January, the AFP claimed Hapilon had been injured in a government airstrike after being sighted in the town of Butig, Lanao del Sur province, but the report could not be confirmed. In early April, 11 members of the ASG clashed with government troops in Inabanga, Bohol province – an island north of Mindanao and well outside the group's usual area of operations. Four ASG members, three soldiers, two civilians and a police officer were killed in the clash. The reported presence of the ASG in these areas provided evidence of the ASG's widening geographical reach and fuelled the authorities' concern over the emerging links between Hapilon's faction of the ASG and other ISIS-aligned groups operating in the southern Philippines. These concerns first arose in 2014 when Hapilon pledged allegiance to Abu Bakr al-Baghdadi, the leader of Islamic State, also known as ISIS or ISIL, in Syria and Iraq, and was subsequently declared the figurehead or 'emir' of ISIS in Southeast Asia.

These fears over Hapilon's links to ISIS were fully realised on 23 May when a botched AFP raid to capture Hapilon in the city of Marawi, Lanao del Sur province, sparked an armed uprising by ISIS-linked groups, including the ASG faction led by Hapilon. The AFP initially hoped to quash the insurgency within a matter of weeks, but the conflict soon spiralled into a situation of prolonged urban warfare as the AFP drastically underestimated the strength of the militants – initial estimates in late May of a force comprising fewer than 100–200 militants were dwarfed by the actual strength of more than 900. The militants were able to take over large swathes of the city, setting up base in the central Banggolo district, and declared the establishment of a regional ISIS Wilayat (or province) in Southeast Asia. After the initial outbreak of violence, President Duterte declared martial law across all of Mindanao for a period of 60 days (later extended by the Philippine Congress until the end of the year). The AFP launched waves of air-strikes and ground offensives, yet it took until 16 October for Duterte to declare the city 'liberated from terrorist influence' and a further week for the military to declare a formal end to combat operations. ASG leader Hapilon was shot dead by government troops during the final days of the conflict in mid-October along with Omar Maute, another key planner of the siege and the last surviving senior leader of the Maute group.

After the siege ended, the Philippine government said that the final death toll stood at more than 1,000 people, including 974 militants, 165 government soldiers and at least 47 civilians. Several hundred civilians had been held hostage while 353,000 residents from around 77,000 families had been displaced by the fighting. More than 200,000 residents were still unable to return home as of the end of 2017.

The participation of Hapilon's ASG faction in the siege marked the first time the ASG had been involved in a large-scale insurgency in an urban setting, indi-cating the growing ambitions of Hapilon and the rising military capabilities of his faction, which had been bolstered through the receipt of large ransom pay-ments after a spate of kidnappings in recent years. The decision by Hapilon to join forces with the Maute group and align the ASG more closely with ISIS also constituted a reversion to the group's radical ideological roots based on Salafi jihadism: although in recent years the group had morphed into something more akin to a profit-driven criminal enterprise, when the ASG was founded in 1991 by Abdurajak Abubakar Janjalani it aimed to establish an independent Islamic state centred on the southern Philippines.

However, this apparent reversion to past ideological motivations may turn out to be only a temporary phenomenon. Hapilon's large ASG faction, consist-ing of an estimated 60–200 fighters, was effectively wiped out in Marawi, leaving behind many smaller ASG factions (amounting to a combined total of no more than 200–300 fighters) in the group's traditional maritime strongholds located in the remote islands of Sulu, Basilan and Tawi-Tawi. None of these factions have pledged allegiance to ISIS and neither are they thought to harbour the same bold regional ambitions as Hapilon's followers. The remaining ASG factions are loosely led by Radullan Sahiron in Sulu and Furuji Indama in Basilan, although many other sub-leaders control small bands of fighters and other factions continue to operate in the remote Tawi-Tawi islands near the Malaysian state of Sabah. With the ASG now lacking an overall figurehead and suffering from a leadership void after Hapilon's death, the group is expected to undergo even greater splintering and factionalisation in the coming years. With no apparent centralised hierarchy, the ASG is likely to revert to smaller-scale, localised activities in its island strongholds, consisting of ambushes targeting the security forces and infrequent attacks against the civilian population.

ASG presence in Basilan and Sulu

The activities of the ASG in Basilan and Sulu continued throughout the year and did not recede entirely during the Marawi siege. The ASG routinely clashed with the security forces and launched several attacks against civilians in these areas. March was a particularly deadly month for armed clashes in Sulu: five ASG members were killed and 11 soldiers injured during a clash in Indanan on 1 March, while another ten militants were killed two days later in Patikul. On 5 March, government troops killed a further nine militants in a gun battle in Maimbung. April also witnessed significant violence. A military assault on an ASG hideout in Talipao on 2 April killed at least one militant and left 32 soldiers injured, while on 10 April seven members of the AFP's Citizen Armed Forces Geographical Unit (CAFGU) died during a shootout with the ASG in Sumisip, Basilan. A military assault on an ASG camp in Sumisip then killed at least 20 militants on 11 May. After this major incident, ASG activity in Basilan and Sulu decreased in intensity as the Marawi siege got under way, yet several notable clashes and attacks still took place.

On 31 July the ASG beheaded five loggers abducted the previous week in Lantawan, while a clash the following week in Kalingalan Caluang left five militants and two soldiers dead. On 21 August the year's deadliest ASG attack targeting civilians took place when militants rampaged through the Basilan town of Maluso, setting fire to houses and killing nine civilians while wounding a further 16. Clashes involving the ASG continued into the final months of the year. On 8 November the ASG killed six AFP troops in Sumisip, before killing three civilians during a raid in

Indanan town on 5 December. Three days later the ASG clashed with the security forces in Panamao town, leaving at least three militants dead. Aside from the incidents highlighted, many other smaller-scale clashes with government troops and deliberate attacks on civilians occurred throughout the year. These types of incidents were in line with the historical pattern of violence associated with the ASG, and the threat of attacks shows no sign of abating in the near future.

Regional cooperation

While 2016 saw the ASG launch a spate of kidnappings at sea and draw international condemnation after beheading two Canadian hostages, 2017 saw a reduction in the threat due to enhanced regional cooperation in the maritime domain. In mid-June, Indonesia, Malaysia and the Philippines began conducting regular trilateral naval patrols in the largely lawless waters of the Sulu Sea, having first discussed the possibility a year earlier at the height of the ASG piracy epidemic. In October, the three nations bolstered these measures through the introduction of coordinated air patrols to spot suspicious activity from the skies. In addition, Malaysia indefinitely extended a dawn-to-dusk curfew for civilian vessels in waters off the Eastern Sabah Security Zone in a further attempt to deter kidnappings and prevent maritime crime along its coastline. As a result of these combined measures, the rate of ship-hijackings and hostage-takings at sea in the region slowed dramatically, despite several incidents in early 2017 which on most occasions were thwarted by the fast-responding security forces. The Philippine Coast Guard foiled two attempts to board vessels at the start of the year after responding to distress calls from the container ship *Ocean Kingdom* off Basilan on 4 January and the *Dong Hae Star* off Tawi-Tawi on 22 February. However, the Vietnamese freighter *Giang Hai* was boarded by ASG militants in the Sulu Sea on 19 February and six members of the crew were abducted. The ASG also beheaded German national Jurgen Kantner on 26 February after a ransom-payment deadline passed. Kantner had been abducted the previous November in waters off the Sulu islands.

In response to the authorities' crackdown at sea, a higher proportion of the ASG's hostage-takings in 2017 occurred on land or in close proximity to the coastline. A number of Filipino nationals were kidnapped as well as several groups of Indonesian and Vietnamese fishermen. Among these incidents a local teacher was abducted from Maimbung town in March, while six construction workers were abducted from Jolo in July and a town councillor was seized in the same area in September. On 14 October five fishermen were abducted from their vessel in waters off Pangutaran town, while a month later the ASG abducted six Filipino civilians, including two children, from their home in Patikul. No Westerners were abducted by the ASG in 2017, largely due to tougher security measures and heightened awareness about the dangers of traversing the region. The total number of hostages held by the ASG declined significantly after a succession of rescue operations carried out by the AFP in the final months of the year. On 10 November the military rescued four Vietnamese captives during a raid on an ASG hideout in Languyan, before freeing five fishermen a week later after launching a second raid on Sugbay island. However, at the end of 2017 the ASG was thought to still be holding at least 12 hostages.

ASG's overall capabilities downgraded

By the end of 2017 the ASG's overall operational capabilities had been significantly downgraded as a result of sustained offensives by the Philippine military. Isnilon Hapilon's faction was decimated after almost all of his followers were killed in Marawi. In addition, the ASG's funding stream from kidnapping operations had dried up as a result of the new regional measures put in place. These changes were reflected in the declining number of major armed clashes during the last six months of the year and in the steadily increasing number of ASG militants reported to have surrendered to the authorities.

Several senior ASG leaders were also killed or arrested during 2017, further degrading the group's capabilities and damaging morale among its remaining fighters. Sub-group leader Buchoy Hassan was killed in a security operation in Tawi-Tawi on 14 March, while senior ASG leaders Abu Rami and Alhabsy Misaya were killed in separate clashes with AFP troops in April. On 3 September, faction leader Abu Asrie was arrested by the Malaysian authorities in Kuala Lumpur, while one of the most-wanted members of the ASG, Boy Indama, was detained by Philippine troops on 30 September in Lamitan.

Following the end of the Marawi siege in late October, President Duterte and General Guerrero vowed to combat radical Islamist groups across Mindanao, including the surviving remnants of the ASG which were still active in Sulu and Basilan. In December, the Philippine Congress approved Duterte's request to extend martial law in the south for a further 12 months until the end of 2018 to aid the AFP in their counter-terrorism operations. As of the end of 2017, at least ten AFP battalions – a force consisting of around 5,000 troops in total – had been deployed to tackle the ASG in the group's Sulu stronghold.

However, although the ASG may now be under substantial pressure on the battlefield, the group will be difficult to defeat as long as the underlying drivers of recruitment persist: rates of poverty, unemployment and underdevelopment remain far higher in Basilan, Sulu, the Tawi-Tawi islands and across the broader Mindanao region than elsewhere in the country. Compounding these long-term recruitment drivers, state presence and administrative control remained weak in the southern Philippines, while corruption among state officials continued to represent a substantial hurdle to improving the situation. The ASG retains a degree of local support among the most marginalised communities, in part due to its practice of sharing ransom money with religious/tribal/local community leaders (who in turn provide cover and support for the group). Being clan- and family-centred, ASG factions are also deeply embedded within local communities.

Despite repeated vows from President Duterte and military officials to defeat the ASG within six to 12 months, the military's latest overall security plan for the southern Philippines – announced at the beginning of last year – provided a far more realistic timescale. The AFP's *Development and Security Plan Kapayapaan*, launched on 6 January 2017, stated that the military's counter-insurgency strategy should aim to defeat the ASG and other armed Islamist groups within six years. Yet as the events of 2017 demonstrated, the dynamics of the conflict involving the ASG have the potential to shift in dramatic and somewhat unexpected ways. The authorities must therefore display continual vigilance and be prepared to react to sudden changes on the ground in a region where the long-running armed Islamist separatist movement has recently been characterised by splintering and the emergence of radical offshoots, resulting in increased volatility and unpredictable events such as the siege of Marawi. While appearing unlikely at present due to its weakened offensive capabilities, the ASG's involvement in another similar scenario in the coming years cannot be entirely ruled out.

Philippines (MILF)

The peace process between the government of the Philippines and the Moro Islamic Liberation Front (MILF) overcame several hurdles during 2017. Progress, however, stalled towards the end of the year, causing both President Rodrigo

Key statistics	2016	2017
Type:	Internal	Internal
Fatalities:	90	175
New IDPs:	280,000	290,000
New refugees:	– [b]	– [b]

Duterte and the MILF's leadership to express their shared frustration. Duterte and MILF Chairman Al-Haj Murad Ebrahim warned of the risk of greater violence, extremism and radicalisation in Mindanao should the long-awaited passage of the proposed Bangsamoro Basic Law (BBL) be further delayed. The final terms of the BBL – designed to pave the way for the creation of a new self-governing Bangsamoro entity in the south to replace the existing Autonomous Region in Muslim Mindanao (ARMM) – were still being debated by Philippine legislators as of the end of the year.

Meanwhile, the activities of the Bangsamoro Islamic Freedom Fighters (BIFF) – a radical offshoot of the MILF which broke away from its parent organisation in 2010 – escalated as violent clashes involving the BIFF intensified in western Mindanao. A small cohort of BIFF members participated in the five-month siege of the city of Marawi between May and October alongside several militant groups aligned with the Islamic State, also known as ISIS or ISIL, including the Abu Sayyaf Group (ASG) and the Mautes. Other BIFF factions launched an intensifying campaign of attacks against the security forces and civilians in their areas of influence in 2017. After an eventful year, the southern Philippines' long-running Moro separatist insurgency is approaching a critical juncture as the peace process nears what could be its final stages amid rising jihadist violence.

Peace process edges forward

The peace process advanced steadily during 2017 through several positive steps towards the passage of the BBL – a process which was first set in motion by a prior peace agreement signed between the government and the MILF in 2014. In late

February the Bangsamoro Transition Commission (BTC) – the body tasked with drafting the BBL composed of members of the MILF, the Moro National Liberation Front (MNLF) and other key stakeholders – resumed its work after being expanded to 21 members. In a significant obstacle to progress, the influential MNLF founder and Sulu faction leader Nur Misuari rejected a seat on the BTC and opted instead to discuss the proposed law through a series of one-on-one meetings with President Duterte over the course of the year. On 17 July, the BTC finalised its draft version of the BBL and sent the document to Duterte, who then passed it to the Philippine Congress for the consideration of lawmakers on 4 August. Even at this early stage, concerns were raised over the potentially slow progress of the bill through Congress as it was not accompanied by a certificate of urgency. Duterte responded to these concerns by hosting a meeting with the key stakeholders in Manila on 14 September, during which he vowed to come up with a 'game plan' to ensure the passage of the bill into law. A week later, Duterte formally certified the bill as urgent.

Despite the intention of both sides to see the BBL passed by the end of the year, the hope for a swift passage of the bill through Congress did not materialise. By the end of the year the proposed BBL was still being debated by lawmakers amid disagreement over its final terms. Key issues still to be resolved included ensuring that the BBL falls in line with the provisions of the Philippine constitution; agreeing on the geographical delimitations and final status of the new Bangsamoro region; and deciding whether to include an anti-dynasty provision to ensure the region remains democratic. After several months of intense discussions, in early December a House of Representatives panel began deliberations on four separate versions of the BBL and agreed to establish a new subcommittee with the aim of reconsolidating the proposals into a single bill in the new year. Despite voicing frustration over the stumbling blocks encountered in Congress, both sides exercised considerable restraint in their rhetoric and reiterated their shared commitment to cooperate and push ahead with the peace process. In November, Duterte appealed for the MILF to remain patient and labelled the BBL as his 'personal commitment', vowing to correct 'historical injustices' against the Moro population in the south. Ebrahim, the chairman of the MILF, also reinforced his group's commitment to the peace process, saying that violence would not help in 'achieving our political aspiration for self-government and self-determination'. The calm and restrained response of the MILF leadership in the face of continued delays to the BBL indicated that the group remained committed to pursuing a non-violent approach, which was further demonstrated through the MILF's strict adherence to the ceasefire deal signed with the government in 2014. In the final months of the year, both the government and the MILF expressed confidence that the BBL would be passed in 2018.

Despite this optimism, Duterte and MILF leader Ebrahim separately warned of the potential for rising violence, extremism and radicalisation in Mindanao if the BBL is further delayed, or (in a worst-case scenario) not passed at all. On 12 October, Duterte said that 'there will be fighting in all of Mindanao' if the government fails in its quest to secure a lasting peace agreement with the MILF, warning that 'the mainstream rebel groups would then be joining with the extremist groups'. Echoing these comments several weeks later, Ebrahim warned on 23 October that the delay in approving the new Bangsamoro region – set to cover the Muslim-majority provinces of Basilan, Lanao del Sur, Maguindanao, Sulu and Tawi-Tawi in addition to several smaller pockets of territory – was 'creating discontent in communities', and could aid terrorist recruitment in the most marginalised and impoverished areas. In November Ebrahim further elaborated on his concerns, labelling the BBL as being 'of great importance' for stability and security in Southeast Asia as a whole, while warning that 'the longer this process takes, the more people are going to be radicalised'.

Last year's prolonged assault on Marawi by a collection of ISIS-aligned groups has rendered such warnings more credible and pressing, enabling all stakeholders to visualise the potential consequences should the peace process fail to achieve its central aim of facilitating a new self-governing region in the Muslim-majority areas of the southern Philippines. The Armed Forces of the Philippines (AFP), the MILF and the MNLF all repeatedly voiced the importance of passing the law quickly to avoid a repeat scenario elsewhere in Mindanao, with cities such as Cotabato and Zamboanga mooted as possible secondary targets. To avert such an eventuality, in 2017 the MILF and MNLF not only supported the peace process but also cooperated with the AFP on the battlefield against ISIS-linked groups, including the BIFF. The two main rebel groupings provided additional manpower to support AFP counter-insurgency operations in Maguindanao, while the AFP provided tactical and air support to MILF rebels advancing towards BIFF positions on the ground. In October, Ebrahim said that the MILF remains 'determined to oppose radical groups' in its areas of influence, yet the MILF insists that 'no formal joint operations' have been conducted with the AFP.

The BIFF's escalating campaign of terror

Clashes between the BIFF and the AFP intensified significantly during 2017, particularly in the BIFF's stronghold of Maguindanao province. On 26 January, four BIFF fighters were killed and seven soldiers were injured during a clash in Datu Saudi town, while the following month an army officer was killed after being ambushed by militants in nearby Datu Unsay. In mid-March the AFP launched a sustained three-day offensive targeting the BIFF, shelling militant hideouts and launching a wave of airstrikes on BIFF positions in Datu Salibo. The AFP said the operation killed at least 21 militants and left another 26 injured. A second AFP offensive targeting three Maguindanao towns between 7 and 11 May killed a further 31 militants. In Lanao del Sur province to the north, the BIFF contributed around 40 fighters to the ISIS-led siege of Marawi, which erupted on 23 May and lasted for five months. However, the BIFF played a comparatively minor role in the uprising, which was directed and fought primarily by militants from the ASG and Maute groups. Most of the BIFF's capacity was retained in its rural heartlands further south, where clashes intensified both during and after the Marawi conflict.

On 21 June the BIFF launched a particularly brazen assault on the town of Pigcawayan, North Cotabato province, attacking military installations and schools while taking 15 civilians hostage to use as human shields before retreating. One civilian was killed in the incident, which displaced more than 1,400 local residents. August–September saw major and sustained clashes erupt between the BIFF and members of the MILF across farmland in central Maguindanao. Most of the clashes involved militants affiliated with a radical BIFF faction led by Esmael Abdulmalik. On 6 August, an improvised explosive device (IED) killed five and injured seven members of the MILF, while several days of fierce gun battles in mid-August killed at least 20 BIFF and five MILF members. Sporadic clashes erupted later in the month, killing another 27 combatants on both sides. Armed clashes between the two groups continued to take place throughout September.

Having sustained heavy losses on the battlefield, the BIFF sought to regroup and replenish their ranks between October and November, resulting in a lull in the fighting. The conflict intensified again in December: the month saw 34 people killed, marking a severe escalation of violence. After several minor clashes early in the month, the AFP conducted a succession of targeted offensives from mid-December onwards. On 19 December airstrikes killed at least five BIFF members in Carmen town, North Cotabato province. Four days later another six BIFF militants were killed during clashes in the town, which also left five soldiers wounded and a member of the AFP's Citizen Armed Forces Geographical Unit (CAFGU) dead. In the final days of December, the government launched airstrikes in central Maguindanao's Datu Unsay town, killing a further ten militants. At the end of the year the military claimed to have killed 182 BIFF militants in total during 2017, yet the final figure could not be confirmed as enemy bodies were often unable to be recovered and identified by AFP troops due to the remote and hostile locations of the clashes.

In addition to clashing with the military with increased frequency towards the end of 2017, the BIFF also launched a campaign of violence against ethnic tribespeople. The BIFF clashed repeatedly in late December with members of the ethnic Teduray tribe in Maguindanao province as the militants attempted to seize small pockets of territory in agricultural areas. On 25 December the BIFF set fire to Teduray houses in Iginampong village, before killing two members of the tribe the following day in an IED blast in Datu Saudi town. On 28 December the BIFF abducted and killed two Teduray farmers in Datu Hoffer town while also raiding a small Teduray settlement in nearby Datu Unsay. The BIFF's rampage against the Teduray people continued on 31 December when the group torched 12 houses belonging to the tribe in Datu Hoffer.

The civilian population in western Mindanao also remained at significant risk from the violent activities of the BIFF during 2017. More than 353,000 residents were displaced from Marawi and its surrounding areas during the siege of the city between May and October, with more than 200,000 Marawians still displaced at the end of the year. (The BIFF, however, played only a minimal role in causing this displacement as the majority of militants involved were affiliated to the ASG and Maute groups.) Other instances of localised displacement resulted from armed clashes involving BIFF militants against the MILF or the AFP. Several hundred residents fled their homes near Datu Salibo town, Maguindanao province, during sustained MILF–BIFF clashes throughout August, while another 2,000 residents were displaced in central Maguindanao as clashes erupted between the BIFF and the AFP towards the end of the year. On 5 December, the International Committee of the Red Cross said that it had provided humanitarian aid to 11,600 people displaced by fighting between the BIFF and government troops since mid-August.

Civilians also remained at high risk of death or serious injury due to being caught up in armed clashes and from the growing threat of being deliberately targeted in terror attacks perpetrated by the BIFF. The BIFF's increasing use of IEDs in the final months of 2017 was a particular cause for concern. Civilians were injured in bomb attacks attributed to the BIFF in Datu Odin Sinsuat and Guindulungan in September, while on New Year's Eve, suspected BIFF militants detonated a bomb outside a crowded bar in Tacurong city, Sultan Kudarat province, killing two civilians and injuring 16. In total, at least 11 civilians were killed by the BIFF in the final three months of the year compared to none during the previous three months, indicating the group's increasing disregard for civilian life.

Despite the uptick in violence, the BIFF remained geographically confined to three provinces in western Mindanao: Maguindanao, North Cotabato and Sultan Kudarat. The BIFF also remained split into at least three factions, the most active of which was led by Esmael Abdulmalik, who was touted as a potential candidate to replace slain ASG leader Isnilon Hapilon as the next 'emir' of ISIS in Southeast Asia. In a particularly worrying development, the AFP reported seeing 'foreign-looking' fighters alongside BIFF militants in Maguindanao, raising fears that remnants of the Maute group – which was virtually defeated in Marawi but included jihadists from Indonesia and Malaysia – may now be taking up arms with the BIFF. If these reports are true, it would appear that the BIFF has now assumed the ISIS mantle in the southern Philippines and is the new group of choice for radicalised individuals from across the region looking to engage in jihad. Duterte and AFP chief General Rey Leonardo Guerrero have vowed to tackle the BIFF head-on since the end of the Marawi siege in mid-October. In December, Duterte opted to extend martial law in Mindanao for a further year to aid the armed forces' offensives against groups includ-ing the BIFF, while Guerrero has vowed to redeploy resources from Marawi to combat militant groups elsewhere in western Mindanao. Signs of this bolstered counter-insurgency strategy were already visible through the AFP's intensified operations against the BIFF in December.

MILF and MNLF stay on peaceful path

The region's two largest, more moderate and well-established Islamist rebel groups, the MILF and MNLF, did not clash with the AFP during 2017 and remained committed to observing the ceasefire while pursuing a final peace settlement with Manila. Small sub-factions of these two groups, however, were not always under the direct control of the centralised MILF or MNLF leadership, and on infrequent occasions have clashed with each other in localised clan disputes known as *ridos*. On 12 November, a MILF fighter was killed and four others injured in such an incident. These disputes were often resolved quickly and tensions soon defused after the intervention of senior rebel leaders on the ground, and therefore usually resulted in only a small number of casualties. On a particularly positive note, in early October the United Nations removed the MILF from its list of armed groups accused of recruiting child soldiers, drawing praise from human-rights groups. A UN report noted that 1,869 minors had been disengaged from the MILF's ranks since a UN–MILF action plan to address the issue was signed in 2009.

Mindanao's long-running armed Islamist separatist insurgency reached a criti-cal juncture in 2017. The two largest and most influential rebel groups, the MILF and MNLF, remained committed to the peace process and continued to observe a ceasefire with the government. Despite growing frustration over the delay in securing a final peace deal, the steady progress made towards the passage of the BBL over the past year provides cause for significant optimism. In 2018 there exists an opportunity for the long-awaited BBL to be passed, paving the way for the creation of a new autonomous region in Muslim-majority areas of the south-ern Philippines, thereby removing some of the perceived historical injustices which have long driven recruitment for radical groups in Mindanao. However, the BIFF presents a significant obstacle as it remains committed to fighting for a fully independent Islamic state in the south and appears determined to intensify its campaign of violence in an effort to disrupt the peace process going forward. The escalating violence seen during 2017 makes clear that a failure to pass the BBL and secure a lasting peace with the MILF risks exacerbating political tension in western Mindanao, which in the current climate has the potential to rapidly translate into radicalisation and further bloodshed.

Philippines (NPA)

The long-running conflict between the government of the Philippines and the Maoist insurgents of the New People's Army (NPA) escalated during 2017 as the peace process collapsed and violence resumed across the country. Negotiations first broke

Key statistics	2016	2017
Type:	Internal	Internal
Fatalities:	150	300
New IDPs:	– [b]	– [b]
New refugees:	– [b]	– [b]

down in February and could not be revived, despite several attempts. By the end of November, President Rodrigo Duterte had formally terminated the peace process and announced his intention to list the NPA and its political affiliate, the Communist Party of the Philippines (CPP), as a domestic terrorist organisation. Violence worsened significantly in the final months of the year, with a spike in rebel ambushes targeting state security personnel and more frequent clashes between the NPA and the Armed Forces of the Philippines (AFP).

The NPA also continued to exercise a degree of de facto control in its rural areas of influence through collecting 'revolutionary taxes' from wealthy individuals and businesses (particularly mining and agricultural firms) operating in the countryside. Companies that refused to comply with these payment demands often became the target of armed raids and arson attacks. The NPA also continued to pose a considerable risk to civilian life through launching targeted attacks against specific individuals, while other civilians were inadvertently caught in the crossfire during clashes. Rhetoric between Duterte and the NPA grew increasingly fiery as the year progressed, rendering the possibility of reconciliation increasingly remote.

Peace process collapses

The peace process between the government and the National Democratic Front of the Philippines (NDFP) – which represents the NPA and CPP in formal peace negotiations – collapsed in 2017 after talks broke down. Hopes had initially been raised after the election of Duterte in June 2016 as he had vowed to pursue a negotiated settlement with the rebels to end the long-running insurgency. The revived peace process – which was first initiated in 1986 and involved multiple rounds of failed negotiations under five former Philippine presidents – made substantial progress in its early stages under Duterte, with three rounds of talks having been successfully completed in Oslo and Rome between August 2016 and January 2017. Both sides had declared separate ceasefires at the beginning of the process, resulting in a dramatic reduction in violence on the ground as armed clashes between the NPA and AFP almost entirely ceased.

However, amid heightened tensions between the two sides at the negotiating table, renewed clashes broke out between the NPA and AFP in late January, prompting CPP leader José Maria Sison to lift the NPA's ceasefire on 1 February. Duterte followed suit and lifted the government's own ceasefire two days later. Talks then came to a sudden halt in early February 2017 as the two sides reached a sticking point over the release of imprisoned rebels. The CPP–NPA said the release of those it called 'political prisoners' was a precondition for the process to advance, while Duterte refused to consider the request unless the rebels first agreed to sign a joint ceasefire. Talks were briefly revived in the Netherlands in April but ultimately failed to make any meaningful progress. A fifth round of negotiations scheduled for May was cancelled by the government amid continued rebel ambushes targeting military personnel. In September, the mayor of Davao initiated localised peace talks with NPA leaders in Davao City, yet this initiative was cancelled in early December following Duterte's decision to terminate the peace process at the national level.

While the initial breakdown of talks and resumption of clashes in February were triggered by unsatisfied rebel demands for a prisoner amnesty, several more deeply rooted factors also contributed to the failure of dialogue and hampered efforts to restart the peace process. The factionalised nature and wide geographical areas of operation of the NPA – which has active units in most of the Philippines' provinces – made it difficult for the CPP's leaders at the national level to control fighters on the ground. Impatience among regular NPA members in the months leading up to the breakdown of talks likely contributed to NPA ambushes against AFP troops (which occurred shortly before Sison opted to lift the ceasefire). These incidents provoked retaliatory assaults by the military and resulted in spiralling violence at the local level. The historical lack of trust and long-held suspicions which persist on both sides – rooted in five decades of conflict – inevitably made it more difficult for the already faltering peace process to be revived.

The initial breakdown of the peace process in February led to a swift return to violence across the country, which worsened throughout the year and intensified rapidly following Duterte's decision on 23 November to sign a proclamation that formally terminated the peace process with the NPA–CPP–NDFP. The following month, Duterte ordered the Department of Justice to cancel the bail of 21 NDFP 'peace consultants' who had been freed from custody the previous year to participate in the peace process, including senior CPP leaders Benito and Wilma Tiamzon.

As violence flared and the peace process faltered, divisive rhetoric on both sides intensified, marking a stark contrast from the conciliatory tones voiced in the initial aftermath of Duterte's election in 2016. In August 2017, Duterte declared 'war' against the rebels, saying 'let's stop talking, and start fighting' before describing peace negotiations as a 'waste of time'. Meanwhile, the CPP labelled Duterte's administration as a 'semi-colonial, anti-peasant, anti-people regime', claiming the communist movement had 'no other course but to tread the path of militant struggle and collective action'. In October, Duterte accused the CPP–NPA of attempting to 'destabilise the government' and threatened to launch a 'full-scale war' against the group. After a rebel ambush on troops delivering humanitarian aid to flood victims in Northern Samar on 16 December, Duterte derided the NPA as being 'almost the same as ISIS', stating that the NPA possessed 'no ideology other than to destroy and kill'. CPP leader Sison responded to Duterte's taunts with increasing ferocity in the final months of the year, declaring Duterte 'the number one terrorist in the Philippines' while directing his forces to 'intensify guerrilla warfare throughout the whole archipelago' with the aim of 'overthrowing the Duterte regime and its fascist rule of terror'. The CPP also frequently denounced the US–Philippine defence alliance and branded Duterte a 'dictator', while Duterte often labelled the NPA–CPP–NDFP as 'enemies of the state'. The escalating war of words between the outspoken leaders of the two sides incited further violence.

Talks are highly unlikely to resume in the current climate; even more so since Duterte's decision on 13 December to extend martial law in Mindanao until the end of 2018. Duterte's stated reasoning for the extension centres on confronting the threat from Islamist militant groups in the south following last year's siege of Marawi led by the Islamic State, also known as ISIS or ISIL. However, the CPP believed that Duterte had ulterior motives and viewed the extension of martial law as a veiled threat against the NPA and a direct boost to the AFP's counter-insurgency operations targeting the rebels, given that the NPA was the strongest group in the eastern Mindanao region.

Violence intensifies nationwide

After a quiet start to 2017, violence returned to a familiar pattern immediately after the peace process collapsed in February. The NPA reverted to employing its traditional guerrilla tactics: launching small-scale ambushes targeting the security forces in the countryside. The NPA was most active in the southern Mindanao region, particularly in the provinces of Compostela Valley, Cotabato, Davao del Norte, Davao del Sur, Surigao del Norte and Surigao del Sur. However, sporadic clashes also occurred in rural areas across the entire Philippine archipelago, affecting central and northern provinces including Albay, Batangas and Negros Occidental. The government also claimed in November that the NPA had reactivated its notorious 'sparrow units' – urban hit squads tasked with assassinating AFP personnel in towns and cities – after suspected rebels shot dead a soldier at a market in Daraga, Albay province.

While the majority of incidents caused between one and three deaths, several major armed clashes resulted in a higher number of casualties. On 30 March, 15 rebels and three AFP troops were killed in separate clashes in Quezon and Oriental Mindoro. On 12 July, eight NPA members were killed during a clash with government troops in Compostela Valley, while on 21 July five Philippine National Police (PNP) officers were killed in a rebel ambush in Negros Oriental. The deadliest single incident of the year erupted on 28 November, when government soldiers killed at least 15 NPA rebels during a fierce clash in Nasugbu, Batangas province, which also left five AFP troops injured. The following week, multiple gun battles broke out near Lake Sebu town, South Cotabato province, leaving a further seven rebels and two soldiers dead. Aside from using firearms in most attacks, the rebels also occasionally deployed improvised explosive devices to target the security forces. The final week of the year saw a lull in violence as both sides adhered to a temporary ceasefire declared over the Christmas and New Year period. Yet clashes were expected to resume in 2018, with the NPA vowing to intensify its campaign of resistance and AFP chief General Rey Leonardo Guerrero directing his troops to take on the rebels across the country.

NPA presence blights rural communities

The NPA continued to collect 'revolutionary taxes' from businesses and wealthy individuals in its areas of influence during 2017, a practice which Manila describes as extortion. These payments remained a key source of financing for the NPA in its rural heartlands: in May, the PNP estimated that the NPA earns approximately PHP1 billion (US$19.1 million) annually from extortion activities in eastern Mindanao, while in August Secretary of National Defense Delfin Lorenzana said that the NPA collects an estimated PHP1.2bn (US$22.9m) each year from mining companies alone. The NPA continued to use violence and intimidation against those who refused to meet its payment demands, often launching armed raids and committing arson attacks against non-compliant businesses. These incidents occurred more frequently during the second half of the year as the conflict intensified. On 15 September, insurgents armed with hand grenades attacked a solar power plant in Negros Occidental, causing extensive damage to the site. Later in the month the NPA set fire to a palm-oil tanker in Agusan del Sur, before destroying 11 heavy-duty construction vehicles parked at Bicol International Airport. In the final three months of 2017, 12 further incidents took place, with the lucrative banana industry most frequently targeted. On 3 October the NPA set fire to a banana-packing plant in South Cotabato, while later that month a truck carrying fresh produce was set ablaze in

Surigao del Sur and a banana plantation was torched in Bukidnon. Among a series of other attacks, rebels torched construction equipment at a quarry in Cagayan and attacked a hydroelectric plant in Mountain province, causing power outages in nine municipalities.

While civilian lives are usually spared during attacks on businesses, the economic cost to the firms involved often runs into millions of pesos. The Philippine Banana Growers and Exporters Association sought to highlight the worsening situation faced by companies, asking on 17 October for troops from the AFP's Citizen Armed Forces Geographical Unit (CAFGU) to be deployed to protect plantations from the threat of NPA attacks. Without government help, firms operating in areas affected by the NPA faced a dilemma: either pay the NPA's taxes and risk being closed down by the government for doing so; or ignore the NPA's demands and risk being targeted by the rebels. On 21 November, Duterte warned firms in Mindanao that they could be shut down or have their licences to operate in certain areas permanently revoked if they continued to fund the NPA.

Risk to civilians

In contrast to several of the radical Islamist groups operating in the southern Philippines, the NPA is not known to target civilians indiscriminately. However, civilians remained at risk in 2017 from being caught in the crossfire during armed clashes. On 20 April, two young children and their grandmother were killed by stray bullets in Masbate province, while the following day three civilians died during an encounter in Sultan Kudarat. On 28 July, two civilians were killed in the crossfire during a gun battle in Sorsogon province, while another two were killed during separate clashes in September. The most notorious incident of this kind occurred on 9 November when a baby in a passing vehicle was killed by a wayward NPA bullet as insurgents attacked a police convoy in Talakag, Bukidnon province. The death sparked outrage across the country and was cited by Duterte when he terminated peace talks and announced his intention to declare the CPP–NPA a terrorist organisation later that month.

In addition to the inadvertent killing of civilians, there were several occasions where civilians were directly targeted in 2017. In April, a local government official in Palawan and a village chief in Zamboanga del Sur were shot dead by the NPA;

the village chief had reportedly expressed support for a new military detachment being built in his area. In August, the rebels assassinated a further two village chiefs before killing three private security guards working for a construction firm in Sultan Kudarat, with the NPA having described the firm's logging operations in the area as 'environmentally destructive'. On 5 September, an indigenous Lumad leader was shot dead in Agusan del Norte after speaking out against the NPA's activities and violent tactics. In October, a local village councillor was killed in Magpet, North Cotabato province, after voicing support for the government's rural development initiatives. Rebels shot dead a farmer suspected of being a military informant in the same town later that month. On 17 November a tribal leader who had refused to pay the NPA's 'revolutionary taxes' was shot dead in Kapalong town, while on 2 December a town councillor suspected of being a police informant was killed in Baggao, Cagayan province. These incidents demonstrated how the NPA was able to maintain control over local communities through the fear of reprisals for anyone who sought to disrupt the group's activities. However, the NPA maintained a degree of support in impoverished areas of the countryside where many people remained frustrated over economic inequalities and state corruption.

Overall, there was a severe escalation of the NPA insurgency in 2017, characterised by the total collapse of peace talks and rising levels of violence across the country; the number of deaths and injuries soared after the ceasefires were lifted in February. This was in stark contrast to 2016, when there was real hope that the five-decade-long conflict could be ended by negotiation with President Duterte. With the peace process stalled and tensions high on the battlefield, the conflict looked set to enter a new and dangerous period of heightened violence, possibly on a scale not witnessed since the height of the communist insurgency in the 1980s.

Southern Thailand

Violence in Thailand's southern insurgency declined in intensity in 2017. The diminished number of attacks and fatalities was linked to several factors, including the strengthening of the state security apparatus, the evolving strategy of

Key statistics	2016	2017
Type:	Internal	Internal
Fatalities:	300	250
New IDPs:	– [b]	– [b]
New refugees:	– [b]	– [b]

the main militant group and the ongoing peace process between the junta-led government and the umbrella insurgent group Mara Patani.

While Mara Patani continued to present itself as the main insurgent negotiator, the Barisan Revolusi Nasional (BRN) remained the most powerful active militant group and was believed to be responsible for most attacks. The Thai government claimed credit for the reduction in violence due to its increased security presence, which was partly borne out by the situation on the ground, but there were indications that changes within the BRN also contributed to evolving tactics and fewer attacks.

There was a broad-based consensus that the Mara Patani peace process had dim prospects of succeeding due to the umbrella organisation's inability to influence militants on the ground. Critics of the process also pointed out that while government negotiators focused on symptoms of the conflict and short-term goals, the fundamental grievances of the Muslim Malay ethnic community remained largely unaddressed.

Tighter security

The number of fatalities and attacks in Thailand's southern insurgency both declined to 14-year lows in 2017. The government put this down to its expanded security presence in the country, with 61,000 regular army soldiers stationed in the region at the end of the year. The Internal Security Operations Command (ISOC) prioritised local recruitment from within the southern provinces, which helped to cultivate a network of informants that made successful attacks more difficult. The ISOC also advertised job postings for paramilitary rangers euphemistically known as 'defence volunteers' to expand the locally recruited security forces, although top-down policy-making continued to originate from Bangkok.

The junta-led government prioritised establishing security in seven economic centres in Southern Thailand – Muang Pattani, Muang Yala, Muang Narathiwat, Betong, Tak Bai, Sungai Kolok and Hat Yai – while increasing the number of checkpoints on main transit routes and in villages. Late in the year, an unidentified BRN insurgent told the media that militants had been ordered to carry out attacks but were limited in doing so because the Thai military was 'everywhere'. In September, the Thai defence minister also announced plans to increase unmanned aerial vehicle surveillance in the region.

However, while the violence tapered off towards the end of the year (with the exception of the last week of December), deadly attacks continued on the security forces, often using tactics in which responders to an initial incident were targeted by subsequent attacks. In terms of fatalities, the worst attacks were an improvised explosive device (IED) blast and subsequent ambush that killed six paramilitary soldiers in April, an IED blast that killed six soldiers in June and an IED attack that killed four rangers in September.

Analysts attributed the relative decrease in attacks to the BRN having achieved its goals of driving Buddhist residents out of some districts and proving that it could make the region ungovernable. Towards the end of the year, the BRN's stated strategic shift to avoid civilian casualties seemed to be evident, with a reduced number of civilian fatalities and injuries appearing to result from collateral damage. The exception towards the end of the year was the targeting of a family in a car in November, in which a young girl was shot in the arm.

The first half of the year, however, was troubled by the continued targeting of civilians, with the most egregious examples being the murder of a family of four – including a child – in early March, and the killing of three teenagers in June, both of which were blamed on insurgents. In turn, the Thai military was accused of continued abuses, including the summary execution of insurgent suspects in March and the torture of detainees. In November, charges were dropped against three human-rights campaigners who had published a 2016 report about the systematic torture of detainees, which was widely seen as a tacit admission of the accuracy of the report.

Although it did not cause any fatalities, the most noteworthy attack of the year was a bombing that injured 79 civilians at a Big C chain-store outlet in Pattani province on 9 May. A small initial bomb triggered a panic within the store and the subsequent major car bomb seemed intended to target people fleeing through the exits.

While the BRN and other insurgent groups have targeted civilians in the past, this attack was widely seen as counterproductive because Muslim civilians were among the injured victims. Both Mara Patani and the Patani United Liberation Organisation (PULO), formerly a major insurgent force on the ground and participant in the peace process, condemned the violence. The principal rationale for the indiscriminate attack appeared to be an effort to discredit and disrupt the ongoing peace process.

An evolving insurgency?

In September, official peace talks between Thai government negotiators and Mara Patani ended prematurely, apparently over a disagreement about the initial parameters of the discussions. The government had proposed the establishment of 'safety zones' in the southern provinces, in which militants would theoretically cease attacks in return for greater local autonomy and limited self-rule. While the Thai government's chief negotiator General Aksara Kerdphol expected to proceed with designating areas as 'safe', Mara Patani instead focused on defining precisely what such a designation would entail. Talks ended abruptly.

Aksara subsequently blamed Mara Patani for the breakdown in talks, saying it was not ready for safety zones, while later reaffirming the Thai government's commitment to the peace process. Mara Patani representative Abu Hafez al-Hakim described the interruption in talks as a minor problem, although there was little apparent progress for the rest of the year. BRN sources told the media that the organisation opposed the present peace process, and a spike in attacks in mid-September seemed to be an attempt to discredit the negotiations.

Throughout the year there continued to be a debate about whether the BRN was represented in the peace process and consequently how much Mara Patani could influence active militants. While both the Thai government and Mara Patani insisted that three BRN members were among the five insurgent organisations represented in the umbrella group, BRN sources continued to disavow participation, which seemed to be substantiated by continued attacks. Analysts widely questioned the extent of Mara Patani's influence on BRN cells, which cast the credibility of the entire negotiations process in doubt.

However, while the BRN broadly did not support the negotiations, there were signs that the organisation was changing in ways that could precipitate a different track of talks. In January 2017, a key leader of the group, Sapae-ing Baso, who was described as its 'spiritual leader', died from complications related to diabetes. It is worth noting that Sapae-ing's family denied that he had played a leadership role in the group, but he certainly was a prominent member. In March, Thai authorities said that Doonloh Wae-mano, a former school headmaster and a fugitive wanted in connection with the insurgency, had assumed command of the organisation. While BRN militants operate in cells that do not uniformly respond to a unified command structure, it seemed clear that Doonloh was exerting increasing influence.

His influence was linked to indications of a strategic shift within the organisation. According to research by security analyst Don Pathan and Deep South Watch, there appeared to be preparations under way for negotiations involving the BRN separate from, or at least redefining, the Mara Patani process. The Malaysian facilitator of peace negotiations between the Thai government and insurgent groups, Ahmad Zamzamin Hashim, reportedly met with Doonloh three times in the latter half of 2017 in a continued effort to induce the BRN to join talks.

The same sources indicated a potential meeting between Doonloh and Thailand's negotiator Aksara in Indonesia at an unspecified future date, while another round of peace negotiations taking place in Saudi Arabia instead of Malaysia has been broached.

The BRN has traditionally been a shadowy operation averse to making public statements, but in April group spokesman Abdul Karim Khalid made a rare announcement that the BRN was amenable to negotiations. He also suggested preconditions for talks, including a 'neutral' third-party facilitator and international observers, in a model patterned on successful peace talks in Indonesia's Aceh province and in the Philippines. The group's leaders were also reportedly seeking international assistance to train them in strategic-negotiating competencies.

Lack of common ground

The BRN's overture in April was immediately dismissed by the junta-led government, with Prime Minister Prayut Chan-o-cha reiterating the official position that the conflict is a domestic issue. The security situation and perception of the armed forces as protectors of national sovereignty, Buddhism and the monarchy are crucial to the legitimacy of the military, which seized power in Thailand in 2014. As such, authorities appeared to be constrained in what concessions could be made, particularly regarding any decentralisation of power that could be perceived as ceding sovereignty.

More general political developments over the course of 2017 indicated that the junta planned to hold on to power even after national elections, which were tentatively scheduled for November 2018. With an appointed senate and ongoing campaign to maintain Prayut in his position, it seemed likely that the military-led government would continue to set counter-insurgency policy for the foreseeable future.

The junta's two-track counter-insurgency approach included both tightening the security situation to quell the violence, for which it claimed credit in 2017, and continuing to pursue economic-development projects to address historic wealth inequality in the region. However, the success of the latter strategy was questionable, with corruption allegations affecting some projects in 2017. Two key infrastructure projects – the construction of coal-fired power plants in Songkhla and Krabi provinces – faced widespread grassroots opposition based on environmental concerns.

During Prayut's visit to Songkhla in November, protesters opposing a planned power plant in Thepa district clashed with police. Following the incident, Mara Patani's Hakim condemned the authorities' draconian response, linking the insurgent groups to more mainstream community concerns in the region. More generally, opinion polls at the end of the year showed the junta government's popularity falling in the southern region, suggesting a continued recruitment pool for the insurgency.

Chapter Seven

Europe and Eurasia

Armenia–Azerbaijan (Nagorno-Karabakh)

The conflict in Nagorno-Karabakh changed little in 2017. The parties continued to participate in diplomatic initiatives, although no major breakthroughs were achieved. Armenian and Azerbaijani officials met separately and jointly with the co-chairs of

Key statistics	2016	2017
Type:	Internationalised	Internationalised
Fatalities:	200	50
New IDPs:	– [b]	– [b]
New refugees:	– [b]	– [b]

the Organization for Security and Co-operation in Europe (OSCE) Minsk Group several times during the year to discuss recent developments in the conflict zone. In June, the OSCE co-chairs and the personal representative of the OSCE chairperson-in-office revisited the region to conduct a monitoring mission along the border in Armenia's Tavush district. According to the report, no ceasefire violations were registered. During this time, the co-chairs also engaged in a series of diplomatic efforts, meeting first with Armenian President Serzh Sargsyan and next with Nagorno-Karabakh President Bako Sahakyan in Stepanakert. Later that month, the group also travelled to Baku to meet with Azerbaijani President Ilham Aliev. The OSCE co-chairs reiterated the need for re-engagement in negotiations and called for the immediate reduction of tensions between the two sides. While the presidents expressed their desire to resume dialogue, little substantial political progress was made. The efforts of the Minsk group were also focused on attempting to persuade the Armenian and Azerbaijani presidents to hold a bilateral

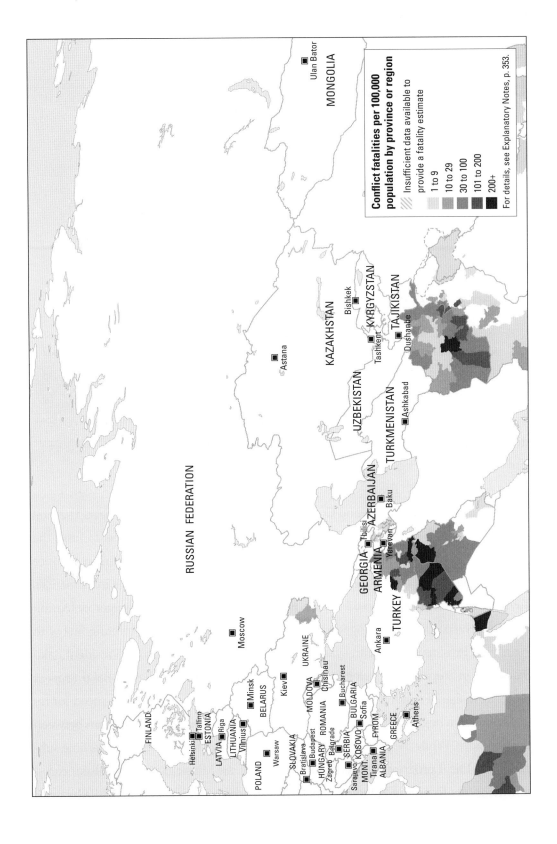

Conflict fatalities per 100,000 population by province or region

Insufficient data available to provide a fatality estimate

1 to 9
10 to 29
30 to 100
101 to 200
200+

For details, see Explanatory Notes, p. 353.

MONGOLIA

Ulan Bator

KAZAKHSTAN

Astana

Bishkek
KYRGYZSTAN
Tashkent
TAJIKISTAN
Dushanbe

UZBEKISTAN

TURKMENISTAN
Ashkabad

AZERBAIJAN
Baku

RUSSIAN FEDERATION

GEORGIA Tbilisi
ARMENIA
Yerevan

TURKEY
Ankara

Moscow

BELARUS
Minsk

UKRAINE
Kiev

MOLDOVA
Chişinău

ROMANIA
Bucharest

BULGARIA
Sofia

GREECE
Athens

FINLAND
Helsinki
Tallinn
ESTONIA
Riga
LATVIA
LITHUANIA
Vilnius

POLAND
Warsaw

SLOVAKIA
Bratislava
HUNGARY
Budapest
Zagreb
Belgrade
SERBIA
Sarajevo
MONT.
KOSOVO
Tirana
ALBANIA
FYROM

meeting. Such a session took place in Geneva in mid-October, and was significant in being the first bilateral interaction at this level for over a year. At the same time, the importance of the meeting should not be overstated, given that it took place not because of any genuine movement on the substantive issues but simply to demonstrate to external audiences and conflict observers that something was happening on the diplomatic front. After the meeting, Aliev and Sargsyan released a joint statement stressing an agreement 'to take measures to intensify the negotiation process'. In an atmosphere of low expectations, it was unclear whether the meeting achieved anything beyond purely rhetorical commitments. Earlier in October, Andrew Schofer, the new United States co-chair of the OSCE Minsk Group, visited Nagorno-Karabakh to discuss the conflict's negotiation process, and reiterated the OSCE's willingness to support the parties.

In the same month the Armenian government approved a draft of a new agreement with Russia stipulating the provision of a defence loan of US$100 million to buy as-yet-unspecified modern arms from Russia, with a repayment period of 20 years. Azerbaijan also continued to enhance its military capability.

A new military-academy building was inaugurated in Armenia in November and will provide specialised military training alongside the current state curriculum. The facility began housing students from the tenth to 12th grades, who will enlist in the Armenian armed forces when they reach adulthood. The school's inauguration was part of a larger plan to modernise the armed forces. However, many in Armenian civil society expressed concern with the measure, considering it a sign of a militarisation of Armenian society.

Throughout the year Armenia indicated that it would adopt a tougher military doctrine as a response to the 2016 'Four-Day War' with Azerbaijan, in which Armenia lost some territory. The military doctrine signalled Armenia's preparedness to expand the security belt further into Azerbaijan's territory in the event of an attack. The sides continued to accuse each other of using heavy weaponry and constant ceasefire violations along the Line of Contact, with several incidents of intense escalation resulting in casualties throughout the year.

The overall rhetoric in Armenia, Azerbaijan and Nagorno-Karabakh remained highly hostile towards the 'other'. In mid-December, Azerbaijani news outlets reported that Ramil Safarov, a 40-year-old major in the Azerbaijani Armed Forces, had been promoted to lieutenant colonel, although evidence suggested the rank was granted four months prior. Safarov became a controversial figure in 2004 when he killed Armenian officer Gurgen Margaryan with an axe while both men were attending a NATO Partnership for Peace programme in Hungary. A Hungarian court sentenced Safarov to life in prison, but in 2012 he was extradited to Azerbaijan to serve out the rest of his sentence. In Azerbaijan, Aliev immediately pardoned Safarov, awarding him an apartment and eight years of back pay for the time he spent in prison. The promotion of Safarov therefore undermined confidence and trust-building between Armenia and Azerbaijan, adding to Armenian concerns of state-sponsored anti-Armenian discourse among Azerbaijani society.

The general balance of forces in the conflict did not fundamentally change in 2017. Both the risk of an all-out military confrontation and the likelihood of achieving a comprehensive and mutually acceptable political solution remained low.

Ukraine

The conflict in Ukraine continued without abatement or diplomatic improvement in 2017. Attempted ceasefires were systematically broken throughout the year and, despite political efforts to resolve the conflict, the Minsk agreement

Key statistics	2016	2017
Type:	Internationalised	Internationalised
Fatalities:	700	600
New IDPs:	110,000	21,000
New refugees:	–[b]	–[b]

remained unimplemented. The total death toll surpassed 10,000 lives. In September, Russia's President Vladimir Putin proposed allowing United Nations peacekeepers into the conflict area, but this suggestion was under debate among the Minsk signatories and an agreement was not reached at the end of the year. The beginning of the year saw some of the heaviest shelling since the start of the conflict, in particular around the city of Avdiivka in Donetsk district, but overall civilian casualties and the rate of violence in 2017 were comparable to prior years. From 1 January to 15 November 2017, the Office of the UN High Commissioner for Human Rights recorded 544 conflict-related civilian casualties – 98 killed and 446 injured

– representing a 3.6% increase from the previous year. In December, Ukrainian officials exchanged 246 prisoners for 74 separatist-held captives in the largest prisoner exchange since the conflict began. Although this was a positive step in establishing communication between the two sides, the exchange was unlikely to signify any meaningful progress in the conflict. The Trump administration's decision to sell weapons to Ukraine, allegedly including anti-tank missiles, was condemned by Russia and will likely further complicate diplomatic attempts to end the conflict.

An opportunistic conflict

Heavy fighting throughout late January and early February in the government-controlled city of Avdiivka resulted in electrical and water outages in freezing temperatures. This level of violence was not sustained throughout the year, however, decreasing throughout May to September and tapering off in October. Ukrainian government troops established their presence in Travneve and Hladosove, and increased their presence in Verkhnyotoretske in Donetsk district. Despite an upsurge in violence in November, the pattern of fighting remained largely unchanged from previous years, and there were no significant changes in the conflict lines nor any territorial gains for either side. Shelling of infrastructure, such as water-filtration plants, continued to pose a key risk to the quality of life for civilians.

The majority of ceasefire violations reportedly came from the separatists, although the Ukrainian army was also accused of ceasefire violations as it became increasingly assertive in testing the front-line. Both sides continued to deploy heavy weapons in direct violation of the Minsk agreement. Both combatant sides also showed signs of internal problems: the Ukrainian armed forces were rife with corruption, and 500 suicides had been reported in the previous three years, while in July, pro-Russian separatists in the Donetsk region announced the formation of a new state named Malorossiya, for which Luhansk-based separatists did not show support, with some leaders openly criticising the decision. Moscow also disavowed the announcement.

A coup among the leadership of the Luhansk People's Republic (LPR) in late 2017 saw the ousting of leader Igor Plotnitsky by Igor Kornet. Alexander Zakharchenko, Plotnitsky's counterpart in the Donetsk People's Republic (DPR), sent troops to Luhansk to lend Kornet support. While this change in leadership looked unlikely to impact the ongoing conflict, it may be indicative of the limits of Moscow's control over the LPR. The coup was taken as an indicator of the infighting between LPR elements that had the support of Moscow's security services and those that were supported by Moscow's military. Continued infighting of this sort could lead to Moscow reconsidering the level of its support for, and involvement with, the separatists.

UN peacekeeping proposal

In September Russia proposed a draft resolution asking that the UN Security Council consider the authorisation of a UN peacekeeping-force deployment to the Donbas. While peacekeeping appears to be an appealing option, it was too early to be optimistic about the feasibility and effectiveness of this proposal due to the inconclusive and narrow nature of the core provisions. On 11 September Putin expressed willingness to consider a wider mandate for UN peacekeepers that might be deployed beyond the contact line. This statement represented a welcome rapprochement between Russian and Ukrainian positions on one of the key contentious issues regarding the proposed UN force's parameters. The proposal entailed the deployment of a UN protection force armed with small and light weapons to provide enhanced protection to the existing OSCE Special Monitoring Mission to Ukraine, thereby enabling the mission to concentrate on and be more effective in the monitoring of the situation on the ground and to contribute to the implementation of the Minsk II security provisions.

The consideration of such a proposal itself was not new. The idea was discussed during Track Two meetings between Russian and US experts in November 2014, and Ukrainian President Petro Poroshenko had repeatedly called for the deployment of a UN-authorised peacekeeping force, including shortly after the signing of the Minsk II agreement in 2015. The timing of Putin's public support for the idea of a UN peacekeeping deployment appeared to have been largely driven by his pragmatic desire to project an image as a leader who was willing and able to devise constructive conflict de-escalation strategies, as well as to make compromises. A softer international position on Ukraine was important in the context of the potential easing of EU sanctions, and could also boost Putin's domestic popularity among the electorate in the run-up to the presidential election in March 2018. The financial cost of supporting the separatists in the self-proclaimed republics of eastern Ukraine was likely to be an additional, increasingly unbearable burden on the already strained state budget.

However, while this proposal was a welcome shift that to a limited extent re-energised peacemaking efforts in the conflict, with the potential to contribute positively to longer-term conflict management, several major problems remained with its implementation. Firstly, it was uncertain whether concrete steps would be taken on this proposal. Russia conditioned the peacekeeping deployment on the removal of heavy weaponry from the Donbas, a condition that has yet to be fulfilled despite it also being part of Minsk II. Any deployment would need to be authorised by the UN General Assembly and sanctioned by the UN Security Council – a process that is likely to take significant time and will not begin until the other core conditions have been firmly agreed upon. Secondly, the short-term nature of the peacekeeping force (six months) is highly problematic given the duration, magnitude and increasingly entrenched quality of the conflict itself, and is unlikely to be sufficient to proactively add to pacification. Thirdly, the scope of the force's mandate needed to be better and more robustly specified. As the experience of UN peacekeeping elsewhere demonstrates, forces that are too constrained and too ambitious or ambiguous in terms of the range of objectives tend to be ineffective. Finally, the sequencing of steps and involvement of the Russian-backed areas in eastern Ukraine remained a contentious issue, unlikely to be resolved in the near future. Without some form of consent and regular contact with the self-proclaimed republics in the east, UN deployment will not be possible. Yet the authorities in these areas are unlikely to agree to such a deployment without the prior granting of special-autonomy status – a parameter that, although already present in Minsk II, remains as yet unfulfilled and is quite widely seen in Ukraine as a reward for the rebels and a dangerous step towards the break-up of the state. Despite all these stumbling blocks, the very evidence of movement on the idea after a long period of deadlock indicated that there was an opening for more meaningful dialogue.

Trade blockades

In February, Ukrainian 'volunteer battalions' (coalitions of former Ukrainian soldiers, missionaries and members of nationalist political parties) blocked coal supplies from separatist-held areas, supplies which were a significant energy source for the rest of the country and therefore a major source of revenue for eastern Ukraine. Despite initial condemnation from the Ukrainian government, the blockade was adopted as official government policy and the embargo sustained. The government's freezing of rail and road cargo links may shave 0.6% and 0.7% respectively off Ukraine's GDP. Also in February, separatists seized control of approximately 53 private and state-owned Ukrainian companies across Donetsk and Luhansk, including some belonging to Ukrainian billionaire Rinat Akhmetov. In April, Kiev cut the electricity supply to Luhansk and Donetsk.

The blockade resulted in a contraction of industrial output, slowing down Ukraine's economic growth and causing increased economic hardship for local residents in the occupied territories. The expected slowdown in GDP also affected Ukraine's ability to receive the next billion-dollar disbursement from its rescue loan. Only once an economic forecast has been agreed – requiring the Ukrainian government to decide whether it will keep the blockade – will the IMF provide funding.

Citizens living in the occupied and non-government-controlled territories faced difficulties receiving pensions and other aid from the Ukrainian government, being increasingly seen as Ukrainian 'non-citizens'. The UN Human Rights Council estimated that 560,000 people living in non-government-controlled areas had lost access to their Ukrainian state pensions. Despite being Ukrainian citizens, those who lived in non-government-controlled territories did not have the right to vote in elections. The blockade compounded problems for those who needed to move across the conflict line regularly – a weight limit of 75 kilograms and a list of permitted goods that people could carry were introduced. People who traded across the border were severely limited and access to aid, basic goods and services became increasingly limited for those living near the contact line. Human-rights abuses, harassment and arbitrary detention conducted by all combatant sides were serious and ongoing concerns.

The Ukrainian conflict moved no closer to meeting the Minsk agreement requirements in 2017. The conflict line remained relatively static: despite occasional upticks in violence, it has essentially become a frozen conflict. A lack of political will continued to characterise the Ukrainian government's response to the fighting. Increasingly, it appeared that the Ukrainian leadership benefited from the conflict as a distraction from its poor domestic performance and accusations of widespread corruption. Russia's suggestion of a UN peacekeeping mission was a positive step, but requires agreement and commitment from all sides. The humanitarian situation for those living near or in the conflict zones worsened with no abatement in sight. Without a significant political breakthrough, the Ukrainian conflict will remain in this state for the foreseeable future.

Chapter Eight

Latin America

Brazil (Rio de Janeiro)

The security situation in the metropolitan area of Rio de Janeiro deteriorated further in 2017 due to increased
clashes between armed criminal
gangs and the government's security
forces. There were 1,032 homicides
in 2017 resulting from police inter-

Key statistics	2016	2017
Type:	Internal	Internal
Fatalities:	– [c]	2,000
New IDPs:	– [b]	– [b]
New refugees:	– [b]	– [b]

ventions – i.e., those resulting from clashes and gunfights occurring in relation to a
police operation – representing a 23% rise compared to 2016 and equating to 8.4 deaths
per 100,000 inhabitants in the metropolitan area of Rio de Janeiro. This trend formed
part of the general rise in intentional homicides in Rio that has taken place since 2013,
when organised criminal groups (OCGs) started to challenge the Pacifying Police Units
(UPPs) – the bases established by the police to stabilise and enforce state control over
previously violent areas – for control of the *favelas* (as the slums are called in Brazil). The
homicide rate resulting from these interventions, sometimes supported by the army,
more than doubled between 2013 (when criminals groups stepped up their attacks) and
2017, jumping from 3.3 per 100,000 inhabitants to 8.4 per 100,000 inhabitants in 2017.

Diversification of gang activity

The oldest OCG in Rio is the Red Command (CV), which was formed in 1979 when
members of leftist guerrilla groups, who had been fighting the Brazilian military

Conflict fatalities per 100,000 population by province or region

Insufficient data available to provide a fatality estimate

1 to 9

10 to 29

30 to 100

101 to 200

200+

For details, see Explanatory Notes, p. 353.

regime, met criminals while in prison. The expansion of the cocaine economy during the 1980s transformed Rio's drug-trafficking scene from a cluster of small gangs operating in marijuana into a thriving underworld dominated by highly organised groups, and contributed to the rise and consolidation of the CV. The CV remains one of the most powerful criminal actors in the city, despite being involved in several wars with a number of smaller gangs over the years, including splinter cells formed by its own former members. One of those splinter cells formed the Friends of Friends (ADA) group, which was created around 1998 by former CV members and is now the most powerful rival of the CV.

The control of territory has been a traditional concern of cocaine-trafficking groups such as the CV, given that at least some level of territorial control is necessary for storing drug shipments and establishing selling points for consumers from the wealthier classes. However, declining prices and rising competition in the cocaine trade during the 1980s and 1990s accelerated the diversification of the CV and its rivals towards other criminal activities, including extortion and the exploitation of unregistered businesses in such sectors as minibuses. These illicit activities – particularly the extortion charged as a 'tax' in exchange for a level of security provided by armed gangsters – have reinforced the need for territorial control and presence. This presence has often been advertised publicly in order to display to local populations the need to obey and respect gang members, and it is common to see graffiti with the initials 'CV' or those of other criminal factions marking their turfs in some *favelas*. The hillside location of most Rio *favelas* further aided this territorial demarcation, as well as presenting a topological obstacle for the security forces attempting to penetrate the territories of these well-armed gangs.

Drug-trafficking gangs such as the CV and ADA make ample and well-documented use of high-calibre weapons such as rifles. A total of 2,757 rifles were seized by authorities in the state of Rio de Janeiro between 2007 and 2017. Given that most clashes take place in *favelas* in the metropolitan area of Rio such as Alemão, Maré and Rocinha, a large proportion of these weapons were likely to have been in the ownership of criminal organisations. In September 2017, an M60 machine gun was seized during a police operation in two *favelas* in the northern area of Rio city – the first time that this model had been seen in Rio. The gun was capable of firing 550 rounds per minute and possibly arrived from Colombia.

Decline of the pacification strategy

The year 2017 saw further deterioration in the state government's commitment to the UPP strategy. The UPP project was created and implemented in 2008 by Rio's then-security secretary José Mariano Beltrame, who described it as 'a logic to implode the power of drug trafficking by shaking its territorial structure'. The UPP strategy marked a clear shift from the prevailing approach in previous decades, which had consisted of occasional raids by the Military Police of Rio de Janeiro State (PMERJ) into *favelas* to arrest specific targets or punish gangs for certain acts of violence. Because such raids did not establish state control of the *favelas*, they almost always involved heavily armed officers and the use of armoured vehicles entering and quickly exiting the slums, usually on the same day. Often these operations were conducted by an elite squad of PMERJ known as the Special Police Operations Battalion (BOPE). BOPE gained a reputation for excessive use of force, while its aggressive stance was also foregrounded in its official insignia that showed a skull with a knife driven through it on top of two crossed handguns against a black background.

By contrast, the UPP strategy centred on the permanent presence of police in UPP bases in gang-dominated *favelas*. The pacification project achieved impressive results in its first few years. In 2010, for instance, the police invasion of Vila Cruzeiro *favela*, with support of armoured vehicles provided by the armed forces, was broadcast live and gathered public praise due to the images of alleged gang members fleeing the area in face of public authorities. As opposed to the previous approach, a permanent police presence and a UPP base was then established in the *favela*. With the steep decline that followed in several criminal indicators (including homicides), the pacification project was considered a success and expanded in Rio. The federal government also expressed interest in taking the project to other states.

The decline of the programme came as the UPPs expanded to some of Rio's largest *favelas*, such as Maré, Alemão and Penha, where criminal groups started to pose low-intensity but regular opposition through ambushes and targeted killings of officers during 2014. With reduced fiscal income due to falling oil prices, the state of Rio was unable to step up its security presence in face of this increased criminal violence. The PMERJ, which is the main institution tasked with law enforcement across Rio de Janeiro state, also struggled with dwindling resources that even reduced the number of vehicles available for its patrol duties. The problem also affected the funding of public services and infrastructure works – which, under the UPP strategy, were supposed to be a developmental counterpart to the policing presence in the *favelas*. Several high-profile disruptions in the city's functioning during 2017 – including rising assassinations of police officers and gunfights affecting the Red Line (a critical highway linking the city centre to the international airport) – led to an order by the federal government in late July that directed the armed forces to aid local police in their fight against organised crime. Unlike previous military operations in Rio, which focused on establishing a permanent presence in specific slums to support a UPP base, this time soldiers were deployed to support police operations across the city.

The increasing hostility towards the UPPs in the *favelas* took place against a backdrop of rising violence between the gangs themselves. During 2017, reports by local media – citing police intelligence and the authorities of Brazil's prisons, where many gang leaders are located – mentioned that ADA's boss in the Rocinha area, Rogério 157, had turned and joined the CV. This sparked fears of an escalation in a gang war in one of Rio's largest *favelas*, which is located in the southern part of Rio near wealthy areas and places visited by tourists.

The security crisis escalated in August, when the two groups clashed in Rocinha. In September, ADA organised an operation that utilised dozens of armed men from other areas of Rio in an attempt to retake Rocinha from Rogério 157, resulting in seven days of frequent gunfights both between the two gangs and between the gangs and the security forces, resulting in the deaths of seven people. The clash also garnered international headlines as it took place a little after the first anniversary of the 2016 Olympic Games, which were hosted by Rio. The police and military presence helped to de-escalate the confrontation in Rocinha but the spectre of gang violence remained. In December, just as the CV gang had consolidated its control of Rocinha, Rogério 157 was arrested by authorities, paving the way for renewed attempts by ADA to retake the slum.

The violence between the CV and ADA was also linked to the nationwide dispute between the CV and its São Paulo-based rival the First Capital Command (PCC). The PCC supports ADA – support which reportedly includes shipments of weapons. Given that the PCC is by far Brazil's largest and richest criminal organisation, its backing can provide a significant lifeline to ADA, raising the possibility that ADA's battle against the CV may continue for some time.

Rise of the militias

Militias form an additional aspect of non-state armed activity in Rio. Originally formed as self-defence groups by current and former members of the armed forces, militias now operate in extortion and illicit provision of services such as gas, water, transportation (mainly through minibuses), internet and cable television.

Militias have experienced enormous growth in Rio in the past 15 years. They have spread through areas not yet occupied by drug traffickers, but have also increasingly been joining forces with drug traffickers or recruiting them. However, despite the period of rapid expansion, the militias have attempted to maintain a low public profile: they have understood that the visibility resulting from frequent and overt use of armed violence is bad for business. The Justice League, Rio's largest and richest militia, realised this after Jerônimo Guimarães and state lawmaker Natalino José Guimarães, two of its original leaders, were imprisoned in 2007 and 2008 respectively following an investigation by the general prosecutor's office. The police operation to arrest Natalino Guimarães was followed by a gunfight involving the lawmaker's bodyguards. Since then, the militia has been focusing on corruption rings that co-opt local politicians rather than armed confrontation.

Despite the desire of the militias to avoid public exposure, the relationship between militia groups and the political elite has often been resolved violently. Research by the Federal University of the State of Rio de Janeiro revealed that 79 candidates who ran for office between 2000 and 2016 were murdered in Rio de Janeiro. In the last election year, 2016, there were 13 murders. Of the total number of those murdered, 63 ran for the position of councilman, six for the City Hall and three were candidates for vice-mayor, meaning that 91% of the fatalities were related to the Rio municipality.

With a combination of the intensification of gang-related violence, the rise of the militias and the corruption of key security institutions from which the militias originate, Rio experienced a volatile security environment in 2017. The decline of the UPPs and public-security funding in general meant that authorities were left without a clear replacement strategy, a situation that was exacerbated by the fragile financial situation of the Rio state government, which is in charge of law enforcement. The state suffered not only with the decline of international oil prices during 2014 and 2015, but also with the economic recession hitting Brazil between 2014 and 2016, when Brazil's GDP shrank by a total of 8.2%. Despite a recent rise in international oil prices, Rio still faces significant obstacles to recover a level of economic and institutional strength that would allow it to revive the pacification strategy – or a worthy replacement.

Colombia (BACRIM)

Established organised criminal groups (otherwise known as BACRIM) operating throughout the country continued to pose a threat to Colombia in 2017. Areas in which FARC had been traditionally present faced insecurities as a result of FARC's demobilisation and

Key statistics	2016	2017
Type:	Internationalised	Internationalised
Fatalities:	– c	125
New IDPs:	– b	90,000*
New refugees:	– b	– b

*The IDP figure for 2017 is a share of the total estimated number of IDPs in Colombia due to both the FARC/ELN conflict and the BACRIM conflict.

the resulting power vacuum. Moreover, delays in the implementation of the FARC peace agreement and its delivery to rural areas created strategic areas which illegal armed groups sought to enter. This was particularly relevant to areas in which illicit economies flourish that have not yet been transformed as part of key rural and integral reforms. Tackling these groups proved problematic in the face of their fluid structure, with membership, affiliations and alliances often shifting depending on who held the monopoly over certain stages in the illicit drug process and territory at any given time. In 2016, Colombia's Minister of Defence Luis Carlos Villegas declared that several BACRIM groups had been reclassified as 'organised armed groups' (GAO), a designation that would permit an increased role for the armed forces in combatting the threat of these groups.

The most organised of these groups was the Gulf Clan, which was reported to have at least 51 regional commands and control at least 45% of Colombia's global drug output. The organisation was also responsible for illegal mining, extortion, murder and forced displacement. The Gulf Clan was allegedly present in more than 200 municipalities throughout the country, with strong consolidation in 142. By the end of 2016, the Colombian police estimated that the Gulf Clan had around 3,000 members, although this differed from the estimates of the Gulf Clan itself (which suggested that the number was around 8,000 individuals), as well as the office of the prosecutor general, which announced in September 2017 that they expected the organisation had approximately 7,000 members. However, the fact that the Gulf Clan employed both formal fighters and subcontractors (local gangs hired to carry out specific activities for the organisation) could perhaps explain this discrepancy, although the Gulf Clan's criminal subcontracting posed an additional security challenge for law enforcement. While subcontracting allowed the Gulf Clan to consolidate power through local structures, it also contributed to disputes and clashes at the local level between gangs and common criminal groups. It was likely that violence carried out by organised criminal organisations would continue to be a long-term challenge in Colombia's security domain, particularly over control of the most important nodes within the country's illicit drug economy.

While the Gulf Clan continued to expand across the Atlantic and Pacific coasts – important embarkation points in the drug economy – the group declared in September 2017 that it was willing to negotiate its surrender, with the group's leader Dairo Antonio Úsuga (alias 'Otoniel') saying that he would hand himself in. Up until this time, the armed forces had been successful in either killing or arresting key figures in joint police and military operations. The year ended with the Gulf Clan declaring a unilateral ceasefire in December. However, President Juan Manuel Santos stated that while he welcomed a surrender of the organisation, military activities against the group would not stop.

The drug economy showed signs of expansion in 2017. There was an increase in the number of hectares being used for coca in the country, with a record number of 188,000 hectares being recorded in 2016 by the United States Office of National Drug Control Policy, marking a 133% increase over a three-year period. While the rise in coca hectares could partially be attributed to the Colombian government's decision to abandon aerial fumigation, another factor was the exploitation by organised-crime groups of the power vacuums left by FARC's demobilisation. For example, although the Gulf Clan remains the most powerful of these actors, other BACRIM groups such as Los Rastrojos and La Cordillera continued to operate and exert influence throughout their areas of strategic interest.

In response, the Colombian government vowed to destroy 100,000 hectares of coca in 2017 – five times the goal of the 20,000 hectares that the government aimed to destroy in 2016, although it ultimately failed to reach the 2017 objective. According to the Colombian armed forces, there was success in manually eradicating 52,001 hectares, marking an eight-year high. Throughout the year, the US government put pressure on Bogotá, with Washington saying that it 'seriously considered' returning Colombia to the blacklist of countries failing to play their role in cracking down on the illicit drug trade, thereby placing the state on a par with Venezuela and Bolivia.

Despite this, the problem of BACRIM appears to be a key security challenge in the mid- to long term. Although provisions in the peace agreement deal not only with rural reform but also substitution of illicit crops, at present it appears that the power struggle for illegal economies is consolidating more quickly than programme and security delivery. A notable factor that suggests this has been the increase in killings of social and community leaders who have been in support of these types of programmes, with at least 54 cases allegedly being carried out by members of criminal groups or structures of paramilitaries in 2017 alone. Unless there is an acceleration of delivery and a consolidation of state presence, this will continue to impact on the exacerbation of endemic violence carried out by these actors.

Colombia (FARC and ELN)

Despite the final peace agreement in 2016 between the government and FARC, 2017 marked a challenging new stage in the Colombian conflict. The political and security environment throughout the year was largely characterised by the difficulties of implementing the

Key statistics	2016	2017
Type:	Internationalised	Internationalised
Fatalities:	200+	70
New IDPs:	170,000	50,000*
New refugees:	_ b	_ b

+The fatality estimate for 2016 includes some deaths due to violence involving the BACRIM, which this year is included as a separate conflict.
*The IDP figure for 2017 is a share of the total estimated number of IDPs in Colombia due to both the FARC/ELN conflict and the BACRIM conflict.

agreement, a situation that was further impacted by uncertainty pertaining to the outcome of the 2018 elections. While FARC made its transition from insurgency to legal political party, negotiations continued with the National Liberation Army (ELN), the country's second-largest armed group, resulting in a temporary bilateral ceasefire by the end of the year. There were, however, ongoing attacks by the ELN and FARC dissidents. Violence continued to impact on the civilian population, with the Colombian Single Victims Registry reporting that 83,560 individuals had registered as victims of the armed conflict in 2017. Forced displacement due to the violence continued to remain a systemic issue, with 78,650 individual cases recorded in 2017 alone.

Ongoing challenges to the implementation of the peace agreement

The implementation process of the peace agreement faced several challenges throughout 2017. Due to the vote against the peace agreement in the 2016 plebiscite, the Colombian government relied on the 'fast-track' mechanism (which reduced the number of debates required for the approval of laws and constitutional reforms) to implement provisions of the settlement. However, the fast-track mechanism expired on 30 November 2017, with one of the most important provisions in the peace agreement, the Special Jurisdiction for Peace, being approved by the Senate on the day of its expiration.

According to the Kroc Institute, which was tasked with providing the technical verification and monitoring of the agreement, implementation was more successful in short-term provisions, such as the bilateral ceasefire, the surrender of weapons and FARC's demobilisation, along with the creation of verification mechanisms. However, the institute reported in November 2017 that implementation had been activated in only 45% of the 558 stipulations as of 31 August 2017; moreover, only 17% of the provisions had been fully implemented. There was no observed implementation in 61% of provisions relating to reparations for victims and more than 80% of provisions dealing with democratic and social participation guarantees. The lack of implementation for this last provision was especially significant as the year also saw an increase in attacks on social and community leaders, resulting in the deaths of an estimated 170 Colombian leaders. As part of the peace agreement, the government vowed to set up the National Protection Unity, a body designed to protect against threats and killings of social-rights leaders throughout the country. However, it was alleged that there was often no effective state response when leaders reported threats, with such threats often being considered as 'personal' rather than as a result of Colombia's political situation. In order to counter this, as part of the overall military *Plan Victoria* the government announced *Plan Orus*, a major security offensive consisting of 63,000 troops tasked with providing security in 67 municipalities and 595 villages. *Plan Orus* can mostly be interpreted as a continuation of promises by the government to comply with certain points of the peace agreement which are directed towards guaranteeing the political participation of the leaders. According to the president, army commanders were to establish contacts and generate trust in order to combat the killings more effectively.

There was, however, broader resistance to the implementation of the peace agreement by various stakeholders, from formal actors within the Colombian political system and segments of the civilian population to the country's illegal actors and FARC dissidents.

FARC: transition from insurgency to political party

The main change in Colombia's political and security environment in 2017 was FARC's transition from armed group to a legal political party that will contest the 2018 elections. On 18 February, Major-General Javier Pérez Aquino, the chief observer of the United Nations Mission, announced that FARC's movement into 26 demobilisation zones was complete. On 27 June, the UN declared that the formal disarmament of the group had been achieved. On 31 August, FARC changed its name to the Common Alternative Revolutionary Force, although it maintained its original acronym. FARC's long-standing emphasis on the importance of a party helped it achieve the transition in a relatively brief time frame, with the new party inheriting a pre-existing, consolidated political entity.

The peace agreement also included provisions to facilitate FARC's transition: between its date of registration and 19 July 2022, the new political party is due to receive an allowance equivalent to 7% of the annual operating budget reserved for political parties and movements. This sum, alongside access to media and security guarantees under the Comprehensive Security System for the Exercise of Politics, was designed to support the party's endeavours to contest future electoral campaigns. Moreover, FARC was granted two key concessions for the two constitutional periods 2018–2022 and 2022–2026. Firstly, the agreement formally permitted FARC's new political party to register its list of candidates for the upcoming 2018 election. The candidates would compete under equal electoral conditions and the party would be allowed to enter into coalition with other political parties or movements. The second concession was that while FARC candidates were able to contest seats at the 2018 election, the party was nevertheless guaranteed a minimum of ten seats (five in the Senate and five in the House of Representatives) for the two constitutional periods.

Groups of FARC dissidents opposed to both the signing of the peace agreement and the disarmament and demobilisation of the group continued to operate in the country. It was, however, difficult to ascertain the numbers of dissidents involved and how they were linked to and interacted with other groups. For example, while government figures suggested that around 5–7% of FARC fighters (approximately 500–750 fighters) refused to demobilise, the investigative organisation InSight Crime reported that this number was more likely to be around 1,000–1,500, or double the official estimates. (Other estimates placed the number at around 800–1,000.) Reports suggested that these groups were primarily operating in the departments of Cauca, Caquetá, Meta, Nariño, Guaviare, Vaupés and Guainía.

Individuals linked to these dissident groups were responsible for a variety of attacks throughout the year, such as an improvised explosive device attack on a vehicle transporting members of the armed forces in Guaviare in April, the kidnapping of a Colombian UN worker in Miraflores and an armed confrontation that resulted in the death of six former FARC members who were ambushed as they were attending a meeting in Nariño. The presence of the dissidents also had longer-term implications for Colombia's security environment, with some of the groups mutating into actors involved in the illicit drug trade.

An uncertain future with the ELN

After several false starts, negotiations formally commenced on 7 February between the Colombian government and the ELN, the country's remaining insurgency, in Quito, Ecuador. A 'first accord' was announced during the first week of talks between the two sides regarding progress towards a ceasefire, the role of social and civil leaders in the peace process and general humanitarian measures that would be applied towards the de-escalation of the conflict. However, the ELN's ongoing attacks throughout 2017 posed a key challenge to the progression of talks, raising questions about the commitment of the organisation to reaching a final settlement. Shortly after negotiations commenced, the ELN claimed responsibility for setting off a bomb in La Macarena, Bogotá, on 19 February that killed one policeman and injured 25 others (23 policemen and two civilians). It also claimed responsibility for attacking a military patrol on 14 February near Villavicencio, and continued an array of attacks on the Caño Limón Coveñas pipeline throughout the year.

The Colombian government and the ELN finally agreed to a bilateral ceasefire that lasted for 102 days (from 1 October 2017 to 12 January 2018), but the outcome of the negotiations remained uncertain. With the Colombian elections looming in 2018, many expressed doubt that a final settlement between the ELN and the Santos administration would be reached. The situation was further complicated by internal division within the ELN. Unlike FARC – which traditionally operated under a strong, hierarchical command-and-control structure where decisions from the leadership bound the entire organisation – the ELN operates in a horizontal-organisation format that emphasises collective decision-making. When the ELN originally voted on whether or not to negotiate with the government, the outcome was only marginally in favour of negotiation, a situation that could challenge the robustness of the group's collective decision-making process. Many analysts argued that if the ELN did not sign a final settlement with the government, the result could be dire for the organisation, as sections within the ELN – particularly on the border of Venezuela – would continue to operate on the premise that the war with the government was continuing. Given that various ELN fronts were not in favour of negotiation, should a final settlement be signed there may be potential for a new wave of ELN dissidents to emerge in response to possible demobilisation, which would further generate insecurities for populations in and around its areas of influence.

El Salvador

The balance of power between the government of El Salvador and Mara Salvatrucha (MS-13) continued to shift in favour of MS-13 in 2017. In November, a survey reported that 42% of those surveyed felt that the

Key statistics	2016	2017
Type:	Internationalised	Internationalised
Fatalities:	– [b]	– [b]
New IDPs:	22,000	300,000
New refugees:	80,000	– [b]

gangs ruled or governed the country, compared to 12% who said the state was the governing power, 6% who believed that the president was in control and 5% who responded that no one was governing. This growing lack of perceived government legitimacy – fuelled by the belief that the government cannot or will not tackle the expansion of gangs – is part of what drives the violence and desperation among the civilian population. The expansion of MS-13 to rural areas, the significant growth of internally displaced persons and the gang's increasing brutality – the use of beheadings, torture and dismemberment are now commonplace – has led to MS-13's transition from a local actor to an armed group with international reach. The acquisition of new, more sophisticated weapons, alongside the investment of millions of dollars in seemingly legitimate businesses such as car lots, restaurants and hotels, added another dynamic to the long-standing conflict.

Political negotiations

Although MS-13 in El Salvador has not reached the level of political sophistication demonstrated by its counterpart in Honduras, the year still witnessed sustained attempts by the group to influence the political agenda in the run-up to the March 2018 legislative elections. Instead of aligning itself behind a particular ideology, the gang sought negotiations with all major political parties. This strategy dates from the ill-fated gang 'truce' between the major gangs in El Salvador from 2012 to 2014, when the gangs negotiated directly with the government, then continued to negotiate blocs of votes with both major political parties. Given the proven ability of the gangs – primarily MS-13 and to a lesser extent Barrio 18 – to deliver votes to whichever party will pay the most for them, such negotiations – often taking place in fits and starts – are now a regular feature of the political landscape.

MS-13's negotiations in 2017 indicated the extent of the gang's increasing involvement in the political process. Throughout 2017, MS-13 posted audio recordings and YouTube videos of its leadership negotiating with leaders of the two main political parties – the right-wing Republican Nationalist Alliance (ARENA) and the Farabundo Marti National Liberation Front (FMLN) – in order to secure monetary gain and more formal political power.

While willing to engage in political activity, MS-13 often resorts to using violence as a negotiating tool, raising or lowering the number of homicides in order to influence government behaviour. The group's traditional tactic of leaving bodies on the street continued to be successful in 2017. This strategy was evident during a huge spike in violence in September, when the daily homicide rate rose from 11 to 40 as MS-13 demanded that the group's imprisoned leadership be given conjugal visitation and other privileges (including ordering fried chicken and pizza), as well as telephonic communication with the outside world. The demand for communication access was particularly important because the imprisoned MS-13 leadership orders executions and other actions by mobile phone. Once the concessions were given, MS-13 ordered the homicides to cease and the rate dropped dramatically.

State crackdown amid rising insecurity

A total of 3,947 homicides were reported by the National Police of El Salvador in 2017. A number of organisations estimated what proportion of those deaths were considered to be related to organised crime, ranging from 65%, according to newspaper sources, through to 70% according to World Health Organization reports. Given the extreme difficulty of obtaining up-to-date data and drawing a clear distinction between deaths resulting from organised criminal violence and those resulting from other forms of criminality, we have decided to refrain from providing a fatality estimate for the armed conflict in El Salvador.

In late April, Howard Cotto, head of the National Police, reported the splintering of MS-13, with the emergence of a new group calling itself MS-503 (503 is El Salvador's international country code) due to internal disagreements within MS-13 over the distribution of extortion money and drug trafficking. The emergence of the rival factions, one loyal to the MS-13 imprisoned leadership and the other to the MS-503 leadership, largely out of prison, caused instability in El Salvador's criminal underworld and contributed to a significant increase (16.3%) in intentional homicides during the second quarter in comparison to the preceding three months. In June, Cotto publicly acknowledged that violence was indeed rising and blamed it on the settling of scores among MS-13 members. He added that additional security measures had to be taken in prisons, where many of the gang leaders resided. However, most of these measures have not been actually implemented.

The scale of the challenge faced by El Salvador was highlighted in July when the national police and the attorney general's office announced that 593 suspected gang members had been arrested as part of a nationwide operation; the authorities stated the majority of them would be charged with homicide and extortion. Cotto said the majority of those arrested belonged to MS-13 and were suspected of taking part in attacks against police and military officers. In September Cotto announced a further 406 arrests linked to gangs as part of *Regional Shield*, a joint operation undertaken with Honduras and Guatemala. Guatemala's attorney general announced 163 arrests as part of the same operation, with 14 people also being arrested in Honduras.

MS-13 grew in tactical, financial and political sophistication in 2017, rendering the states of the Northern Triangle – El Salvador and Honduras in particular – increasingly impotent in their efforts to control the growth of the gang and re-establish territorial control, despite several mass arrests. The group's increasing political awareness and territorial control marked a significant stage in its development, placing it closer to an insurgency than the traditional definition of a criminal gang. In the absence of a concerted political effort from national and international actors, the havoc wrought by MS-13's activity looks likely to pose a threat to the security of the region for years to come.

Honduras

The Mara Salvatrucha (MS-13) gang made historic political, territorial, social and economic gains in Honduras in 2017. The security situation deteriorated across the region as the state was challenged in, and often pushed out of, an ever-growing swathe of territory. MS-13 engaged in a widening array of illicit activities, including control of key routes in the region's multibillion-dollar cocaine trade, direct political action to protect the gang's interests and a multi-pronged strategy of territorial expansion to govern areas where the state was absent or had lost legitimacy.

Key statistics	2016	2017
Type:	Internationalised	Internationalised
Fatalities:	–[b]	–[b]
New IDPs:	16,000	–[b]
New refugees:	45,000	–[b]

Regional violence

In recent years, the Northern Triangle (El Salvador, Guatemala and Honduras) has been the setting of a violent, multi-sided armed conflict comprising inter- and intra-gang warfare, vigilante groups and state–gang warfare, all of which has shredded the social fabric of the region. Violence in the Northern Triangle claimed more than 12,000 lives in 2017, including more than 140 policemen, with it generally being agreed that gang violence was the primary driver of homicide rates. The number of internally displaced persons rose to 667,000 in 2016, while 31,754 unaccompanied minors (children under the age of 18 with no adult) from the Northern Triangle crossed the southern border of the United States in 2017, almost all claiming to be escaping gang violence.

In Honduras, official sources reported a total of 3,791 homicides in 2017. A number of organisations estimated what proportion of those deaths were considered to be related to organised crime, ranging from 65%, according to newspaper sources, through to 70% according to World Health Organization reports. Given the extreme difficulty of obtaining up-to-date data and drawing a clear distinction between deaths resulting from organised criminal violence and those resulting from other forms of criminality, we have decided to refrain from providing a fatality estimate for the armed conflict in Honduras.

Although all accounts point to a drop in the overall number of fatalities in 2017 compared to 2016, this decrease was due to MS-13 successfully taking territory from enemy gangs or the state, rather than any increased effectiveness of law enforcement or prevention programmes. The year saw extreme, short-term spikes of localised violence as the battle for control was waged, then a sharp drop in the homicide rate once MS-13 had taken control of the territory and eliminated its enemies.

The country also experienced violence against members of the armed forces and police. Three members of the military and two of the police-investigations directorate were killed during the first quarter of 2017 by suspected members of organised-crime groups. The National Inter-Institutional Security Force (FUSINA) – a security task force composed of civilian and military personnel – warned in February that criminal groups were deliberately targeting military and police agents in response to recent security operations that had resulted in the seizure of weapons from gangs. In its battles with the state in both Honduras and El Salvador, MS-13 regularly used

AK-47 assault rifles (newly purchased from Colombia and Nicaragua) and other automatic weapons, as well as rocket-propelled grenades and C4 explosives. The gang also regularly used commercially purchased drones equipped with smart phones to survey police patrols or enemy territory and transmit real-time location intelligence on movements that might threaten the gang's territorial position.

The changing nature of MS-13

MS-13 was able to establish itself more robustly in the drug trade in 2017 as it exploited a power vacuum created by successful US law-enforcement actions in Honduras over previous years, which had disrupted several of the biggest cocaine-transport networks and purged the Honduran police of more than 2,000 members suspected of corruption and human-rights violations. In addition to transporting cocaine, MS-13 began unloading shipments arriving by air from Venezuela and running laboratories that transform coca paste – mostly from Colombia – into cocaine hydrochloride (HCL), the white powder that is consumed. This has shifted the dynamics of the conflict between the gang and the state, as well as between MS-13 and rival gangs, including the bloody turf battle between MS-13 and the Atlantic Cartel that helped cement the gang's role as a transport network.

The most immediate and predictable impact of the increased participation in the cocaine traffic was to give MS-13 access to economic resources it had never before enjoyed, enabling the group to buy new weapons and enhance their military capabilities, mainly by hiring dozens of highly trained police personnel expelled from the force as instructors. This allowed the group to defeat rival gangs such as Barrio 18, as well as to take control of key rural cocaine-trafficking routes on the Guatemalan border, including numerous *pasos ciegos* (informal border-crossing spaces).

New revenue streams also precipitated a transformative change in resource allocation and political activism, as MS-13 sought to halt extortions of local businesses in areas under gang control. Extortion remained in effect for large companies, service providers – such as water trucks, liquefied natural gas delivery vehicles and soda and beer distributors – and wealthy individuals.

By relying on cocaine-trafficking profits and forgoing what had traditionally been the gang's main source of revenue, MS-13 attempted to change its approach in order to build social capital and a political base for the organisation. The strategic shift was also innovative, given that no Central American gang had adopted such a policy before. The gang leadership correctly calculated that the group would be viewed in a much more favourable light by removing the most onerous form of economic abuse of the lower- and lower-middle-class communities from which most gang members originate and still reside. The transformation was palpable in gang areas in and around San Pedro Sula, with most residents of communities controlled by MS-13 referring to the group as *la mara buena* ('the good gang') to differentiate it from other gang structures. MS-13 itself eschewed being called a *mara* ('gang') and insisted on being called *La Familia* ('The Family'), indicating both how the gang viewed itself and how it hoped to be viewed in its areas of control.

MS-13's new approach to extortion was carried out alongside other strategies designed to fulfil roles the state could not. These included ruling on local disputes (such as domestic violence, theft, vandalism or violating gang rules) via bi-weekly hearings; providing protection from other gangs and local law-enforcement groups; running basic literacy programmes (primarily designed to help their members communicate with each other through mobile telephones, but with some community participation permitted); and helping families run hundreds of small *maquilas* (garment factories) which illegally mass-produced T-shirts, underwear and other clothing items. The gang supplied most of the material for these family-run *maquilas* by stealing it from the large international *maquilas* in San Pedro Sula.

MS-13's new array of illicit activities, maturing political strategies and enhanced weaponry greatly strengthened the group as a political and military actor in the course of 2017. The group's broadening portfolio of capabilities was a major contributor to evaporating state control, legitimacy and the rule of law, as well as the renewed wave of illegal Central American migrants attempting to cross the border into the US. The group also demonstrated an increasing degree of coordination and adaptability, with gang members communicating extensively across all three countries in the Northern Triangle and with members in the US, ensuring a broad awareness of how each individual street-level group functioned and what lessons could be learned from each victory and defeat. With MS-13 becoming ever more entrenched in the social and political fabric of Honduras, the state faced complex and deep-rooted challenges in countering the group's increasing influence in the country.

Mexico (Cartels)

Mexico experienced rising levels of criminal violence in 2017, driven by the fragmentation of the large cartels and subsequent competition for territory and influence between smaller criminal gangs. The army and navy remained at the forefront of the

Key statistics	2016	2017
Type:	Internal	Internal
Fatalities:	– [b]	– [b]
New IDPs:	23,000	20,000
New refugees:	– [b]	– [b]

state's response to the threat posed to peace and security. The state continued to focus on targeting the leadership of the largest armed groups.

Rising insecurity

The rise in homicides in 2016, driven by criminal violence and confirmed by data from the National Public Security System (SNSP), was a source of concern for policymakers at the start of 2017. Although most of the leaders of the country's leading criminal gangs had been killed or arrested, insecurity was rising. In late January, the defence ministry sent 500 troops to Ciudad Mier in Tamaulipas, the northeastern border state, to reinforce security. Insecurity was also high in the state of Veracruz on the Gulf of Mexico, which registered 130 murders in December 2016 and 100 more in January 2017 as a result of a turf war between criminal gangs that appeared to be linked to the internal weakening of the Zetas cartel and the departure from office of the state's governor, who was a Zetas ally.

Shortly thereafter, the federal legislature resumed its debate on the draft Internal Security Law, which was intended by lawmakers to tackle the legal ambiguity surrounding the deployment of the army and navy against criminal gangs. Separate bills had been presented by senators from three of the main political parties, but after months of wrangling the government decided to shelve the legislation because of the controversy it generated. Critics alleged that the draft law amounted to the militarisation of the country by subordinating municipal and state authorities within Mexico's federal system to the armed forces, and that it was likely to further erode the observance of human rights.

In March, the federal authorities reviewed the initial results of President Enrique Peña Nieto's initiative to tackle violence in the 50 municipalities most affected by violence in 2016. The president had announced the plan in August 2016, when he noted that 42% of all homicides took place in just 2% of Mexico's 2,448 municipalities. To this end, the federal government increased funding to support security-sector efforts, social programmes and institutions in those municipalities. However, between September 2016 and February 2017, homicides rose in 37 of the 50 municipalities when compared with the period between September 2015 and February 2016. They were unchanged in one municipality and fell in the remaining 12. However, in some areas the number of homicides doubled or tripled. The city of Chihuahua in the eponymous northern state experienced a 232% increase in homicides. Tecomán, in the Pacific state of Colima, saw homicides rise by 300%, leading the federal government to deploy 500 of Peña Nieto's military police force in February in order to stabilise security in the face of a conflict between the Sinaloa Cartel and the Jalisco New Generation Cartel (CJNG).

In May, data came to light on the extent of federal spending on internal security. Since the government announced a war on the cartels at the end of 2006, Mexico has spent far more on security measures than the budget approved by Congress each year. In 2013, the budget was US$43 million but the out-turn was US$205m; the figures for 2014 were US$38m and US$496m; and for 2015 US$30m and US$445m. Even in this context, however, the difference in 2016 was vast: lawmakers allocated US$42m but spending amounted to US$965m. The largest portion went to the defence ministry in 2016, whereas in 2015 the interior ministry had received the majority. That shift appeared to underline the government's continued reliance on the armed forces to combat the cartels and provide security to the population in areas most deeply affected by criminal violence.

The importance of the armed forces was underscored in June when the Mexican Navy regained control of all the country's 103 ports, which the navy had surrendered to the Secretariat of Transport and Communications in 1977. The navy's Marines are regarded as the most effective and professional element of the armed forces and their return to the ports was intended to check and roll back the progress made by criminal groups in taking over ports. Also in June, the security forces in the state of Sinaloa engaged in a battle with armed criminals, killing 17 of them.

The authorities recovered 14 AK-47 assault rifles, four AR-15 semi-automatic rifles and one G3 rifle from the scene, highlighting how well equipped many of the gangs had become. In July a detachment of Marines clashed with members of the Tláhuac Cartel while on patrol in the outer reaches of Mexico City. Eight gang members were killed. According to the authorities, the gang members were carrying weapons that should have been exclusively for the use of the military. Seizures of weapons by the authorities have fallen sharply in recent years, but this probably does not reflect a reduction in the number of weapons held by criminal gangs. According to one report, published in 2015, there are some 13m illegal arms in circulation, brought from the United States and Central America. In the last ten years the army claims to have recovered 13,000 grenades and 150,000 firearms. Over the last five years, more than 60% of seizures have been of heavier weapons, including automatic and semi-automatic rifles, machine guns and grenade launchers.

Although the federal government had paused in its efforts to push the Internal Security Law through Congress, it remained committed to its military-first strategy. Peña Nieto came to office in 2012 proclaiming a change to the strategy of his predecessor, Felipe Calderón, but aside from increasing spending on social programmes and development in affected areas in the early years of his term, and striking a less belligerent rhetorical posture, he has continued to deal with cartel violence through military instruments. In early June the presidential administration announced that 107 of the top 122 senior cartel figures had either been arrested or killed. However, the president's decision to persist with a military-led kingpin strategy attracted growing criticism from commentators. The kingpin strategy, also known as decapitation, weakens a cartel and can trigger an internal struggle for control, often leading to the fragmentation of the cartel into smaller groups. This fragmentation of cartels has called into question the continuing efficacy of a decapitation strategy. In 2007, the government faced six large cartels; today, there are several hundred smaller gangs as well as a few cartels.

The anatomy of conflict

In 2017, the drivers of violence were appreciably different from those a decade earlier. When Calderón first sent the army into his home state of Michoacán, the largest cartels were primarily involved in drug trafficking to the US. While that remains a lucrative business, many of the smaller criminal groupings active today lack the logistical sophistication for the task. Others, meanwhile, are focused on other criminal activities, including smuggling of other goods, from foodstuffs to metals; cultivating and supplying the growing domestic market for drugs; stealing fuel; and engaging in kidnap and extortion. The growth in domestic demand for illegal drugs, for instance, has created opportunities in some parts of the country that are more lucrative than shipping narcotics to the US. Changes in the make-up of drug demand in the US and Mexico have also encouraged in recent years the manufacture of synthetic drugs such as methamphetamine as well as the cultivation of opium poppies in the southwestern Pacific state of Guerrero. Fuel theft by *huachicoleros* (criminals who siphon fuel from pipelines) is also a major challenge, driving lethal violence in Guanajuato and Puebla states which involves the armed forces as protectors of state-owned pipelines that are regarded as strategic infrastructure. In 2016, thousands of taps and small pipelines attached to the Pemex pipeline system cost the company an estimated US$1.5 billion.

An unintended consequence of the kingpin strategy is that it regularly creates opportunities for criminal groups to challenge incumbents for control of these illicit activities and markets. In 2017, the principal factions fighting over these criminal spoils were the Sinaloa Cartel, the CJNG, Los Zetas and the Gulf Cartel, although it should be noted that the federal government announced the emergence of new cartels at various points during the year. In 2017 the CJNG – which emerged in 2010 from infighting between two factions of the Milenio Cartel (part of the Sinaloa Cartel's federation) – was engaged in an ambitious expansion in many areas of the country. It was boosted by substantial profits generated from the US drug market and also its growing arsenal of high-capability military-grade equipment and weapons that the group imported from gun shops and gun shows in the US. According to US and Mexican authorities, the CJNG operated in at least 22 of the 32 Mexican states, while the group was also reported to have operations or alliances in Bolivia, Brazil, Central America, Colombia, Peru, Uruguay and the US.

In 2017, the CJNG continued its campaign to become the largest criminal grouping in Mexico. Along the Pacific coast, the group looked to secure complete control of key cities in Nayarit, Jalisco, Colima and Michoacán states, clashing with remnants of the Knights Templar and La Familia Michoacána cartels. The port cities of Manzanillo and Lázaro Cárdenas were at the centre of the campaign, being key entry points for illegal methamphetamine precursors from Asia which would then be smuggled onwards to service increasing consumption of methamphetamine in the US. Elsewhere, the CJNG's ruthless efforts at consolidation were marked by large increases in executions. In Nayarit State, 337 individuals were executed by organised-crime groups in 2017 compared to 31 in 2016, while a significant increase also occurred in Guanajuato State, where there were 1,983 cases in 2017 compared to 670 in 2016; the majority of these increases were likely attributable to the CJNG. The CJNG competed with Los Zetas in various towns and cities on the east coast, and continued its especially brutal campaign in Veracruz to suppress any challenge to its dominance. In Veracruz, the cartel used frequent executions, involving decapitation and dismemberment of victims, to assert itself.

Meanwhile, the CJNG's campaign against the Sinaloa Cartel focused on the border towns in the northern states of Baja California, Chihuahua and, to a lesser extent, Coahuila and Sonora, and was fought primarily by the CJNG's local partners, the Tijuana New Generation Cartel and the Juárez Cartel. Fighting was at its most intense in Tijuana, Juárez City and Chihuahua City, where the groups sought control of local narcotics sales as well as smuggling routes into the US. Occasional fighting also took place further south in Sonora and Sinaloa states between the Sinaloa Cartel and CJNG partner the Beltrán Leyva Cartel. The CJNG's offensive against the Sinaloa Cartel came as the latter struggled with internal divisions, caused by the re-arrest of its leader, Joaquín 'El Chapo' Guzmán, in January 2016 and his extradition to the US in January 2017.

In northeast Mexico, although fragmented and weakened, Los Zetas and the Gulf Cartel continued to compete for control of strategically valuable cities. In May, Marines killed the Gulf Cartel's regional leader in Reynosa, a border town in Tamaulipas, during a gunfight with Gulf Cartel members. The disruption to the Gulf Cartel's operations in the area induced Los Zetas to begin a campaign to take control of Reynosa and nearby Matamoros and Rio Bravo, all located along the US–Mexico border, to secure the narcotics- and human-smuggling routes for themselves. Significant clashes ensued, with the Gulf Cartel and Los Zetas splinter groups (Los Zetas Grupo Bravo and Los Zetas Vieja Escuela) on one side and Los Zetas Cartel del Noreste on the other. The fighting prompted the Mexican government to deploy soldiers and Marines to the area to combat the groups. Although large-scale gun battles in the streets between the cartels declined as a result of the Marines' deployment, they continued their competition by other means, undertaking targeted attacks and executions throughout the remaining months of 2017, and ambushing the security forces.

New legal mandate for armed forces amid rising violence

Data released at the end of 2017 confirmed that the year had witnessed an increase in the level of violence throughout most of the country. According to the SNSP, there were 29,168 homicides in the year, which represented a 27% rise compared with 2016. Homicides increased in 26 of the country's 32 states. Shootings rose in 30 of the 32 states. According to the count of the newspaper *Milenio*, just under 13,000 homicides were connected with organised crime. A count by the newspaper *Semáforo Delictivo* and the consultancy Lantia Consultores, which includes homicides not featured in the SNSP dataset, put the figure at just under 19,000. It identified Guerrero, Guanajuato, Veracruz, Michoacán, Chihuahua and Baja California as the states with the highest levels of organised-crime homicides.

Under our methodology, not all of these deaths fall within the parameters of an armed conflict between organised adversaries. Because the Mexican authorities do not provide data on the number of 'civilians' killed by the army, navy and police, and because of the difficulty in isolating the deaths that result from fighting between the larger organised groups, we cannot arrive at a satisfactory method for reporting an estimate of total annual fatalities.

Data are available for deaths suffered by the army, navy and police. According to the National Security Council, just under 550 police and security agents were killed during the year, some 80% of whom were state or municipal police. In total, 38 soldiers and Marines were killed, which was a marked increase on the 24 deaths recorded in 2016, although it was far below the 89 military fatalities seen in 2010. Politicians were also a particular target of the violence. In 2017, 34 politicians were killed, including 18 mayors and former mayors. Guerrero was the epicentre of this phenomenon. This brought the total number of killings of citizens holding political office between 2004 and 2017 to 176.

At the end of the year, the government presented the draft Internal Security Law for consideration by Congress. The bill was adopted in December. In simple terms, it provides a firmer legal basis for the deployment of the army against the most vicious criminal organisations. It was intended to make the decision-making process connected with deployment of the armed forces transparent and open. The law makes a distinction between public security, which is the preserve of the police force, and internal security, for which the application of military force is appropriate. It allows the president to deploy the armed forces to tackle threats to internal security for up to one year at a time. The president is supposed to obtain the approval of the National Security Council and to notify the National Commission on Human Rights (NCHR). However, article 16 of the law allows the president in situations of crisis to issue a Declaration of Protection of Internal Security, thus deploying the armed forces, without the need to obtain the approval of the National Security Council or notify the NCHR. The law was criticised by opposition parties, human-rights organisations and the United Nations High Commissioner for Human Rights. The NCHR moved swiftly to petition the Supreme Court to consider the constitutionality of the law, and Peña Nieto committed to not make use of the law until a decision was handed down.

The passage of the law underscored the determination of the outgoing president to reaffirm the primary role of the military in the fight against organised criminal groups, especially as progress in developing police forces has been limited. However, the rise in homicides on a yearly basis since 2015 has bolstered concerns that the use of the armed forces may be stoking violence in the country. The presidential election on 1 July 2018 might lead to a change in approach, particularly if the front-runner, Andrés Manuel López Obrador, wins. López Obrador has promised a comprehensive review of the current strategy; indicated that he favours development policies to curb violence; and expressed a willingness to consider offering amnesties to criminals in order to reduce the violence, provided that the families of those affected were not opposed to the amnesty. The amnesty idea has been firmly attacked by the other presidential candidates, although it is not clear whether it would extend beyond drug smuggling to violent crimes. Separately, López Obrador has welcomed the efforts of one bishop to negotiate a truce in Guerrero, and there have been instances in the past of governors reaching an understanding with criminal gangs to offer impunity in return for guarantees that violence will be curbed. The presidential election may thus prompt a fundamental reappraisal of the state's approach.

Chapter Nine

Explanatory Notes

The IISS Armed Conflict Survey provides analysis and data on active armed conflicts involving states and non-state armed groups across the world. The data in
the current edition is accurate according to IISS assessments as at June 2018, unless
specified. Inclusion of a territory, country, state or group in *The Armed Conflict Survey*
does not imply legal recognition or indicate support for that entity.

Individual conflict entries in *The IISS Armed Conflict Survey*

For each conflict, there is an analytical essay identifying and critically assessing key
developments in the political, military and humanitarian aspects of the conflict. This
is complemented by an analysis of the type of conflict and data on fatalities, refugees, internally dispaced persons (IDPs) and returnees. However, there are many
conflicts for which data is limited or unavailable. We have indicated these issues as
appropriate in the conflict data boxes with two superscripts: −[a] [data limited] and
−[b] [data unavailable]. No fatality estimate is given for 2016 where a conflict is a new
entry in *The IISS Armed Conflict Survey 2018*. This is indicated in the data boxes by
the superscript −[c].

Fatalities

For each conflict in *The IISS Armed Conflict Survey*, we present an annual estimate
of fatalities that are a direct result of armed conflict. We publish rounded numbers,
according to this formula:

- 15–60 rounded to the nearest five;
- 61–100 to the nearest ten;
- 101–200 to the nearest 25;
- 201–500 to the nearest 50;
- 501–1,000 to the nearest 100;
- 1,001–2,500 to the nearest 250;
- 2,501–10,000 to the nearest 500;
- 10,001–50,000 to the nearest 1,000
- 50,001–200,000 to the nearest 5,000; and
- 200,001–400,000 to the nearest 10,000

We produce our estimates on the basis of open sources, where possible building a fatality count through reports of individual clashes over the course of the year, preferably on the basis of three separate, reputable sources. For some conflicts, we have to rely on fewer than three reputable sources.

In some cases, an international or regional organisation or a government will provide a fatality estimate that we can use to measure against our own open-source count, or in the case of high-fatality conflicts as the primary source. We do so only if we are convinced as to the rigour and impartiality of the organisation in that case.

We will also, on occasion, take into account fatality estimates provided by a non-governmental organisation (NGO), university or research institute when generating our fatality estimate – provided that we are satisfied as to the independence and rigour of the source.

The type of estimate is categorised as either a count (compiled by building a fatality count from media sources over the year); a reported annual figure (a fatality figure supplied by a government, international organisation or NGO); a projection (where a ratio is applied to a total figure); or a combination of the above.

Table of Sources			
Middle East	Type of estimate	Source	Notes
Egypt (Sinai)	count and reported annual figure	IISS/ACLED, Tahrir Institute	
Iraq	count and reported annual figures	IISS, UNAMI, AP	civilian deaths – UNAMI, AP; combatant deaths – media count
Israel–Palestine	count and reported annual figure	B'Tselem, IMEMC, OCHA	
Libya	counts	IISS, IISS/ACLED	
Syria	reported annual figure	Syrian Observatory for Human Rights	
Turkey (PKK)	count	IISS/ACLED	

Table of Sources

Yemen	count		Yemen Data Project	The significant difference between the 2016 and 2017 fatality estimates is partly accounted for by a change of source from IISS media count figures to Yemen Data Project figures. (YDP figures were unavailable in 2016.)
Sub-Saharan Africa	**Type of estimate**		**Source**	**Notes**
Central African Republic	count		IISS/ACLED	
Democratic Republic of the Congo	count		IISS/ACLED	
Mali (The Sahel)	count		IISS	
Nigeria (Farmer–Pastoralist Violence)	count, reported annual figure		IISS/ACLED, Amnesty International	
Lake Chad Basin	count		IISS/ACLED	
Somalia	count		IISS/ACLED	
South Sudan	count		IISS	
Sudan (Darfur)	count		IISS	
South Asia	**Type of estimate**		**Source**	**Notes**
Afghanistan	reported annual figure		Pajhwok News	
India (Assam)	count		IISS	
India (Manipur)	count		IISS	
India (Nagaland)	count		IISS	
India (Naxalites)	count		IISS	
India–Pakistan	count		IISS	
Pakistan	count and reported annual figure		IISS/ACLED, SATP	
Asia-Pacific	**Type of estimate**		**Source**	**Notes**
Myanmar (ARSA)	projection		IISS/ISCI, MSF	
Myanmar (EAOs)	count		IISS	
Philippines (ASG)	count		IISS	
Philippines (MILF)	count		IISS	
Philippines (NPA)	count		IISS	
Southern Thailand	reported annual figure		Deep South Watch	
Europe and Eurasia	**Type of estimate**		**Source**	**Notes**
Armenia–Azerbaijan (Nagorno-Karabakh)	count		IISS	
Ukraine	count and reported annual figure		IISS, government	
Latin America	**Type of estimate**		**Source**	**Notes**
Brazil (Rio de Janeiro)	reported annual figure, projection		government, IISS/government	
Colombia (BACRIM)	reported annual figure		government	
Colombia (FARC and ELN)	reported annual figure		government	
El Salvador	n/a		n/a	Insufficient data available to provide a fatality estimate

Table of Sources			
Honduras	n/a	n/a	Insufficient data available to provide a fatality estimate
Mexico (Cartels)	n/a	n/a	Insufficient data available to provide a fatality estimate

Acronyms and abbreviations	
ACLED	Armed Conflict Location & Event Data Project
AP	Associated Press
IMEMC	International Middle East Media Center
ISCI	International State Crime Initiative
MSF	Médecins Sans Frontières
OCHA	United Nations Office for the Coordination of Humanitarian Affairs
SATP	South Asia Terrorism Portal
UNAMA	United Nations Assistance Mission in Afghanistan
UNAMI	United Nations Assistance Mission in Iraq
YDP	Yemen Data Project

Refugees

According to the 1951 Refugee Convention (Article 1A(2)), the term 'refugee' is applied to a person who 'owing to well-founded fear of being persecuted for reasons of race, religion, nationality, membership of a particular social group or political opinion, is outside the country of his[/her] nationality and is unable or, owing to such fear, is unwilling to avail himself[/herself] of the protection of that country; or who, not having a nationality and being outside the country of his[/her] former habitual residence as a result of such events, is unable or, owing to such fear, is unwilling to return to it'.

The refugees entry refers to the number of people that as a result of conflict moved out of the host country in the last year. It measures the flow rather than the total number, or stock, of refugees created by a conflict.

Although multiple sources are consulted as part of our analytical process, refugee data used in *The IISS Armed Conflict Survey* is sourced from the United Nations High Commissioner for Refugees.

Returned refugees

The term 'returnee' is applied to a refugee who has returned to his/her country after taking refuge in another country. Voluntary repatriation is often under-reported, as many refugees return spontaneously, without informing the authorities of the asylum country.

Internally displaced persons (IDPs)

IDPs are individuals or groups who have been forced or obliged to flee their homes as a result of, or in order to avoid, the effects of armed conflict, situations of generalised violence or violations of human rights. The IDP figures in the tables correspond to the number of people displaced that particular year, and not to the total number of IDPs since the beginning of the conflict. IDP figures and information come from the Norwegian Refugee Council's Internal Displacement Monitoring Centre.

Attribution and acknowledgements

The IISS owes no allegiance to any government, group of governments, or any political or other organisation. Its assessments are its own, based on the material available to it from a wide variety of sources. Some data in *The IISS Armed Conflict Survey* is estimated. Care is taken to ensure that this data is as accurate and free from bias as possible. The Director-General and Chief Executive and staff of the Institute assume full responsibility for the data and judgements in this book. Comments and suggestions on the data and textual material contained within the book, as well as on the style and presentation of data, are welcomed and should be communicated to the Director of Editorial at: IISS, 6 Temple Place, London WC2R 2PG, UK; email: publications@iiss.org. Application to reproduce limited amounts of data may be made to the publisher: Taylor & Francis, 4 Park Square, Milton Park, Abingdon, Oxon, OX14 4RN; email: society.permissions@tandf.co.uk. Unauthorised use of data from *The IISS Armed Conflict Survey* will be subject to legal action.

Key to regional maps

Conflict fatalities per 100,000 population by province or region

- Insufficient data available to provide a fatality estimate
- 1 to 9
- 10 to 29
- 30 to 100
- 101 to 200
- 200+

Index